ANCIENT ROME

THE RISE AND FALL OF AN EMPIRE

ANCIENT ROME

THE RISE AND FALL
OF AN EMPIRE

Simon Baker

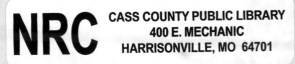
BBC
BOOKS

20

First published in 2006
This edition published in 2007 by BBC Books, an imprint of Ebury Publishing.
A Random House Group Company.

Copyright © Simon Baker 2006
Foreword by Mary Beard © Woodlands Books Ltd 2006

The Random House Group Limited Reg. No. 954009

Addresses for companies within the Random House Group can be found at
www.randomhouse.co.uk

A CIP catalogue record for this book is available from the British Library.

ISBN 978 1 846 07284 0

The Random House Group Limited makes every effort to ensure that the
papers used in our books are made from trees that have been legally sourced
from well-managed and credibly certified forests. Our paper procurement
policy can be found on www.randomhouse.co.uk

To buy books by your favourite authors and register for offers visit
www.rbooks.co.uk

Commissioning editor: Martin Redfern
Project editor: Eleanor Maxfield
Copy editor: Trish Burgess
Designer: seagulls.net
Maps and family trees by HL Studios, Long Hanborough, Oxon
Picture researcher: Sarah Hopper
Production controller: David Brimble

Printed and bound in the UK by Clays Ltd, St Ives plc

CONTENTS

For my mother, Patsy

Your task, Roman, and do not forget it, will be to govern the peoples of the world in your empire. These will be your arts – and to impose a settled pattern upon peace, to pardon the defeated and war down the proud.

Vergil, *Aeneid*

So power and greed ran riot, contaminated and pillaged everything, and held nothing sacred or worthy of respect until [the Romans] plunged themselves to their own destruction.

Sallust, *War with Jugurtha*

FOREWORD

Rome was a city founded on murder. In 753 BC the twin brothers Romulus and Remus – at the head of a small band of exiles and malcontents – dug the defences of the tiny village that was to become the capital of an empire that stretched from Scotland to the Sahara and beyond. But excitement soon turned to tragedy. The brothers quarrelled, and Romulus killed his twin.

More problems were soon to follow. Romulus had only a handful of supporters. So where were the citizens for the new city to be found? The answer was: from all-comers. Romulus declared his city an 'asylum', and welcomed any exiles, refugees, runaway slaves and criminals who chose to take up residence. Rome was a city populated entirely by, in the ancient sense of the term (which is not so very far from our own), asylum-seekers.

That took care of the men. But where were the women to be found to make the wives and mothers in his new state? Here Romulus resorted to mean trickery. He invited some of the neighbouring peoples to a religious festival and, when he gave the signal, had his lads run off with the young female guests. This so-called 'Rape of the Sabine Women' has appealed to writers and artists ever since as a story of violence, lust and hard-headed political expediency.

We have no idea how much of this lurid tale is actually true. The precise date of 753 is the result of an elaborate and frankly unreliable calculation more than five hundred years later by Roman scholars, who were as interested as their modern equivalents in working out when exactly Rome began; but it does fit roughly with evidence that has been recovered by archaeologists for the earliest phases of the city. Romulus himself was no more or less an historical person than King Arthur of Britain.

But, accurate or not, this is how the Romans for the rest of their history, over more than a millennium, told the story of Rome's origins. They saw in the story many of the questions that were to dominate their political life ever after, and for that matter still dominate ours. These are the exciting themes that underlie this book. How should a state be governed? Can violence ever be justified in politics? Who has a right to citizenship and to benefit from its privileges?

When Romans reflected on the civil wars that sometimes scarred their political life, they looked back to the quarrel of Romulus and Remus and saw their city as destined from the very beginning to suffer the nastiest kind of internecine strife. The death of Romulus also provided them with food for thought. They could not agree whether he had in the end been taken up to heaven by the grateful gods, or hacked to death by angry citizens. This was a story debated with even greater intensity after the murder of Julius Caesar (see Chapter II) in 44 BC – hacked to death by his enemies in the name of liberty for becoming an autocrat, yet made into a god by his supporters and honoured with his own temple in the heart of the city.

This book concentrates on six pivotal moments in the history of Rome, from the second century BC to the fifth century AD – a time of dramatic, sometimes revolutionary, change. During this period, Rome came to be the dominating power around the Mediterranean and much further afield (traces of the presence of Roman traders have been found as far east as India). It turned from a more or less democratic republic into an autocratic empire. And – most dramatic of all perhaps – Rome was finally transformed from a pagan to a Christian city. Formally baptized only on his deathbed in 337, Constantine (see Chapter V) was the first Roman emperor publicly to sponsor Christianity. Indeed, he was the original founder of several of the churches and cathedrals that define the sacred landscape of Rome even today, including the first St Peter's.

Each of the pivotal moments touches on big questions of political change and conflict. The story of Tiberius Gracchus (see Chapter I), for example, and his controversial attempts to redistribute land to landless peasants, raises issues of the gap between rich and poor and who should benefit from the profits of a wealthy state. The story of Nero (see Chapter III) explores the consequences of autocracy gone mad. But these particular moments have been chosen for another reason too. For they offer us a vivid glimpse of some of the key personalities in Roman history. They let us get close to individual characters, their human motives, their political dilemmas, and their attempts to change the world in which they lived.

Modern professional historians tend to stress how little we know about the Roman world. True, we are almost completely in the dark about what life was like for the slum dwellers of the city (though we can make a fair guess!) or for peasants struggling to find a livelihood in the countryside. And we are not much better off when it comes to understanding the feelings of women or slaves, or how the Roman empire's balance of payments actually worked, or – for that matter – what Romans wore under their togas or how they disposed of their sewage (the miracles of Roman drainage have, I am afraid, been grossly exaggerated). But on a wide range of other aspects we are probably better informed about Rome than about any other society before the fifteenth century. We have direct access to the writings, the thoughts and feelings of Roman politicians, poets, philosophers, critics and commentators.

Take Julius Caesar, for example, and his decision to march on Rome – a decision that launched the civil war that effectively ended democracy and ushered in the one-man rule of the emperors (see Chapter II). We still have his own autobiographical account of these events, published in his multivolume memoirs, *On the Civil War*. In some ways it makes strange reading; for example, he refers to himself throughout in the third person: 'Caesar decided...', not 'I decided'. In other ways it is a stirring story, and a clever justification of his actions.

But not only that. From the run-up to the outbreak of war and through the conflict itself we can still read a series of private letters written by – and sometimes to – one of Rome's most weighty statesmen (or so he would have liked to think). This was Marcus Tullius Cicero, who was also a notable philosopher and orator, as well as a supporter of Pompey, Caesar's rival. It is still something of a mystery how these letters were preserved and published. But they certainly give us an extraordinary insider's view of a man wrestling with his doubts and indecisions about whom to support and how to make the best of it when he found himself on the losing side – all interspersed with the day-to-day problems of disloyal slaves, divorce, the death of a daughter, and shady property deals.

As it turned out, Caesar was characteristically generous to Cicero; whatever his political ruthlessness, 'clemency' was one of his slogans. But after Caesar's assassination, his apparatchik Mark Antony (of 'Friends, Romans, countrymen...' fame) had him summarily 'removed'. The story was that after Cicero's death, his hands and tongue (his most powerful political weapons in writing and speaking) were pinned up on display in the Roman Forum, and that Antony's wife took particular pleasure in piercing them with her hairpins. It's a story that speaks as much about Roman views of women as about the hatred of Antony and his wife for Cicero.

Of course, none of these accounts is as simple as it seems. Neither Caesar's own memoirs, nor Cicero's published correspondence, are any more reliable than the equivalents penned by a modern politician. We cannot take them straightforwardly on trust. But they do bring us directly to the heart of Roman history and politics. And they are not alone. We get our most detailed and vivid information about the unsuccessful Jewish Revolt against the Romans (see Chapter IV), which ended with the destruction of the Temple of Jerusalem in AD 70, from the history written by one of the participants – Josephus – a Jewish rebel and then notorious turncoat, who ended up living comfortably in Rome under the patronage of the emperor Vespasian. Most stories of unsuccessful rebellions are told by the winners. There is, in fact, no other such detailed account by a rebel against an imperial power from any empire before the modern period.

And even if nothing significant survives from the mouth or pen of the emperor Nero himself, there are still extraordinary pieces of writing by members of his court circle and by key players in the politics of that notorious reign. We have, for example, a philosophical treatise addressed to Nero by his tutor Seneca, giving some clear and level-headed advice on how to be an emperor. Clemency usually works better than cruelty was the general message – following the example of Julius Caesar. As we shall see, Seneca did not in the end win clemency from his old pupil; in fact, he was to die a slow and agonizing death at Nero's behest.

Some people think that a hilarious skit on Nero's predecessor, the emperor Claudius, becoming a god was also written by Seneca while he still enjoyed Nero's favour. Claudius was apparently an unpromising candidate for immortality by Roman standards (he limped, stuttered and was believed to be a fool). And the satire – which now goes under the English title *The Pumpkinification of Claudius* (a pun on 'deification') – pokes cruel but hilarious fun at him in particular and, more generally, at the whole Roman institution of making 'good' emperors (and some not so 'good' ones) into gods. One of the characters in the skit is the first emperor Augustus, the gold standard against whom all future emperors were measured. He was made a god on his death in AD 14, but decades later, Seneca jokes, he still hasn't nerved himself to make his maiden speech in the heavenly senate, so in awe is he of all the 'proper' deities. It is one of the very few pieces of ancient comedy that can still make you laugh out loud. Humour doesn't usually travel well across cultures, but *The Pumpkinification* works for me at least.

In addition to this rich and varied evidence from some of the leading characters themselves, there are also detailed accounts by later Roman historians of the incidents discussed in this book. In the forefront is the cynical analysis of the early years of the Roman empire, written in his *Annals and Histories* by Tacitus, himself a Roman senator of the late first century and early second century ad. This account is as much a meditation on corruption and the abuse of power as an historical narrative. It contains, for example, the chilling tale of Nero's murder of his mother, Agrippina, with which Chapter III opens. After an unsuccessful attempt at doing away with her by sending her out to sea in a collapsible boat, Nero resorts to sending in some armed thugs. As matricide, this was one step worse than the fratricide that marked the very beginning of Rome.

But Tacitus is only one point of access to the ancient historical tradition. From roughly the same period as Tacitus we have a series of racy 'Lives of the Emperors' by Suetonius, who worked for a time in the palace bureaucracy and seems to have had some access to the imperial filing cabinets, or their ancient equivalents. Then there are the moralizing biographies by Plutarch, a Greek inhabitant of the Roman empire, who produced a series of life stories of famous Romans going back to

Romulus. Most of these were paired with an appropriate figure from the Greek world. Julius Caesar, for example, pointedly turns up as the biographical twin of Alexander the Great, the most successful conqueror the world had ever known, with a similarly tragic end, and – admittedly unproven – suspicions of assassination.

All in all, we have a lot for which to thank those medieval monks who painstakingly copied these ancient texts in an unbroken tradition since antiquity, and thus kept them alive to be rediscovered in the Renaissance – later to be interpreted and reinterpreted by us.

It is these precious survivals from the Roman world itself that have made it possible for the BBC television series to re-create in a compelling and dramatic way some of the key turning points in Rome's history. Of course, we shall never know exactly what it was like to be there, or be able to reconstruct all the complicated motivations and aspirations of the characters concerned. And we have to recognize that the ancient historians on whom we partly depend were themselves sometimes resorting to imagination and guesswork; after all, how could Tacitus possibly have known what actually happened at the secret murder of Nero's mother? But we have enough evidence to let us begin to get inside Roman heads, and to see the problems, dilemmas and conflicts from their point of view. We can tell a very good – and historical – story indeed.

This book complements the television series, as well as being a marvellous read in its own right. Focusing on the same pivotal moments, Simon Baker has put them into a broader context. He has filled out the historical background to each, and exposed some of the intriguing problems of the evidence on which the dramatic reconstructions are based. Sometimes we are confronted with conflicting versions of the same event. How do we choose between them? Sometimes the evidence simply dries up. Then, like Tacitus and all historians, we are forced to make good guesses and to use our imagination. The result is a history of Rome that combines vivid drama and a gripping story-line with a keen alertness to bigger historical questions, and to the challenges of drawing a clear narrative thread out of the evocative, but complicated and diverse, ancient evidence.

Ever since ancient times, people in the West have been retelling the history of Rome and re-creating it for their own purposes in fiction, painting and opera, and latterly in film and television. There have always been good and bad versions of this – cheesy clichés as well as powerful and arresting images and narratives. The figure of Julius Caesar has been a particular catalyst of such reconstructions. For centuries he has prompted some of the sharpest analyses of the nature of autocracy and liberty, and raised a question that remains with us even now: can political assassination ever be justified?

William Shakespeare's *Julius Caesar*, itself loosely based on a translation of Plutarch's *Life of Caesar*, is only one of many reflections on the rights and wrongs of the case. The audience's interest is divided between the title role of Caesar, killed less than halfway through the play, and the fate of his assassins, which dominates the second part. Do we feel that we are on Caesar's side – a legitimate ruler illegally put to death? Or is the killer Brutus our hero for being prepared to murder even a friend in defence of popular liberty? How far do patriotism and political principles demand that we sometimes flout the law and ride roughshod over personal ties of friendship and loyalty?

Predictably enough, the answers proposed for these particular historical and literary conundrums were especially loaded around the period of the French Revolution. Voltaire, for example, presented a dramatic version of the events, which clearly had one eye on the execution of the French royal family when it unequivocally backed the assassins' deeds as honourable.

But twentieth-century politics also found good food for thought in the dilemmas raised by the events of the Ides of March, 44 BC. Orson Welles's debut production at the famous Mercury Theatre in New York in 1937 was a staging of *Julius Caesar*, which (in a then daring experiment with modern dress) had the cast of Caesar's supporters kitted out as Mussolini's fascist thugs.

Not all the characters discussed in this book have had quite such an enduring shelf life. Tiberius Gracchus, for example, is not exactly a modern household name. In fact, outside academic ancient history, posterity has served his mother Cornelia rather better than it has served him. A model of devoted (and ambitious) parenthood, she is supposed to have turned her nose up at the rich jewels being shown off by a friend – pointing to her sons instead as her 'treasures'. In her doting maternal role she starred in a whole series of eighteenth-century paintings, usually depicted with a pair of (to us) rather priggish boys at her side, and looking decidedly sniffy at the strings of pearls and suchlike being trailed in front of her. And, again in her parental role, she makes a striking appearance alongside other Western heroes, from the Greek tragedian Sophocles to the emperor Charlemagne and Christopher Columbus, in the famous nineteenth-century memorial stained glass at Harvard University. But even Tiberius has recently enjoyed a certain celebrity, being used as a pointed comparison for the occasional modern politician (such as Hugo Chávez of Venezuela) known as a radical or revolutionary reformer.

The emperor Nero, however, has had almost as busy an after-life in Western culture as Caesar. One of the greatest and earliest Italian operas, Monteverdi's *Coronation of Poppaea* (1642), explores the intense relationship between the emperor and his mistress Poppaea. A case study in devious manipulation, as well as in the power of passionate love, she is depicted cynically disposing of all the obstacles in her path towards marriage with the emperor – including the opposition of the moralizing but virtuous Seneca. The opera ends with Poppaea being gloriously crowned as empress of Rome. But a well-informed audience will already know that this victory will be short-lived, as Poppaea is destined soon to die after a vicious blow from Nero himself (a scene powerfully dramatized in the BBC series). It is a chilling and timeless exploration of passion, ruthlessness and immorality.

More often, though, Nero has found a decidedly lurid role in modern popular culture, especially in film. The classic image of a luxury-loving and decadent emperor, he has been portrayed countless times consuming unlikely foods (dormice and pretty little songbirds, as the usual cliché of Roman dietary habits would have it) amid grape-strewn orgies, cackling over his mega-lomaniac schemes to rebuild Rome after the great fire of AD 64 and 'fiddling while Rome burned'.

Much of this is the product of modern elaboration and the projection of all our stereotypes of Roman luxury on to the convenient figure of Nero. But the theme of 'fiddling' (that is, 'playing the violin' – not, as it is often now taken to be, 'footling aimlessly') goes back to an ancient story that, while Rome was in flames, the emperor climbed up a tower to get a good view of the blaze and sang a song on the destruction of the legendary city of Troy. True or not, this was no doubt meant to portray the emperor as a self-obsessed artist, utterly out of touch with prac-tical realities. In fact, as recounted in Chapter III, whatever his artistic ambitions, Nero seems to have taken eminently sensible steps to cope with the immediate aftermath of the fire.

There was also a story that he looked for scapegoats to blame for starting the fire, and picked on the early Christian commu-nity in the city – whose view that the end of the world was nigh may well have made the accusation more plausible. To make an example of the Christians, according to Tacitus, he crucified them or burnt them alive (using them, it is said, as lamps to brighten the night). It was the first Christian 'persecution', and St Peter may have been one of the victims.

This has given another distinctive theme to modern portrayals of Nero. Film and fiction have indulged in touching but entirely implausible fantasies of Christian heroism in the face of Neronian tyranny – often enlivening the picture with the subplot of a pretty young Christian girl converting her young pagan boyfriend, and taking him with her to a noble but gory death (usually involving lions). Many of these stories are versions of a best-selling novel, *Quo Vadis*, by the Polish writer Henryk Sienkiewicz, which was published in the nineteenth century and quickly translated into almost every European language (the title, meaning 'Where are you going?', is taken from words addressed by Peter to Jesus).

The most famous film version of this book was made in 1951, starring Peter Ustinov as a villainous Nero with an upper-class English accent (the goodies were American). But, as always, even if villainous, Nero did retain an aura of glamour too. In fact, the film's makers, MGM, promoted it with a series of 'tie-in' products. These included some gaudy boxer shorts and pyjamas, advertised under the slogan 'Make like Nero!' Persecutor of the Christians he may have been, but – or so the implied message was – it was still fun to feel like ruler of the world by sporting Nero's brand of underwear.

As we look back, some of the ways that past generations (even relatively recent ones) have re-created the Romans and Roman history can seem strange, unappealing or downright laughable. We can hardly see how Shakespeare's actors strutting the stage in their own Elizabethan costume could ever have done plausible duty as Romans – though we are, I suspect, more sympathetic (inconsistent as it may be) to Orson Welles's fascist thugs. It is almost equally hard to take seriously those wooden paragons of virtue in so many Hollywood movies, dressed up in white sheets, and orating in a pretentious fashion – as if they had jumped straight out of the nineteenth-century House of Commons or a schoolboy's Latin textbook.

But we do still retain a soft spot for the marvellous images of Roman debauchery and cruelty set in luxurious baths, at dinner parties or the amphitheatre. Ridley Scott's *Gladiator*, for example, staged some really compelling scenes of butchery and mass crowd dynamics in the Colosseum; though, interestingly, these were largely based not on the ruins themselves, but on nineteenth-century paintings (which Scott found more convincing and impressive than the real thing). We can enjoy too those fictional re-creations of Roman life 'below stairs', such as the classic musical *A Funny Thing Happened on the Way to the Forum* (which first appeared on Broadway in 1962, was made into a film in 1966, and was revived at the National Theatre in London in 2004). This drew on the traditions of ancient Roman comedy itself, but owed much of its appeal to the glimpse it offered of what might have happened beneath the glittering marble veneer of the city.

Part of the reason that some of these older visions of Rome now seem to us so unconvincing is that our understanding of Roman history and culture has changed in the interim. New information continues to be discovered. For example, our picture of life on a Roman army base has been enriched in the last few years by private letters and other documents (including the famous invitation to a birthday party from one officer's wife to another) unearthed at the fort of Vindolanda in northern England. In Italy one of the most impressive discoveries of the twentieth century was the excavation of a large villa at Oplontis, near Pompeii, which seems to have belonged to the family of Nero's wife, Poppaea, and allows us to reconstruct her background with much greater confidence. And it was only in the mid-nineteenth century that we obtained a full, reliable text of the autobiography of the emperor Augustus, which had been discovered inscribed on the wall of a Roman temple (dedicated to Augustus as a god) in Ankara.

No less significant are the changing interpretations of old evidence. One particular debate, which is acutely relevant to our account of Tiberius Gracchus and Julius Caesar, concerns the underlying motivations of Roman politicians, especially in the hundred years or so before Julius Caesar's rise to power. One view, prevalent for much of the last century, is that there was very little ideological difference between the opposing political leaders. What was at stake was no more and no less than naked, personal power. If some (such as Gracchus or Caesar) chose to rely on the support of the people rather than the aristocratic Senate, that was simply because it offered the most direct route to the power they yearned for. Increasingly, this has come to seem to a new generation (as, in fact, it had already seemed to our predecessors of the eighteenth and nineteenth centuries) an inadequate way of seeing the debates and political struggles of the period. It is hard to make sense of the violent clashes around Tiberius Gracchus without imagining that a meaningful conflict about the distribution of wealth in the state was at stake. And it is this view that the television series and this book have followed.

In many ways, though, changing images of Rome are a consequence of each generation looking for something different in Roman history. True, some things remain fairly constant. It seems very unlikely, for example, that we shall ever shake off our notion of Rome as a culture that is somehow larger than life, for good or ill. The sheer extent of its empire and the size of its monuments, such as the Colosseum, will probably ensure that. But recent historians have tended to shine their spotlight on aspects of Rome that their predecessors left barely illuminated.

They have, for example, chosen to look beyond the monumental centre of the city. Certainly, from the period of Augustus onwards, the heart of Rome was packed with temples, theatres and public buildings of all sorts, constructed not just from white marble, but also from precious multicoloured marble embossed with gold and occasionally encrusted with jewels. It must have been a staggering sight to any visitor from more 'barbarian' provinces, such as Britain or Germany. But there was always a seedier side. This was not only the poor back-street world that *A Funny Thing...* tried to capture. But also, before the age of Augustus (who boasted that he had transformed Rome from a place of brick to one of marble), the whole city was much less glittering and grand, certainly not full of the planned urban spaces, promenades and porticoes of popular perception. Frankly, with the exception of just one or two neighbourhoods, it probably looked more like Kabul than New York. And it was about as violent.

Part and parcel of these changes of vision is a growing tendency to question the image of ancient Romans as somehow very like us (or perhaps more like our imperialist Victorian ancestors) – different only in the sense that they wore togas and, picturesquely but no doubt uncomfortably, ate their dinners lying down. Historians now tend to find their fascination with the Romans lies as much in their foreignness as in their comfortable familiarity. Their norms of sexual behaviour, of gender difference, of ethnicity were quite different from ours. They lived in a world (as one historian recently put it) 'full of gods', and the élite were served by battalions of slaves, a whole subordinate population of humans who lived outside the rights and privileges of humanity. The account given in this book, and in the television reconstruction, tries to incorporate some sense of that difference between them and us.

Of course, all reconstructions are inevitably provisional. And the implication of these changing attitudes to Roman culture (and they are bound to go on changing) is that our own modern version of Rome, however historically grounded it is, is likely to appear in a hundred years' time as quaintly old-fashioned as nineteenth-century reconstructions now look to us.

But why bother with the Romans at all? Partly because, in Europe at least, they are still with us. Their precious treasures, artworks, bric-a-brac and kitsch fill our museums. The monuments sponsored by several of the key players in this book are still prominent landmarks in Rome: the great arches of Titus and Constantine are the best known of the city; the Colosseum, built with the profits of the Jewish War, is visited by millions of tourists a year; Nero's extravagant Golden House can still be explored underground. Further afield, the traces of their activity mark the landscape across their empire – in our road networks, our town plans and our place names (it is almost certain that any British town or village whose name ends in '-chester' is sitting directly on top of a Roman camp or *castra*). And, of course, their surviving literature – from elegant love poetry to thundering epic, from hard-headed history to self-serving memoirs – is as impressive, acute and provocative as any in the world, and it is worth all the attention we can give it.

The Romans also have a lot to teach us. I do not mean that in terms of direct relevance or comparability. Intriguing comparison though it is, the Venezuelan president Hugo Chávez is much more different from Tiberius Gracchus than he could ever possibly be like him. But we share with the Romans many fundamental political dilemmas, and can usefully watch them wrestling with solutions. They, after all, were among the very first to wonder how to adapt models of citizenship and political rights and responsibilities to vast communities that transcended the boundaries of a small, 'face-to-face' town. By the first century BC the population of the city of Rome alone, excluding Italy and the more remote territories of the empire, was in the order of a million.

One-man rule, in the shape of emperors good or bad, was only one of their solutions – but the best known and to us the least palatable. More crucially, they reformulated the idea of citizenship in the context of the nearest thing to a global state the ancient world ever knew. Unlike the exclusivity of, for example, ancient Athens, which restricted citizenship to Athenians born and bred, Rome came to unite its huge empire through sharing its political rights. Slaves who were freed by their masters, as many were, became citizens with political rights. Citizenship was gradually extended throughout the empire, until in 212 the emperor Caracalla granted citizenship to all free populations within the Roman empire. Rome, in other words, was the first multicultural megastate.

It was also the inspiration of those men and women who are more directly responsible for shaping the political world in which we live today. The founding fathers of the United States saw a model in the republican politics of Rome before the advent of one-man rule. Hence American 'senators' and the 'Capitol' (after the Roman Capitoline Hill) as seat of government. In Britain the Labour movement saw resonances of its own conflicts with a land-owning and industrial aristocracy in the struggle of the Roman people against aristocratic conservatism. Hence the left-wing *Tribune* newspaper (called after the office of tribune held by Tiberius Gracchus and other radical politicians), and the 'Tribune Group' of Labour MPs. To understand our world we need to understand how it is rooted in Rome.

In many ways we are still living with the legacy of Romulus's murder of Remus.

MARY BEARD
June 2006

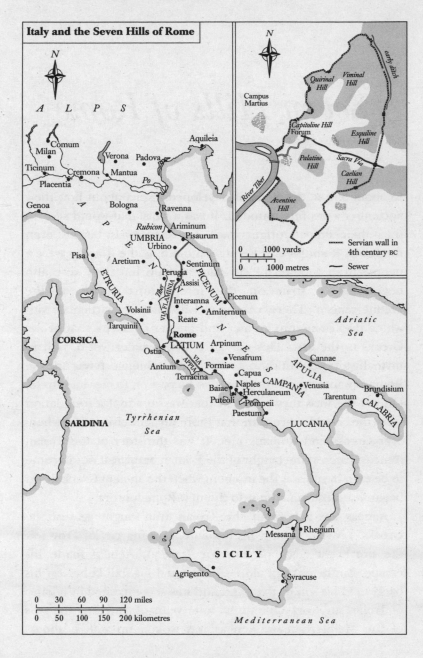

Italy and the Seven Hills of Rome

N

A L P S

Comum
Milan
Verona
Ticinum
Cremona   Mantua   Padova
Placentia   *Po*   Aquileia
Genoa   Bologna
Ravenna
Rubicon   Ariminum
UMBRIA   Pisaurum
Urbino
Pisa   Aretium   Sentinum
Perugia   PICENUM
VIA FLAMINIA   Assisi
Tiber   Interamna   Picenum
Volsinii   Reate   Amiternum
Tarquinii   S A M N I U M
Rome
CORSICA   Ostia   LATIUM
Arpinum
VIA APPIA   Venafrum
Antium   Formiae
Terracina   Capua   APULIA   Cannae
Baiae   Naples   CAMPANIA   Venusia
Puteoli   Herculaneum   Tarentum   Brundisium
Pompeii   CALABRIA
Paestum
*Tyrrhenian
Sea*   LUCANIA

SARDINIA

Messana   Rhegium

S I C I L Y

Agrigento   Syracuse

Mediterranean Sea

*Adriatic
Sea*

| 0 | 30 | 60 | 90 | 120 miles |
| 0 | 50 | 100 | 150 | 200 kilometres |

Inset map

N

Campus
Martius

Quirinal
Hill   Viminal
Hill   *early ditch*

Capitoline Hill
Forum   Esquiline
Hill

Palatine
Hill   *Sacra Via*

River Tiber   Caelian
Hill

Aventine
Hill

- - - - Servian wall in
4th century BC
———— Sewer

| 0 | 1000 yards |
| 0 | 1000 metres |

Seven Hills of Rome

In about 350 BC the Romans developed a story about how their ancient city was first founded. It was a story that would seek to trace their ultimate origins back to a remote past beyond even the age of Romulus and Remus. At the time the Romans were a people from a powerful city-state in Italy, but they were also beginning to strut on the international stage of the Mediterranean. There was one civilization in particular with which they came into greater and greater contact – that of the Greeks in the east. This was an enticing, older world, rich in myth, history, sophistication, wealth and influence. It was one the Romans wanted to connect with, to be part of, to measure up to. One of the ways they achieved that was to adopt a foundation story they could share with that more ancient civilization whenever Greeks and Romans met. It was the story of the Trojan Aeneas. Later, at the height of the Roman empire, it would come to be seen by some as the moment when the ancient Greek world began its transformation into the new Roman order.

Aeneas was a hero of the Trojan War fought against the Greeks. Leaving behind his desolate, burning city of Troy (on the northwest coast of modern Turkey), Aeneas made his escape. But he was not alone. He carried his frail father on his back, held his son by the hand and was accompanied by a band of Trojan survivors. One night, after years of travelling the seas of the Mediterranean, Aeneas was woken up with a shock.

The god Mercury appeared before him and delivered a stern message from the god Jupiter. Aeneas's destiny, he said, was to found the city that would become Rome. His old home destroyed, Aeneas was set on a mission to found a new one. It was no less than a heaven-sent task. Continuing their travels, he and his followers eventually reached Italy. Sailing upriver, the greased pine timbers of their ships gliding gently over the water, they laid eyes on the future site of the city. Here they found an idyllic rural land called Latium, its quiet green woods standing in contrast to the bright colours of their boats and the shine of their armour. But in this Eden-like land events quickly spiralled out of control. The Trojan settlers who came in piety and peace quickly turned invaders, began a bloody war and found themselves murdering local countrymen.

Although the story is a myth anchored in the very ancient past, its theme gets to the heart of early Roman history: conflict and the Italian countryside. It would not be the first and only time that war and the rural 'quiet land' of Italy bled into each other. Indeed, in 350 BC, at the time of the myth's creation, those two spheres of Roman life were fast becoming stitched into a single fabric. Early Roman citizens were both farmers and part-time soldiers. In both war and agriculture Romans humbly and piously called upon the traditional gods to sanction their endeavours and bring success to them and their families. The cycles of the agricultural year and the season of military campaigning were the same too: March (the month of Mars, the god of war) heralded the period of greatest activity. By the time October came around, the tools of the farmer and the weapons of the soldier were put away for the winter.

Above all, however, it was the characteristics of soldier and peasant that had become fused in the Roman. The virtues that made a good farmer also made a good fighter. Patriotism, self-lessness, industriousness and a hardy ability to persevere in the face of adversity would not only make a farm or a plot of land productive. These were the same virtues that would build the greatest empire of the ancient world. This, at least, is how the Romans liked to see themselves. It was a comforting view. The poet Virgil, who composed the epic story of Aeneas's foundation of Rome, neatly summed this up. The Roman peasant-soldiers, he said, were like bees. They were not individuals, but a highly organized community striving together. Like Aeneas, these 'little Romans' worked hard, were dutiful and patriotically repressed their private desires to the greater good of the group. Yes, some died from their exertions along the way, but the race as a whole flourished. And the glowing, lucent honey they produced? This was pure gold, the product of a golden age, the riches of an entire empire.[1]

However, as in the story of Aeneas's violent struggle to found Rome, the rural ideal of the bees clashed with the reality. Away from the hive, observed Virgil, the bees were also capable of waging venomous war on outsiders. But outsiders were not their only enemy. With their wings flashing, their stings whetted and their arms ready for battle, they reserved their most vicious attacks for inside the hive, for an internecine war on themselves.[2] Lurking behind the rustic virtues of the hardy peasant, behind his honour and his steadfastness, said Virgil, was something quite opposite: the chaos of passion, the irrationality of war and, worse, the messy brutality of civil war. This was the true theme of Rome's foundation. It was one that would reverberate throughout the history of the empire that the city-state would create. It would characterize the eventual fall of Rome as much as its earliest foundation and its incredible rise.

The site of the city that the mythical Aeneas first set eyes on was located 24 kilometres (15 miles) inland near a river, the Tiber. Made up of seven compact hills, it seems today like a small, unprepossessing place for the capital of an empire that would rule over the known world. There was no immediate port giving on to the sea's trade routes, and the marshes lying at the bottom of the hills, subject to overspills from the Tiber, had to be drained before settlement could spread there. Nonetheless, on the Palatine Hill, the future residence of Roman emperors, a series of stone and wooden shepherds' huts formed the first settlement at the very start of the Iron Age in 1000 BC, and from that time on it would be continually inhabited. By the seventh century BC that community on the Palatine joined together with others on the Quirinal, Aventine and Caelian hills. Soon the Esquiline and Viminal hills also were deforested, levelled and terraced to make homes for other settlers. The Capitoline Hill, which was nearest to the river, became the settlement's acropolis and the home for the temple of the shepherds' principal deity, Jupiter. The area at the foot of these hills, once the place where the shepherds grazed their flocks, was drained and filled, and the meeting-place of the Roman Forum soon formed the city's epicentre.

But while the site of the capital of the future Roman empire was perhaps unexpected, it did have natural advantages for an expansion into Italy. Those hills, for example, formed a natural defence against invaders, while the Tiber valley opened out on to the rich agricultural plain of Latium. The site also formed a natural bridging point between Latium (and hence the Greek colonies at the foot of Italy) and another region, called Etruria, to the north. Its sandwiching between these two civilizations is reflected in the language the Romans used: they spoke a dialect of the language of the Latins, but it was the Etruscans, themselves influenced by the Greeks, who predominantly gave the Romans their alphabet. However, the Etruscans gave the Romans much more than writing: they gave them their early rulers too.

Between 753 and 510 BC Rome was ruled by kings, the last three of whom were Etruscan. The first, according to legend, was Romulus, and his story is in keeping with the rootless, belligerent theme of his ancient ancestor Aeneas. Romulus and his twin brother Remus were the sons of Mars, the god of war. Abandoned by their jealous great-uncle and exposed to the wilderness of Latium, they were saved when a she-wolf, an ancient figure of ferocity, suckled them. Later the brothers were looked after and raised by shepherds. It was a start in life that made the twins tough but also unforgiving. When they were adults the brothers quarrelled over who should be the founder of the city they decided to establish. In the course of this argument Romulus killed Remus and became the first king. Although the Romans believed that after Romulus there were six more kings of Rome, the reality is that perhaps only the last three (Tarquinius Priscus, Servius Tullius and Tarquinius the Proud) were real historical figures. Under these Etruscan kings, key characteristics of the political system of early Rome were established, and these would resonate throughout the city's history.

One political principle arose from a clash of loyalty among the leading aristocrats; they felt they owed their primary loyalty not to the state or the wider community, but to their clan. The noblemen were known to walk around the city with their associates, relatives and retainers, whose families could all trace their descent from one common ancestor. These dependants were known as 'clients', and the informal network of which they were part became a key nub of political power, status and influence in the state. This is reflected in the names of Romans then and through the centuries to come.[3] Appius Claudius, for example, was a prominent politician in Rome of the 130s BC. His family name shows how, alongside his personal name of Appius, he could trace his ancestry back to Attus Clausus, the man who founded the clan. The Claudii would not only become the leading men of state throughout the Roman republic, but would also form one branch of Rome's first dynasty of emperors, the Julio-Claudians.

But it was not just the ancient names and the associated prestige which began under the Etruscan kings that would echo through the centuries to come. The authority invested in the kings was their most important legacy. It was this that would become the foundation stone of the Roman imperial mentality. The Romans called the kings' executive authority *imperium*. This was their right to give orders to ordinary people and to expect those orders to be obeyed. *Imperium* allowed them to punish and even to execute people for disobedience. Crucially, it also included the power to conscript citizens into an army and lead them to war on people outside the boundary of Rome who challenged that authority. The holder of *imperium* carried a symbol of his power, and this too was of Etruscan origin. The *fasces* was a bundle of elm or birch rods 1.5 metres (5 feet) in length; they were tied together with red leather thongs, and in among the rods was an axe. The authoritarianism symbolized by the rods survives today in our word 'fascism'.

Long after the Etruscan kings had gone, the authority of *imperium* would remain. In Roman eyes it would legitimize and justify conquest. Be it Julius Caesar's annexation of Gaul or the emperor Trajan's invasion of Dacia, *imperium* carried with it the honourable appearance of the execution of justice. The first Roman emperor Augustus was also the first to regularly use the title of *imperator*, from which we get our word 'emperor', the man to whom that authority is attached. The reality of *imperium*, however, would be much more self-serving. It would result in the mass shedding of blood, not just within Italy, but throughout the entire Mediterranean world. How Romans other than the Etruscan kings came to hold the power of *imperium* is the central story of the first great revolution in Roman history: the foundation of the Roman republic in *c.* 509 BC.

CREATING THE REPUBLIC

The great revolution that spawned the political system of Rome is told in a famous story. Sextus, the son of the king Tarquinius the Proud, made sexual advances to Lucretia, the wife of a nobleman. When she resisted, Sextus threatened to kill both her and a slave in her company, and claim that he had caught her committing adultery with the slave. Lucretia gave in. Unable to live with the dishonour, however, she soon committed suicide. Personal tragedy quickly escalated into a very public revolution. A nobleman called Lucius Junius Brutus, enraged at the death he had just witnessed, was spurred to take action against the Tarquins. With a band of aristocrats, he drove Tarquinius the Proud and Sextus out of the city of Rome. While the details of the story might more comfortably belong to the world of romantic fiction, the fact remains that Roman nobles mounted a *coup d'état* in the final decade of the sixth century BC against the last of the Etruscan kings and crystallized a crucial political change. This revolutionary moment would become the most pivotal point in early Roman history. From it was forged another key cornerstone in the Roman mentality: a desire for political freedom and a hatred of domination by one man.

The solution the Romans devised to the problem of rule by kings was the republic. The word does not imply a democracy (although it would have democratic elements), but means literally the 'public good', the 'state' or the 'commonwealth'. It was a system of government that evolved slowly over a long period of time, and was subject to continual tweaks and improvements as Rome's influence and power in Italy and the Mediterranean world increased. Above all, the republic would see the power of *imperium* exercised not by kings, but by two annually elected office holders called 'consuls'. Under the men who held this office and their powerful clan-networks of clients, the small city-state of the Roman republic would build an empire.

The magistracy of the consulship approximated to the role of a prime minister or a president today, although, unlike that modern parallel, there were of course two consuls. The simple fact that two men were elected to the consulship meant that one could act as a restraint on the other. They were elected by a vote in a public assembly, and held power for a year. When presiding over official business, they, like certain other office holders, wore a light woollen toga distinguished by a purple border. Once their term of office was over, the consuls were called to account by their peers in the aristocracy. The basis of their authority, the power of *imperium*, was as strong and personal as it had been under the kings. For example, reflecting their aristocratic clan background, the consuls were accompanied by a group of twelve attendants wherever they went. Just as they had done under the Etruscan kings, these attendants, like a band of bodyguards, heralds and policemen rolled into one, carried with them the consuls' rods and axe of office, and cleared the path for the consuls to pass through. Now, however, that power of *imperium* was circumscribed by the limitations of the office.

For all their attempts to move decisively away from the kings, the aristocratic Roman nobles who founded the republic were careful not to abandon entirely the rule of one man. For times of emergency, they created the office of dictator, to which the consuls could appoint someone to restore control over affairs of state. Once the republic had been safely returned to order, the elected consuls would resume office. Indeed, as the responsibilities of the two consulships increased throughout the fifth and fourth centuries BC, the leading men of state sought to share out the burden of the consuls' duties by developing subordinate magistracies with more specific tasks. The origins of these other offices are obscure but later in the republic they come to form a clearly defined hierarchy.

One such office was that of praetor. This post was perhaps created to ease the responsibility of consuls in hearing private legal cases – at first within Rome, but later in trials brought by Romans elsewhere in Italy and abroad. The fact that praetors were also accompanied by attendants (though only six), also carried the power of *imperium*, and had the privilege of consulting the gods shows that they were like junior consuls. When Rome's empire developed, the post of praetor would be held by military commanders and governors of Rome's provinces abroad.

Several other posts were important to the smooth running of the republic. The office of quaestor originally carried with it the responsibility of assisting the consul in hearing and judging legal trials. (This is suggested by the meaning of *quaestor*: literally 'investigator'.) Later it too took on a different character: it came to be associated with managing financial affairs, and, as a result, the post of quaestor became an office akin to that of a minister of the treasury in a modern state. An aedile, on the other hand, was the magistrate who supervised the markets in the city. Perhaps the modern equivalent would be a minister in the Department of Trade and Industry.

Finally, the responsibility of the censor was to compile a census of Roman citizens every five years. This office, loosely an ancient version of the General Register Office, was much more important than perhaps its task implies, particularly in a military context. The Roman army at this period was not a professional body; it was comprised of simply citizens of the republic. However, because soldiers had to provide their own armour, the process of registering Roman citizens and their respective wealth and property had the consequence of dictating their military obligations to the state. The wealthier had a greater influence within the Roman republic because they brought more wealth and prestige to its army.

Out of all the holders of these offices a key body of the republic was formed: the Roman Senate. The Senate was a debating chamber and the collective voice of the political élite, and was presided over by the year's consuls. However, the Senate was not at all like a present-day parliament, such as the US Senate. It was not made up of representatives of Roman citizens; instead it comprised simply ex-office holders. Indeed, senators did not pass laws and had no legal powers. As we shall see, sovereignty belonged not to the Senate but to the adult male citizens who voted in the assemblies of the people for elections and the passing of bills.

Rather, senators were an advisory body whose decisions were formulated and passed on as guidance to the current office holders. This, however, should not belittle the importance and authority of the Senate. Future and past office holders relied on the approval and support of their colleagues in the aristocratic ruling class for political influence and success in elections. Considering that the office holders would most often come from the Senate, and return to it once their term of office was over, magistrates in the Roman republic ignored the wishes of their fellow senators at the peril of their future political careers.

This, then, was the basic formation of the Roman republic. The Greek historian Polybius provided an astute analysis of this political system, which he based on knowledge gained while he was held hostage in Rome during the mid-second century BC. It had, he said, using Greek concepts, elements of democracy (elections and the passing of bills in the popular assemblies), oligarchy (the Senate) and monarchy (the consuls). The harmony between these three parts was the source of the republic's great virtue, its unequalled strength and dynamism. When the three elements worked together, there was nothing that

Rome could not achieve, no emergency it could not overcome. Two critically important questions remained, though. Who was eligible for these offices – the aristocratic heads of the leading Roman clans or ordinary Roman citizens? And how did the Romans vote for them? Answering these questions would be the cause of the next great revolution in the development of the Roman republic.

CONFLICT: PATRICIANS AND THE PLEBS

In the earliest period of the republic the aristocrats of the old Roman clans held all offices. These men called themselves 'patricians', and one argument was typical of the way they justified their complete monopoly on power. Since the time of the Etruscan kings, they explained, they had held all the ancient priesthoods. Their unique knowledge of the gods made them best placed for the decisions of political office; only with that knowledge could the gods' favour on Rome in the future be guaranteed. The success of the state was considered to be dependent on the gods' goodwill, making Roman religion of critical importance, both then and throughout Roman history. In the early republic, however, said the patricians, they alone were the gatekeepers to the gods and they alone should hold power.

The rich leading plebeians (namely, the non-patricians from the rest of the Roman people, known as the plebs) vehemently disagreed with this claim. In the mid-fifth century BC they organized and agitated for reform. Although they campaigned on a platform of alleviating the economic problems of the poorest plebs, the reality was different: they too wanted their hands firmly on the levers of power. By 366 BC they had notched up their crucial victory: one of the consulships was opened up to candidates from the plebs, and in 172 BC for the first time plebeians held both the consulships. However, this was not quite the radical, meritocratic reform it might appear.

Wealth was the key to office holding. To secure election to a magistracy, to build up political alliances and support among the plebs and the aristocracy, prospective candidates needed lots of money. As a result, only the richest two per cent of adult male Romans ever reached the consulship. This situation seemed to get worse with the enfranchisement of the rich plebeians because they quickly closed ranks with the patricians and formed a new nobility, admission to which was carefully policed. That, at least, is what noble Romans liked to think. More recently, scholars have shown that the new élite was actually more open than even the Romans thought; the reform of rules relating to eligibility for the consulship helped achieve this. Another consequence of allowing plebeians to become consuls and office holders was not immediately recognized by the Romans, but lay some way off in the future. Later in the history of the republic, when Rome built its empire in Italy and throughout the Mediterranean world, candidates from Roman élites in Italy and the provinces of the empire would be eligible to run for the top offices of the republic. Later still, those provincial élites would even furnish Rome with its emperors.

It had taken the best part of a century for rich plebeians to find their way to sharing with the patricians the top offices of the Roman state. The struggle of the ordinary plebs in fighting for their political voice also began in the fifth century BC. In order to curb the power of the patrician élite, they used the only leverage they could: an old-fashioned strike. When Rome's security was being threatened by invading forces in 494 BC, the citizens simply laid down their weapons en masse, took up a position on the Aventine Hill and refused to fight. The plebs' secession from the republic resulted temporarily in the formation of a state within a state. Instead of asking the rich nobility to provide them with an office in the republic to serve their interests, the Roman citizens, holed up in protest on their hill, simply made up their own. The magistrates they created were called 'tribunes of the people'. Only when that office became formally recognized by the patricians as part of the state did the struggle, known as 'the conflict of the orders', come to an end.

The new office would prove crucial to the history of the republic. It would radically change the balance of power between the political élite of the Senate and the people. Ten tribunes were elected annually by the plebs alone, and it was their responsibility to protect the plebs from abuse of power at the hands of the office holders, especially the consuls and praetors in possession of *imperium*. If need be, a tribune was empowered to intervene physically to defend a citizen who was being wrongfully punished or oppressed, and to bring help. It is important to stress, however, that whereas today the roles and jobs of figures in a modern state are highly stratified and specialized, in ancient Rome they were entwined in one person. A consul was at once a military commander, a prime minister, a chancellor and a bishop, while a tribune combined the roles of a Member of Parliament or a US senator with defence lawyer, policeman and trade union representative. Although the new office was radical in origin, later in the history of republic it would come to be held by the lackeys of the noble élite. Nonetheless, by the mid-fourth century BC the political voice of the plebs had found its teeth. Now its bark was recognized too.

The second crucial consequence of the plebs' great strike was the strengthening of their tribal assemblies. Before the secession the dominant assembly of the people was called the Assembly of the Centuries, but it was not very democratic. It was organized around military units known as 'centuries', and because military obligations were dictated by a citizen's wealth, the assembly was dominated by the rich. A relatively small number of citizens from the highest class of soldier controlled over half of the 193 centuries, while the mass of the poorest citizens held only one. Considering that each century had one vote, the political voice of the poorer citizens amounted to a whisper.

After the conflict of the orders, however, the tribal assemblies became more powerful. They were classified according to regional districts, known as 'tribes'. Each tribe thus contained both rich and poor. Thanks to the electoral college system of 'one tribe, one vote', these assemblies were altogether more representative. As Rome increased its rural territory throughout Italy, the city's original four tribes expanded accordingly to thirty-five. A new assembly, the Assembly of the Tribes, was called by a high-ranking magistrate from the élite (a consul, for example) and could be attended by patricians as well as plebeians. The Plebeian Assembly, however, was convened by a tribune of the people, attended only by plebs and became a standard place for passing laws. At first the votes of these popular assemblies were nothing more than plebiscites – a way for the élite to gauge the majority opinion of the Roman citizens. By 287 BC, however, the decisions of both tribal assemblies, whether expressed in elections or in the passage of bills, had the force of law and were binding on the entire Roman people.

In both the office of tribune and the newly empowered popular assemblies the Roman republic had grown the great paradox of its 'two heads': those of the Senate (the collective voice of the aristocratic and moneyed political élite) and the Roman people. A system that mixed an aristocratic élite with the fundamental principle that power also lies in the hands of the people seems puzzling today. In the ancient world, however, the partnership was potent. It was the concept hammered into the initials 'SPQR' (*Senatus Populusque Romanus* – the Senate and Roman People), the logo emblazoned on the Roman military standards and the slogan that would, in time, authorize Rome's march into the domains of its future empire. That march had begun before the conflict of the orders, in the fifth century BC. It was the start of an extraordinarily aggressive period of expansion. One of the greatest problems of ancient history is explaining exactly why it happened.

WINNING ITALY

Where that expansion was aimed is certainly clear. Between 500 and 275 BC, in piecemeal fashion and through a combination of war and diplomacy, the citizen armies of the Roman republic brought first Latium and then the rest of the Italian peninsula under its control. The original motivation for war was perhaps land. With the peasant holdings of most Roman citizens too small to sustain a large family, the Romans of the early republic were on the lookout for new territory. But the first concerted military campaigns were driven perhaps more by the defence of land rather than its acquisition. In 493 BC Rome joined an alliance of Latin communities, known as the Latin League, to defend their cherished region of Latium. It was being invaded by the hill tribes of central Italy: the Volsci, the Sabines and the Aequi. This war, provoked by aggression from outside Rome, would provide the republic with a very convenient and useful theme for all future wars in Italy and beyond. To ensure the favour of the gods in their military campaigns, the Romans would look for instances to justify taking action in 'self-defence'. Indeed, the legitimating mythology of the 'just war' was fostered by the elaborate religious ceremonies with which Romans declared hostilities. These eccentric demonstrations of their attentiveness to justice were rituals with which Rome's Italian neighbours would become very familiar.

Once the assaults of the hill tribes had been checked, Rome and its Latin allies turned their attention to the region of

Etruria to the north. Perhaps because the family trees of the leading Romans had Etruscan roots, there was no shortage of old friendships and feuds with which to justify both alliances and declarations of war. Some Etruscan cities promptly came to terms with Rome; others were defeated in battle and annexed. Accused of arrogance by its Latin partners for claiming to have carried the lion's share of the fighting, Rome turned on them next. The increasingly powerful city-state went to war with the Latin League in 340 BC, defeated it, and then dismantled the league two years later. Next in line were the Samnites. Perhaps Rome's greatest Italian adversaries, the Samnites were a powerful and organized confederation to the south of Latium. They proved so hardy that the name 'Samnite' would later be accorded to one of the four types of gladiator in the Roman arena. In three wars that endured until 290 BC, and in which Rome had mixed success, huge swathes of Samnite territory eventually came under its control. The once diminutive city-state was now pushing at the borders of the Greek colonies at the foot of Italy.

The fruits of all these wars of conquest were varied. Sometimes the territory won became a Roman colony: the land was annexed, divided up and allotted to Roman citizens. Sometimes Rome came to an alliance with autonomous Italian communities, its basis being the agreement to come to each other's military aid. Sometimes Rome conferred the privilege of citizenship (either with or without the right to vote), and in this instance, while these communities had two citizenships at once, they had also become absorbed into the Roman commonwealth. The language, customs and culture of the Romans were thus slowly spread throughout Italy.

All these forms of conquest demanded one thing: loyalty to Rome. That loyalty would create Rome's greatest asset in building an empire beyond the perimeters of Italy – an endless supply of citizens and allies, and hence an endless supply of military manpower. In analysing the superior power of the Roman citizen militia over other armies of the Mediterranean, the Greek historian Polybius wrote: '... even if the Romans have suffered a defeat at first, they renew the war with undiminished forces... Since the Romans are fighting for country and children, it is impossible for them to relax the fury of their struggle; they resist with obstinate resolution until they have overcome their enemies.'[4]

In the fire of these wars of conquest, the military mindset and culture of the resilient Roman peasant-soldier was forged. The Roman consuls who wielded the power of *imperium* and led the campaigns were on a quest for glory, seeking to bring honour to the ancient family names of their more humble ancestors, the shepherds and farmers of Etruria and Latium. Above all, the character of the tough, unwavering peasant, in whose work there was no quarter for comfort or self-indulgence, was reflected in the Roman attitude to these wars. As they liked to see it, the conflicts were undertaken with pious respect for the gods, with integrity, honour and, above all, justice.

The war that completed Roman control of Italy in the south was sparked in 280 BC. The Greek city of Tarentum, on the heel of Italy, had sent out messages of defiance towards Rome. Indeed, fearing Roman expansion into their territory, the Greeks of Tarentum had called for military aid from overseas, and Pyrrhus, the Greek king of Epirus (in northern Greece) had agreed to help them. He had ideas for a western Greek empire of his own.

Furious at this impertinent show of disrespect from Tarentum, Rome wanted reparation for the so-called 'insults' levelled at it. Here was another opportunity to act in 'self-defence' and to requite what Rome considered its due. A new and very real Trojan War was beckoning. It was not now between the mythical

Trojan hero Aeneas and the legendary Greek kings Agamemnon and Menelaus. This time it pitted their descendants, the 'Trojan' Romans against the Greek army of King Pyrrhus.

Tarentum was too far away from Rome for the meticulous rituals with which Roman priests now traditionally initiated hostilities. There was, for example, no time for the arrival of a herald-priest on the enemy's frontier. Here such a man would bind his head with wool, call upon Jupiter as his witness that he came lawfully and piously, and announce that the 'guilty' party had thirty-three days to surrender.[5] Neither was there time to ensure the favour of the gods by throwing a spear into the designated enemy's territory. The Romans found an expedient solution to this problem, however. They forced a prisoner seized from Pyrrhus's army to buy a small plot of land in Rome and the priests threw their symbolic spear into that.

Pyrrhus invaded Italy at the start of the campaigning season in 280 BC. In two brutal and bloody battles he successfully defeated the Romans. The Greek king, though, having seen so many of his soldiers slaughtered in achieving this success, was said to have remarked, 'With another victory like this, we will be finished!' (Hence our modern phrase 'pyrrhic victory'.) By 275 BC, however, the Romans had turned their fortunes around. They defeated Pyrrhus at Beneventum near Naples, expelled his invading army, and were now free to consolidate their grasp over the rest of southern Italy.

With the ambitious Greek king Pyrrhus defeated, however, the Mediterranean world outside Italy had been forced to sit up and take notice. There was a new player in the region. Breaking over their seven hills, the waves of Aeneas's Romans were now lapping at foreign shores. The power of Rome had arrived.

I

REVOLUTION

In 154 BC the grand public funeral of Tiberius Sempronius Gracchus, a hero of the Roman republic, took place. His corpse was carried into the Forum dressed in the clothes of a triumphant general: the purple toga was covered in silver stars and accompanied by the rods and axes of office that befitted his exceptional career. The noblemen in the procession, unshaven as a mark of respect, wore black and their heads were veiled; the women beat their breasts, tore at their dishevelled hair and cut their cheeks with their fingernails in grief. There were also professional mourners in attendance, as well as dancers and mime artists imitating the dead man with exaggerated gestures. The most haunting feature of many men in the procession, however, was the funeral mask they wore, each one moulded from beeswax to an eerie likeness of Gracchus and his ancestors, each one faithful in colour and shape. In this way the men who wore them bore a striking family resemblance to the dead man now propped up on the speaker's platform of the Forum before the onlooking rich and poor of Rome.

As the ancestral representatives of the family took their ivory seats on the platform, one of them delivered an oration celebrating the dead man's achievements in life. There was much to commemorate. Gracchus had twice achieved the office of consul, the highest post in the republic, as well as the distinguished and influential office of former consuls, that of censor.

As a soldier, he had led successful campaigns on behalf of the republic in Spain and Sardinia. For both of these he had been awarded a triumph, the name given to the famous procession in which a conquering general crossed the sacred limits of the city and returned to civilian life in Rome. Yet despite the achievements that had covered his name in glory, Gracchus was not reputed to be someone who looked to personal success. His funeral was a public celebration of one virtue above all. The Romans liked to think of him as having put the service of the republic before his own ambitions, for making the welfare of the Roman people his first and foremost guide. The funeral speech would therefore have had the same effect as the wax masks. It reminded the onlookers that 'the glorious memory of brave men is continually renewed; the fame of those who have performed any noble deed is never allowed to die; and the renown of those who have done good service to their country becomes a matter of common knowledge to the multitude and part of the heritage of posterity'.[1]

But the renewing of Gracchus's achievements, both through the masks of his family and the speech in his memory, had another, more specific function. It served as a reminder for his sons, grandsons and subsequent descendants to live up to those achievements. The desire to honour the glory of one's father by emulating his success in the service of the republic, whether in war, empire-building or politics, was among the key motivations of the Roman aristocratic élite. It is easy to imagine that nowhere did this desire burn more brightly than in the heart of a nine-year-old boy, Gracchus's son, also named Tiberius Sempronius Gracchus.

The boy would have stood alongside his mother and the leading aristocratic senators before the blazing pyre outside Rome; it was here that, after the public funeral orations, his father's body would have been cremated. As he watched the ceremonies

45

come to an end, the boy would have been instilled with the desire to endure hardship and even death to earn a eulogy similar to that accorded his father. He now carried the responsibility of upholding the paternal name and glory. It was a burden outstripped only by the obligation to uphold the prestige of another family: his mother Cornelia's.

Through both his mother and father, the young Tiberius Sempronius Gracchus was related to three of the great aristocratic dynasties of the Roman republic. Together, in the space of less than a hundred and fifty years, these families had led the way in turning the republic from its position as master of Italy to master of the entire Mediterranean. By the time of Gracchus the elder's funeral, the Romans referred to that expanse of sea as *mare nostrum* (our sea) because of their undisputed dominion over it and the lands surrounding it.

And yet this boy's path in life would radically diverge from the pattern established in his family. The young Tiberius himself would have no grand funeral like his father's: just twenty-two years later his mutilated corpse would be slung unceremoniously into the river Tiber. The men who would carry out his

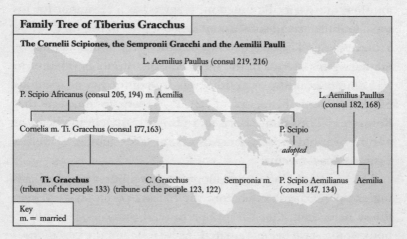

Family Tree of Tiberius Gracchus

The Cornelii Scipiones, the Sempronii Gracchi and the Aemilii Paulli

L. Aemilius Paullus (consul 219, 216)

P. Scipio Africanus (consul 205, 194) m. Aemilia

L. Aemilius Paullus (consul 182, 168)

Cornelia m. Ti. Gracchus (consul 177, 163)

P. Scipio

adopted

Ti. Gracchus (tribune of the people 133)   C. Gracchus (tribune of the people 123, 122)   Sempronia m. P. Scipio Aemilianus (consul 147, 134)   Aemilia

Key
m. = married

murder would not be foreign enemies of Rome on the battle-field, but the same aristocratic senators who had lined up behind him watching his father's funeral pyre burn. For Tiberius's short, controversial life intersected with a key turning point – a crisis – in the history of the Roman republic. This crisis centred on the question of who would benefit from the empire Rome had so quickly acquired – the rich or the poor? The aris-tocratic architects of Rome's empire or the ordinary citizen-soldiers who had built it? It was a question that would lead to a soul-searching investigation into the nature of Rome's empire and what the process of acquiring it had done to the moral character and values of Romans. Extraordinarily, this crisis would see the young Tiberius take not the side of his own family and the aristocratic élite, but the side of the poor.

After the funeral the wax masks of the elder Gracchus and his ancestors were laid in a shrine in the family home. They would serve as an 'inspiring spectacle for a young man of noble ambi-tions and virtuous aspirations. For can we conceive anyone to be unmoved by the sight of all the likenesses collected together of the men who have earned glory, all, as it were, living and breath-ing? What could be a more glorious spectacle?'[2] Yet in 154 BC no one would have imagined what a revolutionary path the young Tiberius, in seeking to match the example represented by those masks, would take, or how it would change Rome for ever.

The great convulsion in Roman history epitomized by Tiberius's career is a morality tale. In becoming a superpower, Rome, so it was said, abandoned the very values with which it had won its supremacy. At the pinnacle of its achievement, the virtues that had made the Roman republic so successful failed it and were lost for ever. To understand the significance of this turning point, however, one must begin with an account of how Rome reached it.

CONQUEST OF THE MEDITERRANEAN

The Greek historian Polybius, detained as a prisoner in Rome between 163 and 150 BC, wrote a history aimed at helping Romans to answer one question: how did Rome achieve supremacy over the Mediterranean in the space of just fifty-two years (219–167 BC)?[3] Although Polybius's work fed Roman myths and legends about this period in their history, this should not diminish the extraordinary success of Rome. The Romans' mastery of the Mediterranean was so complete that by 167 BC the Senate was able to abolish direct taxation in Italy, replacing it with the riches that the republic received in revenue from its provinces abroad.

The leading politicians in Rome who had achieved this feat were a small clique of aristocratic families. Although access to these families – through the practice of adoption, for example – was more open than the Romans liked to think, between 509 and 133 BC just twenty-six families were said to have provided three-quarters of those elected to the consulship, the highest annual office in the republic. A mere ten had provided half of them. The young Tiberius Sempronius Gracchus was related to the three interconnected families who had blazed a trail during the great period of Roman expansion: the Sempronii Gracchi through his father, and both the Cornelii Scipiones and the Aemilii Paulli through his mother (see family tree, page 48). By tracing a brief history of Rome's conquest of the Mediterranean, we can see how all the young Tiberius's relatives spearheaded Rome's empire-building abroad. This extraordinary story begins in North Africa and with the challenge posed by a rival.

In 265 BC the ancient city of Carthage was the most significant power in the Mediterranean. It was founded by Phoenicians (from what is now Lebanon) around 800 BC. Their

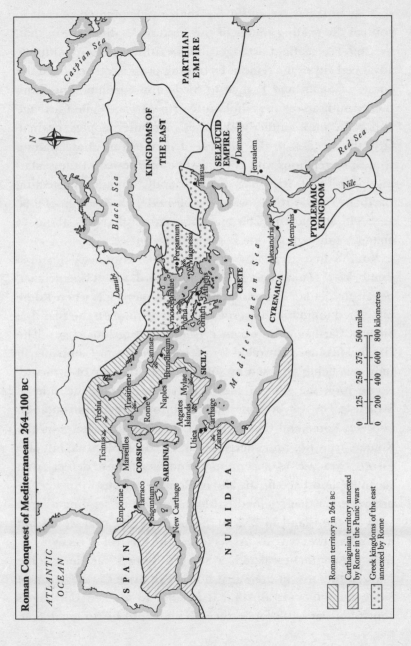

Roman Conquest of Mediterranean 264–100 BC

ATLANTIC OCEAN

Caspian Sea

N

PARTHIAN EMPIRE

KINGDOMS OF THE EAST

Black Sea

SELEUCID EMPIRE

• Damascus

Tarsus

Jerusalem •

Red Sea

Danube

Nile

Pergamum

Magnesia

PTOLEMAIC KINGDOM

Cynoscephalae

Pydna

Memphis •

Corinth Athens

Alexandria •

Ticinus

Trebia

Trasimene

Cannae

Brundisium

CRETE

CYRENAICA

Marseilles

Rome •

Naples

Mylae

SICILY

Aegates Islands

Mediterranean Sea

CORSICA

SARDINIA

Carthage

Utica •

Carthage

Zama

SPAIN

Emporiae

Tarraco

Saguntum

New Carthage •

N U M I D I A

| | 0 | 125 | 250 | 375 | 500 miles |
| | 0 | 200 | 400 | 600 | 800 kilometres |

⬚⬚⬚ Roman territory in 264 BC

⬚⬚⬚ Carthaginian territory annexed by Rome in the Punic wars

⬚⬚⬚ Greek kingdoms of the east annexed by Rome

skill lay in seafaring, and it was their single-minded pursuit to control the trading routes of the western Mediterranean that, by 265 BC, made Carthage the wealthiest, most culturally advanced city of the region. Its trading posts stretched from the coasts of Spain and France to Sicily and Sardinia, and from there south across the whole of North Africa. While Carthage had come into conflict with other maritime peoples, particularly the Greeks, in the process of establishing these trading routes, its relations with the city-state of Rome and the seafaring peoples of Italy had been friendly: treaties protecting Carthage's trade routes were established with Rome in 509 BC and 348 BC. Now in 265 BC, however, all that was about to change, although no one knew it at the outset.

Rome's first great war with Carthage, known as the First Punic War (*Punic* being the Latin word for 'Phoenician'), began in 264 BC. The moment of incitement was when Rome was called upon to help resolve a small dispute on the island of Sicily, a Carthaginian province (see map, previous page). The city of Messina, controlled by mercenaries from Campania in Italy, was being attacked by soldiers from the city of Syracuse. Rome took the side of Messina; Carthage took the side of Syracuse. The war by proxy blew up into a direct confrontation between Rome and Carthage after the consul in charge of the Roman army not only succeeded in relieving Messina, but also forced Syracuse to accept his generous terms, defect from Carthage and become an ally of Rome. Anxious to protect its province, Carthage joined battle in earnest by sending a large army to the island in 262 BC. So began a war that would last more than twenty years. At stake was the control of Sicily.

As the conflict escalated, so too did Rome's war aims. Rome realized that to win the war it needed to drive Carthage out of Sicily altogether; to do that it needed to weaken Carthage's control of the seas around Sicily. This would be no mean feat, for it required developing a weapon Rome had not yet tried out, let alone built: a navy. According to Polybius, the Romans seized the opportunity to build a war fleet for the first time in their history when a Carthaginian ship harrying the crossing of Roman troops to Sicily ran aground on the coast of southern Italy.[4] The Romans seized it, copied its design and within a year produced a navy of one hundred oared warships. They even took the opportunity of enhancing the ships with a secret weapon: a rotatable, spiked boarding bridge. Thus armed, the Romans, led by their admiral Gaius Dulius, won their first sea battle at Mylae in 260 BC.

Despite some major setbacks, including an ill-advised invasion of North Africa, the destruction of their fleet by storms no less than three times, and near financial ruin, the Romans responded to adversity in typical, never-say-die fashion: they rebuilt their ships. Crucially, they were given a much-needed breathing space when, in 247 BC, the Carthaginians chose to focus not on defeating the Romans, but on restoring the loyalty – wavering towards Rome – of the Numidians and the Libyans in the interior of North Africa. When, on 10 March 241 BC, Rome won a decisive victory over a Carthaginian relief fleet off the Aegates Islands to the north of Sicily, the Romans finally achieved mastery of the sea. At that time the Carthaginian general Hamilcar was conducting a successful guerrilla war against the Roman army on Sicily. Even though he himself had not been beaten, he was instructed by the political leaders in Carthage to come to terms.

The undefeated general's submission to the Romans symbolized the unresolved nature of the first war. If striking the peace treaty rankled the Carthaginian leadership, there were more bitter pills to swallow. In the immediate aftermath of the war Carthage evacuated Sicily and, with the exception of the kingdom of Syracuse, which remained an ally, the island became

Rome's first overseas province. Harsh conditions were imposed, principally the indemnity that Carthage had to pay Rome: 3200 talents of silver, the equivalent of 82,000 kilograms (80 tons), to be paid over ten years. Rome then took advantage of Carthage's weakness to expel Carthaginians unceremoniously from both Sardinia and Corsica. In the space of a few years Rome had moved seamlessly from a position of seeking to 'defend' its allies in the region by excluding the Carthaginians from 'Italian' waters to exploiting the three wealthy islands for its own enrichment. Corn, as well as other riches, flowed into Rome from the islands. And yet despite this naked show of imperialism, the question of who controlled the Mediterranean had still not been answered.

The region of contention between the established Carthaginian empire and Rome's fledgling overseas empire now became Spain. The general Hamilcar headed up an expeditionary force and went there in 238 BC with the express purpose of building a new empire to make up for the loss of Sicily, Sardinia and Corsica. The mines of Spain were rich in gold and silver, a new army could be recruited from the local tribes there, and the country's grain supply could compensate for the loss of Sardinia's. Through a combination of campaigns, treaties and alliances, Hamilcar with his sons expanded their control of Spain, while Carthage continued to supply his expeditionary force with officers, elephants and colonists to populate the new cities being built. Nervous of the growing power base that Carthage was building in Spain, Rome sent envoys in 226 BC to New Carthage (modern-day Cartagena), asking the Carthaginians to limit their expansion to the river Ebro (see map, page 49). They agreed, but the peace was only temporary because Rome then strategically established an alliance with the independent city of Saguntum on the Mediterranean coast north of New Carthage. By making an ally of a city on the periphery of Carthage's expanding Spanish empire, Rome could eventually justify a war once again by claiming to come to Saguntum's defence. A time bomb for a future war was thus set ticking.

The man who was prepared to take on Rome for a second time and try to reverse the result of the first war was Hamilcar's younger son, Hannibal. In 221 BC he had assumed command of the Carthaginian forces in Spain. When he was nine, went one famous story, his father had dipped his hand in the blood of a sacrifice and sworn him to an eternal hatred of Rome. Now the twenty-seven-year-old general had his excuse to vent that wrath. To his mind the city of Saguntum, which had begun harassing neighbouring Carthaginian towns, was a threat, an impediment to their control of Spain and the security of the western empire. So, with authorization from the leaders of Carthage, Hannibal crossed the river Ebro and took the city by storm. War had been declared.

The Romans expected the Second Punic War to be fought in Spain. They were utterly wrong-footed. This conflict, which lasted from 218 to 201 BC and was the greatest of the wars between the two rival empires, is legendary for Hannibal's extraordinary decision: to invade Italy and march on Rome. In the spring of 218 BC he set out on the 1600-kilometre (1000-mile) journey across hostile territory with 12,000 cavalry, 90,000 infantry and thirty-seven war elephants. Such a feat demanded courage and resourcefulness. At the river Rhone, 500 metres (1650 feet) wide and too deep to wade across, the elephants were enticed on to rafts by mahouts. The animals were deceived by a covering of soil laid on the rafts to make them look like solid ground. Once two females had floated across, the others, despite some casualties, overcame their panic and followed. However, the greatest challenge to Hannibal was not a river, but the snowcapped mountains of the Alps.

Enduring ambushes, falling rocks and boulders, steep, slippery tracks, low food supplies and freezing temperatures, Hannibal headed his army through the narrow passes with ingenuity and inspired leadership. When his men were cold he spent the night in the open with them; when a road was blocked by a landslide he rallied them to heat up sour wine, pour it over the obstructing rocks and thus break them up; when his army was flagging from exhaustion he raised their spirits by reminding them of the opportunities for glory and loot that lay ahead: 'You are passing over the protective barrier of Italy – nay more, you are passing over the very walls of Rome!'[5] After four weeks crossing the whole Alpine range, Hannibal walked into Italy in the company of (at the lowest estimate) 20,000 infantry, 6000 cavalry and a minority of the elephants. The infantry might have been double that size. He rested them all for two weeks before proceeding to match the great feat of reaching Italy with another: destroying every Roman force he met there.

Between the winter of 218 BC and the summer of 216 BC, at the battles of Ticinus, Trebia and Trasimene (see map, page 49), the young general Hannibal surpassed the Romans in military flair, strategy and daring to consistently crush armies far larger than his own. The climax to his Italian campaign, however, was the battle of Cannae, a place that became synonymous with Roman tragedy. At this confrontation in the region of Apulia he succeeded in surrounding an army double the size of his own with both flanks of his superior African cavalry. As the encircling Carthaginian alliance closed in, a prolonged period of butchery ensued; 45,500 Roman and allied infantry were killed, along with 2700 cavalry. The battle cut a massive swathe through the officer corps of the aristocratic élite too: no fewer than eighty senators died on the battlefield. Indeed, it is said that perhaps no Western army has suffered higher casualties in a single day of fighting before or since than the Romans did at Cannae. The defeat sent shock waves through southern Italy, where many of Rome's allies and colonies now defected to Carthage. This had always been Hannibal's plan, and now it was paying off. To all appearances, Rome, the precocious fledgling empire, was doomed to be short-lived.

And yet, in the immediate aftermath of the battle, one man would show the never-say-die spirit of defiance with which Rome would turn events around. His name was Publius Cornelius Scipio and he was the man who was to become the grandfather of Tiberius Sempronius Gracchus. Although the then nineteen-year-old junior magistrate had just witnessed his father-in-law killed on the battlefield, he rallied the surviving officers. Scipio's energy and authority checked the impulse of the terrified soldiers who were threatening to flee. In fear now of Scipio, they promptly pulled themselves together and swore their loyalty to the Roman republic. The same indomitable spirit was echoed at the gates of Rome too. Here the victorious Hannibal sent a delegation to sue for terms in the expectation that his enemy would capitulate. The Romans responded by refusing to allow the Carthaginians even to enter the city. When Hannibal himself subsequently drew up his army outside the city walls, so the story goes, the land on which they camped happened to be for sale. Such was the confidence of the Romans that, before Hannibal and his army left, a buyer for it was found.[6] The message was clear: the Romans were determined to fight on and fight to win.

The man who would lead their comeback between 216 and 202 BC was Scipio. The key to his success in reversing Hannibal's achievement was the Romans' ability to draw on a seemingly endless supply of high-quality manpower. Although the Italian allies of Rome in the south defected to Hannibal, many others remained loyal, and it was from these and other allied communities throughout Italy that Rome created new armies. With them at their disposal, the Romans now adopted a different tactic altogether. They allowed Hannibal free rein in the south of Italy to try to raise a coalition of new forces, and meanwhile set out to defeat the Carthaginians in Spain. The plan was to prevent a second invasion and to stop Hannibal from acquiring much-needed reinforcements from abroad. At the age of just twenty-six, Scipio took New Carthage, won over many Spanish tribes and drove the Carthaginians out of Spain altogether. Such was his popularity that, despite opposition from the Senate in Rome, the charismatic and highly motivated young general was then able to raise another army of volunteers and set his sights on the one feat the Romans had not achieved during the First Punic War: an invasion of North Africa.

With Hannibal and his army recalled to Carthage to help defend the country, Scipio finally came to face to face with the great Carthaginian general at Zama, about 120 kilometres (75 miles) from Carthage, in 202 BC. At a meeting with his adversary, Hannibal attempted to negotiate a peace. Scipio refused. The Roman knew that the advantage was now with him. As the lines of the battle drew up, he and his army knew too what to expect from a fight with the Carthaginians. When, for example, Hannibal released the elephants the Romans, under orders from Scipio, stood firm and allowed them to pass through clearly marked lanes in their formation. Then, when the two sides joined battle, the envelopment tactic was used, but this time it was Hannibal and the Carthaginian army who were trapped inside. With some 20,000 Carthaginian deaths and only 1500 Roman losses, the battle of Zama brought about a stunning Roman victory and concluded the Second Punic War beyond all expectation. Rome's extraordinary comeback was capped by the terms of the peace. Carthage was allowed to retain the territory in Africa that it had held before the war, but its overseas empire was taken away for ever. It was forced to surrender its fleet and its elephants, to pay 10,000 talents (250,000 kilograms or 245 tons) of silver in indemnity and, crucially, to agree, in a way similar to a nuclear non-proliferation treaty today, never to re-arm or declare any war without permission from Rome.

Zama marked a key turning point. While Carthage lost a western Mediterranean empire, Rome – now master of the two new provinces of Spain and the sole power in the region – gained one. For his inspired leadership and brilliance in warfare Publius Cornelius Scipio was honoured with the name 'Africanus'. He was not the only one who bathed in glory. For their instrumental part in winning the west the ancient aristocratic family of the Cornelii Scipiones shot to pre-eminence among the Roman élite. So, one branch of young Tiberius Sempronius Gracchus' family tree was thus established. However, it was another of his ancestors who would go on to match Scipio's conquest of the western Mediterranean. He would do so by concluding the conquest of the Greek east.

The strategy by which Rome came to dominate the east between 197 and 168 BC was a little different from that used in the west. In the aftermath of the Punic Wars, the signs of an empire were plain to see. Roman garrisons and standing armies were now dotted around Sicily, Sardinia, Corsica and Spain; taxes from these provinces were being raised; and the annually elected Roman office holders allotted to govern those provinces immediately began to exploit their mineral wealth for the benefit of Rome. In the east, by contrast, the Roman Senate took a slightly more subtle, gradual and diplomatic path to asserting Rome's supremacy.

The eastern Mediterranean was at this time made up of a series of kingdoms. They were known as the 'successor kingdoms' of Alexander the Great, because the dynasties that ruled them were founded by Alexander's Greek generals when the great conqueror died and his vast but brief empire collapsed. One of these kings, Philip V of Macedon, had already incurred the anger of Rome. He had taken advantage of the republic's weakness after Cannae and made an alliance with Carthage. By 197 BC, with Carthage subdued, Rome was in a position to declare war proper on Philip. The excuse it chose was a familiar one: the defence of its Greek friends who were being tyrannized by him. Within the year Philip was defeated at the battle of Cynoscephalae and Rome had won the right to dispose of his kingdom as it saw fit. Instead of making the kingdom of Macedon a province of the republic, however, the Roman commander in the region attended the Isthmian Games at Corinth, received the rapturous welcome normally accorded to Greek kings, and cleverly declared Greece now to be 'free'. Then he withdrew his army.

Another opportunity for such Roman generosity soon presented itself. When the Greek king, Antiochus of Syria, expanded his Seleucid kingdom with attacks on Asia Minor (modern-day Turkey) and northern Greece, the Roman army returned to the region again with the stated purpose of aiding the Greek cities under threat. Antiochus was defeated at the battle of Magnesia in 190 BC, his kingdom was returned to its former limits and the Greek lands he had overrun were allocated to Rome's loyal allies in the war. Then, once again, the Roman troops were evacuated. Although both these brief wars gave the impression that freedom and autonomy remained with the Greek cities of the east, the reality was quite different. The consequence of Roman intervention was that the Greek cities were now bound by an unspoken obligation to Rome. In exchange for their 'freedom' the Greek cities of the east owed Rome their loyalty.[7]

The actions of one king, however, would provoke Rome into letting the mask of its benevolent eastern policy slip. When

Philip V's son Perseus came to the throne he sought to re-establish the prestige and authority of the Macedonian kingdom in the region. Through interventions in the local wars of Greece, he duly won influence and widespread popular support among the Greek city-states. His gain in influence, however, was to the cost of Rome's and in the eyes of the Roman Senate that was simply unacceptable. A new excuse for a 'just war' was devised and hostilities were declared in 171 BC.

At first Perseus's Macedonian phalanx was successful. By June 168 BC, however, the close-packed battle formation of infantry soldiers that had conquered the known world under Alexander the Great was fighting its last battle. At Pydna on the northeast coast of Greece the Roman legions of Lucius Aemilius Paullus won a decisive victory; 20,000 Macedonians were killed and 11,000 were taken prisoner. The once-mighty Greek kingdom was broken up into four republics loyal to Rome; it was only a matter of time before Macedonia became a Roman province in its own right. King Perseus himself, the last royal descendant of Alexander, was captured and taken to Rome. Here he was paraded as a trophy of Rome's dominion in the eastern Mediterranean. The stage on which the prisoner walked was the triumphal procession of Lucius Aemilius Paullus; the triumphant general was the future great-uncle of Tiberius Sempronius Gracchus the younger.

For the glorious part they played in Rome's conquest of the Mediterranean, in the wars won and in the numbers of the enemy killed, the family of the Aemilii Paulli joined the Cornelii Scipiones at the forefront of the Roman élite. Tiberius Sempronius Gracchus the elder ensured that his family too rivalled them for glory and prestige. His own father had been a consul and a hero from the war against Hannibal. Now he too injected the family name with new glory. In 180 BC Gracchus senior subjugated northern Spain, and three years later crushed an 80,000-strong rebellion in Sardinia. For these achievements Gracchus was considered worthy to marry Cornelia, the most eligible noblewoman in Rome. She was the daughter of Scipio Africanus and the niece of Lucius Aemilius Paullus. In Cornelia the three illustrious families united. They were the three wings of the ancestry of Cornelia's son, Tiberius Sempronius Gracchus the younger, and they came together at Gracchus's funeral in 154 BC. But despite the families' extraordinary success in conquering the Mediterranean a question mark loomed over their achievements.

It centred on the uncertainty of what the empire they had built was doing to Rome. Were the wars they had waged really defensive and just, as many claimed, or were they simply naked expressions of the desire for gain? Who really benefited from that gain? The Roman republic as a whole or just a few aristocrats who had profited while holding office? Above all, what effect did winning an empire have on the moral character of Rome? Was it encouraging virtue in its soldiers and leaders, or simply greed and corruption? Indeed, were personal ambition and the pursuit of glory now being set above the interests of the republic and the Roman people? This was the great debate that the conquest of the Mediterranean had ignited. In 146 BC one single event would fan its flames to a roaring blaze.

TURNING POINT:
THE SACK OF CARTHAGE

By the end of the year 148 BC, the Third Punic War was going badly for the Romans. The consuls leading the attack on Carthage and the neighbouring countryside had initiated rash assaults, resulting in defeat and failure, while the soldiers themselves were growing idle, greedy and selfish.[8] Of the three wars against Carthage, the third was the most controversial and, to many minds back in the metropolis, the Romans were now paying the price. The historian Polybius, who was an eyewitness to the later stages of this war, addressed the nature of the controversy. Opinion in the Mediterranean world, he said, was divided over the Romans' decision to go to war with their old rival for a third time:

> There were some who approved the action of the Romans, saying that they had taken wise and statesmanlike measures in the defence of their empire. For to destroy this source of perpetual menace [Carthage] …was the act of intelligent and far-seeing men. Others took the opposite view, that far from maintaining the principles by which they had won their supremacy, they were, little by little, deserting it for a lust of domination.[9]

The war had been controversial from the very start. Before any decision to launch hostilities was taken, heated arguments divided the Senate. On one side were the doves: they argued vehemently that, far from seeking to destroy Carthage, Rome needed a strong Carthage to act as a counterbalance of power in the Mediterranean. In this way, went their argument, Carthage would actually restrain Rome from becoming so powerful that it gave way to the 'avarice' that destroyed 'honour, integrity and every other virtue'.[10] The hawks countered this line of argument by playing on old Roman fears. Carthage, they said, was resurgent and wealthy and would always pose a threat until it was absolutely destroyed. Led by Cato the Elder, this side glossed their case with bright rhetorical brush strokes. The Carthaginians were untrustworthy, degenerate and effeminate child-sacrificers.The suggestion was that they were, in effect, subhuman and should be treated as such. Relentlessly keeping the issue at the top of the agenda, Cato ended every speech he made in the Senate on whatever subject with the statement '*Delenda est Carthago*' (Carthage must be wiped out).[11] In this way he ground down the opposition, and eventually the hawks swayed the majority of the Senate in favour of war. Now all the senators needed was a justification. Establishing this would only make the controversy worse.

A pretext was soon found. Following an inspection of the city of Carthage and surrounding countryside, a Roman commission reported to the Senate an 'abundance of ship-building materials' and alleged that Carthaginians had built up their fleet beyond the legal limits set by the treaty of the Second Punic War.[12] However, the archaeological and historical evidence for the development of these ancient weapons of mass destruction is inconclusive even to this day. Then, when the Carthaginians did eventually break the treaty in an irrefutable way (by going to war with their neighbour Numidia without the permission of Rome), even here the case against Carthage was far from convincing. There was one simple reason: Rome, acting behind the scenes, had been the one to incite Numidian aggression against Carthage in the first place. But this was by no means the last instance of Roman cynicism. In its diplomacy, too, Rome would bring the controversy of the decision to go to war to an even fiercer pitch of intensity. For the Roman senators were about to violate one of the republic's most ancient and divine virtues: *fides* or 'reliability' – the ability in political affairs to keep one's word.

As the Roman war machine geared up for action, with ships shuttling between Italy and North Africa and the number of troops and cavalry deployed swelling to over 80,000, the Carthaginians sent no fewer than three embassies to the Romans in 149 BC. Each of them offered their surrender, each was a desperate bid to prevent war. On the first occasion the Roman consul agreed to peace and to give Carthage its freedom under Roman rule. There was, however, one condition: that the

Carthaginians surrender three hundred hostages, specifically the sons of their noblest families. The Carthaginians, in good faith, agreed. Then, when this was done and the flower of their élite had sailed for Rome, the Roman consul in Africa, Lucius Marcius Censorinus, stipulated a further condition: the surrender of 200,000 sets of armour and 2000 catapults. Distraught, the ambassadors returned to Carthage and oversaw the arms being collected by the wagonload and taken to the Roman camp. However, the wily Censorinus had one more trick up his sleeve.

A final condition was stipulated before peace could be agreed: the removal of the city of Carthage from the coast to 16 kilometres (10 miles) inland. Censorinus's argument for this was an extraordinary piece of hypocrisy. The sea, he said, with its prospects for trade, had corrupted Carthage. It had given it 'a grasping disposition'. Carthage needed to be more like Rome: 'Life inland,' he claimed, 'with the joys of agriculture and quiet, is much more equable.'[13] Dumbstruck, the ambassadors broke down in tears of frenzy and mourning. It was impossible to meet this condition without, in effect, destroying the city for ever. It now dawned on them that the Romans had never sincerely intended to come to terms. They had simply sought to gain an advantage in a war that was now – and had always been – unstoppable.

Two years later, the treachery of the Romans at the outset of the war was deemed by many to be the reason for their lack of success in it. The Roman people paid great attention to the rightness of their wars in the building of the empire. 'When the inception of war seems just,' ran the logic, 'it makes victory greater and ill success less perilous, while if it is thought to be dishonourable and wrong, it has the opposite effect'.[14] So it was proving to be at the end of 148 BC. But, with the arrival in Africa of a new and iconic general in the spring of the following year, all that was about to change.

To resolve the miserable, grinding stalemate in Carthage, the Roman people and the Senate had turned to a young aristocrat. The credentials of Publius Cornelius Scipio Aemilianus were impeccable. He came from the patrician family of the Cornelii Scipiones; he was the grandson of the consul who fell at the battle of Cannae; the adopted grandson of Scipio Africanus, the victor of the Second Punic War; and the son of Lucius Aemilius Paullus, the vanquisher of Perseus in the war against Macedon (see family tree, page 38). Aemilianus had proved his own abilities in the early stages of the war against Carthage. Indeed, leading the fourth legion, he was the only officer who had achieved any significant victories. Now, even though he was thirty-seven, five years below the official age for the office of consul, the demand among the Roman people for him to be elected was so overwhelming that the Senate eventually agreed to make an exception to the traditional laws of the republic and allowed him to stand. Once elected to the consulship, his responsibility was simple: to take charge of the war in Carthage and win it.

With that aim in mind, Aemilianus returned to North Africa, brought discipline back to the army and adopted a new strategy for the war. He ordered the Roman campaigns in the interior to be abandoned. All Roman units were now to focus on taking the city first by siege, then by assault. During the summer of 147 BC he created an impregnable seal around Carthage to prevent any reinforcements and provisions from reaching the city. On the land approaches, he ensured that a double wall of earthworks was built across the isthmus in just twenty days. On the harbour side, he was no less ambitious. In order to block up the entrance to the port, a barrier was created by depositing 15,000 cubic metres (52,000 cubic feet) of rocks and boulders. Siege engines were then placed on top of the wall rising out of the sea. Despite some brave

Carthaginian resistance and attacks, the city was effectively made watertight by the winter. Aemilianus spent the next few months clearing up pockets of resistance in the country, and when spring came again in 146 BC, he and his army were ready to take the city. To help them, new recruits arrived from Italy. One of those green soldiers was Aemilianus's seventeen-year-old cousin, Tiberius Sempronius Gracchus.

As a close relative, Tiberius shared Aemilianus's tent and table. The boy was, after all, not only Aemilianus's cousin, but also his brother-in-law; earlier Aemilianus had married Tiberius's elder sister Sempronia. But the two men had more in common than family. The war presented both of them with a unique opportunity to prove themselves. For Aemilianus, holding the annual consulship gave him a limited window of time to silence his critics. In his youth he had avoided taking the proper route to success in politics and had once confided in his friend and tutor, the historian Polybius: 'Everyone regards me as a quiet and lazy person with no share in the energetic character of a Roman because I do not choose to plead cases in court. They say that the family does not need the sort of representative that I am but someone just the opposite. That is what hurts me most.'[15] His single year as consul and general in charge of the war in Carthage was his one shot at the big time, his once-in-a-lifetime opportunity to prove himself worthy of his family, to renew the fame of the Cornelii Scipiones. Glory was there for the taking so long as the weight of expectation did not get to him first.

Much too was expected of his cousin. Since his father's death, Tiberius, along with his sister and younger brother, had been brought up by their renowned mother Cornelia, the daughter of Scipio Africanus. She had ensured that Tiberius had received the best Greek education in rhetoric and philosophy; it suited the young man's intelligent, generous and idealistic nature.

But she had also fired him with ambitions for a glorious career and a desire to excel in the Roman virtues of self-discipline and courage. As a result, although gentle, thoughtful and by no means a natural fighter like his cousin Aemilianus, Tiberius was a fiercely determined young man.[16] This latter quality would prove an asset during his summer in Carthage.

Tiberius joined Aemilianus's staff to learn the art of war, to study his actions and follow his example. However, this war also presented him with a chance to get his foot on the political ladder known as the *cursus honorum*, the annual electoral competition for honours. Since in ancient Rome political and military careers were not separate as they usually are today but entwined as one, ambitious young men needed to have served in a number of campaigns before they could stand for even the lower offices in the hierarchy of magistracies. But there was much more to building a political career than simply notching up one military campaign after another. As Aemilianus himself was known to observe, power in Rome began with earning integrity. An ancient aristocratic code followed on from this: 'Dignity of rank,' said Aemilianus, 'arises from integrity, the honour of holding office from dignity, supreme authority from holding office, and freedom from supreme authority.'[17] Liberty to do what one wished was the value most cherished by Roman aristocrats. It was the very essence of the free republic. But how to set foot on such a daunting, political path? How to begin building such character? How to emulate one's ancestors? As Aemilianus and his officers made the final preparations for the assault on Carthage, Tiberius found out.

There is no record of what Aemilianus told his officers before battle, but it is easy to imagine that it centred on an old theme. The battle ahead was about liberty and justice winning out over tyranny. It was about decent Roman values surpassing the treachery and deceitfulness of the Carthaginians. It was, in short, about civilization vanquishing decadence and corruption. With the final assault on Carthage, 120 years of war, hatred and suspicion would come to an end. The questions of who controlled the ancient world and how it was to be run would at last be unambiguously answered. As incentives for his officers to show valour in a conflict of such proportions, perhaps Aemilianus reminded his entourage too of the usual decorations. Ancient Romans awarded acts of bravery not primarily with medals but with crowns, bracelets, necklaces and miniature spears. Depending on the nature of the achievement, the crowns took different names and forms. Some were of grass, some of oak leaves, others of gold. Only one, however, fitted this momentous occasion. The Mural Crown was to be awarded to the first person to scale the walls of the city.

Perhaps with this in mind, Tiberius and his unit waited in the dawn light for the horns to blare. With his thirst for glory contending with terror, Tiberius was about to experience his first taste of war. Then the signal came. The Romans broke cover, quickly set timbers, scaffolding and siege engines against the city wall, and took on the 30,000 Carthaginian defenders. Against the shower of arrows, spears and weighted nets trapping the Roman climbers below, Tiberius's unit began the long scramble up the city wall some 9 metres (30 feet) wide and 18 metres (66 feet) high. Despite the swathes of Roman casualties crashing to the ground around him, Tiberius achieved what perhaps had seemed impossible: he became the first to lead his detachment to the top of the wall of Carthage. But as soon he and his men were over, they would have realised that the fight had only just begun. They now faced the enemy in gruelling, mechanical hand-to-hand combat. In the moment of his great triumph Tiberius found himself in hell.

The horrific conflict lasted six days and nights. Once inside the city, killing squads advanced house by house, narrow street by narrow street. They cut and stabbed their way from the Forum of Carthage along three streets and forced the enemy back on to Byrsa, the citadel. When the determined Carthaginians, fighting for survival, began attacking the Romans with missiles from the roofs of their close-packed houses, the Romans captured the first few tenements, murdered their occupants and mounted the roofs too. Throwing planks over the narrow alleyways, they continued to wage the war from rooftop to rooftop, leaving a trail of mutilated corpses in their wake or tossing them to the streets below. Then, amid the cries, shrieks and animal-like groans, Aemilianus raised the intensity of the brutal assault and ordered the streets to be set on fire. The booming noise stepped up the confusion. Houses came crashing down and the elderly, the wounded, women and children were forced out of their hiding places.[18]

Squads of Roman 'cleaners' now attempted to bring order to the scenes of frenetic activity. They cleared away the bodies of the dead and wounded alike, mixing them with the rubble and sweeping them into holes in the ground. The streets needed to be clear to make way for the cohorts of army and cavalry charging forward. Horses trampled over the dismembered limbs and severed heads that remained in their way. This warfare was a far cry from the bloody field engagements of Hannibal, or the naval clashes of the First Punic War. It took the horror to another level. At all costs, however, Roman discipline had to be sustained. Although the troops were rotated in order to maintain the ferocity of their attack, Aemilianus, snatching morsels of food and sleep whenever he could, worked around the clock.[19]

By the seventh day the Romans' efforts had paid off and 50,000 exhausted, starving Carthaginians approached Aemilianus bearing garlands of the god of healing, Asclepius, a signal that they wished to surrender in exchange for their lives. Aemilianus agreed. After the respite, the Roman army focused its full force on the sacred Temple of Eshmoun. This was situated at the height of the citadel and it was the fortified bolt-hole to which Hasdrubal, the Carthaginian general, and a defiant army of nine hundred defenders had retreated. The Romans surrounded it and for some time were unable to penetrate the temple's natural defences. The grind of war – fatigue, want of food and fear – eventually forced the Carthaginians on to the roof. There was nowhere left to turn. When Hasdrubal, realizing that they were doomed, secretly deserted, Aemilianus was quick to drive home the advantage. In full view of the rebels, he staged the abject surrender of their cowardly leader before him. After that demoralizing spectacle it was only a matter of time before the rebels, including Hasdrubal's wife and children, gave up hope and threw themselves to their deaths in the fire enveloping the temple below.[20]

The Romans had sealed their victory. What was utterly striking about the aftermath of the ruthless sack of Carthage, however, was the reaction of Aemilianus. The moment was not cause for thoughtless, impulsive celebration but pessimism, doubt, even guilt. Polybius, an eyewitness to the events, recorded it. Aemilianus took him into his confidence, climbed to a point where he could survey the spectacular devastation below and burst into tears. He even quoted some lines from the *Iliad*, the ancient Greek poem of Homer:

> A day will come in which our mighty Troy,
> And Priam and the people over whom
> Spear-bearing Priam rules, shall perish all.[21]

When Polybius asked him what he meant, Aemilianus replied that one day Rome would meet the same fate as Troy and its king, Priam. The ancient city of Carthage, after all, had been the centre of an empire that had lasted seven hundred years. It had 'ruled over so many lands, islands and seas, and was once as rich in arms and fleets, elephants and money as the mightiest empires'.[22] Now, however, it lay in ruins. It is astonishing that a Roman general should respond so differently from his all-conquering ancestors. He reflected not on the glory of Rome, not on the success of the just and free republic but on its future and inevitable demise. The echo of Homer's poem was poignant for another reason. The sack of Troy was the moment that had provoked the flight of the Trojan Aeneas. That flight had resulted in the legendary foundation of Rome. The 'Trojan' Romans, said Aemilianus, would go the same way not just as the Carthaginians but as their distant ancestors too.

Over the next few days, Aemilianus reserved much of the city's gold, silver and sacred objects for the Roman state. He made sure too that none of his friends and associates participated in excessive looting so that neither he nor they could be accused by their political rivals in Rome of privately profiting from the war. Such behaviour would be tantamount to dishonour, the great mistake of putting one's own interests above those of the republic. Only after the richest slice of the plunder had been saved for Rome, did Aemilianus turn over the remainder of the city to the grasping hands of the Roman soldiers.

Ten commissioners soon arrived from Rome with one final request for the great conqueror. Nothing of Carthage, they said, should remain. So, after the city was burnt for ten days and demolished stone by stone, brick by brick, the Roman army concluded the most comprehensive, painstaking eradication of a city and its culture in all of ancient history. Archaeological evidence of the burning and demolition can be seen to this day. From a city of approximately a million inhabitants, the surviving 50,000 Carthaginians were sold into slavery. The towns that had supported the city were likewise destroyed, while those that had sided with Rome were rewarded. The new Roman province of North Africa was now established. It was, however, becoming harder to see where were those ancestral virtues of piety, justice and honour and what role, if any, they played.

In the same year as Carthage was razed to the ground, the rich city of Corinth in Greece was also methodically sacked by the Romans. It was punishment once again for challenging their power in the region. The two events took place within months of each other and for this reason the year 146 BC would prove a major watershed in Roman history. Across the breadth of the Mediterranean Sea, from the Atlantic coast of Spain to Greece's border with Asia Minor, Rome was now the supreme master. It could do anything it wanted to whomever it chose and it could do so without fear of reprisal. It did not even have to keep its word. In the war with Carthage, the ancient virtue of *fides* had been violated and yet, in spite of this, Rome was still victorious. The Roman gods still seemed to smile with favour and grant success.

Before leaving North Africa, Aemilianus attended to one last duty. Tiberius had been popular and held in affection by the soldiers. Now the young man's success in the war was capped when Aemilianus awarded his cousin the Mural Crown for his courage in being the first over the walls of Carthage.[23] In years to come, however, the consequences of destroying Carthage would haunt those who had carried it out, both the doubting general and the seventeen-year-old, decorated soldier. Indeed, with time, the cost of this Roman atrocity would tear the cousins apart.

CRISIS IN ROME

When Tiberius returned to Rome he stepped into glory. Wearing his golden Mural Crown, the young idealist walked through the main streets of the city as one small part of a grand procession. All the temples were open and filled with garlands and incense. Sunlit rose petals streamed down from the rooftops, and the attendants of officials did their best to control the tide of the crowds. For pouring into the streets, cheering, laughing and embracing each other, was the multitude of the Roman people.[24] All this excitement and celebration was in honour of one magnificent event: Aemilianus's triumph, the illustrious prize awarded by the Senate to honour the general's victory in Carthage.

Trumpeters led the way, sounding out the same martial music with which they had previously roused the soldiers to war. Oxen, their horns gilded and bearing garlands, were present too. Some soldiers, in their finest armour, held aloft models, plans and pictures depicting the city they had conquered and critical scenes from the war. Behind them others carried a forest of placards inscribed with the names of foreign places now subdued. After the parade of captive Carthaginians, the spoils of their city and the piles of their armour, came Aemilianus on his chariot. He wore a purple toga into which silver stars had been woven, and his face was daubed with red paint. Thus attired, he was the personification of Jupiter, the greatest of the gods who protected Rome. However, there was no question about the conqueror's quasi-divinity. The state slave, standing behind him, may have held a heavy gold-leaf crown over Aemilianus's head, but every time the crowd cheered, he murmured to the general: 'Remember you are only a man.'

The procession ended with a ceremony at the Temple of Jupiter on the Capitoline Hill, the place from where Aemilianus had set out the year before. The chief prisoners from Carthage were dragged to the prison at the foot of the hill and executed. Once their deaths were confirmed, Aemilianus supervised the sacrifice. He climbed the temple steps, poured wine over an ox's brow, sprinkled its back with salted flour, then traced a knife slowly along its spine. Then, as a signal to the attending slaves to slit the animal's throat, he pulled a loose fold of his toga over his head in the manner of a priest, and the beast was duly killed. The sacrifice was perhaps a way of giving thanks to Jupiter for Aemilianus's success in Africa, something he had promised to do before he left Rome. That promise now fulfilled, the triumphal procession came to a close with celebratory banquets and feasting.

With her heroic son Tiberius now safely back in Rome, Cornelia would have encouraged him to accompany her to the dinner parties and social gatherings hosted by the élite. To help his career progress, the young man now needed to network voraciously, gain more military experience in the company of great generals like his cousin Aemilianus, and build on the prestige of the Mural Crown he had won at Carthage. A political 'career' for a young aristocrat in the Roman republic of the second century BC was not in any sense like a modern career. There was no salary for holding office. There was no nine-to-five routine or basic five-day week. All prospect of success in a Roman aristocrat's political life depended on one narrow window of opportunity: winning an election for an annual public office.

Once successful in discharging the duties of that office, the holder found that rewards flowed freely – fame, glory, prestige and the possibility of great wealth. As a result, the competition was intense, and increased even further as the offices higher up the chain of magistracies became fewer and thus harder to obtain. Aemilianus had reached the top. Now it was the turn of Tiberius. Indeed, Cornelia was so famous for reproaching both her sons that she was still referred to as the mother-in-law of 'Scipio Aemilianus' rather than as the mother of 'the Gracchi'.[25] However, while his networking and nascent political career may have been on his mother's mind, there was one debate in Roman high society that would perhaps have interested the young Tiberius a great deal more. It centred around the wealth that everyone had just witnessed flowing into Rome.

The booty from the cities of Carthage and Corinth, the tribute from the new provinces of Sicily and Sardinia, and the income from the mines of Spain brought a massive injection of money into the city, so Rome was flourishing. The city became a hive of industry and expenditure: new docks and markets were constructed, the water supply was doubled, and large building projects sprang up. And yet, despite Rome's newfound prosperity, not all sections of the population shared in its wealth. The city that Tiberius found on his return to Rome reflected the ever-widening gap between rich and poor.

Rome during this period was not yet the glorious, marbled city of the high empire, of organized public spaces and cool colonnades. It was a city of extremes and contradictions. As soon as Tiberius strayed from the Forum, temples and public assembly areas, leaving behind the main thoroughfares of the Via Sacra and Nova Via, he could easily have got lost in the warren of chaotic, claustrophobic streets. Alleys were so narrow that houses with balconies and upper floors almost touched; from their windows people would throw out waste and sewage. In very poor districts, such as the Esquiline, houses built from cob and wattle were so rickety that they often stood up only by leaning against each other for support. As a result, they regularly collapsed or burnt down when fire spread rapidly from building to building. The sight of a charred house standing next to a temple beautifully restored by a wealthy aristocrat was nothing out of the ordinary.

In spite of their poor quality, the houses were divided into apartments so that tenants could crowd into attics, basements and even shacks on flat roofs. Romans advertised rental property by painting 'For Rent' on the outside of the building, and the rents they charged were increasingly exorbitant. Those who could not afford to pay them set up lodgings in the nooks and crannies of public buildings, under stairs or even in large tombs. As there were no kitchens in the cheap tenement housing, the activity of Rome's poor citizens and slaves spread out to the streets, and the numerous bars and restaurants heaved with people. And all this activity took place against a background of mayhem and constant noise from carts, wagons, litters and horses. Rome at the end of the second century BC really was a city that never slept.

Into the pulsing metropolis the majority of Rome's population, which was approaching one million, was crammed. The aristocratic élite, however, in whose circles Tiberius moved, had a very different experience of the city. While the air was suffocating down in the crowded, messy streets, up on the Palatine Hill it was fresh and clean. It was to these exclusive heights that the wealthy and aspirational, borne aloft in litters, retreated to their luxurious villas and colonnaded gardens. The style of these new residences was strikingly innovative. Empire-building had not only made the élite lots of money, but it had opened their eyes to foreign influences. Greek style had the greatest cachet, as Roman aristocrats admired Greece's ancient, sophisticated and aesthetic civilization.

Befitting Rome's position at the heart of the new empire, the city now became the centre through which Greek art and influence circulated and gained value. The conquering aristocrats beautified not just the city, but also their homes with Greek-influenced monuments, temples and porticoes. Keeping up with the Fabii or the Claudii or any of the aristocratic families was a trick accomplished only by the conspicuous display of an exotic mural of Hellenistic inspiration, or a chic marble statue from Greece. Tiberius's mother caused quite a sensation when she inherited from her uncle

Lucius Aemilius Paullus, the conqueror of Macedon, Rome's largest library of Greek manuscripts.

Such conspicuous displays of prosperity and success served a dangerous purpose. They were not only a manifestation of a nobleman's prestige and political standing. They were a spur, an incitement to others too. When, for example, an aristocrat such as Aemilianus returned from conquest abroad, he might put his new wealth towards a grand monument, a luxurious work of art, or use it to influence his political associates and woo the Roman people. A new benchmark was set. Now other aristocrats had to play catch-up or else lose status. The only way for them to achieve that was to run in elections and win further office. A praetorship might win the successful candidate a chance to profit personally from administering a province. Winning a consulship, of course, was to hit the jackpot. It provided the chance to command the republic's armies and clean up by conquest. Only by holding such an office did an aristocrat stand a chance of matching his rival's success; only in this way could he hope to put his family's status on a par with theirs. Where the families of the Cornelii Scipiones, the Aemilii Paulli or the Sempronii Gracchi blazed a trail, their aristocratic rivals had to follow.[26] By the 140s BC, however, the pattern of self-serving competition was, so it was said, corrupting the republic.

For the more the élite vied with each other for office and prestige, the blinder they became to the growing poverty in Rome. The gap between rich and poor grew wider and wider as the spoils of the empire were unevenly divided. Some feared that the élite would become ever more selfish and grasping, and that the mob of Rome would run riot, frustrated by their own grievances and offended by the greed of the rich.[27] In other words, the great and noble 'free' republic was on the verge of a precipice. It was about to tear itself apart. How had it come to this?

The single inflammatory issue on which the rich and poor were growing increasingly divided was land. It was a source of tension closely connected to the problem of military service. In the second century BC the Roman army was not, as modern armies have become, a professional standing army paid for by the state. It was a temporary militia made up of Roman citizens and allies from Italian communities throughout the peninsula. Participation in the army was the key obligation of being a Roman citizen, and as Rome conquered Italy, it imposed this obligation on those outside the city too. To qualify for service in the army, a citizen had to be able to meet a minimum property requirement. The logic behind this qualification was that ownership of property gave you a stake in the republic, which, as a free-born citizen, it was your duty to protect through service in the army. As a result, the army was made up principally of smallholding farmers.

While Rome fought short, local campaigns in Italy, the system of citizen-soldiers worked well because it allowed the men to return to their farms at regular intervals. However, with the conquest of the Mediterranean, the Roman armies found themselves serving for long periods of time in Spain, Africa or the east. Commanders of the armies also made the problem worse by continually choosing the most experienced soldiers. As a result, these soldiers were kept in the army year after year. Some eventually returned to their land, but many others never did. Inevitably, the farms suffered: they fell into disuse and neglect, and the family members still living on them faced accumulating debt and starvation. To alleviate the pressure, small landowners or their families were forced to sell or abandon their holdings.

The smallholders' loss became the aristocrats' gain. In the Roman republic the safest investment for capital was land. As the élite grew rich from the spoils of conquests and the subsidiary businesses of empire-building (such as state contracts for roads, sewers, buildings and aqueducts, arms manufacture, provisioning of the army and navy, the leasing of mines and quarries), they used their wealth to take advantage of the desperate smallholders and acquire their land 'partly by purchase, partly by persuasion and partly by force, cultivating wide estates instead of single farms'.[28] Exacerbating the problem was another hard fact of empire-building: it made financial sense for the élite to employ gangs of slaves imported from all corners of the Mediterranean as herdsmen and fieldworkers. As a result, even the possibility of work as hired hands on the large estates was closed to free-born smallholders.

Deracinated and dispossessed, some peasants survived on small, marginal plots of land, eking out an existence from what they could produce and from seasonal work, such as harvesting. Others, however, drawn by the prospect of employment in an arms manufactory, in construction or in shipbuilding, increasingly went to where they believed the streets were paved with gold: Rome. They were to be rapidly disappointed. The industries were not big enough to absorb the large influx of peasants, while other potential avenues of employment were off limits too: the expert work of the potter, the textile worker and the artisan was better accomplished by the slaves who came from the skilled, sophisticated societies of the east, and who could provide Rome cheaply with desirable and fashionable goods for the consumer market. For these reasons the unemployed mob of Rome began to swell. The real trouble, as Tiberius would quickly find out during his time back in Rome, was that the aristocratic élite were utterly divided on how to resolve the growing crisis.

Take Publius Cornelius Scipio Nasica, a cousin of both Aemilianus and Tiberius. Waspish, arrogant and a highly practised politician, he was in his fifties and a leading senator of the day. As one of the Roman élite's largest landowners, he was interested in maintaining the status quo. His view was clear. Material benefits flowed through to the lower orders just as they had always done: through the goodwill and generous patronage of the élite. The traditional system worked perfectly well.[29] Aristocratic patrons, he argued, provided the lower orders with large gifts of money for public buildings, food schemes and entertainment, such as gladiatorial games and chariot races. What more could they possibly want?

Others took quite the opposite stance. What was required to resolve the problem, they said, was not the laissez-faire attitude of the conservatives in the Senate. The remedy was active reform and new laws. One advocate of this approach was the senator Appius Claudius Pulcher. He was a passionate, philosophical and ambitious elder statesman, as well as a descendant of one of the oldest patrician families in Rome. The republic, he said, depended upon the concord between the orders, between the Senate and the people. The crisis over land was destroying that concord, and action was now urgently needed. In 140 BC the two factions came to blows. A senator called Gaius Laelius was appointed consul for that year, and in this capacity he put forward a proposal for land reform in an attempt to redress the grievances of the increasing number of landless peasants. When he took it before the Senate, however, the bill was met with such outrage by the majority whose interests were threatened that Laelius abandoned it. For this decision he was rewarded with the name Laelius the Wise.

By 138 BC, with Nasica's conservative faction outmanoeuvring the reformers led by Pulcher, there were clear signs that the crisis over land was not about to go away; in fact, it was getting much worse. A rebellion of 200,000 slaves broke out in Sicily, and, with the Roman army at full stretch elsewhere, a grain shortage consequently struck Rome. In the same year too,

Roman soldiers deserted en masse from campaigning in Spain, frustrated at their length of service and absence from their lands. Many were caught and punished by Nasica himself: they were flogged in public and then sold into slavery for one humiliating sesterce.[30] However, it would not be long before the crisis was witnessed at first hand by another man. Tiberius would soon see for himself quite how bad the situation had become.

While 138 BC may have been a year of political turmoil for Rome, for Tiberius it was the year in which his political career took off. In the summer he was elected to his first junior office, that of quaestor, an office connected mainly with state financial activities. However, his duties would not detain him in the metropolis, but take him off to war once again, this time in Spain. In the northeast of Rome's Iberian province, the republic had been struggling for some years to put down resistance from the semi-independent Celtiberian tribes of the Numantines. The Spanish warriors had shown amazing physical courage and fierce determination. The geography of the land too was something of a metaphorical quagmire; the fighting had been confined to defiles, dangerous ravines and precarious mountain passes. For these reasons, a string of Roman commanders had tried and failed to make any headway in finishing off this nagging, dogged war. In a new expedition Gaius Hostilius Mancinus, the consul for 137 BC, was determined to crush the rebels once and for all. As his financial officer, he took along with him the twenty-five-year-old Tiberius.

With his official account books in hand, and his foot set firmly on the ladder of political office holding, Tiberius was living up to the memory of his father's glorious career. En route to war, however, he saw something that would prove to be his real political awakening. It would also prove crucial to the legend of Tiberius. As his detachment marched through

Etruria, the Italian countryside north of Rome, he was able to see for himself how Roman empire-building had transformed it for the worse. What he saw was not industrious single farms of Roman citizens, but large estates worked by gangs of foreign slaves.[31] It is possible that en route he even met peasants who had been forced off their land through the death of their males, or whose farms had simply fallen into disuse through neglect and shortage of help. The ancient sources certainly make clear that Tiberius's experience in Etruria inspired the dramatic course his life took when he returned to Rome. The events in Spain, however, would be the trigger.

DISGRACE

Mancinus's expedition was ill-omened from the start. The chickens that he meant to sacrifice to the gods escaped from their cage; then, as he boarded a ship for Spain, he heard a haunting shout go up, '*Mane Mancine*' (Remain, Mancinus); after changing ships and choosing to set off from another port altogether, the unlucky general was set back once again when he spied a snake on board, which fled before it could be captured.

As the expedition began, so it continued. In Spain, against the Numantines, Mancinus lost engagement after engagement. The only note of hope was struck by his young quaestor. 'Amid the various misfortunes and military reverses that marked the campaign Tiberius's courage and intelligence shone out all the more brightly.'[32] In addition, the young aristocrat showed his strength of character by always maintaining 'respect and honour' for his commander, in spite of the general's miserable progress. One disaster in particular, however, would prove especially testing for both of them.

One night Mancinus received a false rumour that significant reinforcements from some neighbouring Spanish tribes were about to join the Numantines. Panic-stricken, the Roman general decided to break camp under cover of darkness and move his army to more advantageous ground. As fires were extinguished and the quiet retreat began, the Numantines learnt of his plan and responded with lightning speed: they captured the Roman camp, then attacked the army as it fled. The rearguard infantry bore the brunt of the casualties, but there was worse to come. The 20,000 soldiers of the Roman army soon found themselves trapped in difficult terrain and encircled by an enemy force less than a quarter of their number. There was no escape.

Mancinus had no option but to send envoys to the Numantines and come to terms for peace. The Spanish enemy declared itself unwilling to negotiate with anyone except Tiberius. Such was their respect for his personal qualities and their high regard for his father that he alone would be acceptable. Their reason for this went back to 178 BC, when Tiberius's father had made peace with the Numantines: he had put them in his trust, had become the protector of their interests in Rome, and had staked his own name and honour on the obligation to maintain the peace. Above all, the elder Gracchus 'had always ensured that the Roman people kept the terms of the peace with the strictest justice'. On the basis of his family's prestige, therefore, the young Tiberius now negotiated with the Numantine leaders and eventually, after giving way on some points and extracting concessions on others, he agreed a truce that established 'terms of equality between Numantines and the Romans'.[33] The peace was solemnized by an oath.

With this act, Tiberius saved the lives of 20,000 Roman soldiers, as well as those of their many slaves and camp followers. The army was set free and sent on its way back to Rome, but not before the Numantines had stripped them of its arms and property, and had asked Mancinus also to swear an oath to honour the peace. Once the Roman army had departed, however, Tiberius showed his conscientiousness in executing his duties as quaestor. He went alone to Numantia and asked for the return of his account books, which had been confiscated. The Numantine leaders were delighted to see him again, asked him to enter the city and made it clear that he could now trust them as friends. After dining at their table, Tiberius also left for Rome, his ledger books safely in his custody once more. Given his successes, perhaps he anticipated a hero's welcome. The reality could not have been more different.

In the Senate the Roman treaty with the Numantines was greeted with vitriolic disdain. A savage debate was sparked. Nasica, the cousin of Tiberius and Aemilianus, voiced the dominant hawks' point of view: this was no peace, but a pathetic, ignominious surrender. Indeed, the Numantines were not 'equals'; they were not even an enemy worthy of a peace treaty. Rather, they were rebels in a Roman province and should be crushed at all costs. Mancinus was called to stand trial. He defended himself as best he could: what about the lives saved? If the treaty was not a success in absolute terms, surely it was in the circumstances? Tiberius, standing beside Mancinus, stepped into the debate, using all his rhetorical skill and education to defend his commander. But the Senate was not remotely swayed from its belief in Roman invincibility. Since the destruction of Carthage, Rome was now the only superpower, the master of the Mediterranean. It could do what it wanted to whomever it chose. If the price of defeating the rebellious Numantines was the glorious death of 20,000 soldiers in the service of the republic, so be it!

In response, Mancinus begged the Senate to consider the poor quality of the soldiers he had at his disposal in Spain. The levy had produced an inexperienced, ill-disciplined and ill-provisioned army that the previous commander in Spain, a man called Quintus Pompeius, had failed to improve in any way. But again, this defence was not enough to help his case. One reason was prestige. Pompeius had powerful friends within the Senate, whereas Mancinus's family had far less political clout. A commission, led by Aemilianus and his friends, was appointed to conduct a thorough investigation. Following this, the Senate, to the horror of Mancinus and Tiberius, tore up the treaty.

The rejection was not strictly illegal because all treaties made in the field needed to be ratified by the Senate in Rome. The problem, however, was more a moral one: repudiating the treaty was, in effect, to trounce the Roman republic's reputation for *fides* – good faith and keeping true to oaths. Such a violation would be sure to incur the wrath of the gods. In order to atone for this wrong, the commission put forward two proposals for the Roman people to vote on: either that Mancinus, as the general responsible in Spain, be surrendered to the Numantines, or that his staff be offered in his stead. Aemilianus now entered the ring. He used his powerful influence among the senators to help his cousin and, accordingly, the first proposal won support in the Senate and was ratified by the Roman people. It was decreed that Mancinus alone was to pay the penalty. In a revival of an old military custom, the former consul was stripped naked, bound in chains, taken under military escort back to Spain and handed over to the Numantines. The Celtiberians refused to accept the offering, and Mancinus returned to Rome in shame.

Although Tiberius had been saved from condemnation, this was scant consolation. The young man's life now lay about him in ruins. The first blow was personally wounding. Not only had his own cousin, his brother-in-law and the man who had been his role model in Carthage, failed to save Mancinus. Aemilianus had also been the one to cast the deciding vote against

Tiberius's treaty. The bonds of friendship and family between the two cousins were thus broken apart. Only anger and recrimination were now left.

The second blow was more pummelling still. The Senate's rejection of the treaty had effectively destroyed Tiberius's career. He had staked not just his own integrity and dignity on the treaty, but also that of his dead father. Certainly, the loyalty of the Numantine people had been utterly betrayed. The implications of this, however, went much deeper, much closer to home. With his peace treaty spurned by the senators, Tiberius had irrevocably damaged his family's reputation, his father's and his own. Prestige had always been the essential ingredient of a political career in the Roman republic, the key to getting to the top. Aristocratic families had accumulated it over hundreds of years, driven on by the desire of sons to match the achievements of their noble fathers. Now Tiberius's ability to command the respect and loyalty of allies, associates and the Roman people had been snatched away for ever. Or so it seemed.

The fate of Tiberius Sempronius Gracchus the younger might have become just a footnote in history. Indeed, there are probably dozens of 'Tiberiuses', brilliant young aristocrats who never fulfilled their potential, about whom we know nothing. One simple fact, however, spectacularly altered the course of Tiberius's life: his personal disaster intersected with the crisis enveloping Rome. This coincidence sparked the greatest upheaval in the republic's long history thus far. Single-handedly, it turned Tiberius against the Senate, against the friends and allies of his family and forebears, and emblazoned his name in the history books. An illustrious, honourable career in the manner of his father's and mother's ancestors was now out of the question; that road to fame was closed. Another, however, lay waiting for him.

As Tiberius left the Senate House in disgrace, he received a very different reception from the Roman people. The wives, mothers, fathers, children and grandparents of the 20,000 Roman citizens whose lives he had saved in Spain now thronged the Forum, cheered his name to the skies and fêted him like a hero. Almost inadvertently, he had won the love and respect of the plebs. Perhaps in this moment the seed of an idea was planted. Tiberius's path to winning prestige, his chance to channel his intelligence, idealism and political skills, and his opportunity to honour the achievements of his father now lay not with the Senate but with 'the cause of the common people'.[34] The ambition of an aristocrat had found another outlet.

Between the summers of 136 and 133 BC events moved quickly. Breaking constitutional precedent, Aemilianus was elected to a second consulship in order to head up the campaign in Spain. Only he, it was fervently believed by the Roman people, could bring this sticky war to a victorious end. As a result, under massive popular pressure, the Senate temporarily waived the constitutional obstacles once again, and Aemilianus became consul for a second time, leaving for Spain in 134 BC. Showing the same military genius, discipline and utter determination he displayed at Carthage, by 133 BC Aemilianus had subdued Numantia after another brutal siege. It lasted eleven months, saw only a handful of Numantine survivors (many of whom had chosen suicide over capitulation) and ended with the razing of that city too.

During the same period of time in Rome, his cousin's life took a radically different path. The first overt sign of Tiberius's change in direction was his marriage to the daughter of Pulcher. This signalled that he was making a clean break with the faction of his cousins Aemilianus and Nasica, who bitterly opposed Pulcher, and was now allied to the reforming faction of the Senate. This group included an eminent lawyer and the revered head of a college of priests – Publius Mucius Scaevola and Publius Licinius Crassus. Tiberius was happy to be associated with these new, high-powered allies. They suited his political outlook and the crisis to which he addressed his ambition. What he had witnessed on his way to Spain had been his political awakening. Now, catalysed by his political humiliation, that consciousness bloomed. According to Plutarch, what motivated Tiberius above all to join forces with Pulcher was the plight of the landless mob in Rome. It was they who 'aroused Tiberius's energies and ambitions by inscribing slogans and appeals' on walls, porticoes and monuments across the city.[35] But the question facing the reformers was how to improve their lot.

The plan for reform was simple: Tiberius would stand in elections for the office of tribune of the people. This was a magistracy that since the early days of the republic had been devoted to protecting the interests of the plebs. Crucially it was also empowered to propose legislation before the Plebeian Assembly, the sovereign body in which the plebs voted. The strategy that would follow his hoped-for election was also straightforward: the reformers would propose a new law. In it a commission would be empowered to work out where state-owned public land had become illegally occupied by landowners in excess of their allotted limit of 125 hectares (300 acres); in addition they would also be granted the authority to redistribute this public land by lot to landless Roman citizens. The fairness of the proposal lay in the fact that it did no more than revive an old law that specified the same limit, but had been ignored for centuries. For the plan to work, all Tiberius needed to do was succeed in the election. After campaigning vigorously and passionately, he was voted into office. For the year 133 BC Tiberius thus became one of the ten tribunes of the people.

The conservative members of the Senate were quick to see danger. Many of them were large holders of public land beyond the legal limit. The man who stood to lose the most from Tiberius's proposed land reform, however, was Nasica himself. Under his leadership, the conservatives in the Senate rallied together and prepared to retaliate. In the same elections for tribune, they too put forward their man to represent their interests in the Plebeian Assembly. Marcus Octavius, a childhood friend of Tiberius, had at first declined to help Nasica's faction and stand in the election. It would have taken a stout, hardy soul, however, to resist the strong-arming of a large clique of aristocrats. Perhaps all that was required was to make it plain to him that he would have no political career in Rome unless he did as he was told. What is certain is that Octavius eventually stood in the election for tribune and also won.

When both men took office at the start of 133 BC, Rome was about to be rocked by the greatest political showdown in the history of the republic. For the first time there would be daggers in the Forum.

MURDER IN ROME

At the start of 133 BC the glorious flow of wealth that had followed the defeat of Carthage thirteen years earlier must have seemed as though it belonged to another age altogether. The aristocrats' building programmes to commemorate their victories in war ground to a halt; the price of grain doubled, then doubled again; and the expensive war in Spain, still unresolved, had drained the state treasury dry. Meanwhile, with the landless swelling the numbers, unemployment in the city rose ever higher.

Into this feverish, tense year the land bill of Tiberius Sempronius Gracchus, tribune of the people, was written on a whitened wooden board and posted in the Forum of Rome.

A day for voting was named and at that appointed time the votes were to be cast by the thirty-five tribes (or electoral colleges) of the plebs. Four tribes represented the urban plebs of Rome, seven the outskirts of the city, and twenty-four the countryside. While the senatorial élite could exert some influence over the urban plebs by virtue of their rank, money and connections, Tiberius needed as many rural voters as possible to come to the city to ensure that his bill would be passed.

The votes would be cast either by word to an official, or by writing on a small wooden tablet covered in wax and presented to the presiding magistrate on a raised wooden bridge – a system designed to prevent voters from being intimidated by any outside harassment. The Plebeian Assembly itself occupied the slope to the north of the Forum. It was made up of a series of concentric stone steps which led up to and abutted the Senate House. From this advantageous perch the senators were able to watch over and cheer or jeer all plebeian business being conducted there.

An opportunity for just such behaviour was not long in coming. Before the appointed day of voting, a series of public meetings was arranged for Tiberius to explain the land bill and allow for views to be expressed. When he mounted the rostra, the inflammatory nature of the bill became apparent in his very first action: he turned his back on the Senate and directed his proposal straight to the assembled plebs. This flew in the face of republican tradition. It was customary to consult the Senate and seek its approval on every piece of legislation before it was proposed. Yet Tiberius's flouting of legislative custom could not have been detected from his utterly composed manner. He stood still, chose his words carefully and then proceeded to speak in an eloquent, courteous tone.

The wild beasts that roam over Italy have their dens and holes to lurk in, but the men who fight and die for our country enjoy the common air and light and nothing else. It is their lot to wander with their wives and children, houseless and homeless, over the face of the earth. And when our generals appeal to their soldiers before a battle to defend their ancestors' tombs and their temples against the enemy, their words are a lie and a mockery, for not a man in their audience possesses a family altar; not one out of all those Romans owns an ancestral tomb. The truth is that they fight and die to protect the wealth and luxury of others. They are called the masters of the world, but they do not possess a single clod of earth that is truly their own.[36]

Tiberius's speech was a tour de force that built to a passionate crescendo. It posed one simple question: who should benefit from Rome's empire? 'Was it not right,' he demanded to know, 'that what belonged to all should be shared by all? Did not a citizen always deserve more than a slave? Was not the man who served as a soldier more useful than the man who did not? Was not the man who had a stake in his country more loyal to its common interests?'[37] The loudness of the applause and cheers from the plebs drowned out the vitriolic heckling from the onlooking conservatives of the Senate. Tiberius had detonated a political time bomb.

To the smallholders gathered in the assembly the benefit of Tiberius's proposal to the Roman republic was clear: by redistributing public land, the land bill would not just share the wealth more equally. Crucially, it would re-enfranchise the plebs, make them eligible once more for military recruitment and inject new energy into Rome's army. And the small price that the wealthy landowners had to pay for this? The surrender not of their privately owned land, but simply of the state-owned public land above the limit of 125 hectares (300 acres) that they had acquired over the last few centuries. Yet the core of the landowning aristocrats would not hear of it, and protested loudly.

This insolent revolutionary with a personal grudge to bear, they said to each other, was undermining the very foundation of the republic. Evicting them from the land they had long occupied and taking away their wealth would surely strip the state of its prime defenders, its leaders in war. Others argued that they and their forefathers were the ones who had invested so much in the public land. Most of it had been ravaged in the Second Punic War, they claimed, and it was their hard toil, constancy and application – not to mention money – that had returned it to productivity. Their ancestral homes had been built on that land, their noble fathers laid to rest in it.[38] The hard truth facing the senators, however, was that the Roman people were sovereign. Only they could vote on laws in the assembly. Now they had found a magistrate who was prepared to break with the customary cooperation between the Senate and the people, defy the aristocrats and put the plebs' interests first. The aggrieved senators could do nothing about it. Or could they?

On the day of the vote, the senators deployed their secret weapon: Marcus Octavius. Before dawn the auspices were taken by the presiding magistrate in order to ensure that the gods looked with favour on the proceedings. Then the heralds took to the streets and the city walls with their tubas, summoning the throngs of voters who had come to Rome in their thousands. Finally, the tribunes mounted the rostra and, amid the air of excitement, the presiding magistrate called the voting to begin. But when the land bill was announced, Octavius stood up and shouted, 'Veto'. The crowd growled their disapproval. Tiberius knew full well that the most effective way to stop the passage of the bill was through the power of veto accorded to all ten tribunes of the people. He never imagined, however, that any tribune would veto what was plainly in the interests of the very people he was elected to represent. Nonetheless, Octavius stood his ground and the voting was temporarily suspended.

Thus began a stand-off between two old friends, now turned adversaries. Day after day the assembly was called, and Tiberius would attempt once again to win over his opponent, but under the threatening gaze of the conservatives on the steps of the Senate House, Octavius persisted in obstructing the bill. The senators had chosen their man well. Octavius was in his late twenties, from an undistinguished family eager to make a name for itself in the Senate, and an owner of much public land himself. So, although discreet and of good character, Octavius stood to lose not just some of his land, but any prospect of a career among the aristocracy he had so recently joined should he fail them.

The highlight of the two tribunes' public struggle came when Tiberius offered to compensate Octavius for any loss of land. To the delight of the crowd, he said he would do so from his own pocket. On another occasion, Tiberius discarded the carrot for the stick, and suspended all state business until the land bill was voted on. As a result, the city came to a standstill. The hearing of court cases was forbidden, the markets were closed and the state treasury shut down. Tiberius's gang of supporters, their blood boiling, were quite prepared to use threats and intimidation to ensure that no one broke the suspension. Yet still the impasse went on; the mob became more agitated and enraged, Tiberius all the more desperate and determined. In total frustration, he finally hit on a solution to the problem of Octavius's veto that would raise the temperature in Rome even higher.

When the masses of riled plebs next assembled and Octavius vetoed again, Tiberius put forward a new motion that no one had ever tried before. He stood up on the rostra and calmly asked the people to cast their votes at once on whether Octavius should be stripped of his office for the simple reason that he was not fulfilling his duty as a tribune of the people. The crowd, baying for blood, let out a loud cheer and immediately began casting their votes. One by one, each tribe voted in favour of deposing Octavius, the presiding magistrate calling out, 'The Tribe of Palatine casts its vote: against Octavius. The Tribe of Fabia casts its vote: against Octavius,' and so on. It soon dawned on Tiberius that after weeks of increasing tension, the mob was about to reach boiling point. Any more heat and it would erupt into a riot.

Tiberius called an urgent halt to the voting and pleaded earnestly and passionately with his old friend. Embracing and kissing him, he begged Octavius to give way and allow the people what they were rightly owed. In response, the young tribune, 'his eyes filled with tears, for a long while did not utter a word'.[39] However, as he looked up to Nasica and his faction observing from the steps of the Senate House, the fear of losing their good opinion gripped him. With this emotion overriding all others, Octavius persisted in his stance one last time and the voting resumed. Just before the final vote was cast, Tiberius, alert to the impending danger, urged his own immediate gang of supporters to drag Octavius from the rostra and protect him. Sure enough, when the voting was complete and Octavius was deposed, the mob rushed headlong at the former tribune. His allies failed to repel them, but under the protection of the bodyguard, Octavius escaped with his life. His servant was less lucky: his eyes were gouged out.

That same day the land bill finally became law with an overwhelming vote. The law stipulated the immediate appointment of three commissioners charged with surveying, recovering and reallocating public land. The three were Tiberius, his younger brother Gaius and his father-in-law, Appius Claudius Pulcher. After the elation of having their bill passed, however, the reformers were stymied from the start. The showdown with Octavius had served only to make the aristocratic faction more hardline and entrenched. Whenever the commissioners requested funds to carry out their work, the Senate successfully sabotaged any progress by refusing to finance it. It is also possible that even Tiberius's allies felt that he had gone too far in exploiting the power of the office of tribune.

Mutterings in the Senate House spread to the streets of Rome, and a smear campaign now gained momentum: Tiberius was not interested in the people, but only in power; he was simply using the plebs to assert his personal ambition and dominion over the apparatus of the republic. In short, went the word, he was a tyrant who wanted to be king. His violent removal of Octavius from the sacrosanct office of tribune proved as much![40] As the rumours grew apace, Tiberius, cresting a wave of popular acclaim and dizzy with direct action, played into the hands of his opponents. Early in 133 BC came news that Attalus, the king of Pergamum, a wealthy Greek city in Asia Minor loyal to Rome, had died. In his will he named the Roman people as his heirs. At a stroke, Rome acquired a rich, cultured economy. But this was not how Tiberius took the news. He saw it as a windfall, the very injection of cash that his land commission urgently needed. He immediately brought another bill before the Plebeian Assembly, proposing to use the royal money to finance the land reform. Since the Roman people were the nominated heirs of Attalus, ran Tiberius's argument, they should be able to dispose of the money as they wished.

Once again, the bill drove Nasica and the conservatives in the Senate to fury. Control of foreign and economic affairs had always belonged to the Senate, and the Senate alone. Tiberius's enemies immediately seized on his action as further proof of his naked ambition for absolute power. In the Senate one of Nasica's faction, Pompeius, stood up and threw fuel on the flames. As Tiberius's neighbour, he said, he had witnessed how envoys from Pergamum had come to the tribune's house, bringing with them a crown and a purple robe from the royal treasures 'in the expectation that he would soon be king of Rome'.[41] The senators erupted in horror. However, there was another reason why Tiberius's controversial bill had played into his enemies' hands: it was grounds for prosecution. No criminal case could be brought against a magistrate while he was still in office, but Tiberius's tenure of the Tribunate was quickly running out. At last, believed the senators, they had their man.

Constantly in fear of his life, Tiberius was now accompanied by a bodyguard wherever he went. Death threats and rumours of plots to kill him had so rattled him that his associates and supporters now guarded his house by camping outside it day and night. Inside, he took advice from them. The only way to avoid prosecution, they said, was to remain in office: why not stand for tribune for the following year? Running for the same office for two consecutive years was unconstitutional by custom, but a vote in the people's assembly could create a new precedent. Fired by this idea and the encouragement of his immediate coterie, Tiberius entertained grand ideas for a new manifesto on which to campaign, a new set of proposals designed to curb the power of the Senate even further.[42] Increasingly, the rumours and slanders against Tiberius and his motives were beginning to wear the look of truth. Was this indeed a quest for personal power, a vendetta of revenge against the very men who had so humiliated him, a quest that was, in the end, out of step with what even the people wanted?

There were certainly signs that his own faction in the Senate was estranged from him, for the ancient sources now go increasingly silent on the role of the eminent politicians who had once backed him. Furthermore, the rural voters whose support had been so critical in passing the land reform bill had returned to the countryside for the harvest. They could not be counted on to come back to the city for the vote on Tiberius's re-election. Nonetheless, the young man went ahead with his crusade and the greatest gamble of his life. The decision would set him on the ultimate collision course with the Senate.

At daybreak on the morning of the elections the auspices were taken. They did not bode well. The birds, although enticed with food, would not even leave their cage. Other bad omens followed. When Tiberius left his house he stubbed his toe so hard on the threshold that it split his toenail. Then a raven dislodged a stone from the roof of a house he was passing on his way to the Forum, which landed on his foot. The signs shook his resolve so much that he thought about abandoning the election. But one of his Greek tutors, who had been influential in shaping his political thought since he was young, told him that 'it would be a shame and an unbearable disgrace if Tiberius, the son of Gracchus, a grandson of Scipio Africanus and a champion of the Roman people, should fail to answer his fellow-citizens' call for help because he was afraid of a raven'.[43]

When Tiberius reached the Forum and climbed the Capitol Hill, he walked into mayhem. Amid the cheers and applause for him, the rival gangs of supporters for the tribune of the people and for the aristocratic élite were jostling and pushing each other around. As the voting got under way, a senator loyal to Tiberius threw himself into the mêlée and made his way towards him with a warning: the Senate, he said, was in session, and Nasica and his faction were at this very moment rallying their colleagues to kill Tiberius. Alarmed, Tiberius passed on the word to his nearby supporters, who prepared themselves for a fight. Some of them, however, were out of earshot, caught up in the swarms of people. To them Tiberius signalled that his life was in danger by putting his hand to his head. His enemies took this gesture to mean something else entirely. They rushed to the steps of the Senate House and made an announcement: Tiberius was calling for his crown![44]

In the Senate, Nasica used this news to drive home his case. He shouted at the consul to save the republic and kill the tyrant. The consul, however, stood his ground and defended the principle of justice on which the republic was founded: he would authorize neither the use of violence in politics, he said, nor the execution of a man without trial. At this point, in frustration and fury, Nasica jumped to his feet and declared a state of emergency: 'Now that the consul has betrayed the state, let every man who wishes to uphold the laws follow me!' Then, in the manner of a priest before a sacrifice, Nasica pulled his toga around his head and left the Senate House.[45]

Joined by their slaves and associates who had come armed with clubs, the hundreds of senators following Nasica now tied their togas around their waists to free up their legs, armed themselves with whatever they could find en route – broken staves or legs of benches – and marched towards the Capitol. Many of the crowd gave way out of respect to their rank and seniority, and fear at the sight of so many noblemen bent on a single, violent purpose. Others, even Tiberius's supporters, panicked and trampled over each other in their attempts to disperse. In the confusion and chaos, Tiberius too tried to run. At first someone caught hold of his toga, so he threw it off. Then, dressed only in his tunic, he tried once again to get away, but tripped over some bodies. He fell down and was promptly clubbed to death.

No fewer than three hundred people were killed in this way: not honourably with swords, but ignobly and brutally with clubs, sticks and stones. In the aftermath, Tiberius's younger brother Gaius requested that his dead brother's body be returned to him. But the aristocratic senators refused Tiberius the dignity of a proper burial and threw his bludgeoned corpse into the Tiber that same night, along with those of his supporters and friends. It was the first time in the history of the republic that a political conflict had ended in murder.

EPILOGUE

In foreign wars, campaigns and battles spanning 150 years between 275 BC and 132 BC, the aristocratic élite of Rome had led the republic to victory across the length and breadth of the Mediterranean. They had generated amazing wealth, both for themselves and for Rome; in the process they had won an empire and become a superpower. But the price they paid for this, so a conservative commentator of the time might have said, was the loss of the very principles of justice, decency and honour that they had used to justify their conquests and that had helped to make the republic so powerful in the first place.

Following the destruction of Carthage, the nobles' pursuit of military excellence, riches and prestige served only to intensify the rivalry and competition for office between the families of the aristocracy. As a consequence, they turned in on themselves and, through greed and self-interest, ignored the developing social and economic problems that empire-building had brought in its wake. As a result, they alienated many sections of society – sections that, in the 130s BC, crystallized into a power base for Tiberius and his associates to use in their bid for reform.

Although Tiberius took a controversial political path in championing the cause of the people against the interests of his own milieu, the aristocratic élite, his aim was essentially conservative: to save the republic by alleviating the problems of the needy. Constitutionally too, Tiberius had been well within his rights as tribune in proposing the land bill without the Senate's approval and in deposing Octavius. But in setting the people against the Senate in such a directly confrontational manner, Tiberius was damaging the customary respect that the élite liked to think underpinned the relationship between the Senate and the sovereign Roman people. In the nobles' eyes such behaviour was utterly offensive. Ever since the expulsion of the kings from Rome, concord and cooperation between the political orders had been seen as cornerstones of the republic, its unique source of strength, power and dynamism. For this reason alone it was easy for enemies, such as Nasica, to paint Tiberius as a revolutionary, to pick at the sensitive nerve of the Romans' fear of domination by one man and to suggest that he was capitalizing on the people for his own ends.

In reality, though, Tiberius and his land bill sought only to restore things to the way they had been centuries earlier before Rome had won the riches of its empire abroad. That aim continued after Tiberius's death. The land commission carried on its work for three more years. Six years later, in 123 BC, his proud younger brother Gaius picked up the baton, was also elected tribune and introduced an even more ambitious and comprehensive programme of reform. He too was branded an enemy of the republic by the conservatives in the Senate and murdered. As with his brother, they despised what he stood for. To the mass of the Roman people, however, Tiberius and Gaius were heroes. In their eyes at least, the two sons of Tiberius Sempronius Gracchus the elder and Cornelia had honoured the funeral masks of their father and their dead aristocratic ancestors. Those ghostly likenesses were displayed in cases in the atrium of their family home. The glorious memory of the men they represented had been renewed.

What really motivated Tiberius and Gaius – whether ideological drive or simple ambition – will always remain debatable.

What is clear is that, behind the mud-slinging and the eruption of blood-letting in politics, there was a genuine principle at stake. This was the crucial issue of who benefited from the empire, the rich or the poor, and it was one that Tiberius addressed in the most thrilling, explosive fashion. No one before him (certainly no one who was supposed to be 'one of us') had so extravagantly antagonized the political élite or so bravely exposed their hypocrisy. In doing so, he did much more than stretch the constitution of the republic to its very limit. He also unleashed the potential of an untapped and highly combustible political force – the mob. The sleeping giant of the Roman republic had been awoken.

But where Tiberius's character was by turns idealistic and gentle, stubborn and ambitious, it would take an altogether more meticulous, cold and ruthless mind to harness the power of the people and drive it to its logical conclusion. Such a mind would use the people not simply to take on the conservatives in the Senate, but to rise to power entirely outside the legal apparatus of the republic; it would use them not for the sake of land reform, but to achieve sole mastery of the Roman world. That mind belonged to Julius Caesar.

II

CAESAR

In 46 BC, two years before he was assassinated, Julius Caesar was voted some extraordinary honours by the Senate of the Roman republic. It was decreed that he be called Liberator and that a Temple of Liberty be built and dedicated in his honour.[1] And yet the man who had freed the Roman people was now their dictator. The man who had liberated the Romans was also partly responsible for thousands of their deaths in a civil war. Indeed, Caesar, the great champion of the people, had now become in effect an autocrat, on the verge of being worshipped as a god. Two years after the Senate's vote of honours in 46 BC he would even be murdered in the name of liberty. How had such a state of affairs come to pass? What had happened to the glorious Roman republic? What had happened to its cherished liberties?

In Rome, during the hundred years before Christ, the idea of liberty became the subject of a fierce debate. In that debate two freedoms clashed time and again: the freedom of the aristocratic élite and the freedom of the Roman people. The two different ideas of liberty amounted to two different versions of what the republic was all about. It was this clash of ideas that would entwine the lives of Julius Caesar and Pompey the Great, and that would rock the entire Roman world to its foundations.

Settling the question of which freedom was supreme would bring the state of the Roman republic crashing down in a bloody civil war. The ancient system of public voting, popular elections, annual office holding and joint government by the Senate and the Roman People would cease to function, and would eventually be replaced with a dictatorship, with rule by one man. Elections did indeed continue under Caesar, but now they were no longer free: it was the dictator who influenced them, who had the last vote. It would prove to be one of the greatest turning points in all Roman history.

But the destruction of the Roman republic was not the consequence of a dry clash of ideas. What turned this ideological debate about freedom into a bloody, violent and messy revolution was a highly personal quality, one that went to the very core of Roman aristocratic values: dignity. A Roman noble's sense of prestige, honour and political standing was paramount – prized by aristocrats above everything else. Ironically, it would be the very same quality that would drive Julius Caesar to fight a civil war and to destroy the corrupt aristocratic milieu that so cherished it. It was this quality that would fuel the titanic power struggles of Rome in the last years of the republic. It was this quality that would lie at the heart of the republic's complete meltdown.

POPULAR POLITICS

The murder of the tribunes Tiberius Gracchus and Gaius Gracchus cleaved a fatal divide in the politics of the late Roman republic. Their mother Cornelia declared the Forum of Rome, where both men had been martyred at the hands of the conservative faction of the aristocratic élite, a sacred ground. The very heart of the city thus became their open, public tomb, and around it grew the cult of the popular politician. Henceforth, over the next hundred years, ambitious young men on the make faced a choice: to use the winning of political office to protect the interests of the conservative élite, or to follow the example of the Gracchus brothers and enact legislation that increased the power of the Roman people. One fork of the political path allowed the noble senators to maintain their traditional grip on both the wealth of the ever-increasing empire and the levers of influence in the republic, while the other fork tried to reform the balance of power and wealth in favour of the people.

The contemperorary writer Varro called these factions the 'two heads' of the republic. It is a fitting image, for in the war of attrition that marked the last decades of the republic, there were striking similarities between the two sides. For example, both sides claimed to be defending the republic. On the other hand, they disagreed profoundly over the question of what was to be defended. The conservative constitutionalists claimed they were defending the republic from assault by the revolutionary state-wreckers, while the populists said they were defending the republic from corruption at the hands of a self-serving aristo-cratic élite.

The political slogan for both sides was the same too: 'Liberty'. But, predictably, their definitions of this word were very differ-ent. The constitutionalists were fighting for their traditional freedom to exercise their dignity equally and without interfer-ence from others in the pursuit of a glorious career; the people they feared were tyrants, would-be kings and powerful individu-als who put their interests above those of the republic. The populists, on the other hand, were struggling for the people to have freedom from domination by the élite, and the freedom to pass their own laws. Between these two political groups and their increasingly entrenched positions the pendulum would swing dramatically and violently.

The battlefield of this struggle was the Plebeian Assembly; the weapon of choice for both sides was the popular vote. The legacy of Tiberius and Gaius Gracchus was to give the people's assembly a new, more authoritative role in the republic at the expense of the Senate. But while the Plebeian Assembly had become more powerful, it was also more susceptible to exploitation. Most Roman citizens who made up thirty-one of the thirty-five electoral tribes lived far away from the city, and it was impractical and costly for them to vote. As a result, the majority never did. Those who could afford to leave their farms tended to be the landed gentry whose sympathies lay with the conservative élite in Rome rather than with the needy. Only the urban mob could be counted on to make up the majority of voters, and they could be easily influenced: the poor might see it in their interests to be swayed by a wealthy benefactor with money to spend; small businessmen and traders by the patronage of their aristocratic customers; former slaves by loyalty to their old masters. In one way or another the voters could be bribed. And as money from the empire flowed into Rome, bribery became rampant. The Gracchus brothers may have shown the potential of the people as a political weapon, but in the last decades of the republic that weapon could be used by both sides.[2]

Thus armed, the populists and the conservative aristocrats in the Senate joined battle. Spoiling for a fight after the murders of the Gracchus brothers, it was the populists who landed the first blows. In the 110s BC anti-corruption laws were passed to curb the excesses of provincial governors. Senators were tried and driven out of public life. At the same time the two sides clashed over another flashpoint issue: how were military commands to be allotted – by the Senate or the people? When aristocratic generals proved to be failures in Roman wars against enemies in North Africa and Gaul, the senators responsible were brought to trial by the people for incompetence. They were then promptly replaced with men not of high birth but of proven ability, and on the say-so of the people, not the Senate. On this basis the general Gaius Marius won an unprecedented series of consulships between 108 and 90 BC, even though he had no senatorial ancestry.

The populist cause went as far as all-out war. Between 90 and 89 BC the armies of the Roman republic went into battle with its disgruntled Italian allies. That bloody, violent war, known as the Social War, came to an end when the Senate agreed to extend Roman citizenship to all Italian communities in Italy south of the river Po. Roman citizenship brought with it the benefits of protection against the arbitrary actions of aristocratic office holders. It was another success marked up by those championing liberty for the Roman people.

The backlash came in the 80s BC. When Rome clashed with King Mithridates of Pontus, a contender for power in the east, the Senate appointed an arch-conservative, Lucius Cornelius Sulla, the consul for 88 BC, to take command of the war. The campaign promised much booty for both the general and the soldiers involved. The appointment was short-lived, however. A tribune of the people vetoed Sulla and proposed instead that the great general Marius be enticed out of retirement and once again given command. Conservative generals peremptorily forced from office in this way would usually have acceded to the sovereign will of the people, however outraged they were. Not Sulla. His response was efficient and devastating. First he won the loyalty of the army under his command. He claimed that if Marius were to win the appointment, it would be veterans from his previous campaigns who would be chosen to reap the rich rewards of victory in the east, not they. The appeal to the soldiers' financial interests worked. The allegiance of the army sealed, Sulla then marched on Rome, killed the tribune responsible for the veto against him, took over the republic by force in a lightning coup d'état and appointed himself dictator. This position had its origins in an ancient republican office that gave one man emergency powers for a short period of time. Sulla, however, decided to make the office serve one specific purpose: to destroy his political enemies.

After finally defeating Mithridates in 83 BC and stripping the eastern provinces of wealth, Sulla returned to Rome, defeated his opponents in a battle at the gates of the city, and then proceeded to wreak a brutal and violent revenge on the populists. Proscription lists were posted in the Forum, and Sulla's soldiers and supporters were charged with hunting down his enemies. Many were killed in the city or forced to flee, their property confiscated. The dictator Sulla's raft of legislation, designed to cripple the power of the populists and bolster that of the Senate, was equally reactionary.

Among the new laws was a decree that political offices had to be held in a strict sequence according to the hierarchy of magistracies. It was thus rendered impossible for upstart populists to be fast-tracked straight to the consulship by the people's vote. The Senate was also enlarged from three hundred to six hundred members, swollen by the intake of Sulla's supporters. The most provocative laws, however, concerned the office of tribune of the people. This magistracy became a shadow of its former self. Now no tribune, once elected, could stand for any other office (thus the office was made unattractive to men of ambition); a tribune's every bill had to meet the prior approval of the Senate; and, in addition, the office was stripped of its power of veto. The pendulum of conservative reaction had swung emphatically against the populists.

His clinical and bloody work done, Sulla returned the republic to the Senate, then retired to Puteoli and the pleasures of a private life in 79 BC. It took the best part of the following decade to restore the ancient powers of the tribunes and to untie the hands of the popular assemblies. The consul who won lavish praise from the people for restoring the last of the tribunician powers in 70 BC was a surprise to many people. He was Rome's most successful general of the day, and he had proved it by winning two triumphs before he was forty. His reputation, however, had germinated in a bloodier, darker time: he had once been the savage henchman of Sulla. Indeed, as the general who, on behalf of the conservatives in the Senate, had spent much of the 80s BC going to war against the leading populists of the day, he had earned the nickname the 'Teenage Butcher'. His real name was Gnaeus Pompeius Magnus – Pompey 'the Great'.[3]

Although the son of a consul and the inheritor of the largest private estate in Italy, Pompey should not be mistaken for an aristocrat at the heart of the Establishment. He was a young man on the make and unencumbered by any sentimental attachment to the political traditions of the republican past. He was, above all, an extraordinary soldier. Ambitious, daring and famed for his mane of blond hair, he was called Magnus (the Great) by his own soldiers (in an echo of his boyhood hero Alexander the Great). He had justified the name with his brilliant execution of a campaign in Africa in 80 BC at the age of twenty-six. His greatest gift, however, was an ability to spot an opportunity that might further his glory. As consul in 70 BC, he seized such an opportunity, changed sides and joined the populists. He not only reinstated the power of the tribunes, but reformed the court juries so that they no longer favoured senators. In addition, he saw to it that sixty-four second-rate senators, all Sullan appointees, were struck off the census list. The people fell in love with him. Although many senators opposed Pompey, the great general had the backing of a young senator, Gaius Julius Caesar.

With the entry of Pompey and Caesar into the ring of Roman politics in 70 BC, the pendulum of popular politics was about to swing back in favour of the populists, but this time in the most spectacular fashion. There was one simple reason for this. Learning from the ruthless example set by Sulla, Pompey and Caesar would, over the next two decades, accumulate more personal power and influence in Rome than any politician before them. Unlike Sulla, however, they sought to boost not the power of the Senate, but the power of the populists. It was no coincidence that they had restored the power of the tribunes because now, to win such power, they were going to need them.

POMPEY, CAESAR AND CATO

Pompey blazed the trail. In 67 BC a tribune proposed to the popular assembly that the people's hero, even though he held no office at the time, be awarded a special command to rid the Mediterranean of pirates, who were then profiteering in the lawless wake of Rome's many wars of conquest. The situation had reached crisis point because the pirates' grip on the Mediterranean was now causing a grain shortage in Rome. The job of defeating the pirate fleets over such a vast geographical space was huge. To pull it off Pompey would need more ships, more soldiers and more time in command than any general had been awarded before.

Alarm bells went off in the Senate. The power Pompey would have at his disposal – five hundred ships, 120,000 soldiers and a three-year command – would make a mockery of the equality of members of the élite. Granting him that power was as good as establishing a monarch over the republic in all but name. Nonetheless, the people ratified the bill and Pompey set to work. His success astounded everyone. He not only defeated the pirates, but did so in just three months. He then used the rest of his time in command to outstrip this achievement and carry out the single greatest sweep of Roman conquest in the east. It was a feat to rival the great conquest of Greece in the second century BC. Swimming on a tide of extraordinary success, the general was rewarded with another command. Once again, a tribune put a law before the people that would grant Pompey the command of the war to finish off King Mithridates in Asia.

Pompey was no less ambitious in this task – and his results were even more staggering. Over the next three years, he not only defeated Mithridates, but created and settled – through a combination of diplomacy and war – two new Roman provinces: Syria and Judaea. As a result of both his campaigns, Pompey could boast that he had captured 1000 fortified places, nine hundred cities and eight hundred pirate ships. He had founded thirty-nine cities and, in addition to the 20,000 talents with which the coffers of the public treasury bulged, the public revenue from taxation in the east had nearly doubled – all thanks to Pompey. The senators back in Rome were by turns delighted, amazed and horrified. In Pompey's appointment of a king here, in his striking of a peace treaty there, or in his capture of a foreign city, it was almost as though he was indeed a new and all-powerful Alexander. The senators' fear remained: would he and his army seize absolute power on his return to Rome?

Crucially, when Pompey returned to Italy, he dispersed his troops and submitted to the Senate. It was an acknowledgement that, although at the very height of his popularity and power, he had no intention of wielding these attributes against the republic. He had his terms, however: the settlement of his soldiers on plots of Italian soil as a reward for their service, and the ratification of the treaties he had made in the east. This was still a source of concern for the conservatives in the Senate. To agree to these terms would be to acknowledge the pre-eminence of Pompey in the republic. It would confirm that he had won the personal loyalty both of the Roman army and of kings, potentates and peoples in the east. The conservatives in the Senate did eventually award the people's hero an unprecedented third triumph, but stopped short of meeting his wishes. They delayed and delayed, shutting the general out in the cold.

Here Pompey the Great now languished, with only his growing bitterness for company.

Meanwhile, in the 60s BC Gaius Julius Caesar, six years Pompey's junior, was also building personal power. Unlike Pompey, Caesar came from an ancient patrician family that claimed descent from the Trojan Aeneas, the legendary founder of Rome. Aeneas was thought to have been the son of Venus, so Caesar was also able to claim descent from the gods. This was a claim he lost no opportunity to make; it established him as more blue-blooded than anyone else in the Roman republic could possibly be. At the grand, aristocratic funeral of his aunt and his first wife he laid out the two planks of his political career with the economy and effectiveness of a public relations company. He praised his aunt's divine ancestry (and thus by implication his own too) and also demonstrated his political sympathies, not through words, but actions. As his aunt had been married to the great general Marius, he ensured that mourners paraded her husband's wax masks. In this way Caesar declared that his was the cause of the populists. Such flamboyance was matched by his dress. Caesar had a reputation as a dandy: he wore his hair carefully parted and combed, and sported his toga with a dashing loose belt.[4] Such displays of behaviour offended the conservatives in the Senate. Little did they realize that there was much worse to come.

In the early 70s BC Caesar made his political sympathies apparent when he undertook to prosecute two corrupt aristocratic governors of the provinces of Macedonia and Greece. Although he lost the trials, he gained great popularity with the plebs. Through his eloquence, ebullient charm and friendly good manners, he showed how easily he could win people over.[5] However, he realized that to win sufficient favour with the Roman people to reach the highest offices in the republic it was necessary to make a much bigger splash than that. With this ambition in mind, Caesar exploited office after office for all it was worth.

The post of curule aedile, for example, carried with it the responsibility of staging public games on state holidays. Elected to this position in 65 BC, Caesar duly seized the opportunity to wow the people of Rome by putting on the most spectacular gladiatorial games the city had ever seen. No fewer than 320 pairs of gladiators clad in burnished silver armour prepared to compete for glory and delight the public. The anticipated occasion caused such a sensation with the Roman people that the conservatives in the Senate immediately proposed a bill curtailing the number of gladiators any individual might keep in the city.[6] In this way, they tried to deter the politician from so shamelessly winning popular favour. In the event, the people had to make do with a more modest show, but the impact had been made.

Such lavish events required money – and lots of it. To recoup his massive debts, Caesar next set his sights on being elected to administer a province, plundering it for booty and repaying his debtors on his return. After his praetorship, he did just this – in the province of Further Spain in 61 BC. Straying from his ordinary duties of governor, he set about warring with the independent tribes of northern Portugal, and proved himself to be as much a fighter and general abroad as he was a suave and debonair populist politician at home. So successful was he that he focussed his ambitions on requesting a triumph – the perfect launch pad, the young general thought, for his election campaign to the highest office of the republic: the consulship. However, on his return to Rome, all did not go according to plan.

The man who was determined to scupper Caesar's smooth path to the consulship was the arch-constitutionalist of the day, Marcus Porcius Cato. Inflexible, humourless and much older in character than his thirty-five years, Cato wanted his life to embody an ideal of austere and ancient republican virtue. His hair was dishevelled in the manner of a peasant, his beard hoary and unkempt, and in protest at the fad among the élite for wearing a light, luxurious purple, Cato insisted on wearing black. His contemporary Cicero said of him that he walked around Rome as if he were living 'in the ideal republic of Plato, not the cesspit of Romulus'.[7] Dinner *chez* Cato was no self-respecting senator's idea of a fun night out. Indeed, as Caesar returned to Rome, Cato showed how he lived and breathed the constitutional laws of the republic, how determined he was to use them to stop the populists from gaining power.

Outside the city walls Caesar sent in his formal request to the Senate for a triumph to mark his conquests in Spain. He also stated that he wished to stand for the consulship in the imminent July elections. Cato's reply came back: according to law, he could not have both. Caesar was caught in a dilemma. To receive a triumph he had to wait outside Rome until the day of celebration. To stand for the consulship, however, he had to enter the city immediately and offer his candidacy in person. Caesar, said Cato, had to decide between the two: the glory of a grand popular procession through Rome, or a bid for a top job in the republic.[8]

Caesar chose to stand for the consulship. As we shall see, it was a decision that would change the course of Roman history for ever. However, the outcome of the election was not guaranteed. In order to secure the office of consul and also recoup the popular favour he had lost in forgoing his triumph, Caesar now urgently needed both money and influence. The only man in the republic who was willing and able to provide these things was none other than the sulking Pompey the Great. The two great populists of the day now made a pact. Pompey would give Caesar financial and popular support to win election to the consulship; and Caesar, once elected consul, would give Pompey what he most wanted. On Pompey's behalf, he would propose the very laws that the fearful conservative senators had long refused – the settlement of Pompey's veterans and the ratification of his treaties in the east.

The alliance of the two men was potentially so powerful and threatening that, at the election for the consulship in the summer of 60 BC, the conservatives led by Cato would stop at nothing to prevent Caesar and Pompey getting their way. The two sides, constitutionalists and reformers, conservatives and populists joined battle once more. In the build-up to the election in July 60 BC the deep pockets of Pompey and his wealthy ally Marcus Licinius Crassus ensured that bribes flooded into the Campus Martius, the place where the people voted in the elections for consul. Even Cato, the priggish adherer to the letter of law, resorted to bribery to promote a conservative candidate, his son-in-law Marcus Bibulus.[9] Cato and his conservative allies were so desperate to ensure that at least one of the consuls could be relied upon to restrain Caesar that they were prepared to play as dirty as the populist bloc fronted by Caesar, Pompey and Crassus. In the event, Caesar won a massive majority, but Cato could claim success too. By a whisker, Bibulus was elected as Caesar's fellow consul. But the battle had only just begun.

The year of Caesar's consulship represents the logical conclusion of the long struggle between the populists and the constitutionalists. Above all, it shows how the populists had now gained the upper hand. For the striking innovation of 59 BC was that the leading populist of the day, the man who was prepared to buck tradition and defy the wishes of the Senate, was no longer a tribune of the people. He was a man in possession of one of the greatest sources of power in the republic – the consulship. The radical tactics of the tribunes were now applied to that post. When, for example, Caesar proposed Pompey's land bill to settle his troops, he met with a wall of resolute opposition rallied by Cato. So instead of backing down to the collective will of his fellow senators, as was customary for a consul to do, he simply walked out of the Senate House, took the bill direct to the popular assembly and had it passed there. But Caesar was prepared to go to even greater extremes. When, on other days of voting on Caesar and Pompey's programme, his fellow consul Bibulus repeatedly tried to obstruct the public business by declaring that the omens were not good, Caesar simply ignored him and pressed ahead anyway. Was Caesar breaking the law? Cato certainly thought so.

In the feverish tension of 59 BC Caesar and Pompey compounded their 'illegalities'. They introduced once again an ominous element used by both sides in the war of popular politics: brute force. When Cato obstructed any discussion of the land bill in the Senate, Caesar had his lictors seize the braying senator and throw him into prison. It was a small taste of things to come. The menacing threat of Pompey's veterans, of thousands of former soldiers loyal to one man, now descended on Rome. In order to make sure that the vote on the land bill went their way, gangs of Pompey's thugs simply entered the Forum on the day of voting and cleared it of all opponents to the bill. In one encounter Cato and Bibulus were carried off, their entourage of officials beaten up and the magistrate's rods of office smashed. As a final humiliating insult, a bucket of excrement was thrown over the consul's head.

The next day Bibulus called a meeting of the Senate and complained about how he had been so violently and illegally treated. The sympathetic senators were at a loss how to respond. For the rest of the year Bibulus stayed indoors in constant fear of his life. The energetic Caesar, meanwhile, simply boycotted the Senate House and the normal procedures of politics, and brought all his populist legislation without hindrance direct to the people's assembly. It was an extraordinary year. And it was not over yet.

It was the custom of every consul, once his year in office had come to an end, to govern a Roman province, chosen by the Senate, as proconsul. In one last-ditch attempt at restraining the ambitious, calculating Caesar, Cato and the conservatives decided to send him to the quiet pastures of Italy. Here there were no wars to fight, no mass of booty to plunder and no opportunity to win the loyalty of an army. In short, it spelt the premature end of Caesar's brilliant, show-stealing career. But Caesar had other ideas. He instigated a loyal tribune of the people to bring a new law to the assembly, granting him the more promising provinces of Cisalpine Gaul (Gaul on the eastern side of the Alps, see map, page 119) and Illyricum (the Dalmatian coast) for a period of five years. By an extraordinary stroke of luck, however, the governor of Transalpine Gaul (on the western side of the Alps) died in the spring of 59 BC, leaving that province too in urgent need of a commander. This region of Gaul was the gateway to lands untouched by Roman rule. It offered an appetizing prospect for war, conquest and riches.

In the Senate Pompey proposed that Caesar be awarded the new command of Illyricum and the Gallic provinces. The sad, broken remnants of the aristocratic élite still prepared to show up for senatorial meetings duly granted it. If they had refused, the people's assembly would have given it to him anyway; by granting the command to Caesar themselves, they saved face and gave the impression, at least, of retaining some power over the people's assembly.[10]

But even in their gloom, the traditionalists could find something to raise a meagre cheer. By the time Caesar left for Gaul, he had alienated not just the entire Senate, but even some of the people too. His legislation had not benefited all sections of the plebs, and some were now asking if his methods were not just as corrupt as those of the discredited aristocrats from whom he said he was liberating Rome. 'The truth is,' wrote the senator Cicero at the time, 'the present regime is the most infamous, most disgraceful, most uniformly odious to all sorts and classes and ages of men that ever was... Those "populist" politicians have taught even quiet folk to hiss!'[11] Above all, however, Caesar had successfully galvanized one gritty, single-minded enemy in particular: Cato.

The dour, tenacious senator remained utterly determined to stop Caesar's accumulation of power, and now he believed he had the weapon with which to do it. Cato assured his allies that he had grounds for prosecuting Caesar in a court of law over the illegalities perpetrated during his consulship. Yes, it was true that while Caesar was still in office, Cato could not touch him. But as soon as the term of his commands in Gaul came to an end and he returned to Rome, Caesar would be taken to court like a common criminal.

Nonetheless, Cato's plans for revenge lay a long way off in the future. When Caesar rode off to Gaul in the spring of 58 BC, he and his ally Pompey seemed untouchable. The consuls and tribunes elected for that year were their loyal friends, and in this way they made sure that all the legislation they had enacted would not be undone. The two men had also sealed their alliance in an old-fashioned and aristocratic manner. Caesar had offered Pompey the hand of his only daughter, Julia, in marriage, and in the spring of 59 BC the ageing general had duly wed his charming young bride.

And yet the supreme alliance between the two men was now about to be tested to the limit. For while Pompey remained behind in Rome surrounded by enemies baying for his blood, Caesar was about to win unimaginable glory. And with that glory would come unimaginable power.

THE BALANCE OF POWER

The status of the small Roman province of Gallia Transalpina, in what is now the south of France, is reflected in its modern name: Provence. The Romans called the northern territory beyond it 'Long-haired Gaul' because of the horrendous, unkempt specimens of barbarity said to live there. The simple fact was that although the Roman Senate had made some leaders of the more powerful tribes official 'Friends of the Roman People', and although pioneering Roman merchants had penetrated along the rivers of the Rhone and Garonne to ply a roaring trade in wine, the dank and cold woods of the north were regarded by most civilized Romans as a threatening unknown. Worse, to many minds the region represented the greatest source of danger to Roman rule.[12]

What prompted such fear? In 390 BC, savage hordes of barbarian warriors from Gaul had achieved what even the great Carthaginian Hannibal had not. Rampaging their way through Italy, they had successfully sacked the city of Rome. More recently, those ancient Roman fears were painfully revived when, in 102 and 101 BC, it took the might of Marius's well-drilled, highly organized legions to defend Italy from another fierce invasion of Gallic and Germanic tribes. But with the governorship of Julius Caesar, the legendary fear in which Gaul was held was about to come to a permanent end.

When Caesar arrived in Gaul he had no instructions or legal authority to wage war. Indeed, just the year before a law had been passed curbing the arbitrary actions of Roman provincial governors. Caesar would have known all about this. It was none other than he, as consul, who had devised and proposed the bill. And yet even regarding his own populist laws, Caesar was meticulous in calculating the moment to break them. In 58 BC the tribe of the Helvetii migrated from their home in present-day

Switzerland and passed close to the doorstep of Caesar's province. In response, the proconsul deliberately stationed his army 16 kilometres (10 miles) outside the boundaries of his province, directly in their path. Falling into his trap, the Helvetii attacked the Roman army. To the Roman commander this was a gift. Caesar quickly exploited a time-honoured legal loophole: he was, he said, defending the Roman republic from aggression and repairing the injury done to his dignity.[13]

Caesar called together his three legions stationed at Aquileia in northern Italy, raised two more legions in Cisalpine Gaul, and promptly taught the Helvetii a harsh lesson in battle. There was uproar in the Senate, Cato's being the loudest voice. Caesar, he said, was simply doing as he pleased: illegally instigating wars with independent tribes not subject to Rome; illegally levying troops and filling up his legions with non-Roman citizens; and illegally granting them citizenship. He was becoming, cried Cato, his own self-appointed judge and jury, heaping crime upon crime against the republic!

The reality was that in the war against the Helvetii Caesar had declared in unambiguous terms his true intention as governor in Gaul. On whatever grounds, on whatever pretext, however flimsy, he was going to single- mindedly pursue a series of wars with the Gallic tribes beyond his province until the whole of Gaul, the sprawling and unknown tracts of that dark, sinister northern land, had been completely pacified and brought under Roman rule. Over the course of the next eight years Caesar set about honouring that intention with seemingly limitless confidence and ambition.

In 57 BC he demonstrated to the Gauls the extraordinary might of his legions by defeating the tribe of the Belgae. They were widely considered to have been the hardiest and bravest of the Gauls because they lived in the north 'furthest away from the culture and civilization of the Province'.[14] When, in 55 BC,

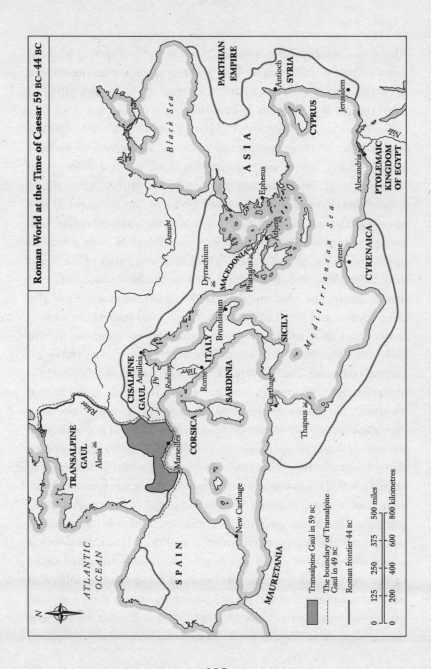

Roman World at the Time of Caesar 59 BC–44 BC

ATLANTIC OCEAN

TRANSALPINE GAUL
Alesia

CISALPINE GAUL
Aquileia

Rhine

Po

Rubicon

SPAIN

New Carthage

Marseilles

CORSICA

SARDINIA

Tiber

Rome

ITALY

Carthage

Thapsus

MAURETANIA

SICILY

Brundisium

Mediterranean Sea

MACEDONIA
Dyrrachium
Pharsalus

Athens

Ephesus

ASIA

Black Sea

PARTHIAN EMPIRE

Antioch
SYRIA

CYPRUS

Jerusalem

Alexandria

Nile

PTOLEMAIC KINGDOM OF EGYPT

CYRENAICA
Cyrene

Danube

N

Transalpine Gaul in 59 BC

The boundary of Transalpine Gaul in 49 BC

Roman frontier 44 BC

| 0 | 125 | 250 | 375 | 500 miles |
| 0 | 200 | 400 | 600 | 800 kilometres |

two Germanic tribes, the Usipetes and the Tencteri, crossed the Rhine and attacked the Romans, Caesar did not simply lead his army in battle, cutting the 400,000-strong enemy to pieces. He used the survivors' retreat into Germany to stage perhaps the most daring action of his command.

Across the 350-metre (1155-feet) width of the Rhine's swelling rapids, Caesar ordered his army engineers to build a bridge. Such a feat of engineering had never before been contemplated, let alone attempted. But as the Romans drove great piles of wood into the river bed to yoke the river, it was almost as though they could control Mother Nature herself. The bridge complete, Caesar then crossed the river with his army and invaded the alien country. The Germanic tribes of the Suevi and Sugambri, who had never seen a bridge before, were so awestruck by the outlandish feat that they retreated into the deep forests and hid. Caesar then burnt and ravaged the nearby lands, and told all those who remained to pass on to the German tribes one very clear message: never again make an enemy of Rome. Then, as quickly as they had come, he and his army disappeared and returned to Gaul, dismantling the bridge en route. The entire exploit had taken a mere twenty-eight days.

A glimpse into what was driving Caesar in Gaul is revealed in his own account of the Gallic Wars. He built a bridge because he considered crossing the river by boat beneath 'his dignity'.[15] *Dignitas* was the pre-eminent quality of a patrician Roman politician, and it was rooted in an historic sense of worth, rank and prestige. The more ancient and aristocratic the Roman family, the greater the dignity accumulated and the higher the point at which that sense of worth was pegged. Caesar's own acute sense of his dignity had been at the heart of his pursuit of office in Rome, had motivated his actions as consul, and was now driving him on to ever greater feats of glory in Gaul. To cap his achievements abroad, in 55 and 54 BC Caesar prepared a fleet, crossed the English Channel and launched an invasion of Britain, a country that many Romans did not believe even existed. On his second attempt, Caesar stayed in Britain for the summer, getting as far as the river Thames and securing tribute from several British tribes. Although no permanent Roman base was established, Caesar had succeeded in making another dramatic statement of his ambition.

The effect of that ambition was to build for Caesar an unprecedented power base both abroad and at home. In Rome the news of his exploits thrilled and delighted the people of Rome: they were the stuff of fairy tales, adventure stories, the kind of fable with which Roman parents would excite and inspire their children. While Cato and his allies were carping on about the deformity and sickness of Caesar's dignity, the people saw that very same thing bringing honour in abundance to the Roman republic. To them, Caesar was putting on the greatest show on earth and the stage was Gaul: ancient, barbaric enemies were being defeated, and not even rivers or oceans could restrain the unfurling arm of Roman power. By the end of 53 BC, Caesar was able to announce that the whole of Gaul was 'pacified'. Accordingly, his glory was not just being restored – it was rocketing.[16]

But Caesar did not rest on the laurels of his foreign exploits to wow the people; he played an active part too. Every winter he set up camp as close to the border of Italy as his province would allow. From there would flow news of extraordinary gifts and benefactions for the Roman people. The centrepiece was Caesar's announcement that in the heart of Rome a glorious new forum was to be built, paid for with the spoils of Gaul.[17] Gifts of a more personal nature also streamed freely into Rome. A rich seam of bribes, as well as letters of recommendation, ensured that Caesar could influence the election of like-minded magistrates prepared to help him and defend his name. Traffic also flowed in the opposite direction. Ambitious young Romans seeking opportunities for wealth and military success thronged in ever-increasing numbers to the one place where the real action was: with Caesar, in Gaul, on campaign. But although Caesar was highly successful in wooing the fast set of Roman politics, Cato and his constitutionalist allies could reassure themselves that at least they had the measure of such opponents. They had been fighting the populist faction in the Forum and the Senate for decades now. What they weren't prepared for, however, and what was new and far more threatening to their interests, was Caesar's power base abroad: the army.

For all the struggle of populist politics, the issue of Rome's citizen-militia fighting long campaigns, only then to discover they had no farms to return to, had never been solved successfully through land reform. Pompey's demobilized veterans may have been settled on plots of land during Caesar's consulship, but they were the exception rather than the rule. Indeed, reforms of the army had only made the problem of rootless soldiers worse: the general Marius may have bolstered the number of army recruits by abolishing any property qualification in 107 BC, but the result of this was to fill the legions with men who had no stake at all in the republic. Their only hope for wealth was an army salary and the chance of winning booty on campaign. In Gaul, Caesar was able to provide both in spades. As a result, a new and very dangerous codependent relationship developed between the general and his men. The soldiers were no longer loyal to the republic and its ancient ideology of freedom. Their only loyalty was to the benefactor who was now responsible for their interests: the general. The historian Sallust put it succinctly:

When anyone seeks power his greatest help is the man in direst poverty, because he is restrained by no attachment to his property, having none, and considers anything honourable for which he receives pay.[18]

The same, of course, was even truer of the Germans and Gauls whom Caesar was levying into his army. These new recruits had never set foot in a Roman province, let alone Rome itself. As the years passed, Caesar's legions grew from the three authorized by his proconsulship to a staggering ten. This put into his hand a weapon more dangerous than any the republic had yet seen: the fierce might of no fewer than 50,000 battle-hardened soldiers, each and every one devoted to his name. It was no wonder, then, that Cato and his allies among the nobles tried to put an end to his power. However, on their first attempt, Caesar, even from his distant outpost of Gaul, knew how to swat it away.

In 56 BC a senator by the name of Lucius Domitius Ahenobarbus announced that he was preparing to stand for the consulship with a view to depriving Caesar of his command in Gaul. With his finger on the pulse of Roman politics, Caesar quickly neutralized this threat by renewing his alliance with Pompey. At a meeting in Lucca in northern Italy, he encouraged him and their ally Crassus to stand in elections and beat Ahenobarbus to the consulship. They would then be in a position to help Caesar: through laws proposed by them in the popular assembly, they could make sure that Caesar would be granted an extension of his command for another five years. In return, Pompey and Crassus would be able to consolidate their power and independence from the Senate with lucrative proconsular commands abroad. They would all get what they wanted.

In Rome Cato spotted the rearguard action of Caesar and Pompey a mile off. He now urged Ahenobarbus not to give in, but to contest the election tooth and nail: 'We are not fighting,' said Cato, 'merely for office, but for liberty against our oppressors!'[19] On the day of voting, Pompey's armed gangs of veterans once again beat up Ahenobarbus and Cato, barred them from entering the Campus Martius and routed their supporters. Pompey and Crassus were duly elected consuls for 55 BC, and Caesar was safe once more. Caesar's friendship and alliance with Pompey had saved the day. However, the next time Cato and his allies launched a strike against Caesar, the general would not be so lucky.

Three years later 52 BC saw a turning point in the relationship between Caesar and Pompey. In this year the fatal flaw in Pompey's character was revealed. The decline in their alliance had begun two years earlier. Pompey's wife and Caesar's daughter, Julia, had died in childbirth, the baby surviving the mother for only a few days. In their grief, both men knew that the one key bond that set their alliance beyond politics was now broken. While Caesar grieved over the news in Gaul, in Rome the depth of what was considered to be Pompey the Great's unbecoming love for Julia was so widely known that even his conservative enemies in the Senate briefly took pity on him.[20]

However, it would take a more cataclysmic event before the conservatives actively wooed the man whom they had long feared and suspected. That event began with the murder of Publius Clodius Pulcher, an ally of Caesar's. As a populist tribune of the people, Clodius had successfully established himself as the chief agitator and benefactor of the urban plebs in Rome. In this bid for power his timing had been perfect: in the mid-50s BC the senators, swamped in a mire of allegations of bribery and corruption, were increasingly discredited. Clodius's sparkling, controversial career suggested that perhaps the people did not want freedom after all, but simply fair, generous masters.[21] When he was stabbed on a street in a brawl with a rival gang, his death triggered widespread fury. His devout supporters – a motley crew of shopkeepers, street urchins, traders, and the needy and poor of the city's slums – united in grief on the streets of Rome in their thousands. They descended on the Forum and proceeded to make a funeral pyre for their champion. The place? The Senate House. The fuel? The wooden benches of the senators. No one could stop them. As the Senate House burnt to the ground, a riot quickly swept across the city.

In the late republic there was no police force. To quell the emergency gripping Rome and restore order, the alarmed senators turned for help to the only man who was able to summon the necessary authority and manpower. That man also happened to be the person whom the conservative majority so despised and mistrusted: Pompey the Great. With the Senate House now a desolate, charred carcass, the nobles swallowed their pride and met in a building attached to a spanking new marble theatre Pompey had built. It was a fitting setting for the meeting. Here the senator Bibulus proposed that the republic's ablest citizen, Pompey the Great, be granted a new appointment: sole consulship, with exceptional powers to end the anarchy consuming the city. In an even more striking volte-face, Cato, biting his tongue, now stood up and urged his colleagues to agree to the proposal. Grudgingly, he – leader of the constitutionalists – was extending an olive branch to his old enemy.[22]

Such an invitation secretly delighted Pompey. Although he had been the people's hero, Rome's greatest general, and the power broker behind Caesar's rise, this had never been quite enough. The reality was that Pompey had always wanted acceptance from the senatorial establishment too. But he wanted the senators to accommodate him on one condition: that they recognized his extraordinary ability, his pre-eminence in the republic, 'his special position'. To acknowledge that, however, went against every instinct, every fibre in every noble senator. It was contrary to their closely held belief in equality among the Roman élite, their belief that power was circumscribed by annual elections. Their ancestors had founded the republic when they expelled the kings from Rome. Why on earth should they welcome one now? Pompey had always been shut out in the cold. Now, at last, the door was fractionally ajar. What would the great general do?

While Pompey appeared modest and unassuming, one clever con- temporary had already got his measure: 'He is apt to say one thing and think another, but is usually not clever enough to keep his real aims from showing.'[23] Pompey accepted his command, and his troops duly marched into Rome. Ten years since his extraordinary, triumphant return from the east, the star of Pompey the Great was rising once more. Would it now eclipse even that of his old ally? The answer would not be long in coming.

ALESIA

While Caesar waited in his winter base near the border of Italy, anxious to see what Pompey would do, in the rest of Gaul the news of the anarchy in Rome spread like wildfire. The leaders of the Gallic tribes now met in a secret forest location. Embellishing and exaggerating the rumours of a Rome in free fall, they spied an opportunity: to take full advantage of Caesar's absence from his legions' winter camps in the north of the country and revolt against their Roman oppressors just when they were at their weakest.[24] There was no time to delay. The Carnutes swore an oath to take the initiative, and they promptly honoured it. They descended on the settlement of Cenabum and slaughtered its Roman citizens. As soon as other tribes heard the news, they rallied in support. Of all the tribes in Gaul, however, the Arverni had the distinction of being mustered by a young noble who would become the leader of the united rebellion. His name was Vercingetorix.

Sending out embassies, Vercingetorix quickly made alliances with the Senones, Parisii, Cadurci, Turoni, Aulerci, Lemovices, Andes and all the Gallic people along the Atlantic coast. Money was raised and armies of Gallic warriors were assembled. Vercingetorix then quickly showed that he had the discipline and determination to match his skills of organization. To bring waverers into line he resorted to cutting off ears, gouging out eyes and even death by burning. Caesar observed respectfully, 'In his command he combined extreme conscientiousness with extreme severity.' [25] In short, Vercingetorix was showing the virtues that Caesar himself most admired – those of a Roman. Vercingetorix was appointed commander of the alliance of Gallic tribes, and within a matter of weeks, most of the tribes of central and northern Gaul had joined the rebellion.

Caesar responded with lightning speed. Cut off from his legions in the north, he rode south through enemy territory and secured his province from immediate attack, before returning north to reunite with his two legions at their winter quarters. His achievement in stabilizing the situation was all the more extraordinary because it was the depths of winter and central Gaul was sunk beneath 2 metres (6 feet) of snow.[26] Rivers were frozen, forests had become impenetrable snowscapes and, where the biting temperatures eased, the rush of flood water from the hills made lakes of the marshy plains.[27] Despite these disadvantages, once Caesar had successfully assembled his entire army, he recognized that the united rebellion in fact presented him with a unique opportunity: to crush the resistance and pacify Gaul once and for all.

With this in mind, Caesar inflicted setback after setback on Vercingetorix's allies. In response, Vercingetorix changed tactics. He decided not to defeat Caesar in battle, but to starve the Romans out of his land by destroying the food supplies of towns close to them. The decisive encounter in the battle of wills between the two men eventually took place in the summer of 52 BC, after Vercingetorix, defeated in open battle, withdrew his army to the town of Alesia.

Alesia was built on an elevated plateau, but despite its vast natural defences Caesar did not hesitate to put the town under siege by building a huge impregnable wall around it. A staggering 18 kilometres (11 miles) in circumference, the wall featured twenty-three forts and eight camps along its length. In addition, the eastern side featured three trenches, each approximately 6 metres (20 feet) wide and deep. Caesar ordered the innermost trench to be flooded. To that end the two rivers that flowed on either side of the town were diverted. Although, after six years on campaign, the tasks of putting up earthworks, walls and watchtowers were routine to Caesar's well-drilled soldiers, the sheer scale and ambition of the siege remain awe-inspiring to this day. But Caesar was not finished yet. When he learnt from Gallic deserters that Vercingetorix was expecting reinforcements, he simply ordered a second wall to be built – facing outwards to protect the besieging Romans from attack in the rear and running parallel to the inner wall. This outer wall was no less than 22 kilometres (14 miles) in circuit.

Inside the city walls, Vercingetorix decided to wait for reinforcements to arrive before launching his attack. However, he knew the clock was ticking. In Alesia the Gauls had enough food for just thirty days.[28] As the weeks passed, the rations were shared out ever more sparingly. When they were nearly finished and the Gallic reinforcements were still nowhere to be seen, a meeting was convened at which some leaders proposed a horrific solution: to survive by eating the flesh of those who were too old to fight in the campaign. Vercingetorix rejected the plan. But the pressure was now on him to come up with a way out. So he did. The outcome of this battle would decide the fate of Gaul for ever, he said. Surrender would mean just one thing: the end of Gallic liberty. To win the battle ahead it was essential to do whatever was in their power to preserve the remaining rations for those who were able to fight. His solution was to hand over all the women, children and the elderly to the Romans. He knew Caesar would then be forced to take the prisoners in, feed them, and thus further deprive the Roman army.

But Vercingetorix had not banked on how ruthless and single-minded Caesar could be. As thousands of Gauls were forced out of the city gates and begged the Romans to take them in, Caesar and Vercingetorix went eyeball to eyeball. Neither man blinked, and as a result, over the coming days, every single one of those women, children and the elderly died from starvation and cold, trapped between the walls of the city they had left behind and the Roman siege wall. One ancient author said of Caesar's conquest of Gaul that one million Gauls were killed and another million enslaved.[29] Today these figures are considered by most scholars to be exaggerated. Nonetheless, in them is the suggestion of the awesome, terrifying coldness of Caesar's decision at Alesia, the extremes to which he was prepared to go in the name of his dignity and that of the Roman people.

Eventually, the Gallic reinforcements arrived and assembled on the heights looking down on the plain below. They numbered more than 200,000 infantry and 8000 cavalry. So it was that one hot day in the summer of 52 BC the full, terrible onslaught of two Gallic armies descended headlong to trap the Romans, the allies attacking the outer wall, while Vercingetorix's armies broke out of the city and assaulted the inner fortifications. The yells and screams of the Gallic allies were matched and echoed by those rising up from inside Alesia. The Romans spread out along their walls. They held out determinedly for the first days of fighting. However, the Roman cavalry did not fare so well, and were saved only when an auxiliary German cavalry routed the Gauls. When night fell, the Gauls once again scampered down the hill under cover of darkness and filled in the trenches with earth; when day broke they attempted once more to breach the Roman wall and unite with their allies. This time, they were repulsed by volleys of sling bullets, heavy-duty catapults and stakes hidden in the ground. On the third day, however, spies alerted the Gauls to a point of weakness at the Roman camp stationed halfway up a hill.

Immediately, the reinforcements of Gallic cavalry massed at the top of the hill and attacked from above, while once again Vercingetorix's men attacked the wall from below. The Romans, terrified by the noise on either side, were running out of strength, numbers and weapons. This was the critical moment of the battle, and both sides fought with utter ferocity. Caesar rode along the ramparts to rally his men in person, shouting at them and explaining how 'all the fruits of their labour depended upon that day, that hour'.[30] Finally, he deployed his reserves of cavalry to attack the Gauls in the rear, and, riding at their head, he now threw himself into the frenetic fighting.

As the scarlet colour of his cloak heralded his arrival, a booming shout went up from the Roman defences. The tables had turned, and it was now the allied Gauls who were trapped on both sides by the Romans. When they saw the Roman cavalry arrive, they turned tail and fled. Under the eyes of Vercingetorix's army still inside Alesia, the huge allied army of Gauls was supremely routed, melting away 'like a ghost or a dream'.[31] Caesar's description of the battle's conclusion was typically terse: 'Massive slaughter followed'.[32] Only utter exhaustion prevented the Roman soldiers from giving chase and killing more.

Completely outnumbered, Caesar had relied on daring, tactical genius, the efficiency of his unprecedented siege operations, and the bravery of his men to pull off one of the greatest victories in all Roman history. Although there were pockets of resistance to mop up, Gaul was now Roman – another province of a vast empire. In due course it would provide Rome with an annual tribute of 40 million sesterces.[33]

The conquest of Gaul also brought its proconsul astounding personal riches, as well as unparalleled glory in the eyes of the Roman people and a quasi-private fighting force of ten Roman legions prepared to do whatever he asked of them. Cato knew it, his allies in the Senate knew it, and even Pompey knew it. The knowledge only brought with it unease. For the question that was now uppermost in Caesar's mind was how to do what no other Roman – not even Pompey the Great – had yet achieved: translate his power into power in Rome.

The day after the massacre of the Gauls at Alesia, seventy-four of the Gallic standards were brought to Caesar. Vercingetorix himself rode out of the city gates resplendent in his Gallic armour of bronze helmet embossed with animal figures, his iron cuirass and gold-plated belt. Halting before Caesar, he stripped himself, handed over his javelin and long broadsword and lay prone on the ground in abject surrender.[34] Caesar's great adversary had been vanquished. And yet, as he looked on, Caesar knew that the real showdown was only just about to begin.

RUBICON

When Caesar's dispatches from Gaul brought the news of his victory to Rome, the Senate decreed an unprecedented twenty days of public celebration. Caesar, too, contributed to the party: he paid for gladiatorial games, as well as a lavish public banquet in memory of his daughter. To give the impression that the feast was his very own special gift to the Roman people, he had some of the food prepared in his house. Indeed, he let slip no opportunity for generosity. Corn was distributed 'without limit or measure' to the plebs, and low-interest loans were given to those in need of money. Senators and knights (the rank below senator) who were in debt, as well as slaves and freedmen accused of crimes, all took advantage of Caesar's largesse.[35]

Later, there would be treats of a more cerebral kind. Caesar's eight volumes of *Commentaries on the Gallic War* were published in 50 BC. These books glorified his dazzling exploits, even eclipsing the collective memory of Pompey's conquests in the east. Easily copied and distributed, they would be a public relations coup like no other. They also showed that Caesar was not just a master general, but a master of literary technique. Written in crystal clear, quotable language accessible to many, Caesar's compositions reminded everyone who read them of the sheer sophistication of his mind. Indeed, he even wrote a scholarly essay on Latin grammar. But the *Commentaries on the Gallic War* were also a timely reminder of the central political principle for which Caesar stood: 'All men by nature desire liberty and hate the condition of slavery.'[36] It was with the liberty of the people in mind – at least the liberty of the Roman people – that Caesar made his first preparations for a return to Rome and to his enemies in the Senate.

The battle lines of the old conflict between Caesar and Cato's conservative allies were now reconfigured in one burning question: when would Caesar give up his command? Caesar knew that as soon as he became a private citizen, Cato would pounce and prosecute him for his alleged crimes as consul in Rome and proconsul in Gaul. Yet the idea that he, Caesar, the man who had sweated blood to win Gaul for the glory and benefit of the republic, might be treated like a petty criminal was absolutely out of the question. Who was the whinging Cato to tell Caesar what to do? Such a prospect was completely beneath Caesar's dignity.

There was only one way out of Cato's trap: to stand again for the consulship. It was not customary to hold the consulship more than once within a ten-year period. It clashed with the principle of republican power-sharing. So, with his sights set on standing for office for 49 BC, Caesar marshalled all his allies in Rome to bypass the conservatives in the Senate and propose a special bill direct to the people. This proposed law would extend his command in Gaul until 49 BC, then allow him to stand for office without having even set foot in the city. Although his enemies in the Senate hissed, such was Caesar's popularity after Gaul that all ten tribunes of the people supported the bill and it was passed in 52 BC. But the law was only the beginning of the debate.

As the months passed, Caesar's command came under attack after attack. Every time a senator tried to revoke the bill and deprive him of his command, a carefully deployed tribune would veto. 'You know the routine,' wrote one contemporary observer. 'There will be a decision about Gaul. Somebody will come along with a veto. Then somebody else will stand up ... So we shall have a long, elaborate charade.'[37] As if by centrifugal force, the members of the Roman élite found themselves forced to take a stand on one side or another. A clique of Caesareans, young, ambitious and growing in numbers, believed that Caesar was the stronger, that reform of the republic and its corrupt, discredited senators was paramount and, above all, that greater political and financial rewards lay with him. Cato, meanwhile, rallied the traditional senators under the banner of defending the constitution of the republic. They came in their droves. Caesar's unprecedented demands made it easy for Cato to present him as the would-be tyrant, as the man bent on destroying the republic, the man whose grotesque greed and ambition were driving him to seize power. But on the question of which side to take, there was one man who had yet to declare his hand.

Since his appointment to the sole consulship, Pompey's behaviour towards his old ally had been highly ambivalent. In the last months of his office in 52 BC he had used his influence to support the bill of ten tribunes granting Caesar the special privilege of standing for the consulship in absentia. However, the warm overtures of the aristocratic constitutionalists, and their appointment of him to stand for the sole consulship, had persuaded him that the path to winning both power and respect did not lie exclusively with Caesar and his maverick ways. So when, after the death of Julia, Caesar offered Pompey his great-niece Octavia in marriage, Pompey turned him down flat.

The woman he eventually chose was beautiful, graceful and cultivated in literature, music, geometry and philosophy. The union caused quite a scandal because his new wife was half Pompey's age. But in Cornelia, Pompey had found not just a woman to love, but also a place in high society, for the blood running in her veins could not have been bluer. She was the daughter of Quintus Caecilius Metellus Scipio, a scion of one of the great patrician families in Rome, a family that could boast among its forebears Publius Scipio, the slayer of Hannibal; a family now at the very heart of the senatorial establishment.

So while he was supposed to have been restoring order to the streets of Rome, Pompey had donned wedding garlands and married Cornelia. As if to spell out just how cosily he was now bedded down with the constitutionalists, in August 52 BC, once peace had returned to the streets of Rome, Pompey willingly gave up his sole consulship before his term of office had expired and invited his new father-in-law Metellus Scipio to join him as his consular colleague.[38] The former gangster was now behaving like a pillar of republican respectability. Cato knew he had Pompey just where he wanted him. Now he went for the kill.

In a bid to drive an unmistakable wedge between Pompey and Caesar, an intense pressure offensive began. While the consuls of 51 BC attacked Caesar publicly in the Senate for holding on to his command, Cato worked on Pompey privately, playing to the general's insecurity. Caesar was now a far more powerful man than Pompey, went his line of reasoning. Was Pompey the Great just going to sit back and watch his old ally return to Rome at the head of an army and tell everyone what to do? What right did Caesar have to dictate to us? No man's dignity was greater than the republic. Cato's sniping soon showed signs of paying off. In September 51 BC Pompey made an announcement. Caesar, he said, should give up his command in the spring of the following year and allow for a successor to be appointed. Pompey was pressed on the matter: what if one of Caesar's tribunes vetoed the proposal? '... and supposing my son chooses to take his stick to me?'[39] With these words, Pompey abandoned the comfort of the fence and severed all ties with Caesar.

Although the conservative politicians had now secured their strongman, it took a massive outpouring of love and support from the people to make Pompey feel like one. When he recovered from a serious illness while in Naples, Roman citizens up and down Italy rejoiced, in bouts of sacrificing and feasting. As he made his way back to Rome, Pompey was mobbed by people wearing garlands, carrying torches and pelting him with flowers. The effect of this enormous public celebration proved intoxicating, even blinding: 'Pompey began to feel a kind of over-confidence in himself, which went far beyond considerations based on facts.'[40]

Pompey's lack of a grasp on reality was now made worse. The Senate requested that both he and Caesar give up one legion from their commands to quell unrest on Rome's eastern frontier in Parthia. As Caesar had borrowed an extra legion from the republic's army, both legions were to come from Caesar's army. The Senate's request allowed him the opportunity to pose as a friend of peace, as the man who wanted to bring about a resolution to the crisis. With that in mind, Caesar willingly handed over both legions. When they arrived in Italy, one of their officers by the name of Appius belittled Caesar's army and his achievements in Gaul. Pompey did not need any troops other than these two legions, he said. They were sufficient to handle the threat posed by Caesar. Pompey's confidence was boosted even higher. He had easily built Caesar up, the great general thought to himself; now he could just as easily pull him down. When, later on, a senator, alarmed at Pompey's lack of preparation, asked him with what legions he would defend the republic should Caesar march on Rome, Pompey serenely replied that there was nothing at all to worry about. 'I have only to stamp my foot upon the ground,' he said, 'and there will rise up armies of infantry and armies of cavalry.' [41]

In mid-50 BC a dissolute ally of Caesar by the name of Marcus Caelius Rufus declared that the love affair between Pompey and Caesar was over.[42] From the slave to the tax collector, from the beggar to the senator, there were now only two words on the lips of every Roman: civil war. And yet as both sides stepped ever closer to outright confrontation in the latter half of the year, the majority of the Senate wanted to pull back from the precipice. In November the senators voted by 370 to 22 for peace.[43] But that meant only one thing: giving in to Caesar's wishes. To Cato that was simply unconscionable.

The weakness of the Senate now served to stiffen the resolve of Cato and his closest allies, provoking even the arch-constitutionalists to actions with no legal authority. After the vote the consul of 50 BC Gaius Claudius Marcellus cried, 'Have your way. Be slaves to Caesar!' and stormed out of the Senate. He and his fellow consul then went to Pompey's house on the outskirts of the city and, in a highly staged piece of melodrama, put a sword in his hand. With it they commanded him to take the field against Caesar in defence of the republic, and granted him both the legions stationed in Italy and the right to levy more. Pompey did his best to avoid appearing the aggressor, replying solemnly, 'If there is no other way.' In reality, though, he too now wanted war.[44]

On the first day of the new year 49 BC Caesar again presented himself as the advocate of peace, believing he had the Senate cowed. The newly elected tribune Mark Antony, Caesar's mouth-piece in Rome, read out a letter from the proconsul: for his many successes in Gaul, the Roman people had granted him the legal right to stand for office in absentia. While he expected that privilege to stand, he was prepared to lay down his arms on the one condition that Pompey did too.

In response, one of the new consuls, Lucius Cornelius Lentulus launched a tirade. Now was not the time to be weak, he said. If the senators caved in, the consuls would have no option but to deploy Pompey and his army anyway. He was the source of the republic's safety and if they did not act now, they could not rely on Pompey's help later. The majority were so stung by these threats that when Pompey's father-in-law Metellus Scipio stood up and proposed that a date should be fixed by which Caesar must lay down his arms or else be declared an enemy of the state, the majority of the Senate agreed with him. When the motion was taken to the people's assembly, Mark Antony vetoed it, so the stalemate continued.[45]

Caesar tried again. If the Senate would not lay down arms, then nor would he simply give up his office and hand himself over to them for prosecution. He was, however, prepared to make concessions. He proposed giving up both provinces of Gaul and the ten legions stationed there so long as he could retain the province of Illyricum and its one legion. Once again, this proposal collided with the steamroller of Cato and his faction. On no account was Caesar to dictate conditions to the Senate, they cried. With this, the political process came to a dead end and war was now inevitable. The consuls passed an 'ultimate decree' of the Senate. Steps must now be taken, it said, to ensure that the republic came to no harm. Bellowing threats and abuse, the consul Lentulus then promptly threw Mark Antony and his followers out of the Senate House.[46]

The lives of Caesar's allies in Rome were now in danger. Mark Antony, Caelius and the former tribune Gaius Scribonius Curio were given six days to leave the city or be killed. They disguised themselves as slaves and made their escape stowed on the back of wagons. Such an unseemly exit was a fitting conclusion to the stand-off, for it gave Caesar one final proof of the Senate's injustice, one last piece of propaganda. The contemptuous, corrupt and arrogant senators had yet again insulted the liberty of the Roman people by threatening the tribunes and violating the sanctity of their persons. To illustrate the point Caesar paraded his humiliated friends before his army, clad just as they were in the clothes of slaves.[47]

The action now moved south. The Rubicon is a small river that once marked the boundary between Gaul and Italy. It was against the law for Roman commanders to bring troops out of their province and into Italy, so the decision to cross the river under arms amounted to an irrevocable declaration of war. But on 10 January 49 BC it was to the Rubicon that Caesar, upon hearing the news from Rome, now sent ahead a detachment of his boldest soldiers. This decision was typical of the man. He was against collecting the full weight of his ten legions from the other side of the Alps because 'better results could be obtained by surprise, daring and taking the quickest advantage of the moment'.[48] On the afternoon before he set off from his camp to join them, Caesar watched some gladiators exercise. He then took a bath, got dressed in the toga of his rank and sat down to make polite conversation with his friends over dinner. It was as though he had no fear. When it became dark he quietly took leave of his guests and slipped away.

Today no one knows where the Rubicon lies or whether it

even still exists. To add to the mystery, the river is not even mentioned by Caesar in his account of the civil war. Nonetheless, all other Greek and Roman historians have focused their accounts on the moment before he crossed the Rubicon. Their attention to this reflects the ancient world's enduring fascination with trying to work out what was going through Caesar's mind at this critical instance. Some say he hesitated and nearly lost his nerve, paralysed at the thought of going to war with his fellow Romans.[49] Others say that a spirit appeared, stole a trumpet from one of his soldiers and, letting out a loud blast, crossed to the other side; Caesar took it as a sign and did the same.[50] All agree, however, that Caesar said, 'The die is cast,' and with those words, he crossed the river.

The republic, with its ancient system of free elections, democracy and concord between the classes of Roman society, was in the hands of Pompey and Caesar. Although they did not yet know it, the very thing that both sides were fighting for was to become the very thing they would destroy. The fight for liberty would reverberate across the entire Roman world.

THE FIGHT FOR LIBERTY

The march of Caesar's thirteenth legion through Italy was as swift and clinical as a bolt of lightning. But just as effective was Caesar's clever campaign of spin. Its slogan was 'Clemency'. Within a day, he had reached Ariminum (now called Rimini); the town voluntarily opened its gate and came over to Caesar without so much as the unsheathing of a sword. Other towns, including Auximum, Asculum, Picenum and Corfinium, followed suit, even though they had troops stationed there who had been levied in Pompey's name. The form these engagements took was the same. The Pompeian officers attempted a meagre resistance; once captured, they were immediately discharged, free to decide which side they were on; the majority of their soldiers deserted to Caesar's army and the towns were thanked. The general himself described his spin offensive in a letter of the time: 'I have of my own accord decided to show all possible clemency and to reconcile myself to Pompey... Let this be a new style of conquest, to make mercy and generosity our shield.'[51] That style was proving very effective.

In Rome, Caesar's enemies were thrown into a fit of panic. They had hoped that the respectable classes in towns throughout Italy would rise up as one in defence of the republic against the invader. But as Caesar waged his blitzkrieg without significant opposition, they quickly realized that they had hopelessly misread the majority view. The senator Cicero was astonished by the complete reversal of advantage between Pompey and Caesar:

> [Do] you see what sort of man this is into whose hands the state has fallen, how clever, alert, well-prepared? I truly believe that if he takes no lives and touches no man's property, those who dreaded him most will become his warmest admirers. Both town and country people talk to me a great deal. They really think of nothing except their fields and their bits of farms and investments. And look how the tables are turned! They fear the man they used to trust and love the man they used to dread.[52]

Militarily too, the constitutionalists were utterly wrong-footed. Pompey did not expect Caesar to attack so swiftly, believing that their forces would not meet until the spring.[53] Blinded by arrogance, Caesar's opponents had failed to complete the levy of the troops in Italy, and there was now no time to wait for Pompey's legions in Spain to reach Rome. The two legions that Pompey did have outside the city walls were simply no match for Caesar's eleven.

A plague of quarrelling and rabid recrimination broke out in the senatorial faction, infecting even the mind of their champion. Indeed it paralysed him. Pompey's old friendship with their common enemy was to blame for arming Caesar in the first place, cried one senator. And where were those armies that he had so proudly boasted would come to him at the stamp of his foot, whinged another. Was Pompey stamping now?[54] The anarchy in the senatorial ranks was echoed on the streets of Rome in one poetic account. All magistrates threw off their robes of office, ordinary people moved through the streets like ghosts heavy with sorrow and fear, and the temples were thronged with women in mourning who threw themselves on the floor and tore at their hair.[55] The city was convulsed with the fear of Roman fighting Roman, of Caesar's unstoppable, relentless advance on Rome.

Finally, Pompey emerged with a plan, painful and shocking though it was to the ears of the senators. To defend the republic, he said, it was necessary to abandon Rome, to evacuate their legions and set sail for the east, where he could rely on his allies in Greece to complete the levy of an army. Only with the support of the friends of the Roman people would he relish the prospect of facing Caesar, not before. Anyone who stayed behind, Pompey added, would be considered a traitor and a partisan of Caesar.[56]

The strategy sank the senators deeper into despair. Although Pompey was proposing a tactical retreat, they could not escape the feeling that they were taking flight before a tyrant. Caesar had forced this miserable plan upon them. Adding to their humiliation and disillusionment, they knew that they would have to abandon every physical manifestation of their cherished republic – their beloved temples, the homes of the city's gods, and, above all their ancestral property. What was the republic if not the city of Rome itself, they protested to Pompey. Cato went about as if in mourning, lamenting and bewailing the senators' losses and the fate of Rome. Cicero, yet to decide whether to stay or go, complained of the indignity of having to walk around 'like a beggar'. Any peace terms would have been better than abandoning the mother city to Caesar and his 'underworld' of disgraced and bankrupt outcasts, he wrote.[57] Nonetheless, they all realized that, with their backs against the wall, they had no choice but to leave.

So, after a night of hurriedly packing up their trunks and bags, laying their hands on whatever property they could 'as if they were robbing their neighbours', and barricading their houses, the majority of the senators, their slaves, friends and dependants kissed the ground, invoked the gods and fled from Rome. There was not even time for the consuls to make the usual sacrifices. The city's poor were left behind, many in tears, morose and resigned to being taken captive.[58] It left the impression that perhaps Caesar was indeed right: the rich did not care for the Roman people, but just for themselves.

But few took any notice of the reproaches of the people. For the Pompeians now formed a massive column of evacuees, making their way along the straight roads that cut through the Italian countryside. Their destination was Brundisium (modern-day Brindisi); their goal, to seize the Roman fleet based there and get to safety as quickly as possible. The port of Brundisium was situated on the heel of Italy, at the point where the crossing to Greece was at its shortest. It became the target of Caesar too. When he received news of Pompey's strategy, he knew that all he had to do was cut his enemy off at the port to bring about an early, bloodless end to the war. The race was on.

By the time Caesar arrived at Brundisium in the company of six legions, Pompey had successfully requisitioned ships and evacuated half his army. The other half now remained with their general. The challenge they faced was daunting: to defend

themselves against Caesar's legions until the ships returned
from ferrying the first dispatch of soldiers. Caesar made the first
move. With typical ambition and clarity of purpose, he immediately blockaded the harbour of Brundisium across the
narrowest part of its mouth by building a causeway made of
rafts. On top of these his army piled earthworks. Pompey immediately countered by commandeering whatever ships he could
and building on to their decks three-storey-high siege towers.
From this great height his harassing legionaries attacked
and bombarded the barricade with arrows, firebrands and
ballistic missiles.[59]

While the battle for the port raged, Caesar pressed home a
slender advantage and sent in one of his officers, Caninius
Rebilus, to negotiate for peace. But if Caesar expected Pompey
to roll over, he was to be quickly disappointed. The retired
general, who was seeing action for the first time in over ten
years, chose to gamble. Believing that he could pull off an
extraordinary evacuation, Pompey fobbed Rebilus off. He gave
the reply that without the consuls present, he could never reach
a settlement with his enemy. Caesar saw through this pathetic
excuse. His verdict on it was unsentimental: 'Caesar finally
determined to abandon these repeated vain efforts at peace and
to wage war in earnest.'[60]

To Pompey's delight, the ships returning from Greece were
now spotted on the horizon. Before long they had smashed
their way back into the harbour. While Caesar organized his
legionaries for a frontal assault on the city, Pompey made every
preparation to restrain such an attack and protect the evacuation. The gates of the town were barricaded, trenches
embedded with vicious spikes were dug in the roads, and the
walls of the town were lined with slingers and archers. Under
cover of darkness, Pompey's soldiers boarded their ships and
looked set to escape. The people of Brundisium, angry at their

harsh treatment by Pompey, had other plans. They signalled to Caesar's men from their rooftops that Pompey was preparing to cast off. Then, helping them up the scaling ladders and over the defences, the townspeople told them where the traps were laid and pointed out the detour to the harbour. Charging headlong through the town, Caesar's legionaries finally managed to reach some skiffs and small vessels just in time to scupper two of Pompey's ships snagged on Caesar's causeway. However, as daylight returned, the rest were nowhere to be seen.[61]

As the bows of his ships beat out spuming foam from the blue of the Adriatic Sea, Pompey knew he had snatched an extraordinary escape from the jaws of disaster. He was now safely on his way to visit friends and allies, the many wealthy kings, dynasts and potentates of Greece and Asia, who would provide him with further levies of soldiers with which to fight Caesar. It now perhaps came as a gentle surprise to Pompey that the plan to abandon Rome was actually working. But Caesar too could reflect on his own success to date. After all, within sixty days and without shedding any blood, he had become master of all Italy. And were it not for his lack of ships, he would without hesitation chase after and attack Pompey and his men before they had time to strengthen their forces abroad. But, on further reflection, he realized that now was not the time to go pursuing Pompey. This would only leave both Gaul and Italy exposed to Pompey's four legions still in Spain.[62] Indeed, Caesar stood to lose everything he had won for his Roman republic unless he dealt with this threat immediately. Before he collected all his legions together, however, and marched north to defeat the Pompeian army in Spain, he had a little stop to make en route.

When Caesar rode into Rome at the end of March 49 BC, he was greeted not by cheering, jubilant crowds celebrating their hero's return, but the sullen faces of a Roman people struck dumb by terror. In this civil war, they wondered, would

LEFT: A bronze bust from the third century BC, often identified as that of Lucius Junius Brutus, the man responsible for the first revolution in Roman history. When, in *c.* 509 BC, Brutus led the *coup d'état* against Tarquinius the Proud, his faction of noblemen expelled Rome's last king and founded the new Roman republic.

RIGHT: The obligation felt by a Roman aristocrat to emulate the achievements of his dead and glorious ancestors was a key motivation of the empire-building Roman élite. In this sculpture from the first century BC, a nobleman, formally dressed in a toga, carries the weighty likenesses of (probably) his forefathers.

ABOVE: Archaeological remains from the third century BC of streets, houses and shops in Carthage. This was the North African capital of Rome's great rival for power in the Mediterranean. The methodical sack of the city in 146 BC was the pivotal moment in Rome's empire-building. In destroying the empire of the Carthaginians, the Romans created their own.

LEFT: Land redistribution (and the question of who should profit from Rome's empire) lay at the heart of Tiberius Gracchus's reforms in the 130s BC. This aerial photograph of Imola in northern Italy shows how the second-century division of land is preserved today in the pattern of fields.

ABOVE: *Cornelia, Mother of the Gracchi* by Jean-François-Pierre Peyron (1781). The high-born mother of Tiberius Gracchus was famous for rejecting tokens of wealth, the fruits of Rome's growing empire. Here she tells a guest that her only 'jewels' are her sons. For her virtuous constancy in rearing them for public life, Cornelia became the first Roman woman to be honoured with a bronze statue.

BELOW: In the last 150 years of the republic, the political front line of the Roman Forum became a very real battleground. In an age before many of the marble ruins shown here were erected, the Forum bore witness to the struggles surrounding the reforms of the Gracchus brothers, the violent menace of Caesar and Pompey's gangs, and the macabre display of the senator Cicero's hands and tongue.

ABOVE: The contrasting sculptures of the two 'mighty generals' and political allies Pompey the Great (left) and Julius Caesar (right). Although it has a comic look, the portrait of Pompey imitates the distinctive hairstyle of Alexander the Great. The bust of Caesar evokes the cold, shrewd character of the man who would defeat Pompey in civil war and bring about both the destruction of the republic and the dawn of the age of the 'Caesars'.

BELOW: *Vercingetorix Throws down His Arms at the Feet of Julius Caesar* by Lionel Royer (1899). Caesar's eight-year conquest of Gaul was secured when he defeated the allied army of Vercingetorix, the leader of the Gallic rebellion, in 52 BC. The glory he won and the devotion of his army made Caesar the most powerful man in the republic.

ABOVE: *The Death of Julius Caesar* by Vincenzo Camuccini (1798). Caesar fell at the foot of a statue of Pompey and in a building paid for by his old rival. Although he was murdered by self-styled 'liberators' who feared the domination of the state by a 'king', the tide towards rule by one man could not be stopped.

LEFT AND ABOVE: Dating from the early first century AD, these contrasting statues of Augustus were seminal in establishing the cult and ideology of the emperor. Above (from Prima Porta, near Rome) Augustus is portrayed as a semi-divine commander-in-chief of the army; on the left (from Via Labicana, in Rome) he is the humble embodiment of religious virtue and pious, traditional, toga-clad Roman-ness.

ABOVE: A first-century AD portrait from Pompeii of a baker with a scroll and a woman with a pen and writing tablets. It is interesting that that this relatively humble couple should portray themselves with the symbols of literacy. Whether they would have enjoyed the classical Latin poets Virgil, Horace, Propertius, Tibullus and Ovid, however, is simply not known.

RIGHT: An unusual gold coin from AD 54. The seventeen-year-old emperor Nero is shown not alone but with his mother, Agrippina. Her names and titles also surround the portraits. This is the first and last time that the mother of a Roman emperor was given such an honour and it reflects her extraordinary influence in this period.

RIGHT: A first-century BC fresco of a garden from Augustus's country villa at Prima Porta, near Rome. This sophisticated painting aims to recreate inside the house the pleasures of the garden. The scene, however, is utopian. The different flowers bloom at once and sixty-nine species of birds have been identified.

ABOVE: A fresco from Pompeii of chariot races. Nero was an avid follower of charioteers, who were divided into factions: Red, White, Green and Blue. As with modern sports, there were diehard fans who would put the name of their team on their gravestone, and snobs who derided fans for their love of the team 'shirt'.

BELOW: A painting showing a riot that broke out in the amphitheatre at Pompeii in AD 59 during the reign of Nero. The fight between local residents and visitors from nearby Nuceria resulted in the Senate banning gladiatorial games in Pompeii for ten years.

Caesar regard Rome as just another foreign city to be captured wholesale, its riches plundered and its gods thoughtlessly desecrated?[63] Over the next ten days, despite the absence of the consuls and praetors, and the emptiness of the chairs of office, Caesar did everything to maintain a semblance of legitimate government. He called a meeting of the Senate in a temple, and a handful of disgruntled senators showed up. But when he asked them to join him in taking over the government they hesitated, still unable to commit to one side. After three days of discussion and excuses, Caesar, despising the weakness of these little men, gave up his patient show of legality and acted according to his own dignity.[64]

To fight the war against the armies of Pompey and Cato, Caesar told the Senate, he needed money from the state treasury. A tribune of the people called Metellus vetoed the request, protesting that it was against the law. Caesar snapped, stormed out of the meeting and declared that in the war against the enemies of the republic he was going to take the money anyway. When the keys to the doors of the Temple of Saturn could not be found, the general ordered his soldiers to take a battering ram to it. The tribune Metellus, however, again tried to stop Caesar by standing in their way. The people's politician, the man whose whole career had depended on his alliance with the tribunes of the people and the defence of their sanctified rights, now forced Metellus aside with the words, 'It's easier for me to kill you than argue with you'.[65] The gold reserves of the republic were Caesar's. But before he left the city, there was time for one last act of illegality. As if a king, he appointed a praetor to take care of affairs in Rome on his behalf. With that, Caesar and his army headed west.

It took a matter of months to defeat Pompey's three armies in Spain. But while Caesar drove his legionaries to the physical limits of exhaustion and endurance, the same could not be said of Pompey. In Greece he recruited his army at leisure. His army coffers were in rude health too, as he had forced the tax-farming companies of the east to hand over their gold.[66] Despite knowing that Pompey held these major advantages, in the winter of 49–48 BC Caesar returned to Brundisium. Here Mark Antony had collected a fleet, and together they prepared to set sail for the great confrontation with Pompey. The republic had come to a fork in the road: would it fall into the hands of the old guard constitutionalists or to Caesar's new order – to those protecting the liberty of the élite or that of people?

Although it was the depths of winter and the Adriatic was crawling with Pompey's ships, Caesar's fleet, shuttling between the two coasts of Italy and modern-day Albania, outwitted the blockade of his enemies and safely landed seven legions near Dyracchium (Durres). When the rest of his soldiers were delayed by the enemy fleet, Caesar was so determined for them to join him that he disguised himself and forced the captain of a twelve-oared fishing vessel to ferry him back to Italy in the midst of a violent storm.[67] Close to being shipwrecked, Caesar gave up the plan and put his trust in his deputy across the water. Mark Antony duly rose to the occasion, ran the gauntlet and successfully ferried over Caesar's remaining legions.

Once in northern Greece, one principle of war dictated the tactics that both sides adopted: the need for supplies. Pompey was in friendly territory, had secure supply lines and was in control of the seas. Caesar, by contrast, was utterly outnumbered, in enemy territory and had very few supplies. As a result, Pompey wanted to wage a war of attrition, to grind down Caesar's men by putting off any engagement with them, and to watch starvation destroy all their vigour. Yes, Caesar's soldiers were experienced and battle-hardened, but the years of war, of long marches, of building camps and besieging cities had taken their toll too. Time and again Caesar tried to lure Pompey into battle to win a quick victory. Time and again Pompey resisted the temptation.

A psychological battle ensued, the Pompeian soldiers testing the endurance of Caesar's gritty, bloody-minded legionaries. When Caesar besieged Pompey's camp near Dyrrachium, Pompey thought he had Caesar's army starved of supplies. However, the soldiers, more wild beast than human, were determined to maintain the blockade in the face of illness, fatigue and extreme privation. They found a solution in a local root called 'chara', from which they managed to bake loaves and survive. When the Pompeian army goaded its enemies with taunts of famine, the Caesareans replied by throwing a few loaves over the walls into its camp just to rattle the enemy with their tenacity, just to prove their invincibility, their superhuman powers.[68] Nevertheless, the Pompeian legionaries would not be rattled for long.

When Pompey finally engaged his enemy at Dyrrachium, he routed Caesar's army. The ninth legion took the brunt of the casualties. Crucially, however, Pompey did not drive home his advantage, but let his enemy's army escape to safety. Distraught at his first defeat in years, Caesar came to a tough realization. He needed to exhaust his enemy, to draw Pompey away from the sea into the mountainous countryside where both armies would be poorly supplied. So Caesar, his risks already running high, gambled on a strategy that approximated to a collective death wish: to march his tired, starving and disease-ridden legions further inland, further into hostile territory, where the chances of finding food were even more remote. In August 48 BC, although the order ran counter to all their instincts, Caesar's soldiers picked themselves up and pressed on through the rocky, forested hills of Thessaly. En route they took the Greek towns of Gomphi and Metropolis, and plundered them for wine and food. Their health and spirits restored, the legionaries finally set camp near a town called Pharsalus.

Believing that he had his enemy on the run and that he now held all the aces, Pompey was quick to follow Caesar. After his first success in battle, he was jubilant, pumped up, giddy with anticipation of victory. But, as his army too set camp near Pharsalus, Pompey had overlooked his one critical weakness: the value he placed on the opinion of the senatorial establishment. That Achilles heel now became fatally exposed. As the days passed and Pompey did nothing, Cato and his faction ran out of patience and turned on the pressure. Surely Pompey had Caesar just where he wanted him, they pestered. Why wouldn't their great general simply engage Caesar and deliver the death blow? Was he too old? Had his judgement gone? Or was he just so glad to be the general once again, so drunk on power that he did not even want to win the war, but only to hold on to his glorious command *ad infinitum*? [69]

Wearily but with steel, Pompey resisted. All the senators seemed to care about, came his acerbic rebuke, was money and whether or not they missed the fig season in Tusculum! His concern, however, was to minimize the loss of Roman life. The strategy of delay, he insisted, was the best way of ensuring that. Besides, what did they, with their soft, metropolitan manners and worries, know about war? Nothing! But as time wore on, and as the insults and nicknames continued to pique, so Pompey showed signs of caving in. [70] Meanwhile, the daily dance was maintained: Caesar and Pompey led out their armies in formation, the bait of battle was offered, and Pompey refused to bite.

On the bright morning of 9 August 48 BC, his supplies again running dangerously low and his strategy failing, Caesar decided to strike camp and march once more inland. But just as the tents were being dismantled and the baggage animals loaded up, scouts rushed in to report that they had noticed something different. Pompey's line of soldiers had advanced further forward from the rampart than usual.[71] The signal was unmistakable. At long last Pompey the Great was ready for battle. The bait had been taken. Caesar was overjoyed, and as a signal to prepare for war he ordered his purple tunic to be hoisted in front of his tent.

The flurry of activity surrounding the two commanders could not have been more different. The politicians in Pompey's camp cried 'On to Pharsalus!' and rubbed their hands at the prospect of witnessing a glorious victory. They argued jovially over who on their triumphant return to Rome would be allocated the priesthoods, who would stand for the offices of praetor and consul, and who would rent which Palatine villa to whom. Caesar and his officers, by contrast, were utterly focused on the task ahead. Buoyed up, they knew they had been handed a lifeline. It was one they were now going to seize.[72]

When the two lines of battle came face to face, the landscape shone with the glitter of their javelins, short swords, bows, slings and quivers full of arrows.[73] Caesar's 22,000 infantry were confronting an army twice that size, while his 1000 cavalry faced an opponent seven times greater. But where his army was smaller, his strategy was shrewder. Seeing that Pompey's cavalry were all aligned on their general's left flank, Caesar knew that his old ally's plan was to encircle one of Caesar's wings. To neutralize that threat, Caesar took a series of cohorts from each of his legions and from them created a fourth line of infantry. Placing them behind his three existing lines, he gave them the following instructions: on the signal of his flag and not before, they were to advance and engage Pompey's cavalry. Above all, they were to use their javelins as pikes and thrust up at the faces of the enemy. Victory that day, he told them, depended on their valour.

Caesar rallied his army with a final speech. To Crastinus, a loyal centurion of the tenth legion who had served with him throughout Gaul, Alesia and Spain, he said, 'Only this one battle remains. After it Caesar will regain his dignity and we our freedom.' Crastinus replied, 'Today, General, I shall earn your gratitude either dead or alive.'[74] And with those words, Crastinus and 120 crack troops, bellowing at the tops of their voices, charged. The impetus lying with Caesar's infantry, Roman now clashed with Roman, each side hacking down the other with mirror-image technique and brutality.

Soon enough, Pompey deployed his cavalry too. Immediately they succeeded in unsettling their enemy. Their assault was so committed, so convincing that Caesar's cavalry was forced to give ground. However, as Pompey's cavalry formed into squadrons and surrounded Caesar's line on its exposed flank, Caesar gave the signal for his secret detachment to break away. Its standards brandished aloft, the fourth line swiftly attacked Pompey's cavalry, jabbing their javelins upwards at enemy faces. It was a moment of military genius. Caesar had correctly guessed that the flower of Rome's aristocratic youth, the scions of senators, might well have the eagerness for battle, but they had neither the experience nor the stomach for it. The decisive action threw them into a panic. They turned and fled to the hills.

Now it was Pompey's flank that was exposed. The fourth line pressed home its advantage and attacked the rear. Caesar, scenting blood, dealt the death blow. He had kept his third line in reserve and inactive. Now, swooping into the bloody mêlée, fresh, unscathed and battle-hardened veterans from Caesar's long-serving campaigns replaced the weary. Without mercy, they smashed and stabbed their way through the bloodied, exhausted Pompeian ranks. Eventually, Pompey's grand coalition, unable to hold the new assault, gave out and was routed.

Seeing his forces flee, Pompey had the look of a man half-crazed or 'whom some god had deprived of his wits'.[75] After waiting silently in his tent while his legionaries outside were slaughtered, he was suddenly taken by the belief that he could regroup and counter-attack. So, in the company of thirty cavalrymen, Pompey the Great also fled from Pharsalus. In reality, he had been utterly defeated. Caesar had decisively won the civil war. Pompey would launch no second offensive.

Caesar ordered his men to storm the fortifications of the enemy camp. The Pompeian cohorts guarding it either joined the flight or surrendered. Once inside Pompey's camp, Caesar's soldiers saw the evidence of a final hubris committed by the senatorial faction. A victory banquet had already been beautifully laid out on silver platters in arrogant expectation of a victory celebration. Every tent was decorated with wreaths of myrtle, the dining couches were strewn with flowers, and drinking vessels were filled to the brim with wine.[76] But now it was not the aristocratic faction, the fathers and sons of the wealthy Roman élite who sat down to feast. That privilege now fell to Caesar and his men.

EPILOGUE

The next day 24,000 of Pompey's army surrendered to Caesar, throwing themselves on the ground, weeping and begging for their lives to be spared. Of the estimated 15,000 dead, 6000 were Roman citizens. To the enemy Romans who survived, Caesar showed clemency once again in a first step to heal the sick republic. He also pardoned the noblemen who had fought against him.[77] Many of them, however, had fled in an effort to reorganize and retrench. Pompey reunited with his wife and set sail from Cyprus, seeking refuge in Egypt. Perhaps he could raise a new army there and fight Caesar another day? Caesar followed him in pursuit. As Pompey stepped ashore at Alexandria, however, he was assassinated. An influential eunuch in the court of the Egyptian pharaoh had decided that the best way to make a friend of Caesar was to murder his adversary. Nothing could have been further from the truth. As Caesar looked on the decapitated head of his old ally and friend and then at his signet ring, which depicted a lion holding a sword, he burst into tears. This was no honourable, dignified way for a great Roman to die.[78]

Although the battle of Pharsalus had decided the civil war in Caesar's favour, it would take further campaigns in North Africa and Spain to mop up the pockets of senatorial resistance. On his return to Rome in 46 BC, Caesar celebrated four lavish triumphs; his veterans were given a lifetime's salary, and there was a gift of money for every Roman citizen. Between 49 and 44 BC Julius Caesar was voted four consulships and four dictatorships. With the power that these offices granted him, he honoured his pledges to reform the republic and restore the liberty of the people. Legislation, ranging from the suspension of rent for a year to the settlement of veterans and the urban poor in Italy and in colonies abroad, was enacted, but it was by no means the revolutionary, radical overhaul that the conservatives feared. Indeed, Caesar could be equally repressive. In a bid to curb the power of the mob in the future, for example, he put a stop to the practice of people gathering in clubs and colleges unless they had a licence.

The dictator also increased the number of senators and knights filling those ranks with new men from ordinary families. As it was Caesar who had made their social rise possible, these men willingly heaped more and more honours on him. In January 44 BC he ostentatiously rejected the title and crown of a king, yet a religious cult and statues suggest that he accepted deification. When, in February, he agreed to the office of dictator in perpetuity, it was hard to escape the reality that Caesar now ruled as an autocrat, as Rome's first emperor. It seemed that rather than reforming the republic by building a relationship with the new senatorial élite, and governing with them towards genuine reform of the republic, Caesar ultimately cared more about his patrician dignity and the honours accorded it than the liberty of the people.

The end of the civil war, therefore, did not mean the end of the debate about liberty. Indeed, Caesar's perpetual dictatorship fanned its flames once more. In mid-March 44 BC, Mark Antony suddenly found himself having a long conversation with a senator outside the Senate House built by Pompey. A strong, physically imposing man, he did not realize that he was being deliberately detained. Inside a group of senators made a pretence of petitioning against Caesar. They approached him and soon they were hemming him in. Then, one of the men broke cover, flashed the blade of his dagger and plunged it into the dictator. The others piled in, frenetically pulling at their togas to release the weapons hidden in their folds. They stabbed their political enemy twenty-three times. Brutus, who was a close family friend of Caesar but who had fought on the side of Pompey at Pharsalus, delivered one of the blows. Afterwards he left the Senate House in the company of some of the conspirators. Their bloody knives still in their hands, they marched to the Capitoline Hill and called out to the people. 'Liberty,' they cried, had been 'restored'.[79]

The lifeless, bleeding body of Caesar now lay alone in the Senate House, the very building that his adversary had paid for and bequeathed to Rome. Indeed, the spot where he had fallen was at the foot of a statue of Pompey. While it might be thought that with this murder Pompey had got his revenge, the truth was that the republic was dead. Although Brutus and all the other patrician senators who wanted to end the 'tyranny' of Caesar and bring back the old idealized republic did not yet know it, Caesar had correctly seen the future. Popular elections and votes in the assemblies of Rome were no way to successfully govern a vast Roman empire. That could only be done by a single head, one ruler – an emperor.

Peacefully winning over both the aristocratic élite and the Roman people to that view, and persuading them to accept that liberty was finished for all of them, was a gargantuan task that required a clever political vision and a clinical, glacial ruthlessness. It was a happy coincidence, then, that the task fell to Augustus. This man's genius for politics would perhaps surpass that of all Romans who came before and after him. So too, however, would his capacity for cruelty, his assiduous ability to do whatever it took to seal power.

Augustus

In the year 17 BC, between 31 May and 3 June, the city of Rome witnessed the greatest show on earth. The Games of the Ages was a festival the likes of which no Roman had ever seen before, nor would ever see again. The buzz surrounding them had been building for weeks. Heralds in ancient, traditional dress had taken to the streets of Rome and had announced in advance the extraordinary scale of events to come: three days of visually spectacular sacrifices at sanctuaries and cult places around the city, followed by seven days of chariot races, tragedies and comedies in Latin and Greek, plus stunning exhibitions of trick riders, animal hunting and mock battles. A special song had been composed for the occasion, and it was to be sung on the last day by two choruses – one of twenty-seven boys and one of twenty-seven girls – all dressed in white. The anticipated mood was of celebration, euphoria and unbounded optimism. Rome, they said, was at peace, prospering and enjoying a new golden age. But the preparations for the games hinted at a more serious purpose at work.

On the day before festivities began the priests went to the top of the Aventine, one of the seven hills of Rome, and received from citizens there the first fruits of the year. These they would distribute to the thousands of Romans attending the festival. But the fruits were not the only handout. They would also dole out sulphur, tar and torches. These were to be burnt by every citizen in a private religious ritual so that every Roman citizen might cleanse himself before the celebrations got under way. The carefully contrived publicity stunt caught on. Behind the public relations drive, however, was a powerful political idea. The real theme of the festival, indicated these preliminary activities, was systematic regeneration, mass renewal, and the purification of the whole Roman state.

The stage manager, host and master of ceremonies was Augustus, Rome's first emperor. The theme of expiation and regeneration was for him the perfect message, the apposite note to strike. For these games would mark a watershed in Roman history. This was the moment at which Romans not only celebrated a new regime of peace and stability, but healed themselves from what had gone before: at least two decades of brutal civil war. From the moment in 49 BC that Julius Caesar had crossed the Rubicon until 31 BC Rome had been devastated by an apocalyptic period of social and political meltdown, a time in which the vast expanse of the Roman empire had seen battlefield after battlefield blackened with blood. It was blood spilt by Romans, not at the expense of their barbarian enemies, but from the veins of their very own Roman friends, cousins, brothers and fathers.

Beyond the aim of healing, however, Augustus ensured that the festival delivered a second, highly sophisticated political message. The key to it lay in the theme of history. For the Games of the Ages were celebrated by Romans every 110 years. They connected the present glorious moment with the very earliest period of the Roman republic. On the one hand, their celebration inspired a belief in Roman citizens that the republic had been 'restored', that there existed a harmonious continuity between Rome's cherished ancient history and the present golden age of Augustus. On the other hand, buried deep in this message, was a quite different reality. The central, most prominent part played at the games was that played by Augustus. It was he who gave the festival to the Roman people. It was he who paid for it. It was he, above all, who at night and before a mass audience took the central role when he sacrificed a pregnant sow to Mother Earth. This starring performance communicated to the Roman people – through their emotions, through their hearts – a completely new political reality. The games were at once traditional and a highly inventive, contemporary take on tradition.

For the truth was that Augustus had not restored the republic, but had achieved just the opposite. He was in the process of ending the political freedoms of the republic. He was rebuilding the Roman state around himself and his power. He was, with subtlety and deft political skill, forging a new age – the age of the Roman emperors. The Games of the Ages in 17 BC were just one example of an extraordinary sleight of hand. They celebrated the arrival of the greatest revolution in all Roman history: Augustus's transformation of the Roman republic into an autocracy – rule by one man.

To achieve this feat he used a whole raft of means, sometimes force, sometimes law. His preferred instrument, however, was persuasion. He deployed it to such effect that the Roman people and the élite of Roman senators and knights would give up their cherished freedoms willingly and hand over power to a single head. It was a brilliant political manoeuvre, the greatest political trick ever to be pulled off in Roman history.

ACTIUM

The anaesthetic which dulled Augustus's surreptitious surgery of the Roman state was peace. In bringing about this peace after so many years of war, Augustus had played a key role too. His part in concluding the civil war was far more gruesome than the one he would later like to play as emperor. Nonetheless it was a role he inhabited with commitment and will power from the very start.

When Augustus heard the news of Julius Caesar's murder in 44 BC, he was known as plain old Gaius Octavius. He was nineteen years old and cut a surprising figure for someone who would eventually win the twenty-year-long civil war. His small, weak frame was prone to illness, his blond hair was unkempt, and his teeth were full of gaps.[1] He was the son of an undistinguished 'new man', but that relatively humble connection to the senatorial élite was dramatically outshone by another family tie. Through his mother Atia, Octavian (as we call him) was the great-nephew of Julius Caesar. More importantly, he was also Caesar's adopted son and heir. Claiming revenge for his adoptive father's assassination, Octavian reignited the civil war in 43 BC. In reality he was making a bid for power.

His first move was bold and calculated. He started calling himself 'Caesar'. In the eyes of the people, the powerful, magnetic brand of Caesar's name had been confirmed by a comet which was sighted just before sunset for seven consecutive days in 44 BC.[2] To most it was proof that Octavian's adopted father was indeed divine. After an initial period of rivalry, Octavian eventually joined forces with the dead dictator's political 'heir', Mark Antony, and together they went to war with Caesar's assassins. As a soldier Octavian was dwarfed by the giant, heroic figure of his new ally. A story did the rounds that at one battle of the civil war Octavian disappeared for two days and cowered in a marsh. He even stripped off his armour and discarded his horse, perhaps to avoid detection. He did return to his army, but long after the action had been decided.[3] Behind the young man's unswaggering manner, however, there was a vicious sting. The puny constitution of Caesar's young heir belied the ruthlessness of his mind and the cold-blooded ease with which he took violent measures.

During the renewed civil war, for example, Octavian (along with Mark Antony) had overseen a notorious wholesale cull of their enemies in the political élite. Some three hundred conservative senators and 2000 knights were named on a proscription list, hunted down and executed.[4] That is just one grim statistic provided by the ancient sources; one can only imagine the severity of punishment meted out to their other enemies. By 42 BC Octavian and Mark Anthony finally defeated the assassins of Caesar at the battle of Philippi. Brutus's severed head was sent to Rome and thrown at the foot of Caesar's statue. With their opponents crushed, the two men had become masters of Rome and her empire. It was only a matter of time, however, before the victorious allies turned rivals again and fought each other for sole control of the Roman world.

Today Actium is located on the tree-lined coast of northwestern Greece, north of the island of Leukada. Over 2000 years ago, on 2 September 31 BC, those silent, green hills bore witness to one of the most pivotal moments in Roman history. This was the battle of Actium. It pitted the navy of Octavian against a combined fleet of Mark Antony and his ally Cleopatra, the queen of Egypt. She was now both Mark Antony's lover and his wealthy benefactor. Since the time of her liaison with Caesar, she had realised that the future prosperity of her country depended on a favourable alliance with Rome. After Caesar's death, she had tied her colours to Mark Antony's mast. Now she was about to find out if her gamble would pay off. For the result of this one battle would not only bring the long civil war to a conclusive end. Actium would also decide the destiny of the Roman empire.

The scale of the encounter was indeed huge: 230 of Mark Antony's ships were blockaded in an expansive bay by an even greater fleet under the command of Octavian's admiral Agrippa. The ninety largest of Mark Anthony's ships were equipped with a state-of-the-art weapon: a pure bronze ram weighing 1.5 tonnes and mounted on the prow. In ancient Rome naval conflicts were won or lost by driving these warheads into enemy ships and sinking them. In spite of this technological advantage, Mark Antony's force was weakened by malaria and desertions: the political tide of support in Rome was turning away from him in favour of Octavian, and Mark Antony's soldiers knew it. Octavian's military steel had improved considerably since his first taste of battle. He was also the greater tactician. After patiently reeling the enemy fleet into action, he now took clinical advantage of its weaknesses.

Octavian and Agrippa first sent in volleys of catapult balls that had been set on fire. Then they surrounded the bronze-prowed ships of Antony and Cleopatra, trapped them with grappling hooks and used their superior numbers of soldiers to dash on board and overpower the enemy force. The battle itself was fast becoming a rather anticlimactic, one-sided engagement. Indeed, Mark Antony's battle plan was perhaps nothing more ambitious than to break through Octavian's blockade. He really wanted to escape to Egypt to create a stronger position from which to win the war. Once Cleopatra had successfully peeled away with a key portion of the fleet, however, the break-up of his allied fleet single-handedly took the teeth out of Mark Antony's naval charge and brought about its complete collapse. There was no epic struggle, only a deflated, easy victory.

A Roman of the time would not have known this from the hype with which Octavian before and afterwards infused the 'titanic' encounter. In Virgil's Aeneid, the epic poem of the Augustan age, Cleopatra's escape was famously cast as a panic-stricken flight, typical of a weak foreigner. But that was just one element in the grandiloquent war of words. The battle of Actium was billed as nothing less than a fight between western and eastern values, between Octavian's vigorous, pious Roman-ness and the immoral debauchery of Antony and Cleopatra's union. It asked Romans to answer one simple question: did they want the vast empire to be saved by a traditional, steadfast Roman military hero, or to become the plaything of an emasculated, oriental king enslaved to a depraved exotic queen? It was presented, in short, as a worldwide clash of civilizations. By winning it, Octavian won something even more important than the military victory. He won the victor's privilege of explaining the meaning of the war's outcome.

THE SPOILS OF WAR

The rich seam of political capital that Octavian drew from his victory was mined immediately. He founded a new Roman city near the scene of battle and called it Nicopolis, the 'City of Victory'. At his old campsite he also ordered the construction of a massive victory monument, from the remains of which archaeologists have recently produced new information. Beautifully carved scenes depict the battle and also the triumphal procession in Rome with which Octavian celebrated his victory in 29 BC. Part of the monument was a 6-metre (20-foot) high wall which contained visually stunning 'souvenirs'. Thirty-six of Mark Antony's bronze prows were set in concrete and fastened on to the limestone blocks that made up the wall. The 'beaks' of the enemy's ships were thus set into the landscape on a hill overlooking the site of the victory. It must have been a spectacular display befitting a spectacular triumph – one never to be forgotten. For although the limp victory did not live up to Octavian's propaganda, its consequences certainly did.

After Actium, the victorious Octavian was master of all Rome's armies. Victory gave him the freedom to conquer Egypt, to provoke the suicides of Mark Antony and Cleopatra (later dramatized by Plutarch and Shakespeare), and to add to Rome's provinces all the extraordinary wealth of that far more ancient civilization. Finally, it furnished Octavian with the greatest personal fortune in all Roman history. It was money he wasted no time in spending. His goal was to honour the promises he had made during the war, and above all to secure the loyalty of the Roman army and the Roman people. It was a goal he accomplished in lavish style.

On his return to Rome he celebrated the closure of the civil war with three spectacular triumphs, he paid off his soldiers with generous cash rewards, and he gave a smaller sum to every Roman citizen. As if that were not enough to win unanimous popular support, the bountiful fields of Egypt's Nile valley were now Rome's granary and a secure, reliable source of the city's grain dole. Octavian thus became the most powerful man in the Roman world. 'At this point,' wrote the historian Cassius Dio, 'Octavian alone held all the power of the state for the first time.'[5] There was a problem, though. The one thing that Octavian lacked within the Roman state was legitimacy.

Winning this would not be the fruit of a single battle, but the great project of his entire life. The result, and the personal reward for Octavian, would be a Roman empire ruled by a single emperor. In achieving legitimacy, however, one question would baffle the ancient world as much as it has done ours. Was Octavian an evil tyrant deviously and quietly dismantling Roman liberty? Or was he indeed a benevolent statesman who, first among equals, shared power with Roman senators and had the consent of the Roman people? Was he, in short, a wicked autocrat in all but name, or a model emperor who restored if not exactly the republic, at least constitutional government? Who really held the reins of power?

In ancient Rome, as in the government of modern states, the question is perhaps impossible to answer. In the case of Octavian the answer lies deep within poor or highly partial historical sources. The evidence that does remain (namely, Octavian's own account of his achievements, plus inscriptions and the wealth of monuments and buildings he authorized in Rome) presents us with only a sustained, ingenious political performance – a performance from which his mask would rarely slip. Whichever view we take of Octavian, what is certain is that he cleverly robed his power in the clothes of the old republican offices. This critical strategy lies behind a meeting of the Senate on the Ides of January 27 BC.

Before he had even entered the Senate House, Octavian had heeded the key lesson of his adoptive father's assassination. The republic had been founded on the moment when the last of the Etruscan kings was expelled by the Roman nobility. That moment crystallized those nobles' hatred of monarchy – their distrust of a single powerful individual who dominated the state. If you exercise supreme power explicitly, suggested the events of the Ides of March 44 BC, you paid the price with your life. If Octavian did indeed hold supreme power he knew he had to disguise it. So at the meeting of the Senate, Octavian renounced all his powers and territories and handed them over to the control of the senators and the Roman people. This extraordinary gesture, however, was highly stage-managed. Just as he had acted his part, so the senators followed suit. In response, they granted Octavian the right to stand for the consulship, and also allowed a fellow consul to put forward his candidacy alongside him. On the surface at least, power had returned to the discretion of the Senate, annual elections and the assemblies of the Roman people. The republic had, it seemed, been restored.

Challenging that appearance, however, were the facts of power. Just as in the last decades of the republic, an office holder's power resided in his authority to command armies and the province in which he could exercise that authority. At the same January meeting, the Senate crucially granted Octavian an 'extended' province: Gaul, Syria, Egypt and Cyprus were all under his authority, and were to be commanded by him for no less than ten years. Not by coincidence, these territories bordered the frontiers of the empire and thus contained the vast majority of Roman army legions. Yes, it was true that senators elected to the second consulship would go on to govern provinces, but these were the peaceful ones. The militarily important provinces were controlled by Octavian and governed by his own appointed deputies. For this reason Octavian outstripped all his consular colleagues in the state.

Octavian's bold balancing act was not easy to maintain. In 23 BC, for example, his holding of the consulship year after year began to smack of supreme power. Although the evidence is murky, a genuine crisis now swiftly gathered momentum, and some senators planned to kill the new 'king'. Octavian was quick to respond. He neutralized the threat by renegotiating his position and simply changing the legal form of words that gave him control of the armies. In winning this bout with the senatorial élite one critical factor weighed in his favour: his unrivalled popularity with the Roman people. He was, after all, the man who had brought stability to a world of chaos. However he knew that the people were fickle and that he could not rely on the vagaries of public opinion for ever. So he turned his attention to cementing his stature in the people's eyes too.

Octavian once again took inspiration from the forms of republican office and made a surprising demand of the Senate. He wanted, he said, the power accorded to a tribune of the people. In relation to the powers which gave him control of the army, this was a relatively modest office to wish for. Certainly it gave him the authority to propose and veto bills before the assembly of the people. That, however, was not the chief attraction of the post. Octavian had spotted its true potential. Drawing on the emotional resonance of its origin in the Roman republic, he would amplify the power of this lowly republican office and elevate it to a whole new status. With it he would become not just any old tribune of the people, but the iconic defender, protector and champion of the interests of all Roman citizens, not just in Rome and Italy, but across the length and breadth of the empire.

Was the creation of such a position the act of a man extemporizing, seeking new ways to ensure that stable, constitutional government was restored? Or was it more sinister? Certainly taking the office of tribune of the people suggested a strategy shared by dictators throughout history: Octavian had stealthily jumped over the heads of the political elite and aligned himself directly with the hearts and minds of the people. Once again, the guise of the old republican office was the key to Octavian's successful adoption of the post. The senatorial heads watched his great leap and consented, if grudgingly and with hatred, all the way.

AUTOCRACY

By 19 BC Octavian had secured the one thing that his adoptive father Julius Caesar had failed to achieve: both unrivalled power and political legitimacy. This unprecedented and deftly created status was summarized with the granting of a solemn, resonant title. Although a change of name might seem superficial, in Octavian's Rome, as in modern politics, the power of a new brand cannot be underestimated.

Octavian first toyed with the idea of calling himself 'Romulus'. It neatly cast him as the new founder of Rome. In this name was both ancient tradition but also the idea of a new age. After some consideration, however, Octavian rejected it. The connotations of a man who killed his brother to found a state left an unpleasant taste. Instead, Octavian simply made up a name. 'Augustus' literally means 'sacred' or 'revered' but stopped short of explicitly calling him a god. That would contradict his theme of being a citizen-leader, of being 'first among equals' in the republic. In the name, however, was the unmistakable hint of a relationship with the gods. It is derived from the Latin word for reading divine signs – augury. It suggested that Octavian was somehow religious, holy and deserving of special, unique respect. The name change was symptomatic of the revolution. It was unobtrusive, but potent. As Augustus's reign continued, as his grip on power became firmer, the rattle sounding the death of political freedom became louder and louder.

It echoed, for example, at meetings of the Senate. Under the republic there was a specific order in which speakers stood up and debated the items of business at hand. Augustus maintained this routine so that everyone appeared to have a voice. Their opinions, it seemed, mattered. To some this must have been a relief. After decades of factional strife and the likes of Julius Caesar and Pompey slugging it out, life for junior senators was imaginably rosier. Ultimately, however the role-playing became tedious. The majority of the senators realized that their opinion counted for little in comparison to the wish of Augustus. To inject into senatorial discussions the show of toothsome debate, Augustus innovated: instead of hearing their opinions in a set order, he asked senators to speak on issues randomly. This made it difficult for them to agree resignedly with what the last speaker had said. He also resorted to imposing fines for non-attendance and to limiting compulsory meetings to twice a month.[6]

Despite these efforts, the old systems of the republic lost their vigour and gave way to autocracy. Indeed, Augustus grew to rely less and less on the Senate for formulating policy. Quite early in his rule, he formulated an advisory body of consuls and senators chosen by lot. They met in his imperial palace and not in the

Senate House. As this body grew in importance, so too did the suspicion of those who were left out of it. Under future emperors, similar councils would become the target of a stock accusation: the empire was run not in tandem with the Senate, but by the emperor's cronies, friends and freedmen. Indeed even by the end of Augustus's life, critical information was kept from the Senate. In his will Augustus left a note about where information could be found relating to the state of the empire, to the numbers and location of Roman soldiers and to the state's financial accounts. 'He added the names of his freedmen and slaves from whom details could be obtained.'[7] Most senators, it seemed, clearly did not know about the fundamental workings of the empire. This top-level information was now out of their hands. Such instances hint at how the substance of the republic ebbed away. Appearances, though, were scrupulously kept up.

Office holders, be they tribunes or consuls, continued to be chosen, but even if they were formally elected, they were at least nominated by Augustus. By AD 5 the lists of candidates for office brought before the people at election time contained only the names of yes-men senators whom Augustus could trust not to rock the boat. When an independent candidate stood of his own free will, Augustus's response was methodical, befitting the unspoken logic of the new regime. A young senator called Egnatius Rufus, for example, won considerable popularity for successfully establishing a private fire-fighting service manned by his slaves. When he refused to withdraw his name from the list of candidates for the consulship, the consequence was fatal. Rufus was tried for 'conspiracy' and executed. The cherished, seminal power of the Roman citizen's electoral vote was reduced to a hollow gesture.

In the administration of the empire the signs of the silent revolution were evident too; power sharing was another carefully coded performance. Men of ambition and standing could, ostensibly, have a legitimate career. Augustus scrupulously maintained the licence of individuals to pursue office in the controlled elections: giving the senatorial élite a role in government was one way to keep potential rivals at bay and, more importantly, he could not manage the empire alone. He needed the experience and the sheer manpower of senators and knights to hear and adjudicate legal cases in the city, to govern the provinces abroad, and to oversee the exaction of taxes. He also needed commanders to fight wars; under his rule the size of the Roman empire's provinces nearly doubled. There was, however, a very fine line circumscribing office holders' power. Those who crossed it, and thus dared to rival Augustus's authority, paid the price for forgetting their lines. In reality, the skills now required of office holders were closer to those of a bureaucrat or a loyal deputy of Augustus. Though their ambitions were perhaps satisfied by the appearance of authority, the élite knew that the real power lay elsewhere.

It was a fact to which the senators and knights slowly grew accustomed. Naturally, the stars of those loyal to the new regime rose; office in the administration, albeit of limited responsibility, made them acquiescent. Those of a more independent leaning simply withdrew and bided their time. Perhaps they consoled themselves that this unhappy state of affairs was temporary, a symptom only of Augustus's personal dominance within the state. At some point in the future he would be gone, they perhaps thought, and at that time there would return both the glorious republic and political freedom. For the time being, they were prepared to play along to keep the ideal alive. Augustus, however, had other ideas.

The old, idealized republic, if it had ever existed, was dead and gone for ever. Dead too was the rivalry among the senatorial élite, and the search for glory in the eyes of the Roman people, which many believed defined it. Just to make sure, in AD 6 Augustus set about implementing the most influential reform of his entire rule.

REFORMING THE ARMY

The reform of the Roman army was the key to stabilizing Augustus's position and the age of emperors to come. The army had always been the source of the empire's security. In the last decades of the republic, however, it had also been the chief source of conflict. This was because it had been in legionaries' interests to go to war even if it meant fighting another Roman army. Recruited and groomed by ambitious generals with the offer of wealth, booty and land, their loyalty had been detached from the Roman state, but had become fatally up for grabs to the highest bidder (as under Julius Caesar). Augustus knew this better than anyone. In the civil war he had repaid his followers in the Roman army by forcibly booting humbler citizens off their Italian countryside properties in order to settle soldiers on them.

Now, however, that relationship changed, and the umbilical cord between commanders and troops was cut. The Roman army was at last taken out of politics and nationalized. Citizens were offered a professional career in army service, a salary and a chance for promotion. The legions, for example, were fixed by law at a core twenty-eight regular units. These were spread along the frontiers of the empire, while a new, 9000-strong élite 'Praetorian' army was stationed in Italy and Rome. Its men were paid three times as much as ordinary soldiers and would with time become the personal bodyguard of the emperor. For the many who chose a career in the regular army, military service was eventually set at twenty years, and, from AD 6, a fixed annual salary of 900 sesterces was decreed, but with the promise of 12,000 sesterces pension upon retirement from the army. (The minimum subsistence for a peasant family is reckoned at 500 sesterces per annum.) At first Augustus paid for the army out of his own personal wealth; his proconsular power did, after all, make him commander of most of the Roman army, and this patronage again underlined his supreme position. In AD 6, however, he took the professionalization of the army to its logical conclusion and created a military treasury, endowed it with a massive initial grant, and then funded it through taxation.

Although Augustus had improved the stability of his own position, the reform of the army was also highly risky. At the end of Augustus's rule the legions in Gaul and Pannonia (modern-day Hungary and the Balkans to the south) seized the opportunity of the emperor's death to renegotiate their terms of duty. Of course there were the usual gripes. They were fed up with their low pay, corrupt superior officers and the paltry prospect at the end of their service, should they live to see it, of some thin-soiled plot of land tucked far away from home; the rewards just weren't as appetizing as they had been under the likes of Julius Caesar. What sparked the mutinies, however, was one grievance above all. Soldiers were being kept on beyond their agreed length of service; the reforms were so expensive that the Roman authorities were desperately trying to save money by delaying payment of the legionaries' retirement bonus.

It is very hard to make financial comparisons across time, but one modern historian has valued the minimum annual state budget at 800 million sesterces. We can calculate that expenditure on the army was in the order of 445 million sesterces each year. This means that the army wiped out roughly half the empire's annual budget.[8] Augustus's initial grant to the treasury was bountiful, but later emperors would not always find it possible to be as generous. An emperor's ability to sustain the professional army would be the critical factor in the future security of the frontiers. Augustus had drawn the sting from the army by destroying its dependency on ambitious, big-hitting generals pursuing their own political objectives. In doing so, however, he had also created the empire's Achilles heel, then and throughout the next five centuries.

If the first lesson of the civil war had been that the Roman army needed to be taken out of the control of ambitious generals, a second lesson followed from the first. In order for the emperor to maintain his ability to pay for the new professional army of the state, he needed to maintain the security of the tax revenues. No longer could the empire afford to allow the wealth of the provinces to fall into the hands of the generals who governed them and lined their own pockets. It was essential that taxes flowed smoothly from the provinces to the centre – to Augustus's imperial coffers. Understanding this was key to the success of an emperor's rule, both for Augustus and for emperors to come.

Even with such a system in place, however, twenty-eight army units were all that Rome could afford. Augustus learnt this lesson too, and it was one he learnt the hard way. For the best part of his rule, his generals had been arduously campaigning to bring Germany between the Rhine and the Elbe under Roman control. That policy appeared to be paying off. Then, in AD 9, disaster struck. As the general Quintilius Varus was concluding a successful campaigning season and returning his army to winter quarters on the Rhine, he took a route through the Teutoberg forest. Within that eerie wood, however, lay a venomous snake: an army of German warriors appeared like ghosts from behind the trees, descended on the Romans and massacred no fewer than three Roman legions. Augustus is said to have been so completely shaken by the news that 'for months at a time he let his beard and hair grow and would hit his head against the door, shouting, "Quintilius Varus, give me back my legions!"'[9]

Although those legions were replaced, the sums did not add up sufficiently to risk pursuing the conquest of Germany. Augustus told his successor as much. He left the emperor Tiberius a handwritten letter strongly advising him to keep Rome within the boundaries of its current frontiers: the Atlantic Ocean in the west, Egypt and North Africa in the south, the English Channel and the rivers Rhine and Danube to the north, and the border of Roman Syria with neighbouring Parthia in the east. Although Tiberius heeded his adoptive father's words, later emperors would not. For the time being, however, Augustus ensured that along these borders his professionalized army maintained the security of the Roman empire. It was a solid platform upon which to cultivate his age of peace.

THE CULT OF PEACE

An essential part of that peace was the creation of the ideology of the emperor. The Greek-speaking eastern provinces of the empire had long been accustomed to worshipping and glorifying the personalities of their individual Roman governors; this was a cultural hangover from the relationship between eastern subjects and their Hellenistic kings. Under Augustus, those provincials continued the practice, but transferred their worship to the figure of Augustus. He was treated like a god. Temples were built to him, and prayers, festivals and sacrifices glorified the names of Augustus and his family. Now that he had successfully weathered the early opposition to his rule, he devised ways of making his glorification an empire-wide trend. It was a task he could set to with flair.

Today, Augustus's genius for presentation would impress even a modern spin-doctor. His favourite tactic was to make skilful use of traditional Roman history. In order to advertise to citizens his successes in foreign policy, for example, Augustus rekindled an ancient custom. He was reminded that in a more ancient era the doors to the Temple of Janus were closed at times of peace, and opened only when a war was being waged. So, when Augustus went to war with Spain in 26 BC, the doors were solemnly opened. In that campaign, Augustus, like modern imperialists, was determined to set reluctant 'friends' straight, and when his generals had completed the job seven years later, he referred to the victory as 'pacification'.[10] At the same time the doors of the small temple in the Forum were ceremoniously closed. It was not, however, his peace with Spain, but with Parthia that was Augustus's greatest public relations coup.

The neighbouring empire to Rome's east had brought about one of the republic's most ignoble and embarrassing defeats. In 55 BC an army, commanded by a leading general of the late republic, Marcus Licinius Crassus, and his son, was utterly anni-hilated by superior Parthian tactics in the deserts of Arabia. Symbolic of the wound gouged into the Roman empire was the loss of Crassus's military standards. These had become a trophy, an emblem of Parthian defiance and a totemic museum piece in that empire's capital city. In 19 BC Augustus set about reme-dying this. His approach, however, did not march to the loud drumbeat of war. It moved to the quieter sounds of a diplo-matic agreement, backed up with the baring of military teeth and a show of Roman force. It was enough of a threat for a new treaty with Parthia to be signed and, critically, the standards to be returned.

Back in Rome, Augustus was quick to spot and exploit the potential of the event. He magically upgraded the Parthian settlement from a peace treaty into a Roman victory to rival Julius Caesar's conquest of Gaul. With exuberant fanfare and pageantry, the standards were brought back into Rome, a triumphal arch was dedicated and the standards themselves were laid to rest. Their location? The new Temple of Mars the

Avenger. The theme of this 'victory' was reiterated in the famous 'Prima Porta' statue of Augustus. Right in the centre of the emperor's richly decorated breastplate was chiselled the scene of a Parthian humbly handing back the standards to a Roman. Without so much as a drop of blood being shed, the Roman 'revenge' was exacted.

Old Roman history put to modern political spin was also the theme of much of Augustus's great marble building programme. In the Rome of the late republic, marble had been used sparingly and only by the very rich in the building of monuments. It was expensive because it had to be transported all the way from Greece. Under Augustus, however, a rich and far cheaper supply had been found and quarried at Carrara, in modern-day Tuscany. For this reason above all, Augustus was able to boast that he found Rome a city of brick and left it a city of marble.[11] He would oversee Rome's extraordinary transformation from the dirty, chaotic rabbit warrens of the late republic into a capital city worthy of a Mediterranean-wide empire. The Altar of Peace, the Pantheon, the city's first stone amphitheatre, and a new Temple to Apollo were just some of the fruits of his building programme. It was, however, the new Forum of Augustus that was perhaps his greatest achievement. In it, the same genius for rhetorical effect can be detected.

Two long porticoes, housing a reverent parade of historical statues, flanked either side of the Forum. On one side were the statues of Romulus, the first kings of Rome, and a series of grand Romans of the republic. On the opposite side were the marble images of Augustus's ancestors – and a formidable, blue-blooded line-up they made too. Beginning with Aeneas, the legendary founder of Rome, it continued with his descendants, the kings of the city of Alba Longa, which Aeneas's son Iulus had founded, then on to his descendants, the family of the Julii, and right down to Julius Caesar, Augustus's adoptive father. No chance was missed to exploit his divine ancestry too. At one end of the parallel porticoes stood the great Temple of Mars the Avenger. As Aeneas was said to be the son of the goddess Venus, this deity took pride of place both inside the temple and also in its pediment. Within she stood alongside Julius Caesar and Mars; outside she was next to Romulus. Crucially, however, the Forum's rich, sophisticated panorama of Roman history encircled one figure. Right in the middle of it, almost certainly, stood a statue of Augustus himself.

One clear political statement rang out. Augustus was the pinnacle, the summation of Roman history; he was the favoured one of the gods; he was the guardian of ancient Roman values, and the embodiment of those values in the future. The new Forum of Augustus was thus the forerunner of more recent monuments of imperialism. For example, the Victorians erected monuments that reflected the belief that their own age was the peak of civilization, and in the 1920s and 1930s, when Mussolini was seeking to assemble his new Italian empire, he too took inspiration from Augustus's building programme.

The life of the city that flowed around this sophisticated and elegant space served only to underline Augustus's carefully crafted script. Everywhere a Roman walked as he went about his civic administrative duties in the Forum he would see images, names and incarnations of Augustus and his glorious ancestry. The Temple of Mars also had a specific state function. Augustus suggested that whenever the Senate met to decide on declarations of war and peace, they should do so in the appropriate surroundings of that temple. Although the meetings were ostensibly collegiate affairs, the senators would not be allowed to forget one simple thing: this was Augustus's temple, and the glory of the wars declared and the peaces agreed in it was Augustus's too. His name was emblazoned across the front above the columns and even the building's incarnation was rooted in his early career. The first citizen had piously vowed to build this religious precinct, so he claimed, after the battle of Philippi in 42 BC, the event that concluded the son's war of revenge against the assassins of his father, Julius Caesar.[12] From the seed of this vow had grown an oak tree of political ideology. Yes, it evoked the traditional past, the ancient virtues of the Roman republic. But it also glorified Rome's kings, a dutiful line of succession that wove together centuries of history and reached its highest point with Augustus.

Augustus's manipulation of history was perhaps matched only by his self-proclaimed restoration of Roman religion. His adoptive father Julius Caesar had reformed the Roman calendar in the last decades of the republic because it had grown completely out of step with the seasonal year. He corrected it by putting in place a calendar based on the solar year. It's almost exactly the same as the one we use today. Now Caesar's adopted son turned his attention to revitalizing the annual list of Roman religious festivals and events. Old rituals from the republic's early history were dusted down, celebrated in the city and injected with new life. Into this resuscitation of a comforting past, however, Augustus had once again stealthily inserted himself and his family. In among the ancient festivals were less 'antique' moments for Roman citizens to commemorate. Augustus's 'restoration' of the republic in 27 BC, for example, made an appearance. His first closing of the doors of the Temple of Janus was there too. Also deemed worthy of celebration were, of course, the first citizen's birthday and the significant propitious days in the lives of his family. The final touch was the renaming of the month formerly known as Sextilis: now it became August. Furtively, the new age was being mapped on to the old.

Time too became a victim of Augustus's stealth offensive. The defining symbol of this assault was not the Roman calendar but Augustus's Horologium. This massive sundial was erected in the

Campus Martius to the north of the city around 10 BC. Its marker still stands today in the Piazza Montecitorio in front of the modern Italian parliament building, but in the age of Augustus and the emperors who succeeded him it provided Roman citizens with the centrepiece of a magnificent astronomical display. A bronze line scored into the stone-paved ground marked the meridian where the sundial's marker fell at noon, and the lines pointing out from the centre were gradated with cross-lines indicating how the shadow of the sun lengthened and shortened throughout the year. The sun that rose in the empire's east and set in its west thus told the time in that empire's capital city.

Augustus, however, made this very much *his* sundial. The marker was a red granite obelisk brought from the province that was most gloriously associated with him. Egypt was famed for its wealth and was now the bread basket of the Roman empire. It was the jewel in the empire's crown, and the man who had first set it there was Augustus. But that connection was not his only fingerprint on the astronomical display. Augustus's birthday fell on the same date as the autumnal equinox (23 September), and on that day the shadow was said to fall in line with Augustus's Altar of Peace near by – another cornerstone in the ideology of the emperor. It was as if Augustus not only controlled time, but also the very movement of planets and heavenly bodies.

The height of Augustus's association with the gods and the heavens was his Games of the Ages in 17 BC. Their impact followed hot on the heels of earlier measures undertaken by him to establish his piety towards the gods and the work of healing the Roman state. In the minds of many the civil war was thought to have taken place because Romans had neglected the gods. At its conclusion, therefore, Augustus, reconnected the state with divine favour by restoring the city's temples and shrines. At the Temple of Jupiter on the Capitol Hill he went one better. In the inner chamber he deposited 'sixteen thousand pounds of gold, as well as pearls and precious stones to the value of fifty million sesterces'.[13] The year before the Games of the Ages, Augustus's medicine for the state took the form not of gifts to the gods, but of law reform.

Inventing Tradition

In 18 BC Augustus passed a series of moral and social legislation that was both harsh and conservative. This focused on putting into law penalties and incentives to promote marriage, childbirth, sexual fidelity and moral improvement in young men. The new public laws on adultery, previously a private matter, were the most notorious. A criminal court was established to deal with sexual offences, and in certain circumstances punishment could be as severe as loss of property and exile. Women rather than men were the worst off under the law. While it was still permitted for men to have adulterous sex so long as it was with a slave or a citizen with a bad reputation, such as a prostitute, respectable citizen women could not have sex with anyone outside marriage. The law even sanctioned the right of a father to kill his daughter and her lover if they were caught in his house having non-marital sex, and also empowered a husband to kill his wife's lover if that man was a known philanderer. If the law was the bitter medicine to enforce social cohesion, the year 17 BC laced it with sugar.

The Games of the Ages picked up on the theme of traditional Roman values such as chastity and piety. But once again tradition was a useful political instrument. The games supposedly harked back seven centuries to the very earliest history of Rome, and were said to be held every 110 years. It was not possible, therefore, for anyone to see them twice in their lifetime. For once, the billing for a show that no one had ever seen before and would never see again was, quite literally, true.[14] As a result of the festival's cyclical nature, its celebration promised an emotional moment of time travel back to the past. Crucially, however, when citizens witnessed the games in 17 BC there was no one alive who could say they were really authentic. The palette of Augustus was antique, but the paints which he was able to use were all new, bold and bright.

In the three days of sacrifices, gone were the offerings to the gods of the underworld that had been the focus in previous Games of the Ages. New gods were now in fashion. The goddess Diana (associated with fertility and childbirth), and Mother Earth (vegetation, regrowth and bountiful produce), as well the gods of Apollo (associated with peace and art) and Jupiter (Rome's patron god) all took centre stage. The star performer, however, was not a priest or purely religious figure as a Roman might have expected. It was the head of the Roman state himself.

On the first night Augustus sacrificed nine sheep and nine goats to the Fates. It was an atmospheric, holy and magical affair. He recited a long prayer that these goddesses might bestow their favour on the power and majesty of the Roman people, on their future good health and prosperity, on the increase of the empire and, last but not least, on himself and the house of his family. The next night saw an even more spectacular ceremony. The first citizen sacrificed a pregnant sow to Mother Earth. It was as though he was searing into the hearts and minds of the massed Roman witnesses a highly charged moment of legend. This moment was imbued with the distant past, but it was a moment from which would spring the new age of the Caesars. The creation of an orderly, cohesive society of new moral Romans did, however, come apart at the seams.

One might imagine that some among the plebs, adjusting to peace and stability, were persuaded by the festival's emotional power. So too perhaps were Augustus's favoured senators and knights, those loyal to the new regime. The association with Rome's past made their position in the administration seem more rooted than perhaps it actually was. As with any 'back to basics' political campaign, though, the very people expected to endorse it were the ones who flouted it. Most of the survivors from the old Roman aristocracy hated it. The last decades of the republic, that time of extraordinary licence and luxury, were a recent memory. The life of the witty, erudite poet Ovid is a revealing foil to that of Augustus. Ovid was a rich man of equestrian rank from Italy. For someone of his standing and intelligence, a glittering career in Augustus's inner circle beckoned. He opted instead for a very un-Augustan life, one dedicated to sex, fun and art. In due course, Ovid became a celebrity, Rome's foremost poet. One poem, however, proved his undoing. In it he advised young people on how to find a partner – at the theatre and at the games, for example. He even disclosed his tips on picking up respectable women. The poem, called *The Art of Love*, flew in the face of Augustus's moral programme, provoking the emperor to take severe action. In AD 8 Ovid was banished to a miserable backwater of the empire, the frontier post of Tomis (now Constanta) on the Black Sea. But the poet was not the only notorious person to fall foul of Augustus's stern laws.

In 2 BC, the same year that Ovid's *The Art of Love* was perhaps published, scandal surrounding Augustus's daughter Julia could no longer be suppressed. The rumours had long built up and now the dam burst. Julia had sold her body for money, went the riveting chatter; she had had sex on the very public spot in the Forum from which her father had proposed his 'moral' legislation; and one of her many lovers from the glamorous, fast set of the aristocracy was none other than the son of Augustus's old enemy, Mark Antony. The stories may have been no more than rumours seeded in a daughter's rebellion against a father who had long used her as a political pawn. Nonetheless, they put Augustus in a deeply embarrassing situation. They threatened to undo all his hard work. Cracks were appearing in his pious imperial edifice.

The reaction of the first citizen was merciless. He went to the Senate, denounced his own daughter, damned her memory by having all sculptures of her destroyed, then sent her into exile on Pandeteria, an island off the western coast of Italy near Campania. Although she was granted permission to move to a nicer part of Italy, she spent the rest of her life in exile. Eventually, her income withheld, she died of malnutrition. For committing exactly the same kinds of 'crime', Julia's daughter was also permanently banished in AD 8. Augustus's unsentimental show of consistency between his 'children' in the Roman state and his own biological children was perhaps just another performance – one designed to put his family above suspicion. This is suggested by another rumour that was doing the rounds: Augustus, the newly entitled 'Father of the Fatherland', was said to have been regularly provided with young girls and respectable married women for his pleasure. He would strip them naked and 'inspect them as if they were the wares of Torianus the slave dealer.' And the supplier of these goods? His own wife, Livia Drusilla. The stories remained, however, just gossip. The public show of rectitude had to go on.

By the time Augustus died in AD 14 his sleight of hand was completed. The Roman people and the Roman Senate had witnessed the discreet replacement of the republic with a new system of rule by one man. At every step they were persuaded, mesmerized and, if necessary, bullied into accepting that a reassuring, comforting continuity between the two eras existed. Whatever Augustus's intention may have been, be it the sinister deception of a tyrant or a genuine attempt by a statesman to return the state to a traditionally styled constitutional government, depends on one's point of view. It was probably a bit of both. What is certain is that there was no grand master plan. In establishing the new regime Augustus improvised as he went along albeit with inventiveness, genius and cold, sometimes cruel calculation. If some in the political élite were violently dragged into the new age kicking and screaming, the Roman people knew full well who looked after their interests most powerfully. When, in 19 BC, Rome was hit first by a plague and then a grain shortage, it was not only the people who took to the streets begging the saviour Augustus to come to their aid and sort out the crisis; so too did the Senate, and even those in the political élite who hated Augustus. He had, quite simply, made himself indispensable.

On his deathbed Augustus called for a mirror and gave instructions to his attendants that 'his hair should be combed and his drooping features rearranged'. Afterwards he asked the friends he had summoned whether, in the comedy of life, he had played his part well. Before then sending everyone away, he quoted the last lines of a comedy by Menander:

> Since the play has been so good, clap your hands
> And all of you dismiss us with applause.[16]

Soon after his death, Augustus was deified. His corpse was deposited in perhaps his most striking building – his own mausoleum. It was located in the Campus Martius, had been under construction for the last twenty years of his reign, and is still standing in part today. Some 40 metres (130 feet) high, the original monument was crowned with a colossal bronze statue of the first Roman emperor, his most explicit display of self-glorification. The ancient traveller and geographer Strabo considered it to be the one Roman monument most worth seeing.[17]

But it was a typically subtle piece of glorification. The design followed the humble circular shape of an ancient Etruscan burial mound, but its execution and its description as a 'mausoleum' elevated it to rival one of the Seven Wonders of the World – the tomb of the ancient Carian dynast Mausolus. It was one last flourish, one last clever artifice, one last bow. The age of emperors had begun in style. It had been created by a consummate performer. Under another performer, however, that age would reach its greatest crisis.

III

NERO

The mid-March evening at the fashionable pleasure resort of Baiae passed in gaiety and fun. One aristocratic lady had travelled by sedan chair from Antium, further north along the coast, to join a smart coterie of high-society guests. The event that brought them together was the festival of Minerva, the goddess of art and wisdom. After gazing at the beautiful, anchored ships from a waterside mansion and enjoying a lavish dinner, it was now time for the woman to return home. As the night was starlit and the sea flat, she chose to do this not by sedan chair but by boat. Despite the favourable conditions, however, that decision would prove near-fatal. For on board the garlanded ship a death trap had been devised. The deck had been carefully engineered with lead weights to cave in and crush the female guest reclining below. The woman for whom the trap was intended was Agrippina, the mother of Emperor Nero. The man who had set the trap was the emperor himself.

Agrippina suspected nothing. After all, Nero had spent the entire evening in her company in a studied spirit of reconciliation and filial love. As the emperor said his goodbyes on the shore, he spoke intimately, childishly with his mother. Lavishing attention on her, he gave her a long, lingering hug. Then Agrippina boarded the ship, went below deck and the boat set off. As soon as it was sufficiently far out at sea, however, a member of the rowing crew activated the device. To Agrippina's horror, the wood in the deck above her head splintered violently, and suddenly the roof came crashing down. But as the weighted ceiling dropped, it stopped within centimetres of her: the sides of her couch had been high enough and strong enough to protect her from the full impact of the blow. Bewildered, she slowly extricated herself and looked around. One of her companions close by had been killed instantly. While Agrippina gathered her strength below, the crew above made a second attempt on her life by capsizing the boat. Now another companion came to Agrippina's aid. Realizing what was afoot, the imperial freedwoman declared that it was she who was the emperor's mother. The crew of the ship, unable to tell the difference in the dark, duly piled in and clubbed her to death with their oars. Meanwhile, as quietly as she could, Agrippina dived into the sea and slipped away.

As she swam ashore, she realized that the whole evening had been nothing but a piece of theatre. The collapse of the boat was no accident, but rather a case of stage machinery gone drastically wrong: the sea had been calm and there were no rocks nearby that might have caused a real accident. She knew full well who had tried to kill her. But before she worked out what to do next, she bought herself time. Once she had returned home to Antium, she decided to maintain the pretence that she had been the victim of an accident at sea by sending a message to Nero. It stated that even though she knew he would no doubt be distraught over what had happened to his dear mother, she now needed to rest and must not be disturbed.

As soon as he heard the news that his mother was still alive, Nero turned to Anicetus, a fleet commander and the man who had devised the death trap. Now, Nero told him, he must be the one to finish what he had started. Accordingly, Anicetus broke into Agrippina's house with a band of soldiers and surrounded her bed. Her final words, according to the historian Tacitus, were a tragic defence of her son. She knew, she said, that it was not Nero who had sent them to kill her. Agrippina then pointed to her womb and told the soldiers, 'Strike here'. Despite the fear and bitterness that had made mother and son enemies, she perhaps wanted to ensure with her last breath that nothing would diminish Nero's hold on power. That was paramount. Her body was cremated the same night on an open couch in a makeshift funeral more fit for a pauper than a descendant of a deity, the first emperor Augustus.

Nero's final order to kill his mother may have seemed cruelly clinical. In reality, he was rattled to the core. In Roman society piety towards mothers, let alone the mother of the emperor, was an ancient, cherished and sacrosanct virtue. Nero was the fifth emperor of Rome, a member of the Julio-Claudian family, the great-great-grandson of Augustus. He was the man whom many in the imperial palace, the Senate and among the Roman people believed to be restoring the government of the empire to the glories achieved by his ancestor some fifty years earlier. In the year of his mother's death Nero was hugely popular, but if the news got out that he had committed the heinous crime of matricide, that popularity would plummet. But there was another, more complex reason why he now felt painfully vulnerable.

Nero had risen to be emperor not by destiny, but by cold, calculating design. Agrippina had been his kingmaker. It was true that the empire was, despite appearances, a hereditary monarchy: all the emperors of Rome had so far come from the one dynasty established by Augustus – the family of the Julio-Claudians. It was true too that, through Agrippina, Nero was descended from the divine Augustus. However, as the first emperor had left no clearly defined system of succession, the route to becoming the most powerful man in the ancient world was laden with murderous pitfalls. Agrippina had ensured that her son overcame them and then, to her cost, reminded him of that fact in order to control him. In so doing, she had fostered in the young emperor an insecurity, a fear that was symbolic of both the system of government he inherited and his character. It centred on his right to be emperor. That insecurity would be instrumental in the collapse of Nero's regime and the crisis into which he would plunge the Roman empire. Yes, Agrippina, the maker of that insecurity, was now gone, but so too perhaps was the one person who could assuage it.

The last years of Nero's rule created one of the most infamous revolutions in all Roman history. His downfall would fatally discredit the dynasty of emperors founded by Augustus and, to the shock of many Romans, bring it to extinction. It would take the political arrangement of government by a single emperor to the greatest crisis of its history. But that was not all. Of all the fault lines in the Augustan system of hereditary monarchy, Nero's downfall would become notorious for exposing its greatest inbuilt flaw – a flaw that, until his reign, had been brushed under the carpet. What if the man who succeeded as emperor possessed a character so insecure and self-obsessed that he was completely unsuited to governing the Roman empire? What if the one person who could do or have anything he wanted withdrew from his responsibilities into a world of fantasy? What if the most powerful man in the ancient world went mad?

HEIR OF AUGUSTUS, SON OF AGRIPPINA

During the forty long years of Augustus's reign, civil war had become a thing of the past, and the 20 million Roman citizens across the breadth of the empire had enjoyed a new period of stability. They, like he, wanted that stability to continue and for Rome and her empire to prosper long after his death. So great was his dominance of the government, and so integral was he to

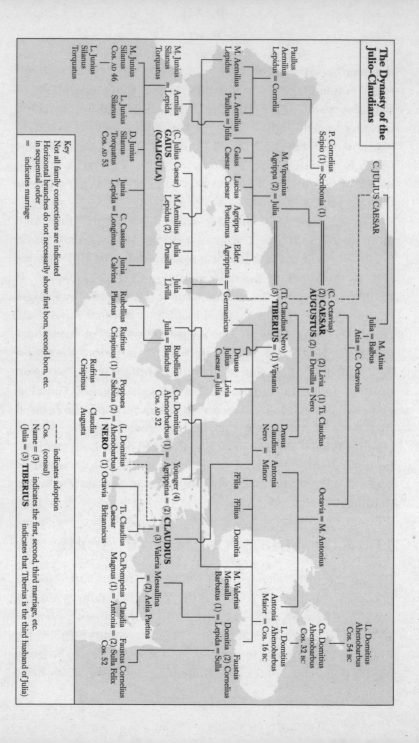

The Dynasty of the Julio-Claudians

C. JULIUS CAESAR

Key

Not all family connections are indicated
Horizontal branches do not necessarily show first born, second born, etc.
in sequential order

= indicates marriage

--- indicates adoption
Cos. (consul)
Name = (3) indicates the first, second, third marriage, etc.
(Julia = (3) TIBERIUS indicates that Tiberius is the third husband of Julia)

the image of Rome, that the people believed the Roman empire depended entirely on him and his family for its future safety and security. Augustus had carefully laid the groundwork for this throughout his reign. In the best court poetry of the day, and on the Altar of Peace, one of the great monuments to Augustus's reign, it was not just the emperor who was honoured, but his family too. The same was true of the oath of loyalty uttered by Romans around the four corners of the empire: 'I will be loyal to Caesar Augustus,' it went, 'and to his children and descendants all my life in word, in deed and in thought.'[1]

However, there was a problem: how to legitimize the succession of Augustus's power and thus maintain the new regime. As his principate was based on the appearance that the Senate and the Roman people were sovereign, and that the mandate enjoyed by the emperor was conferred on him by them, there could be no explicit acknowledgement of the hereditary principle, nor of any law of succession.[2] Indeed, the paradox of a hereditary monarchy with no defined system for succession was just the start of the difficulty. Beneath the propaganda of Augustus's regime, the root of the problem remained: the one-man rule of which Augustus was the architect was at its core more provisional and uncertain than its public image suggested. The emperor had simply innovated as his rule continued, trying one device then another. The question of succession was no different. This state of affairs engendered only uncertainty, an uncertainty that would cast a long, dark shadow over all of Augustus's heirs.

Augustus had no sons of his own. To overcome this obstacle, he chose the time-honoured Roman practice of adoption. In ancient Rome, there was no recognition of primogeniture as a basis for inheritance, so he had a number of people to choose from. During the course of his rule he adopted his nephew Marcellus and the sons of his daughter Julia, Gaius and Lucius, suggesting that the principle of succession was hereditary. But here he was struck by very bad luck. His favoured nephew and his two beloved grandsons all suffered premature deaths (see family tree, page 188). Would Augustus now adopt not from his own family but from the best of the senators? He was said to have considered this, but by AD 4 he had rejected the idea[3]. In that year he had adopted his stepson, Tiberius, and named him as his heir in his will. It was impossible to escape the impression, however, that this was a last resort.

Tiberius succeeded Augustus in AD 14, but the problem of legitimizing the hand-over of power did not go away. In fact, it only grew worse. The question of legitimate succession was again open to competing principles. What was now more important: descent from Augustus or descent from the reigning emperor? In the absence of a clear answer, there were a number of people with potential claims to succeed to the supreme position in the state. The climate of uncertainty bred rivalry, intrigue and murder.

One potential successor to Tiberius was Germanicus. He was the grand-nephew of Augustus, the husband of Augustus's granddaughter Agrippina, and the adopted son of Tiberius. His claim to succession competed with that of Tiberius's natural son, Drusus. In AD 19 Germanicus, a general and a hero of the wars in Germany, died not on the battlefield but ignominiously, by poison. Many suspected Tiberius. This left the path open to Drusus, but he too was murdered by poison in AD 23. His assassin was another man making a bid for power: Sejanus, the low-born commander of the Praetorian Guard. His claim depended on his affair with Tiberius's daughter Livilla, whom he hoped to marry and thus enter the dynastic struggle. The emperor refused the marriage of his daughter to a man with the rank of mere knight, so Sejanus's claim foundered too.

By the time Tiberius died in AD 37, having ruled for twenty

years, he still had not made up his mind about a successor. As a result, the decision of who would now rule the Roman empire was eventually made not by an emperor, but by the officers of the Praetorian Guard. It was in their interests that the system of dynastic succession should continue, so now they played their part. The man they chose as the third emperor of Rome met at least one of the criteria for succession: he was the great-grandson of Augustus and the son of Germanicus. His name was Caligula.

It was during Caligula's reign that the sheer scale of the problem posed by dynastic succession came to light. Throughout Roman history it was the custom of ancient aristocratic families to intermarry. This was how the old families of the republic held on to power, political position and wealth. In the period of the early empire, however, this habit had a new and potentially dangerous consequence. The longer the Julio-Claudian dynasty continued, the greater the number of people who could claim some descent from Augustus. So when, following an illness, the new emperor grew unhinged and tyrannical, there was an ever-increasing pool of rival aristocrats with legitimate claims to the principate who were ready to pounce.

In AD 41 Caligula was assassinated and his wife and daughter murdered. Once again, the Praetorian Guard stepped in to secure a smooth succession, and once again they stuck to the formula for hereditary monarchy, despite its flaws. With the backing of the Roman army they appointed as emperor Caligula's uncle and nearest surviving male relative, Claudius. Rome's fourth emperor ruled for thirteen years and brought stability after the short and turbulent rule of Caligula. However, the problem of competitors and rivals within the Julio-Claudian circles of the aristocracy did not disappear. The new emperor's protected existence before his accession was in part to blame. Claudius had grown up not amid the cut and thrust of public life, but in the imperial palace, surrounded by a coterie of compliant freedmen and slaves. This made his fear of rivals all the greater. It was said that he was responsible for the deaths of thirty-five senators and more than two hundred knights during his time as emperor.[4] But his fear of rivals actually stemmed from another source: direct descent from Augustus was still viewed as the golden seal on an emperor's position. Other aristocrats could boast such a family connection, but not Claudius. Now that was about to change.

When a conspiracy involving Claudius's third wife was uncovered, she and her lover were executed for treason and Claudius became a widower in search of a new wife. The woman who presented the strongest, most persuasive case was Julia Agrippina. She was Claudius's beautiful young niece and, more importantly, the great-granddaughter of Augustus. By this one union, Augustus's dream of an imperial royal family at the heart of Roman government and the empire would once again be alive and well. But that union would also prove crucial for another reason. Agrippina would bring to the marriage a son from her first husband – an eleven-year-old boy called Lucius Domitius Ahenobarbus, the future emperor Nero.

In AD 50 Claudius adopted the young boy as his own son. Lucius Domitius Ahenobarbus now became Tiberius Claudius Nero Caesar. The boy could claim descent from both the reigning emperor and Augustus. It was a claim that had the potential to outshine that of Claudius's own son, Britannicus, and that of all other rivals. It could even be enough to make Nero Rome's fifth emperor. However, given the absence of any defined succession criteria, Agrippina knew the many slips between cup and lip. To make her son's rise to power a certainty, she needed single-minded ruthlessness. It was one quality she appeared to have in spades.

Her first victim was the aristocrat and senator Lucius Junius

Silanus. He was young, popular and successful in public life. Agrippina, however, viewed him simply as a rival to Nero. Silanus posed a significant threat to the future of her son because he too was a descendant of Augustus. Worse, he was already engaged to Claudius's daughter Octavia. Agrippina was quick off the mark. She ensured that a rumour was let loose that accused Silanus of committing incest with his notoriously promiscuous sister Junia Calvina. Although the rumour was utterly untrue, Silanus's name was struck from the roll-call of senators, and his career ended abruptly in disgrace. Claudius cancelled the engagement to his daughter and Silanus committed suicide – on Agrippina's wedding day. The point was not lost on many people.

Next Agrippina tackled the problem of Nero's other serious rival, Claudius's son from his previous marriage, Britannicus. All that was required to destroy his prospects was to establish Nero's prominence in public life before Britannicus's. Nero was three years older than his stepbrother, and the small matter of this age difference allowed Agrippina to make rapid progress. Between AD 50 and 53 the young Nero first slipped into the dead Silanus's shoes and married Claudius's daughter Octavia. He was then given a raft of honours that reflected his swift ascendancy. In March AD 51, at the age of thirteen, Nero assumed the toga of manhood a year before it was due, and in the same year he marked his debut in public life when he made a speech in the Senate thanking Claudius for these honours. This was followed by statesman-like addresses in both Latin and Greek on behalf of petitioners from Rome's provinces. The speeches showed the boy's precocious intelligence and philhellenism. When, in AD 53, he appeared at games given in his honour wearing a triumphal toga alongside Britannicus, who was still wearing the toga of a boy, Nero's supremacy over his younger stepbrother was plain for all to see.

There now remained only one task to seal her son's future as the next ruler of the Roman empire: the murder of the present emperor. In AD 54 Claudius was sixty-four years old. Perhaps as a result of cerebral palsy in childhood, he had always suffered from a limp, constant trembling and a speech impediment. Now he was a doddering old man. But Agrippina could not wait for his death to come naturally. Time was against her. Britannicus was about to reach his fourteenth birthday and was eligible to receive the toga of manhood from his father. The natural son of the emperor might still eclipse Nero, so Agrippina seized the initiative. At dinner one evening, so the story goes, some mushrooms were sprinkled with a lethal substance. Claudius ate them under Agrippina's watchful eye, but the poison resulted in nothing more than a coughing fit. At this point, her doctor stepped in. Ostensibly helping Claudius to vomit, he inserted a poisoned feather down the emperor's throat and thus completed the job.

On the morning of 13 October AD 54 the palace was buzzing with tense, surreptitious activity. Only Agrippina and her closest confidants, of course, knew that Claudius was dead. While her son was being dressed and readied for the formal accession, Agrippina spent her time deviously detaining Claudius's children, Britannicus and Octavia, who were waiting to hear about the state of their father's health. She pretended to seek solace in them during this anxious time; Britannicus, she said, touching his cheek, was the very image of his father. The Praetorian Guard too she kept at bay, fobbing them off with regular messages about the deteriorating health of the emperor. The truth was that she was desperately buying time, 'waiting for the propitious moment forecast by astrologers' to make the announcement of the succession.[5] Agrippina had been plotting towards this moment all her adult life. Nothing, not even a poor omen, was going to ruin it now.

At midday the doors of the imperial palace were flung open. The emperor was dead, and now before the expectant Praetorian Guard stood not Claudius's son Britannicus, but Tiberius Claudius Nero Caesar. Although the sight of the boy took some of the soldiers by surprise, the arranged ceremonies of that day allowed no time for hesitation or doubt. The company of soldiers cheered Nero and speedily put him in a litter to be taken to their camp in the Servilian Gardens in the southeast part of Rome. Here Nero addressed the soldiers and, after promising them the usual gifts of money, the seventeen-year old boy was hailed emperor. With the passing of a decree in the Senate House on the same day, the senators followed suit. No one would ever know whom Claudius himself had intended to succeed him because his will was immediately suppressed.

Agrippina had achieved her greatest ambition. Her son was the most powerful man in the Roman world. At that moment, however, she could not have imagined that the tools she had used to secure power for him were now about to be turned on her. For not long after the young Nero's rule began, a bitter power struggle developed between mother and son. Publicly Agrippina was given honour after honour. She was allowed a private bodyguard; she was made priestess of the cult of the deified Claudius; she was permitted an indirect hand in government by sitting secretly behind a sheet at council meetings held in the palace. Coins from the first years of Nero's reign even bear heads of both the emperor and Agrippina. However, behind the polite courtly gloss of this mother–son relationship, the adolescent Nero began to lose patience with his influential, controlling kingmaker. His habitual obedience to her, he realized, was fast becoming a burden.

His mother was hard to please. She disapproved of Nero's interest in horse racing, athletics, music and theatre. By the second year of his rule, they had clashed over his girlfriend, a former slave called Acte. Motivated perhaps by jealousy, possessiveness and fear of a rival to her son's affections, Agrippina scolded him for having a love affair with such a vulgar, low-born woman. Nero responded, as a teenager would, by intensifying his relationship with Acte and coming close to making her his lawful wife.[6] His next action, however, was tantamount to declaring all-out war. When Nero was still a boy Agrippina had scrupulously filled the imperial household with staff loyal to her. Now Nero attacked that power base by removing one of his mother's key allies – Antonius Pallas – a freedman in charge of financial matters. Agrippina retaliated, fighting fire with fire. She knew how to win power in the palace. More than that, however, she knew how to hit the new emperor of Rome where it hurt.

One day Agrippina, in a display of anger, went around the palace, flinging her arms about and shouting out loud that she favoured not Nero, but his stepbrother Britannicus. The divine Claudius's son was now grown up, she said, and was 'the true and worthy heir of his father's supreme position'.[7] The cold blade of that remark opened a wound – namely, Nero's insecurity over his claim to be emperor. The reaction Agrippina provoked in her son, however, may well have taken even her by surprise. At dinner one evening a drink was brought to Britannicus, who sat at a junior table with the children of other noblemen. Any poison in it would have been detected by the imperial tasters, so the drink was harmless, but it was deliberately made too hot, and the young boy refused it. Cold water, secretly spiked with poison, was added at the table. Thus cooled, the drink was handed back to Britannicus. Before the eyes of both Agrippina and his own sister the fourteen-year-old boy was soon convulsing uncontrollably. The person who had ordered the murder was widely believed to be Nero.

Reacting with a studied lack of worry, Nero casually claimed that Britannicus was simply having one of his epileptic fits; it was nothing out of the ordinary. The other diners saw through this excuse, but did nothing. There was nothing they could do. Containing their horror beneath glazed, outwardly normal expressions, they were paralysed: to have protested or denied it was a fit would have been to suggest murder. But equally, to have conspicuously agreed that it must have been an epileptic fit would also have been to suggest a crime because it would have been so patently a lie. While everyone hesitated, the teenage boy died. 'Octavia, young though she was, had learnt to hide sorrow, affection, every feeling... After a short silence, the banquet continued.'[8]

The aptitude for the crimes required to hold on to imperial power had now passed from mother to son. Nonetheless, Agrippina, the determined and seasoned intriguer, did not give up the covert war against Nero for control of the palace. On the contrary, the death of Britannicus now prompted her to lend her support to Octavia; perhaps she could become a political figurehead around whom aristocrats with rival claims to be emperor would rally. A rumour circulated that Agrippina was also promoting the cause of the aristocrat Rubellius Plautus; he was in a position to claim descent from Augustus because his mother was Tiberius's granddaughter, and Tiberius was the adopted son of Augustus. In response, Nero had Agrippina expelled from the palace and her bodyguard removed. However, it was not long before he devised a more permanent solution to the problem of his mother.

The final straw stemmed from Nero's love life. He did not feel anything for his wife, Octavia. He wanted passionately to marry his mistress, Poppaea Sabina, the wife of his close friend Marcus Salvius Otho, and the woman who would become the great love of Nero's life. Nero knew that his mother would never allow him to divorce Claudius's daughter and marry his mistress. Poppaea knew it too. In private she 'nagged and mocked him incessantly.

He was under his guardian's thumb, she said, master neither of the empire nor of himself.'[9] Poppaea's skill in needling Nero was reinforced 'by tears and all the tricks of a lover'. Thus provoked, in the spring of AD 59 Nero summoned Anicetus and sent his mother the fatal invitation to join him for the festival of Minerva at Baiae.

With Agrippina dead, Nero felt released, free at last. The domineering influence in his life had been eliminated, and he could now rule and behave as he pleased. Indeed, there was much to celebrate. Despite the strife within the imperial palace, the first years of his rule had been far from disastrous. In fact, according to all the ancient sources, the empire thrived during Nero's early years as emperor. Contemporary poets hailed them as a new golden age. Nero rivalled even Augustus for sheer popularity. The people loved him for the games he held, and the Senate for the respect he showed them. Abroad too there were successes to count: Rome was strengthening her eastern frontier in a successful campaign with Parthia. The empire was flourishing.

Given Nero's youth and inexperience at governing during those first few years, how had this happened? Perhaps the empire, administered by senators and knights, ran itself? Perhaps it did not even need an active, industrious emperor, but simply a celebrity figurehead? Another answer to the question of who, if anyone, was really in charge of the empire can be traced to the two men who, according to Tacitus, had taken control of government in the first years of Nero's rule. Their names were Lucius Annaeus Seneca and Sextus Afranius Burrus, and they had been the fledgling emperor's two closest advisers. While the adolescent Nero was growing up, he had sought refuge with them. They protected him from his mother and indulged his interests. In exchange, he listened to their advice. However, these two men were much more than allies with good advice to offer. They were astute politicians on whom the emperor depended entirely for his popularity, for his new golden age.

Now all that was about to change. While Agrippina lived, she had taken the heat off Seneca and Burrus. With her gone, they stood exposed. Now it was they, not she, who were the spoilers of Nero's fun. With Nero having slipped his mother's leash, however, they were about to realize that there was nothing they could do to control him. The Roman empire was about to discover what kind of man its emperor really was.

NERO'S NEW FRIENDS

AD 62, the eighth year of Nero's rule. According to the historian Tacitus, 'the forces of good were in decline'. Those forces were the voices of Seneca and Burrus. To date, their control over the emperor had been clever and highly successful. Burrus was a knight, born in Gaul, who had risen to become the head of the Praetorian Guard. Severe in character and disfigured in one hand, he acted as a moral barometer for Nero. Agrippina had once been Burrus's sponsor, and out of loyalty to her he had vehemently opposed Nero in his murder plans, refusing to have any part in her death. Nonetheless, once the murder had been committed, he dutifully ensured that the Praetorian Guards stayed loyal to the emperor. This support was critical to the success of Nero's regime. But it was his tutor who was perhaps an even more pivotal figure.

Seneca was a senator from an Italian family of Córdoba in Spain. He was also one of the greatest philosophers in Roman history. Urbane, charming and fatherly, he used his intelligence to guide and educate his adolescent charge. In so doing, he became one of the most influential voices in the Roman empire. The importance of Seneca to Nero can be seen in the variety of roles he played. He composed Nero's inaugural speech to the Senate and people. It was rapturously received. For the festival of Saturnalia in AD 54, he entertained the emperor by composing a satire lambasting the regime of the buffoon Claudius. Playing on the word 'deification', it was called *The Pumpkinification of Claudius*, and it had the court in stitches. As *amicus* (friend) of the emperor, Seneca also sat on the imperial council, which met in the palace with the leading senators. As a result, those senators heartily approved of Nero's wise decisions.

Perhaps Seneca's greatest role, however, was damage limitation; he knew how to clear up Nero's mess. His greatest coup was to manage the senators' reaction to the murder of Agrippina. His deft handling of the situation meant that they duly bought the official version of events: Agrippina had been plotting the murder of Nero, the plot had been detected, and Agrippina had paid the price. The emperor was now safe. His public relations exercise was so effective that, far from expressing horror at the matricide, Rome gave thanks to the gods. The state, after all, had been saved. Seneca, one might have supposed, was indispensable to the emperor. But there was one task he set himself that would ultimately prove his undoing. The key lesson he set for his young charge was how to be a good emperor. It would become his life's greatest project and his life's greatest failure.

We know what Seneca taught Nero because his great work of political philosophy, *On Clemency*, has survived. The lesson began with a simple statement of fact. The position Nero held, Seneca would have told the young emperor, was one of supreme power. He was the 'arbiter of life and death for the nations'; in his power rested 'what each person's lot and state shall be'; by his lips Fortune proclaimed 'what gifts she would bestow on each human being'.[10] The key to being a good emperor, however, was not just to acknowledge that power, but to exercise it with restraint. If he could show clemency, he would become a good emperor, like Augustus; if not, he would be nothing more than a despised tyrant. In fact, Nero would do well to emulate Augustus in following this argument to its conclusion: above all, instructed Seneca, the emperor must disguise his absolute power.

Nero at first had been an obedient student. He had revived the traditional partnership with the senators: they and not the cronies of the imperial palace were, after all, the true pillars of justice, political wisdom and administrative experience. Together, Nero and the Senate ruled Rome as if they were equals. The idea that Seneca had sown in the young man was that of *civilitas*: the affability and accessibility of the emperor 'that helps to conceal the fact of autocratic power'.[11] Nero had at first played his role well, giving the impression that he was just another senator, another ordinary citizen. And yet, despite Nero's promising start, by AD 62 he was forgetting his lines. By character he was just not cut out to be a politician. Maintaining the pretence, the theatrical illusion, that he cared what the senators really thought was fast becoming yet another burden. The truth was that, despite Seneca's best efforts, Nero's passions lay elsewhere.

One of these passions was for a good night out. It would amuse the young emperor and his dissolute playmates from the palace to put on a disguise, such as a freedman's cap or a wig, and rampage around the streets of the city, drinking, carousing and getting into fights. 'For he was in the habit of setting upon people returning home from dinner and would hurt anyone who fought back, throwing them into the drains.'[12] Another of Nero's passions from a young age was for horses. With great enthusiasm, he would follow the chariot races and their different teams. He supported the Greens over the Reds, the Whites or the Blues, much as fans follow football teams today. To attend the races and gratify his passion, he slipped out of the palace in secret, so it was said. However, his greatest love was reserved for the Greek arts: for music, poetry, singing and playing the lyre.

Nero was not only very knowledgeable about these subjects, but pursued his own practice and study of them with determination. As soon as he had become emperor, he hired as his tutor the most famous and skilled lyre-player of the day, a man called Terpnus. He even undertook the voice-strengthening exercises of professional singers: '...he would lie on his back, holding a lead tablet and cleanse his system with a syringe and with vomiting.' Diet too was important for improving the quality of one's singing. Apples were to be avoided as they were deemed harmful to the vocal cords, but dried figs were beneficial; and every month for a few days the emperor lived on just chives preserved in oil.[13] Nero's pursuit of these Greek interests worried Seneca and Burrus. It was not the pursuits themselves that were the problem; it was rather that Nero was dangerously close to achieving the standard of a professional performer. In the conservative circles of Roman high society of the day that just would not do.

At that time, when Rome had been the great cultural exchange centre, the exciting cosmopolis of the entire Mediterranean world for nearly two hundred years, and Greece had long been reduced to a Roman province, many Romans in the élite still laboured under an illusion. They were at heart, ran their self-serving myth, a people of tough, sturdy, self-reliant peasant-soldiers who, through grit, determination, fortitude and discipline, had forged their brilliant empire. Roman character and virtue, above all, were revealed in achievements on the battlefield and in public life. Yes, the Greek arts were good for education, perhaps even for relaxation too, but devotion to them would lead only to a breakdown in the moral fibre of Rome, turning a nation of soldiers into one of cowards, gymnasts and homosexuals. Toning up one's oiled muscles for athletics, prancing around in a theatrical costume or singing poetic compositions to the accompaniment of a lyre had not prevented the fall of Greece. In fact, such pursuits probably caused it.[14] The conservatives need only look around the streets of the city to make their point: professional actors were nothing but slaves and common prostitutes.

The chic taste-makers of the fashionable set disagreed. Music, theatre, singing and performing in the Greek style were exquisite, the height of sophistication, the pinnacle of civilization. In ancient Greece aristocrats and citizens had competed to win honours and social status through artistic contests; those contests had been glorified in the works of Homer and Pindar, the founders of epic and lyric literature. So why not in Rome too? To their absolute delight, the hip crowd now at last had a patron. As chance would have it, he was none other than the emperor himself – and he was prepared to lead from the front. In AD 59 Nero celebrated a set of games called the Juvenalia, held to mark the first shaving of his beard and his transition to manhood. They were private games for the government élite, so when the emperor chose to play his lyre on stage, his advisers had been able to pretend it was acceptable. Burrus, who was forced to lead a battalion of the Praetorian Guard on to the stage, grieved as he applauded. The next year, however, Nero really pushed the boundaries of what was proper for the emperor of Rome. He was determined to take his passions to the people.

He first set up a training school for the Greek arts, then asked the sons of the aristocracy to attend it, and later encouraged its graduates to perform in public in a brand new festival of his very own creation. All of Rome was invited. For these games, aristocrats joined professional Greek performers on stage in ballet, athletics and musical contests. To the conservatives of the élite it was a national scandal. The sons of ancient, great, virtuous families, 'the Furii, the Horatii, the Fabii, the Porcii, the Valerii', were being forced to dishonour themselves![15] Nero's view of his novelty games, however, was quite different. He was seeking to lay the foundations of a new age, beginning at year zero. He was civilizing Rome, re-educating the public, weaning them off barbaric gladiatorial games and reorientating the grand sweep of Roman history away from war, conquest and empire towards the more refined ideals of Art. He named the games the Neronia, and decreed that they were to be held every five years. This was how he wanted to lead his people! This was how he wanted to be a good emperor!

The public loved the games. If Seneca and Burrus despaired, they could at least console themselves that, despite the rapturous reception, the emperor had restrained himself from performing before the Roman people – at least for now. By AD 62 Nero showed no sign of outgrowing his Greek habits, his new vision for Rome. This was the year in which he opened his grand Hellenistic gymnasium complex and extravagantly handed out free oil to senators and knights so that they might set an example to ordinary people to take up the very un-Roman, unmanly activities of wrestling and athletics. Seneca and Burrus were fighting a losing battle. The previously harmonious relationship between Nero and his advisers was at breaking point. Two events made it snap.

When a senator by the name of Antistius Sosianus wrote some verses satirizing the emperor and read them out at a high-society dinner party, he was tried for treason and found guilty. Although he narrowly avoided execution, his case spelt the return of the treason law that had so discredited the regimes of Caligula and Claudius. Under its vague terms, an individual could be charged with any form of 'conspiracy' against the emperor. To Seneca the law was a clear indication that his life's project – to make Nero behave and act like a good emperor –

was failing. The real impasse, however, for Burrus and Seneca came soon afterwards. Nero told them that he had decided, at last, to divorce Octavia, the daughter of the divine Claudius, and marry Poppaea. Seneca and Burrus were against it: Nero might well be descended from Augustus, but to divorce Octavia was to sever his principal tie with the deified Claudius, a cornerstone in his claim to be emperor. When Nero argued, stamped his feet and insisted, Burrus retorted succinctly, referring to the throne: 'Well, then, give her back her dowry!'[16] With that, the rupture was final.

Events now moved quickly. Burrus soon fell ill with a tumour and died. The rumour went around that Nero had speeded his death by instructing someone to poison him. What is certain is that the emperor wasted no time in replacing the critically important head of the Praetorian Guard. Nero realized that to make the divorce a reality, he did not need nay-sayers, nuisances and pests with 'right' on their side, people spoiling his fun and burdening his life with responsibility. He needed new friends. To this end he held a nervous meeting of the council of leading senators and palace advisers. Who on earth, they asked themselves, would Nero choose for the recently vacated post? The emperor was quick to reassure them. His first appointment was a person of integrity and experience – a man named Faenius Rufus. He was popular with the Praetorian officers and had a good track record in efficiently managing Rome's corn supply without profiteering from it. The council breathed a collective sigh of relief. However, they were soon to be disappointed by the next appointment. Also taking his place as joint commander of the Praetorian Guard, declared Nero, was the emperor's good friend Ofonius Tigellinus.

Tigellinus's track record was, to say the least, a little unorthodox. While it was true that he had been prefect of the watch (the head of the fire service in Rome), his reputation rested on totally different credentials. He and the emperor had met during Nero's childhood on the estate in Calabria belonging to Nero's aunt. They took to each other instantly, perhaps because they shared a common interest in racing and breeding horses. More than this, however, Nero was fascinated by Tigellinus's character, by his capacity for evil. He was good-looking, some fifteen years older than Nero, and, although from a poor Sicilian background, had friends in high places. He had insinuated himself into the houses of two aristocrats, where he had earned a reputation for depravity. It was said that he seduced first the men, then their wives, and in this way he rose into the echelons of Roman high society. Now, in the imperial household's rounds of orgies, revelries and drinking parties, Tigellinus was Nero's most debauched partner, his trusted playmate, his devilish, amoral master of ceremonies.

The appointment spelt trouble for another reason. With it, a key principle in Seneca's vision of what made a good emperor was sacrificed. To help him successfully administer the Roman empire, the first emperor, Augustus, had at least given the impression that he relied on independent-minded people from the upper orders. The aristocratic Seneca had maintained that tradition under Nero. He was able to be honest towards the emperor because he had nothing to fear from speaking his mind. His wealth and position in Roman society were not dictated by his status in the eyes of the emperor. The appointment of Tigellinus, however, was the clearest indication that Nero was now surrounding himself with servile cronies. Tigellinus was from an ordinary family and owed his place entirely to the emperor. The fear grew in Seneca that far from standing up to Nero, Tigellinus would slavishly tell him whatever he wanted to hear. He would certainly not advise him on what was right. But Tigellinus was not Seneca's only fear. His greatest worry was for his own life.

The ascendant Tigellinus set to work. He knew how to play to Nero's insecurities. He tormented him by saying that Seneca's wealth and property stood as an insult to the pre-eminence of the emperor of Rome because it rivalled the imperial estate. Nero was duly piqued by envy. Time was running out for Seneca, but he was paralysed – caught in a distinctly unpleasant dilemma: he could either continue advising the emperor but risk offending him, or else compromise and go along with Nero's whims and fancies. Neither course of action made an appetizing prospect. Eventually, he struck on a solution: he would graciously ask the emperor leave to retire. Seneca found Nero in the imperial palace. In his polished, charming way, he began by citing the example of the divine Augustus. The first emperor, he said, had allowed even his closest advisers leave to retire. Perhaps the emperor might consider granting him the same reward?

Nero politely refused. 'My reign is only just beginning,' he said. 'If youth's slippery paths lead me astray, be at hand to call me back. You equipped my adulthood; devote even greater care to guiding it!'[17] Seneca thanked the emperor and left. His charm offensive had failed. Nonetheless, he found ways to stay out of the line of fire. Under the pretence of ill health and philosophic study, Seneca spent more and more time on his estates in the countryside. He might well have lost his privileged position of adviser, but he was still in possession of his life – for the time being. Now Seneca's distance from the palace gave Nero time to turn his mind to a third new appointment. This one would be a little trickier than replacing the head of the Praetorian Guard. Now he wanted to promote Poppaea from mistress to imperial wife.

Poppaea was six years older than Nero, a beauty from a wealthy, if not entirely aristocratic, background. While her mother was noble, her father was a knight who had suffered disgrace during the rule of Tiberius. Reflecting her ambitious nature, Poppaea ditched her father's name in favour of her maternal grandfather's, and set about taking Roman high society by storm. She married two aristocrats in succession and had a child from the first marriage. Her love of extravagance and luxury made her the talk of the town. Her lavishly appointed family house near Pompeii, the Villa Oplontis, has been discovered and testifies to that reputation; she had the hoofs of the mules that pulled her litter shod in gold, and she bathed daily in the milk of 500 asses to preserve the beauty of her skin, so the rumours went.[18] Nero was madly in love with her. Now, without the voice of his dear friend Seneca to advise him, without the conscience of loyal Burrus at his side, Nero took his next gamble alone.

The emperor knew full well that if he divorced Octavia he ran the risk of exposing himself to rivals. Other members of the Julio-Claudian clan among the aristocracy were, like Nero, descended from Augustus, and could therefore legitimately claim descent from the royal and divine bloodlines. As a result, Nero took no chances. There were two potential claimants whom Tigellinus, seeking to cement his position, warned him about. Rubellius Plautus was the great-great-grandson of Augustus via the emperor Tiberius; Faustus Cornelius Sulla Felix was the great-grandson of Augustus's sister. If Nero was without the connection by marriage to Claudius, argued Tigellinus feeding his friend's paranoia, it meant that either man could challenge him.

Nero was won over. Assassins were immediately dispatched to Asia and Gaul. When they returned to Rome, they carried with them the heads of their victims, Plautus and Sulla. Their crime, according to the emperor, was by now a familiar one: treason. But how on earth would the Senate react to the terrible news that two of the best, most virtuous men from their number were suddenly dead? Not with great integrity, was the short answer. With Seneca gone, the senators knew that any meaningful partnership between Senate and emperor was now as good as dead. So, driven by fear of offending the emperor, they toed the line. In honour of what was put about as Nero's narrow escape from death, they decreed that thanks be offered to the gods. With his two most prominent rivals dead, Nero now focused on his divorce. All he needed was a pretext.

The imperial rumour machine went into overdrive. Its target? Octavia. A charge was concocted of adultery with a flute-player from Alexandria. To lend the accusation credence, Tigellinus tortured Octavia's maids to produce testimony. One of them defied her torturer: 'The mouth of Tigellinus,' she shouted, 'was filthier than every part of Octavia.'[19] Soon Nero's wife was banished to Campania under military surveillance. In Rome there was uproar. Nero had underestimated the affection in which the daughter of the deified Claudius was held. Protests quickly turned into riots. Nero panicked. More than the respect of the Senate, he craved the love of the people. He did not want to lose it, so he made a shocking announcement, cancelling his divorce from Octavia. The people's response was equally wild. They gave thanks on the Capitol, smashed the statues of Poppaea, and, in their exuberance, even invaded the imperial palace. But their joy was to be short-lived. Nero changed his mind again: Poppaea would be his wife after all. One might imagine that Poppaea was relieved and delighted. Far from it. Even though Octavia had been divorced and exiled, she still presented a problem.

Now it was the turn of Poppaea to press Nero's buttons, to feed his old fear. Octavia, she reminded him, was blue-blooded, popular and the daughter of an emperor. Even in exile, nagged Poppaea, she could become a figurehead for a rebellion and challenge Nero. The emperor agreed. He needed someone to fix the problem. There was one man he could rely on. He summoned Anicetus, the murderer of his mother, to the palace. The offer of a safe, comfortable retirement was on the table, said Nero, but on one condition: Anicetus must confess to adultery with Octavia. With the blood of Agrippina still on his hands, Anicetus had no choice but to agree. All the pieces of the murder plan were at last in place.

Nero called a meeting of senators and advisers at which he made an announcement: Octavia, he declared, had planned a coup, and to effect it had tried to seduce the fleet commander. As the words fell from Nero's lips, a virtuous girl of twenty, exiled on an island thousands of kilometres from Rome, was restrained by Roman soldiers and her veins were cut open. She who had witnessed her father and brother murdered before her eyes, now faced her own death. But it was too slow in coming. When the Praetorian Guards ran out of patience, they suffocated her in a steam room. Her head was cut off and taken to Rome just so that Poppaea could see it.

Nero was drawing ever closer to a precipice. He was on the verge of exposing what lay beneath the carefully constructed veneer of the emperor's supreme position. The appearance, devised by Augustus, that the emperor was subordinate to the institutions of the state was now wearing decidedly thin. Nero was, in reality, above the law; he was answerable to no one, and had always known that. What was changing was that he seemed to care less and less about hiding it. This was a highly precarious position – one liable to raise an army of enemies like ghosts from Hades. Nonetheless, fortune was smiling on Nero. Chance would soon throw the young ruler one final opportunity to prove he could yet be a good emperor – that he could live up to the name of Augustus.

CRISIS

With his two new key advisers, Tigellinus and Poppaea, secured in their positions of influence, the good times rolled. In the lake of Marcus Agrippa the height of Roman engineering was put to the uses of pleasure in the most spectacular way. First, the lake was drained so that Nero might put on an entertaining public exhibition of wild beast hunting. Then it was filled once more with water and a stunning sea battle was enacted. Drained again, it became an arena for gladiators to do combat, but even this was not the last piece of theatre to be stage-managed there.[20] Nero now appointed Tigellinus to direct the most notorious banquet of the age.

The lake was once more filled with water and a vast platform floating on great wooden casks was created in its centre. Round about it taverns and secret places for trysts and assignations were constructed. In the middle Nero, Poppaea and Tigellinus played host to senators, knights and the general public in the most exquisite fashion. Birds and animals in myriad colours and from all corners of the empire populated the temporary island. For further amusement, role-playing was, appropriately, the tenor of the entertainment: high-born women behaved like prostitutes, and no man, be he an aristocrat or a lowly ex-convict gladiator, was to be refused his pleasure. At the party were all Nero's aristocratic friends and senators, who were used to enjoying and indulging themselves on such occasions. However, Nero and his court were about to be given a sharp wake-up call from their decadent pleasures.

The fire began in a small shop on 19 July AD 64 in the area of the Circus Maximus. It would quickly swell to become the greatest conflagration that ancient Rome would ever know. As it gathered momentum, it rampaged through the narrow streets, tenement blocks, porticoes and alleyways in the heart of Rome between the Palatine and Capitoline hills. The fire continued for six days and then, just when it was believed to have died out, it reignited and continued for three more days. By the time it had finished, only four of Rome's fourteen districts would still be intact; three were completely destroyed, and the others largely devastated but for the charred shells of a few buildings. Many people died and thousands of homes were destroyed, from the tenements of low-born plebs to the grand town houses of landed senators. Rome also lost some of her ancient history: the temples and ancient cult sites associated with the city's forefathers – Romulus, Numa and Evander.

Nero was in Antium, 50 kilometres (30 miles) from Rome, where he could now see the fire due to the raging intensity of the flames. He may have paused to play the lyre while the city burnt, but he also responded effectively and with urgency. He ordered immediate relief to be provided for those fleeing the fire. To the homeless he opened up the Field of Mars, including Agrippa's public buildings as well as the private gardens of his own palace. The Praetorian Guard, under the leadership of Rufus, was ordered to construct temporary accommodation to house those who had lost everything in the fire. Tigellinus too, who had been the head of Rome's fire brigade, swung into action on Nero's orders, responding effectively to the crisis. However, it was only once the Senate had had the opportunity of assessing the extent of the damage to Rome that Nero's best leadership was revealed.

After surveying the ruins, taking advice from senators and advisers, and agreeing to pay personally for the clearance of debris, Nero stated his desire to make sure that such a tragedy never happened in Rome again. He proposed building regulations that included restricting the height of houses and tenements, and specifying permissible types of timber construction. By law streets were to be a certain width and carefully laid out according to plan. New buildings would have to feature an internal courtyard to ensure that there were breathing spaces between them. They would be in sharp contrast to the rickety tenements that had so recently and tragically collapsed. Porticoes and colonnades along streets and at the front of houses were to be added. The emperor ensured that he paid for these personally. In the event of another fire, Romans must at all costs be protected from falling debris. But such steps were just the beginning. As he formulated all these measures, Nero realized that this terrible tragedy actually presented Rome with an opportunity. To the assembled senators the emperor proposed not simply to rebuild Rome, but to make it more impressive than it was before – even greater than the city built by the first emperor, Augustus. This was going to be a city fit for the new age of Nero.

The emperor's visionary leadership in the face of Rome's greatest challenge was met with jubilant, rapturous applause. Nero made good his promises too: there were generous incentives for private investors to complete their building projects, and, as coins of AD 64 describe, Nero ensured the swift restoration of the Temple of Vesta, the Market for Provisions and the popular Circus Maximus. But the applauding senators would soon discover that Nero's new public plans for Rome included a more personal, private building project: a new palace for the emperor. This was an architectural project that would come to symbolize both the inspiration and tyranny of Nero's reign.

Nero had already built an elegant mansion for himself on the Palatine Hill, where Augustus had his residence, and which was thereafter associated with imperial homes. Nero's mansion now became merely an entrance, an elaborate vestibule leading to the vast complex of his proposed new residence. The Golden House consisted of several lavish villas and buildings centred on a lake. The magnificent landscaped gardens featured not just lawns but 'ploughed fields, vineyards, pastures and woodlands, and a multitude of all sorts of domestic and wild animals'. This was a kind of fashionable high artifice formed from nature, a style of 'faked rusticity' affording exquisite views.[21] There were numerous fanciful and playful flights of folly too: grottoes, colonnades, pavilions and arcades. The complex filled the valley between the Palatine, Esquiline and Caelian hills, and is estimated to have covered somewhere between 50 and 120 hectares (125 and 300 acres).

The centrepiece was Nero's main palace – two grand wings of intricately designed rooms built over two storeys and flanking a central courtyard. Some of it survives today. The architects Severus and Celer introduced daring new styles and techniques, demonstrated by an octagonal hall in the east wing that was topped by a dome incorporating the latest developments in cloister vaulting. Even the lighting was revolutionary: a series of apertures in the circular crown between the eight walls of the hall and the dome above. At ground level too the eight walls lent further sophistication: the front three gave on to the park, four gave on to vaulted rooms, and the last, at the back, featured a flight of steps down which water streamed. The sections of the palace that are visible today reveal that Nero also employed the greatest painters of the day. They provided exquisite paintings, chic frescoes and decorated panels in the many bedrooms and reception rooms that led off the hall.

The palace was also a showcase of technical innovations and novelty gadgets. The baths boasted both flowing salt water from the sea and sulphurous water from natural springs. In the dining rooms movable ivory panels released flower petals on to the guests seated below, while disguised pipes sprayed them with perfume. The pièce de résistance was a constantly revolving ceiling in one banqueting hall, the design of which reflected the day and night sky.[22] The Golden House was the very height of fashion and good taste, utterly exquisite in every detail. Anyone entering it would have been seduced by its mesmerizing elegance and artistic ambition. But outside lay a reality check: to most Roman citizens, Nero was simply turning the very heart of the city into a private residence devoted to his pleasure.

The Golden House robbed the plebs of places to live; graffiti and satirical verses claimed that the palace was swallowing up Rome itself. Conservatives denounced the break with Rome's ancient history; Nero's pleasure palace had even devoured the site dedicated to the temple to his adoptive father, the divine Claudius.[23] This, said Nero's critics, showed that filial piety, a traditional Roman virtue, had been destroyed. Accordingly, people spread malicious rumours suggesting that the fire had been started deliberately to clear Rome for Nero's megalomaniac vision. This accusation was fuelled by a further rumour that the second fire had begun on the estate of Tigellinus. Indeed, such was the persistent power of the rumours that Nero resorted to drastic measures. He made scapegoats of the sect of Christians in Rome. They were arrested and, as a form of public entertainment, Nero hosted the spectacle of their deaths in his own gardens and in the restored Circus Maximus. The Christians were dressed in wild animal skins and ravaged to death by dogs, or else crucified, their bodies torched to light up the night sky.[24]

A fitting symbol of Nero's excesses was provided by the sculpture that was erected in the vestibule of his new palace: a bronze statue 36 metres (120 feet) high portraying the emperor, a crown of sunrays around his head. With such extravagances as this, it soon became clear to Nero, his advisers and the Senate that the rebuilding of Rome and, above all, the dream palace was going to cost a vast amount of money. What the senators did not reckon on, however, was that Nero would sanction outrageous means to obtain it:

Italy was ransacked for funds, and the provinces were ruined – unprivileged and privileged communities alike. Even the gods were included in the looting. Temples at Rome were robbed and emptied of the gold dedicated for the triumphs and vows, the ambitions and fears of generations of Romans.[25]

To pay for his new Rome Nero was not only riding roughshod over every ancient tradition. To inaugurate his new age he seemed prepared to bankrupt the empire. On his orders, a financial and political crisis was beginning to envelope the management of Rome and her provinces. Why was Nero doing it? The significance of the Golden House runs deeper than the financial crisis that the spiralling costs brought in their wake. At the same time it provides an insight into why opposition to Nero now accelerated.

The Golden House was an artistic endeavour to prove Nero's primacy, his superiority over others, his right to be the most powerful person in the Roman state. He felt the need to do so because of the insecurity that Augustus's hereditary monarchy promoted and that Agrippina had fostered. Now Nero believed he had found the way to settle this issue once and for all. When the palace was partly habitable, Nero was reported to have said, 'Good! Now at last I can live like a human being'.[26] Only the grandest palace the world had ever seen could mean normal living for Nero. Underlying this attitude was the reality and expression of Nero's superiority to all others in the Roman state. Yes, parts of the palace grounds were open to the plebs, and yes, Nero certainly gave the impression of opening up his home to ordinary citizens. But even these concessions painted a picture not of a people's palace, but of a monarch generously bequeathing gifts from his position of supremacy.[27] The change in style of government from Augustus to Nero could not have been more clearly expressed. The first emperor had stressed the modesty of his villa. His house on the Palatine said, 'I am just like any other senator.' Nero's said, 'I am like no other; I am better.' Why did he need to stress this?

When Augustus ended the civil war and established a new state around his position of emperor, the lion's share of power was self-evidently in his hands: he had the loyalty of the army, and he had amassed an incredible personal fortune by conquering the wealth of Egypt. That power set him above all others in Rome as the first citizen, and gave him the licence to dominate the state. So long as Augustus behaved tactfully and disguised his supreme power within a form of constitutional government, others in the élite tolerated this situation. By contrast, Nero's claim to the same position was not self-evident. He enjoyed no great respect among the armies, having had neither opportunity nor interest in winning it through military conquest. He had no outstanding sources of wealth. Heredity alone was responsible for his position. He was there by birth – just.

By AD 64 the murders of his mother Agrippina, the great-granddaughter of Augustus, and of his wife Octavia, the emperor Claudius's daughter, had further weakened Nero's claim to the throne. He feared that other descendants of the Julio-Claudians could make as good a case as he, and that they were now waiting in the wings, potential rivals for power. The final straw was Seneca. Increasingly estranged, Nero's old tutor was no longer at hand to advise him on how to conceal his power, handle the Senate and govern affably with tact, openness and clemency. For all these reasons, in order to assuage the insecurity he felt over his right to be emperor, Nero turned to one solace above all: pursuing a style of rule that asserted explicitly, and offensively, his primacy over his rivals.

Through the unrivalled glories of the Golden House, through its artistic virtues and ambitions, Nero stressed not just his excellence, but his superiority and eminence over everyone else. It was utterly unpalatable to senators and knights with ambition. By the following year a small core of them were plotting in earnest to get rid of him.

THE PLOT

What turned the grumblings and mutterings of a few disaffected aristocrats looking to improve their lot into a serious attempt on the life of the emperor was the participation of the joint head of the Praetorian Guard, Faenius Rufus. In AD 65 the able and efficient Rufus had suffered three years of insults and slanders from Tigellinus while watching him grow more powerful as the whispering voice in the infinitely suggestible emperor's ear. Rufus brought with him other key members of Nero's guard: colonels, company commanders and officers. Their support was critical.

The plotters were led by the senator Flavius Scaevinus, and their plan was simple: to replace Nero with one of their own, Gaius Calpurnius Piso. To their minds Piso was the ideal candidate. He came from an illustrious, aristocratic family of the republic; in more recent times it could trace associations with the Julio-Claudian dynasty as far back as Julius Caesar and Augustus. He was also popular with the plebs as a senator and lawyer who had often acted in their defence. Affable, suave and a sparkling guest at high-society parties, he was a politician who counted even Nero among his friends. But now he was preparing to betray that friendship, forced to this extreme plan, he said, by the need to rescue the freedom of the state from a tyrannical, avaricious emperor who was running Rome into the ground. Others, meanwhile, said he was motivated by pure self-interest.

The plotters hesitated until their plan was in danger of being exposed. A freedwoman named Epicharis had tried to win over Proculus, a captain of the fleet, mistaking his disaffection with

Nero's regime for a willingness to join the plot. In response, Proculus, though he had none of the conspirators' names warned Nero, and Epicharis was kept in custody. The pressure to act was now on. The plotters gathered discreetly to decide how to kill Nero. One person suggested inviting the emperor to Piso's luxury villa in Baiae, but Piso refused to defile the sacred guest–host relationship: it would, he said, look bad. Secretly, however, he feared that if Nero's life were to be taken outside Rome, another rival aristocrat, Lucius Junius Silanus Torquatus, a descendant of Augustus, could take control of events and rob him of the fruits of the plot. Finally, the conspirators settled on taking action during games at the Circus Maximus, a place that Nero could be counted on visiting.

Before they dispersed, they acted out how they would attack the emperor. The strongest of the senators would approach Nero with a petition for financial assistance. He would then seize Nero and pin him to the ground while the disenchanted Praetorians would stab him to death. In this bloody act they would be led by the senator Scaevinus, who had taken to carrying a dagger in his toga as a totem of his intent. He had taken the weapon from a temple dedicated to the deified virtue 'Safety'. The murder in the name of the state's welfare, thought the assassins, would thus be lent extra credence. In reality the enactment was closer to a piece of macabre theatre – an unimaginative rerun of the assassination of that other tyrant, Julius Caesar.

The night before the crime was to take place, Scaevinus was in melancholy mood. He signed his will and settled his affairs, even freeing his slaves and giving them gifts. One slave, Milichus, was charged by his master with two final tasks: to sharpen the dagger and to prepare bandages for wounds. Milichus's suspicions were immediately aroused, but then some guests arrived for dinner and the senator gave the impression of being as entertaining as usual. His cheerful conversation, however, could not disguise his distraction.

Milichus too was distracted that night. Encouraged by his wife to reveal any danger to the emperor in the hope of receiving a reward, and tormented by the possibility that he would miss the opportunity to be the first to reveal the danger, Milichus sneaked out of the house the next day to report his suspicions to Nero. At first he was ignored by the gatekeepers, but eventually his perseverance prevailed. Accompanied by one of Nero's freedmen, Epaphroditus, he finally won an audience with the emperor.

Immediately Scaevinus was arrested and brought to the palace. Here he faced Tigellinus. The senator, a picture of calmness and ease, denied all the allegations; the dagger, he said, was a family heirloom that this ungrateful, dishonest ex-slave had stolen. And the will? Well, came the reply, I have often added new clauses and freed slaves to stave off my creditors. These responses undermined Milichus's evidence and gave the advantage to Scaevinus. The official investigation of treason had been transformed into a scene of social awkwardness and embarrassment. But just as the whole sorry business was winding down and Scaevinus was preparing to leave, Milichus spoke up one last time. He had one last suspicion to voice. He had seen Scaevinus, he said, talk at length with the knight Antonius Natalis.

Scenting blood, Tigellinus agreed to see if Scaevinus's and Natalis's stories matched up. The knight was promptly arrested and brought to the palace. The two men were interrogated separately and their stories immediately differed. To get at the truth Tigellinus now exchanged the nicety of questioning for the sharper tool of torture. And sure enough, in a short space of time, he learnt a great deal. With only the slightest threat of pain, Natalis broke down first – in Nero's presence. He denounced Piso, but then, in his panic, he also blurted out the name of another: Seneca. Tigellinus quickly went to the other interrogation room and confronted Scaevinus with Natalis's confession. Defeated, the senator duly named the others involved. The discovery of such a widespread plot cut straight to the source of Nero's insecurity: after all his magnanimous generosity, and after all he had given the senators, was this how they showed their gratitude to him?

The notion that Nero's regime was becoming anything other than tyrannical was abandoned in the terror that now followed. The walls of Rome and its neighbouring towns were overrun with the military and blockaded; everywhere there were signs of a state of emergency. Each and every one on the confession list faced Nero's wrath. Tigellinus's soldiers rounded up as many as possible and chained them outside the gates of Nero's palace. Although most at first refused to confess, every one eventually gave way either to torture or the bribe of immunity. In the process, they incriminated their associates and even members of their own families. Trials, such as they were, were informal; people were incriminated on the flimsiest of evidence. In Nero's campaign of terror an association with a known conspirator, 'or a chance conversation or meeting, or entrance to a party or a show together' was tantamount to guilt.[28]

No one, however, had yet denounced the joint head of the Praetorian Guard, Faenius Rufus. To conceal his involvement in the plot from Tigellinus and Nero, he bullied, tortured and interrogated more viciously than the others. During one violent 'trial', a Praetorian officer who had also not been detected, surreptitiously flashed Rufus a glance; he was looking for a sign that he should go ahead and assassinate Nero. But as the officer prepared to draw his sword, Rufus lost his nerve and stopped him. With that last opportunity abandoned, the dying embers of the conspiracy were put out.

Meanwhile, Nero's bloody purge of the aristocracy grew in ferocity. During the early stages of the exposure of the plot, Piso had been encouraged to go to the Praetorian camp, to go to the Forum, to go everywhere he could and rally the soldiers and the people against the emperor. But he had decided against it. Instead, he committed suicide by opening his veins before Tigellinus's soldiers could get to him. The spectacular collapse of the conspiracy was symbolized by Piso's will: in order to protect his wife from the emperor's vengeance, it flattered Nero. Seneca, however, was not so quick to give in.

Nero's tutor had wanted no part in the conspiracy; Natalis had only informed against him because he wanted to please Nero. Although retired, Seneca was a thorn in the emperor's conscience, and Natalis knew that Nero had secretly long wished to be rid of him. Natalis's cowardly attempt to avoid death by ingratiating himself with the emperor worked, and Nero seized his opportunity to silence Seneca for ever. When the guards arrived and surrounded his house, the old senator was at dinner. With nothing to hide, Seneca stated his innocence with dignity. The commanding officer, Gavius Silvanus, reported this back to Nero. Seneca's former pupil, however, chose to ignore the small matter of his tutor's innocence, and sent the officer back to the countryside with a death sentence.

Silvanus, however, was bearing a terrible secret: he himself had been one of the conspirators. Now he found himself perpetuating the crimes that he had joined the conspiracy to avenge. He could not bear to give the order directly, so he sent in one of his subordinates. Like Piso and many others, Seneca too chose to commit suicide by opening his veins. He began by severing those in his sinewy arms. When this failed to work fast enough, he cut the veins in his ankles and behind his knees. Seneca's wife Paulina insisted on dying with her husband, and she had done the same. But, Seneca, fearing that the sight of each other would only weaken their resolve and intensify the agony, asked her to move to another room. Nero had anticipated this marital pact and in a final act of vindictiveness – or was it clemency? – had ordered his soldiers to prevent the death of Seneca's wife. Paulina was resuscitated, her wounds bandaged, and she survived, a living ghost in mourning.

Inevitably, Rufus was betrayed by his co-conspirators; there were simply too many who wanted to see him exposed for his role in their downfall, not least the imprisoned senator Scaevinus. When, during an interrogation, Rufus pressed the senator for more information, he pushed Scaevinus too far. The leader of the plot retorted coldly, 'Ask yourself. No one is better informed than you.'[29] Rufus's stunned silence betrayed his guilt and he was seized. Tigellinus perhaps took most pleasure in seeing his colleague's career come to an abrupt end.

Aided by Nymphidius Sabinus and the fawning senator Petronius Turpilianus, both loyal allies of the emperor, Tigellinus mopped up the remaining conspirators among the Praetorian Guards and the Senate. To ensure the future loyalty of the Praetorians, Nero gave each soldier a reward of 2000 sesterces and a free supply of corn. Honorary triumphs were awarded to Turpilianus and Tigellinus, while Sabinus received a consulship and promotion to succeed Rufus as joint head of the Praetorian Guard. Finally, there was the usual round of congratulations, celebrations and thank offerings to the gods led by Nero. Cowed, the Senate slavishly joined in the ceremony.

With the state secure and the emperor pre-eminent once more, Nero showed a modicum of balance and restraint by pardoning Natalis for his confession and sparing others. However, his progress towards overt tyranny now took a step forward when he declared that he wanted to fulfil the greatest ambition of his entire life. To act. In public. In Rome.

DOWNFALL

In the colonnades of the streets of Rome, in the houses and baths of leading statesmen, the whispering ran rife. The senators were now desperately trying to avert a new crisis. The lowly profession of acting, utterly scorned by the conservative élite of Roman society, was about to be embraced in all earnestness by the emperor of Rome, the most powerful man in the world. The venue? The theatre of Pompey the Great. The occasion? The second Neronia. In the republic and during the early days of the empire, leading magistrates had hosted games as a way of asserting their family prestige and winning influence in the state. Now Nero was asserting his primacy by paying for the Neronia, the greatest games of the age, himself. All Roman citizens from Italy and the provinces were invited, and the humiliation and discrediting of the emperor, went the rumour, would be total.

The senators quickly came up with a plan: at a meeting of the emperor's private council at the palace they gently suggested awarding him in advance the prize for first place in the category of song – and also in the category of political oratory to detract from the show-business nature of Nero's chosen field of expertise. The emperor rejected their hypocrisy outright: he was to perform in public, he said, and he was to be received on equal terms with the other artists competing in the competition. There were to be no special favours.

While the emperor rehearsed assiduously, the games' presiding officer chose a theme: the golden age. This was attributed to the fact that the Neronia was due to coincide with Nero's search for treasure to which he had been alerted by an opportunistic Carthaginian called Caesellius Bassus. So successful was Bassus in convincing Nero of the existence of the treasure that the emperor continued to spend money on the games, as well as the palace and the rebuilding of his new Rome, in the expectation that it would materialize. It never did. Meanwhile, as the theme suggested, the games were going to be glorious and lavish. There would be elaborate sacrifices and extravagant, gaudy processions featuring images of the gods and the emperor. The Greek-style contests between athletes and guilds of performing arts would range from chariot racing and gymnastics to poetry, heraldry, lyre playing and acting in comic and tragic set pieces. There was even a titillating, transgressive element – the athletic games – which featured nude men, and from which Augustus had once banned women. Now they were to be honoured by the presence of not just Roman noblewomen and plebs, but the vestal virgins too. These sacral aristocratic maidens devoted thirty years of their lives to the service of the goddess of the hearth. Their inclusion also had a Hellenic origin: the Greeks included priestesses at similar events, so Nero wanted them too. All his wishes were granted, but disgrace was waiting in the wings.

When Nero took to the stage for his chosen contest, the recital of tragic material, he was accompanied by members of the Praetorian Guard; the military backbone of Rome, the élite police force of the emperor was reduced to carrying Nero's musical instrument. The emperor himself looked unsteady and grotesque in the authentic garb of an actor: he wore the appropriate mask – a haunting face with an elongated forehead, high platform shoes, an ornately embroidered and colourful tunic and, underneath it, padding for his chest and torso designed to emphasize his presence on the stage. Following his recital, he performed a section of his own composition about the fall of Troy. The Roman plebs were rapturous in their applause. Dazzled and delighted that the emperor of Rome was performing for their pleasure, they called him back for more.

In the wings an aristocratic friend called Aulus Vitellius encouraged the emperor to follow their wishes. His entreaty gave Nero the excuse to yield to their demands and return to the stage, this time to play the lyre and sing. Genuinely fearful of the judges' verdict, and convinced that he was competing with the other performers on a level playing field, Nero took his performance seriously and followed the rules to the letter: he maintained the dignified poses required, he avoided using a cloth to wipe the sweat away, and showed no visible clearing of the throat and nose. At the close of his song, on bended knee and deferring to the crowd, Nero awaited the verdict. The judges put on their own very best performances as they made their assessments before awarding the first prize. The winner was Nero.

Again the urban masses of Rome stamped, applauded and cheered. It is recorded, however, that in disgust many knights voted with their feet and walked out. In their urgency to leave, some were crushed. Indeed, beneath the jubilation were sinister signs of tyranny. The more conservative citizens from Italy and the provinces were also horrified by what they saw. Nonetheless, they clapped with the rest. They had no choice: they were chivvied along by Nero's professional cheerleaders, planted in the audience by the emperor. These young and ambitious men were called the Augustiani, and they were a special, 5000-strong division of knights appointed by Nero and formed from aspiring artists. As the emperor's official fan club, they cuffed, cajoled and harassed the bored and the horrified among the audience. They also acted like secret police, for they spied on the crowd and noted down the names of those who did not attend or those who did not look as though they were enjoying themselves.[30]

Lack of support for the emperor's performance was tantamount to treason. But that was just one aspect of the games that the senatorial élite found hard to stomach. For not only was Nero strong-arming them into applauding him; through the Neronia, the emperor was also wooing the people in a way that completely cut out the Senate from the political process. The magnificent games made a mockery of any equality between the first citizen and the Senate. This was a naked example of Nero setting himself above the institutions of the state: he was seeking to win the people over by appealing to their emotions, inspiring awe and exaltation of himself as an individual. No one else, muttered the senators in envy, could possibly put on games that would match these. None of them could ever win favour with the people in the way that Nero did.

Over the next year yet more extravagant and offensive spectacles were staged, and on each occasion the same image of Nero was presented – that of a tyrant retreating into a world of fantasy, unable to distinguish what was real from what was illusion. The state funeral of Poppaea was one such moment. Soon after the games, Nero had kicked his wife and their unborn child to death because he was in a rage when he returned from an evening out at the chariot races. Poppaea had said that she wanted to die before she passed her prime, so she had her way.[31] The public funeral, full of procession and ceremony to reflect Nero's grief, again flouted all tradition and sense of Roman decorum: Poppaea was not cremated in the Roman style, but embalmed and stuffed with spices in the manner of eastern potentates. Nero took the platform, eulogized his love's virtues and announced the deification of a woman whom many aristocrats considered to be of questionable birth and ancestry. Nero saved the final affront for last. He ordered her body to be laid to rest in the mausoleum of the divine Augustus.

Unsurprisingly, one senator found this a desecration too offensive to endure. Publius Clodius Thrasea Paetus was a principled rebel senator who had dared to challenge Nero's decisions in government. He had walked out during the vote on the fictitious charges brought against Nero's mother and now once again he broke cover. He made his disgust public knowledge by not attending Poppaea's funeral. From that day on Nero would look for any excuse, no matter how corrupt, to remove this dignified aristocrat permanently. His chance was not long in coming.

At the start of the year AD 66 Tigellinus's son-in-law, Cossutianus Capito, brought a charge against Thrasea. The senator was accused of not honouring the emperor's welfare: he had not attended the ceremony of swearing the oath that augured the new year. Secretly, Capito was motivated by an old grudge he bore Thrasea; the senator had helped a deputation from the Roman province of Cilicia to successfully bring charges against him for extortion while he was governor. The trial against Thrasea began in May. It was clear from the hundreds of soldiers anxiously guarding the approaches to the Senate House, law courts and nearby temples that there was much more at stake than Thrasea's innocence. In reality, battle lines were being drawn up between two warring factions: on one side the emperor, his cronies and various servile senators; on the other side the backbone of the Senate trying to assert its authority once again. The covert war was breaching the veneer of harmonious imperial government between emperor and Senate. As usual, however, there was only one winner. After a series of vicious denunciations, Thrasea was found guilty and chose his own death: suicide. The fight against corruption and tyranny, and the battle for senatorial dignity, prestige and responsibility in government were being lost quite publicly.

The plebs of Rome, however, did not seem to care. Their attention was distracted from Thrasea's ugly trial by another expensive state occasion that had been timed by Nero for that very purpose: the crowning of King Tiridates of Armenia. The occasion was a piece of political pageantry staged to represent the victorious pacification of the Roman empire's eastern border with her hostile neighbouring empire Parthia. Tiridates was to be installed as Rome's client-king in the buffer kingdom of Armenia, which lay between the two. The general who achieved this successful pacification was the brilliant, honourable Gnaeus Domitius Corbulo. For the ceremony, however, he remained in the east.

No expense was spared for the king's reception. It cost Rome 800,000 sesterces a day for Tiridates and his train of family, servants and 3000 cavalry to make the nine-month journey to the capital. When the royal entourage arrived it was welcomed by a megalopolis decked out in garlands, colourful banners and fancy lights; the Praetorian soldiers guarded the roads in their finest armour, and the citizens wore their best clothes as they flooded in their thousands to the Forum, or thronged streets and even rooftops to catch a glimpse of the grand occasion.[32]

The crowning was to take place in the Great Theatre of Pompey, the interior of which had been gilded with gold leaf for the occasion. On the stage where Tiridates would kneel before Nero, a massive cloth awning had been set up to shade the proceedings from the sun; on it was the embroidered figure of Nero driving a chariot and surrounded by heavenly constellations. When Tiridates compared the emperor to the eastern god Mithras, the disenchanted senators looking on were apalled. The contrast between the trial and suicides of dignified senators and the theatrical glorification and submission of a foreign potentate for which Nero could claim little responsibility was truly nauseating. Surely things could get no worse? Indeed, they could.

The cumulative costs of Nero's Golden House, the second Neronia, Poppaea's funeral and now the reception of Tiridates meant that the finances of the Roman empire were quickly spiralling out of control. To avoid financial ruin the coinage was devalued, but in AD 66 and 67 Nero turned to more extreme measures. He was already fearful of any aristocrat who could rival him for wealth. He believed that his homes, estates and possessions provided the very basis, the proof of his eminence in the state; men of conspicuous wealth were, as a result, rivals who could undermine him.[33] Now, however, he began murdering them for their money. It was like a continuation of the purge that he had carried out the year before, but this time without even the excuse of an assassination plot to justify it.

Tigellinus was again instrumental in the purge, and the process of elimination was simple. An aristocrat whose wealth was desired was falsely accused of treason: some slave, crony, or servile senator or knight seeking to win favour, eliminate an enemy or settle an old score could always be found to turn informer and make the accusation. The charges were many and various. Cassius Longinus was accused of honouring his ancestor Cassius, the assassin of Julius Caesar, the founder of the Julio-Claudian dynasty; the charge against Lucius Junius Silanus Torquatus was that he had given his slaves and staff titles usually bestowed on members of the imperial household, as though he himself were aspiring to be emperor; others were accused of incest, black magic and consulting astrologers about the death of Nero. All the charges, according to Tacitus, were fatuous.

Often the accused would do the honourable thing and commit suicide after signing over much of his wealth to the emperor in order to protect some small part of it for his remaining family. If, however, there was any resistance in signing the will, as in the case of Anteius Rufus, Tigellinus would bring along a lawyer or a witness who would forcibly sanction it and ensure that the money went either to the emperor or directly to Tigellinus himself before the victim died. While many were murdered in this way, others escaped death by 'purchasing their lives' from Tigellinus.[34]

With this spree of tyrannical murders, many below the upper echelons of the élite – the families, allies, associates, friends and dependants of those connected to the persecuted senators and knights – now also turned against the emperor too. The ordinary people of Rome continued to love their populist emperor; they marvelled at his lavish shows and grand spectacles.[35] Those of more substantial means took a very different view. They now saw their money stolen, their chances of inheritance destroyed, and their prospects for future advancement and achievement in Roman public life evaporate. If further evidence were needed, they only had to look at the temples of Rome and Italy. These were further plundered and the ancient sacred relics, statues and treasures won during the centuries of the glorious republic were melted down. It was as if the heart was being ripped out of the character of the Romans and their ancient virtues.

Nero took this growing disenchantment as a personal rejection. He was hurt by the ingratitude he was being shown after all he had done for the Roman people. Far from tackling the mounting crisis head-on, Nero's response was to retreat further into fantasy. He said he wanted to escape from the world of Rome, which he increasingly disliked, to a place of like-minded souls who really appreciated him and who were worthy of his talents. So in September AD 66, with an entourage of servants, freedmen, compliant senators and knights, and some Praetorian guards led by Tigellinus, Nero left for Greece.

Before departure there was one final insult to level at the Roman élite, the clearest sign yet that they counted for nothing. It lay in his choice of the person left in charge of affairs in Rome. The man chosen to stay behind was not the consul for the year, not even a senator, but a vicious former slave from the imperial household: Helius. He was given complete authority to banish, confiscate from and even put to death citizens, knights and senators. The historian Cassius Dio was moved to quip:

Thus the Roman empire was at that time a slave to two emperors at once, Nero and Helius; and I am unable to say which of them was the worse. In most respects they behaved entirely alike, the one point of difference being that the descendant of Augustus was emulating lyre-players and tragedians, whereas the freedman of Claudius was emulating the Caesars.[36]

Away from the capital, Nero saw his tour of the great pan-Hellenic games of Greece as a chance to express the full flowering of his artistic career. And in that ambition the Greek city-states were happy to accommodate him. Although some of the four-yearly festivals, such as the Olympic Games, were not due for the year of Nero's visit, the Greeks simply brought them forward to coincide with it. To Nero, however, his participation in the competitions represented much more than artistic freedom. It was an opportunity to silence his critics and vanquish his rivals in Rome. For a militaristic society that valued virtue and excellence above everything else, Nero would assert once and for all his primacy as emperor; his chosen field to prove his excellence was not the theatre of war, as it was for Augustus, but the theatre itself.

At the Pythian, Nemean, Delphic and Olympic Games, Nero won prize after prize in the contests for chariot racing, lyre playing and recitals of tragic material. Indeed, the organizers of the Olympic Games had to add musical contests to the competition because it traditionally included only athletic events. Through these victories Nero continued to show his ascendancy over the senators. And yet his insecurity never left him. He sent a message commanding Helius to murder Sulpicius Camerinus and his son for simply having the family name Pythicus, believing that it diminished the glory he gained from the Pythian Games. However, Nero saved the most outrageous murder for Greece. He invited the general Corbulo, the man to whom he owed all the successes of Roman foreign policy in the east, to join him in Greece. He addressed him as 'father' and 'benefactor' in his correspondence. When Corbulo came ashore unarmed in Corinth, however, he was not given a war hero's welcome by the emperor. He was met by Nero's henchmen, who forced him to commit suicide. The rumour went that Nero was preparing to go on stage, and while dressed in the long, unbelted tunic of an actor, he simply could not face greeting the man who had pacified Rome's eastern frontier with Parthia, the man who represented all that was virtuous and excellent.[37]

In addition to his fear of rivals, other demons, anxieties and insecurities played on Nero's mind during his grand tour. He refused to take part in the Eleusinian Mysteries near Athens for fear of raising the wrath of his mother's ghost. The ghost of Poppaea loomed large too, as the masks of the female characters he performed on stage were deliberately made to resemble her features. He also called Sporus, one of his freedmen, 'Sabina' (Poppaea's other name) because of his resemblance to her. In fact, Nero even had him castrated and underwent a mock marriage ceremony with him, at which Tigellinus gave the 'bride' away. Henceforth, Nero affectionately called Sporus his 'queen' and his 'lady', as though Poppaea were alive and well and a part of the tour. 'After that, Nero had two bedfellows at once: [the freedman] Pythagoras to play the role of husband to him and Sporus that of wife.'[38]

Thus the rounds of partying, pleasure-making and pursuing the arts continued. Nero was on the trip of a lifetime. He plundered many of Greece's most famous works of art in a nakedly imperialistic fashion, and the subject Athenians emblazoned their emperor's name in bronze above the entrance to their most treasured and sacred building, the Parthenon.[39] In early AD 68, however, Nero was abruptly brought down to earth with a bump when a visitor arrived from Rome with some bad news.

Although Helius had for some weeks been sending Nero messages that a rebellion was being organized, it took his arrival in person to convince the emperor to return urgently to Rome and face the crisis. In Nero's absence, Gaius Julius Vindex, the Roman governor of a province in Gaul, had sounded out opinions of Nero among other commanders in the provinces. Word had got back to Helius in Rome, and now here he was, face to face with Nero, telling him that Vindex's rebellion was serious. Nero dismissed the idea. Vindex, a Romanized Gaul, had no real aristocratic pedigree to mount a serious challenge to the emperor; and anyway, he had no army at his disposal. Nonetheless, Nero agreed to return to Rome ahead of schedule. It was a return that the Roman people would not quickly forget.

Just as Nero had left Rome to conquer his rivals through art, so he now returned as though from war in a spectacular parody of the triumphal procession usually reserved for great generals. This was a triumph to match those awarded to Pompey for his conquest of the east, or to Caesar for his conquest of Gaul. In his lavish train, men carried the crowns that Nero had won, while banners of wood bore the name of the festival and the contest in which he had been victorious. As the herald announced that Nero had won 1808 crowns during his tour, his cries were reciprocated with shouts of 'Hail Olympian victor! Hail Pythian victor!' from the crowds who filled the streets. The finishing touch was Nero's specially chosen vehicle – the triumphal chariot of Augustus, in which the first emperor had celebrated his many military victories.

In all the excitement a theatre producer offered Nero one million sesterces if he would perform in public, not in the state festivals organized by the emperor, but in the producer's private theatre. Nero agreed to appear, but refused the money on grounds of principle – although Tigellinus promptly took the producer aside and demanded the money anyway 'as the price of not putting him to death'.[40] However, behind the warm welcome for the emperor, Rome, half rebuilt and with the scaffolding around its reconstruction lying abandoned, showed signs of financial suffering. Worse was to come. Although the plebs welcomed Nero as a popular saviour, he would soon prove otherwise, for his first decision upon reaching impoverished Rome was to leave it for some more fun in the most Greek of Italian cities, Naples. This was the breaking point.

Vindex now publicly declared his rebellion in Gaul. He minted local coins with the slogans 'Liberty from Tyranny' and 'For the Salvation of the Whole Human Race'. It was clear his cause was not to promote Gallic nationalism and a secession from the Roman empire, but simply the removal of Nero. Of course, Nero had heard all this before. The critical development, however, and the key difference from previously was that Vindex had support on a massive scale: he was able to raise a local army of 100,000 Roman Gauls. Clearly, Vindex was tapping the deep well of hatred accumulated over the previous four years when Nero had raised taxes and plundered the wealth of the provincial élites. He had done so not as a thoughtful king making difficult decisions, but as a wilful, capricious tyrant more interested in his performing career. Now, in Gaul, he was paying the price. Yet when news of the rebellion was whispered to him, Nero blithely showed no concern; in fact, he said he was pleased because it would give him the opportunity provided by the laws of war to despoil Vindex's province even further. Nero returned to watching the athletic competition at hand, stung less by the news of the rebellion than by an insult Vindex had levelled at him: that he was terrible lyre player.[41] But a week later he would be genuinely rattled for the first time.

The news that caused Nero to collapse in a heap and lie paralysed as though dead was that five other provincial commanders had joined Vindex's campaign. Foremost among them were his old friend Otho, governor of Lusitania (modern-day Portugal), and Servius Sulpicius Galba, governor of the Spanish provinces and figurehead of the rebellion. The elderly and arthritic Galba was an aristocrat from an ancient patrician family that had long moved in the most elevated circles of Roman society. Although he was not a member of the Julio-Claudian dynasty, he stood for core, old-fashioned values and a connection with Rome's traditions and history in a time of turmoil, decadence and amorality that was characteristic of Nero's regime. Galba's army proclaimed him 'legate of the Senate and people of Rome' on 2 April AD 68. The rebellion had finally found its leader.

At long last Nero took action. He proposed a military expedition to tackle the rebellion head-on, made himself sole consul and, with the agreement of the Senate, which remained notionally loyal, declared Galba an enemy of the state. The emperor gave orders to organize a military line of defence along the river Po, deploying units from Illyricum, Germany and Britain, as well as a legion from Italy. Nero placed all these troops under Petronius Turpilianus, the senator who had helped uncover the Piso plot. Crucially, however, Nero did not take command of the forces himself.

Perhaps as a result of this, a rumour went around Rome describing the following fantasy. Nero was preparing to go to Gaul unarmed and show the rebelling armies his tears in the hope that this would persuade them to recant. Another rumour had it that he hoped singing a victory ode would do the trick. Finally, to quell the crisis, the emperor had settled on an equally fantastic solution – a full-scale drama production. He would ride out with an army of mythical Amazons (actually prostitutes and actresses dressed up and equipped with bows, arrows and axes), and the vehicles accompanying the expedition would carry not provisions and supplies, but stage machinery.[42] Although the Senate and Praetorian Guard had so far remained nominally loyal, now they waited, primed for the moment to jump. That moment came in May, when the crisis reached its climax in a series of damaging blows.

First, the Roman governor of North Africa, Clodius Macer, joined the rebellion by shutting down the grain supply to Rome. The city was already suffering a shortage of food, and the corn supply was its lifeline. Macer was backed by his one standing Roman legion, an auxiliary force and an alternative provincial senate. They were motivated perhaps by Nero's murder of six North African landowners, who between them owned half of the agricultural land.[43] The prefect of Egypt, the other granary of the Roman empire, also wavered in his allegiance. Then news came that the army once loyal to Nero in Gaul, which had even fought Vindex's recruits on his behalf, had now switched its allegiance to Galba. The final blow was the discovery that Turpilianus, the commander of the armies defending Italy from Galba, had now sided with him. When Nero heard this, while he was having his lunch, 'he tore up the letters brought to him, overturned the table, and hurled to the ground two of his favourite goblets, which he called his "Homerics" as they were decorated with scenes from Homer's poems'.[44]

Tigellinus, now ill, had long realized that Nero was doomed. While in Greece he had lost control of the Praetorian Guard to his colleague Nymphidius Sabinus, and now, in secret, he secured a neat exit (as well as his safety) by ingratiating himself with Galba's envoy in the city.[45] The Senate waited for the Praetorian Guards to declare their position. Sabinus bribed them with money given in the name of Galba, and with that they abandoned their loyalty to the emperor. As with Nero's coronation, so it was with his downfall: the Senate soon followed suit, this time declaring Nero an enemy of the state.

After considering various options for escape, Nero put off his decision until the following day. In the early hours of 9 June, however, he woke up in his palace alone. He quickly realized that the Praetorians had indeed defected. Further investigation of the rooms and corridors showed that his friends and even the caretakers had gone. There remained only four loyal freedmen for company, among them Sporus, Epaphroditus and Phaon. When Nero said that he wanted to hide somewhere, Phaon suggested his own villa 6 kilometres (4 miles) outside the city. The emperor, shoeless and dressed in a plain tunic covered by a dark cloak to avoid being detected by the search parties now looking for him, mounted his horse and set out with the others.

At some point, Nero's horse suddenly reared. It was shying away from the stench of a dead body abandoned on the road. 'Nero's face was exposed and he was recognized and saluted by a man who had served in the Praetorians.'[46]

The last part of the journey was undertaken on foot. The emperor and his petty entourage reached Phaon's villa via a path overgrown with thickets and brambles. A robe was laid on the ground so that Nero could protect his feet. The path eventually led to a back wall. While Nero waited for a hole to be made in it, he picked out the thorns from his torn cloak; then he climbed through the narrow passage. Once inside the villa, the freedmen pleaded with him to put himself beyond the reach of his enemies by killing himself. It was the opportunity for one last piece of stage management – his own death scene. Nero gave instructions about making a grave and the disposal of his body, all the while repeating the words, 'What an artist dies with me'.[47]

Despite news that the search party was getting closer and that he would be punished as an enemy of the state, Nero procrastinated further. He directed Sporus when and how to weep, and begged the others to set an example first. Finally, as the sounds of horsemen drew near, Nero, aided by Epaphroditus, drove a dagger through his throat. He was thirty-one years old. His dying wish for a funeral was granted, and his blotchy, full body was afterwards cremated. At the ancestral monument of his natural father's family, the Domitii, Nero's nurses and his former mistress Acte buried the remains of the last emperor of the Julio-Claudian dynasty.

EPILOGUE

Nero left no heir or successor, so control of the Roman empire was now up for grabs. Between the summer of AD 68 and December AD 69 Rome was shaken by a civil war in which contenders staked their claim to the empire. Hoisted on a tide of support from their armies, three provincial commanders – Galba, Otho and another old friend of Nero's, Vitellius – became emperor in quick succession, only to be defeated by a stronger candidate a few months later. What is striking is that, despite the meltdown of effective government in the empire, there was no suggestion during this time of once again making Rome a republic. Now, as in 31 BC and the end of the great civil war, everyone seemed to agree that in exchange for peace and stability, power had to reside in one man. But what kind of man?

Certainly not an aristocrat of the Julio-Claudian dynasty. Few now existed, for Nero had killed most of them during the last bloody years of his regime. Indeed, the tide of opinion was turning away from the idea that the royal bloodline was the best measure of who should be emperor. While the hereditary principle would in part remain, the élite believed it should be secondary to a new basis on which to choose future emperors: merit. In his history of the civil war of AD 68–9, Tacitus touches on this significant shift. In choosing a successor, the short-lived emperor Galba wanted to cast the net wider than a single aristocratic family: '...my introduction of the principle of choice will represent a move towards liberty.'[48] These were the words that the historian Tacitus, writing less than forty years later, put in Galba's mouth. Whether or not Galba was really able to conceptualize the problem as clearly as this at the time is open to dispute. However, it is revealing that, even with hindsight, the historian was able to pinpoint the change in the tide's direction.

The move away from birth as the criterion for selection was also reflected in the reality of the civil war. Galba, Otho and Vitellius could all claim some high-born ancestry, and this would have pleased some conservative senators. However, what the civil war would show was that their opinion was increasingly irrelevant: it was not the senators who were putting forward candidates to be emperor, but the armies in the provinces. The deciding factor in who should be the next emperor was force of arms and success on the battlefield. The general who could command the greatest and widest support among the army would not only win the civil war, but would also be victorious in becoming emperor.

The Senate and the Roman people would come up with a means of explicitly conferring the supreme power. Where Augustus and his descendants had disguised that power to varying degrees, it was now to be made public and explicit, as an inscription of the time reveals. The new emperor would be conferred 'the right and power...to transact and do whatever things divine, human, public and private he deems to serve the advantage and overriding interest of the state'.[49] This blunt statement perhaps made up for the prestige and authority that the new dynasty, which had risen by merit alone, lacked through ancestry. But there was a more important lesson to be learnt from Nero's life: the successor dynasty to the Julio-Claudians would need to put that power to a different end; it would need to create a new image for the position of emperor.

The new emperor of Rome might not use his power to become a gift- giving monarch or an aristocrat vaunting his generosity to his subjects and asserting his eminence above them and the institutions of the state. Rather, he might become an executive of the Roman people – a man who would restore to them what was theirs by right.[50] In particular, after Nero's extravagance, the new emperor needed to be an efficient administrator and organizer, a leader who could bring discipline to the armies after the civil war, and a statesman who could balance the books of Rome's economy by raising money judiciously and spending it wisely. Part of his proving ground would be the fate of Nero's hubristic folly – the Golden House.

Galba lived in Nero's palace only briefly; Otho spent money putting the finishing touches to it; and Vitellius and his wife ridiculed its grandiose decoration. Nero's ultimate successor, however, had the place demolished, keeping just a small section of it. The father of a new dynasty ordered the palace lake to be drained and here inaugurated the construction of a new, far more public building; a monument not to a private king, but to the Roman people: the Colosseum. The story of who that new emperor was and how he came to power is entwined with the next great revolution in Roman history.

IV

REBELLION

In the southeast corner of the Forum in Rome today stands a triumphal arch dedicated to Titus, the tenth Roman emperor. At each corner of the pedestal are Ionic columns with flowering Corinthian heads, and above the monument's beautifully sculpted cornice is the full, weighty mass of its lintel. It is believed that the arch was once crowned with a glorious statue of Titus on a chariot pulled by elephants. Worn and majestic, the solemn stones that remain of the original arch suggest to passers-by all that is austere, noble and beautiful about the classical world. And yet on the shaded inside of the arch lies a very different story. The ancient panel reliefs that line the passageway through the arch depict in detail one of the most violent, brutal and offensive acts of atrocity in the history of the empire: the Roman sack of Jerusalem in the summer of AD 70.

The panels show Roman soldiers triumphantly carrying booty stolen from the most important site of the Jewish faith, the Temple of Jerusalem. In their hands are some of the most sacred Jewish treasures: the golden menorah (seven-branched candelabrum), silver trumpets and the table for the shewbread. These possessions were so holy that for centuries only priests were allowed to lay eyes on them. And yet depicted here, on the Arch of Titus, the hallowed objects are not only being stolen and defiled by Gentiles, but their theft is celebrated as the greatest triumph of Titus's career. Just as the Arch of Titus has stood as a commemoration of that great Roman triumph throughout the centuries to this day, it also testifies to that cruel act of imperialism.

The destruction of the Temple of Jerusalem was the climax to one of the most dramatic turning points in the history of Rome. The Jewish revolt of AD 66–70 in the Roman province of Judaea involved the single greatest military campaign against a provincial people in the history of the Roman empire. In AD 66 Rome controlled a territory that stretched from the Atlantic to the Caspian Sea, and from Britain to the Sahara. Judaea had fallen under Roman control in 63 BC. And yet, as the imperial government of Rome was to find out in the rebellion of the Jews, the greatest challenge they faced was not conquering and creating their foreign provinces, but administering them. For the Romans, as for many imperial powers through the ages, winning the peace was a much more complex affair than winning the war.

The rebellion of the Jews demonstrated the greatest problems of imperialism: the place, if any, of nationalism within the empire; the coexistence of two religions – emperor worship (a key part of Roman paganism) and Judaism; and, above all, the issue of money – who paid taxes to whom, who profited from the empire and who didn't. Indeed, it was this last question of who really benefited from the celebrated *pax Romana* (Roman Peace), from the protection of being a province within the Roman empire, that would ultimately spark the revolt. The rebellion of Judaea raised all these questions in the most graphic and vivid way for one simple reason: between AD 66 and 70 they led to a war that became a matter of life and death for hundreds of thousands of people. The hard fact of Roman imperialism was that, if challenged and if necessary, the emperor was prepared to unleash a monster. To put down the revolt, the empire released the ferocity and firepower of almost a quarter of the entire Roman army.

At the heart of the story, however, lie highly personal motivations and actions, and an extraordinary reversal of fortune. For the man appointed to command Roman forces in Judaea would seize the opportunity of the war to justify a bid for absolute power. His reward for crushing the Jewish rebels would be to rise from obscurity and disgrace to become emperor – at least that's how he presented it. With his claim secured, he would found an entirely new dynasty and lay the foundations for Rome's glorious golden age of peace. His name was Vespasian. However, success in the war against the Jews and the bid to win power in Rome was not achieved alone. For this Vespasian would come to depend on his son Titus, the man who would succeed him first as commander in Judaea and later as emperor. The legacy of father and son survives to this day, not only in the triumphant Arch of Titus, but also in one of the greatest symbols of Roman power – the Colosseum.

A Roman Province

Some 120 years before the revolt of the Jews against Rome, Judaea was a small monarchical state ruled by a dynasty of high priests, populated mainly by Jews and centred on the holy city of Jerusalem. Previously, Judaea had been part of the Persian empire, and then part of the Hellenistic kingdom of the Ptolemies and, later, Seleucids. The latter took their name from one of Alexander the Great's Greek generals, Seleucus, who founded the new monarchy, and they ruled from the capital city of Antioch in Syria. With time the Seleucids came to encompass smaller kingdoms further south, such as Judaea. Eventually, however, the authority of the Seleucids, like that of the Persians, diminished, and Judaea next fell under Rome's sphere of influence. Between 66 and 63 BC the general Pompey extended Roman control in the east by installing, in the place of

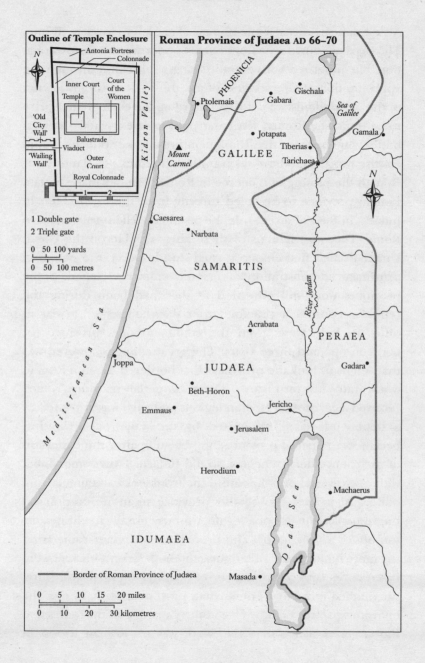

Outline of Temple Enclosure

Antonia Fortress
Colonnade
Inner Court
Court of the Women
Temple
'Old City Wall'
Balustrade
Viaduct
'Wailing Wall'
Outer Court
Royal Colonnade

1 Double gate
2 Triple gate

0 50 100 yards
0 50 100 metres

Roman Province of Judaea AD 66–70

PHOENICIA

Ptolemais
Gabara
Gischala
Sea of Galilee
Jotapata
Tiberias
Gamala
Tarichaea
GALILEE
Mount Carmel
Kidron Valley

Caesarea
Narbata

SAMARITIS

River Jordan

Acrabata
PERAEA

Joppa
JUDAEA
Gadara

Beth-Horon
Jericho
Emmaus
Jerusalem

Herodium
Machaerus

Dead Sea

IDUMAEA

Masada

Mediterranean Sea

Border of Roman Province of Judaea

0 5 10 15 20 miles
0 10 20 30 kilometres

Alexander the Great's successors, client-kings loyal to Rome. The expansion brought Rome great opportunities for exploitation. She inherited both extraordinary wealth and, through the appropriation of Greek works of art, the cultural sophistication of the old Hellenistic world. But there was an even greater prize to be won. The Roman settlement of the east created a critical buffer zone between the Roman empire and her one great rival empire lying in modern-day Iran/Iraq: Parthia.

With the passing of a decree in Rome, Pompey made Syria a Roman province to be ruled directly from the capital, but in Judaea, instead of direct rule, he installed a client-ruler loyal to Rome. The most famous of these kings was Herod the Great. Under Rome's first emperor, Augustus, however, the system of provincial administration across the empire changed. Some provinces were still governed as they had been during the republic: consuls or praetors, after they had served a year in office in Italy, were given the command of a province for between one and three years. The great change, however, was that Augustus took the provinces that bordered the non-Roman world into his own care. These 'imperial provinces' each received a garrison of Roman legions and each was governed by a deputy especially appointed by the emperor. Syria thus became an imperial province, and by AD 6, after the expulsion of the client-ruler Archelaus, so did Judaea. Thus it remained, with one reversal of policy, until the troubles of AD 66.

Because Judaea was a smaller province, its administration was the responsibility not of a legate, who was usually a senior senator, but of a procurator. The procurator of Judaea came from the more junior order of knights, and both he and his staff were based in the Graeco-Roman city of Caesarea on the coast. Here, surrounded more by Gentiles than Jews, he lived in one of the luxurious palaces built by Herod the Great. Again in contrast to the larger province of Syria, there was no Roman legion in

Judaea; there were just 3000 auxiliary troops made up of five infantry units and one cavalry unit, each five hundred strong and drawn mostly from the local population. But for successful administration of Judaea the Romans relied on the locals in other ways too.

Politically, Rome did not govern Judaea on a day-to-day basis. Some towns and villages were run as they traditionally had been, by a small group of elders; others, in the Greek style, elected councils and magistrates. Rome depended on them not only for the smooth management of the province, but also, more importantly, for the execution of the key contract between province and emperor. In return for relative peace, protection and the freedoms associated with being part of the great commonwealth of Rome, the people of Judaea, as in all provinces, collected and paid taxes. This was the cornerstone of the *pax Romana*, the fundamental basis of running an empire. There was a tax on the produce of the land, and also a poll tax. The procurator of Judaea, as both governor and financial officer, was charged with collecting both. However, because the bureaucracy of the Roman empire was so small in proportion to the vast territory it controlled, the Roman procurators needed help in tax-gathering. In Judaea, as in many parts of the empire, they turned to the local élite.

The more lucrative direct taxes were collected by the Jewish high priests and a council of rich Jerusalemite Jews; the indirect taxes were collected by wealthy local businessmen.[2] In practice, only the wealthy could be tax-gatherers. The right to collect taxes was sold at auction, and the successful bidder was required to pay to the procurator a significant sum in advance, with the expectation that he would earn more money through the conscientious execution of his task. This same wealthy élite provided the magistrates in many towns and local councils. Consequently, with a small bureaucratic staff, a small garrison, and dependence on the local élites for the collection of taxes, successful rule in Judaea depended not on Roman force or power, but on the passive compliance of the provincials. Roman administration was, in reality, a delicate balancing act. However, it was an act that time and again the Romans got wrong.

One flashpoint was citizenship. Being a Roman citizen brought with it certain protections from magistrates. St Paul, a Greek-speaking Jew from Tarsus in the Roman province of Cilicia in southeast Turkey, was famously about to be flogged in public after his arrival in Jerusalem in AD 58 stirred up a riot. At the last minute, he was saved from punishment for the simple reason that he was a Roman citizen and as such had the right to a trial in Rome. Jesus provoked a similar reaction in Jerusalem, but because he was not a Roman citizen, he was handed over for crucifixion, even though he had done no wrong. The reality of the *pax Romana* was that it was often easier for Roman officials to put the preservation of order before justice and the protection of the weak against the strong. The tie of citizenship to the Roman commonwealth was then a highly desired prize from which many in Judaea were excluded.[3] Yet Roman administration was far from sensitive to this fact.

When, in AD 63, Jews gathered in Caesarea to protest en masse over systematic discrimination against them, they clashed with the local Greek citizens and a riot broke out. The Roman procurator, Marcus Antonius Felix, responded with extreme repression and sent in the army. To make matters worse, Felix was a Greek as were many of the locally recruited soldiers. As a result, it was the Jews who were violently attacked. Many of them were killed and their property plundered. The fracas, which lasted for days, caused such a controversy that it was given a court hearing before the emperor Nero in Rome. Crucially, Nero, a philhellene, found in favour of the Greeks, and the procurator was deemed not guilty. The Jews were outraged by the verdict.[4]

An even greater source of tension was religion. To the Jews there was only one lord over Judaea, and that was God – Yahweh. Nonetheless, the Jews accommodated the divine Roman emperor by agreeing to sacrifice twice a day to both him and the Roman people.[5] In the Gospels Jesus himself acknowledged that Caesar and God could coexist. But once again the Romans crossed the line of what the Jews could tolerate. In AD 26 the Roman prefect of Judaea, Pontius Pilate, ordered military standards to be displayed in Jerusalem, to which the Roman soldiers would offer sacrifices. Such a display ran contrary to the Jewish Torah, the ancient book of laws central to Judaism, which decreed that there could be no graven images of a pagan deity in the Holy City. Only after five days of protest did Pilate give in and agree to take the standards down. In his desire to promote emperor worship in Judaea, however, the next emperor was determined to go much further.

In AD 38 Caligula ordered Publius Petronius, the legate of Syria, to march on Jerusalem and erect cult statues of himself not just in the city; the emperor wanted one to be put in the Temple enclosure itself. In the face of protest, came the order from Rome, objectors were to be executed and the rest enslaved. In Jerusalem, Galilee and Tiberias diehard protesters gathered in their thousands to confront the soldiers and the carts carrying the imperial marbles. Week after week they told the commander that the whole Jewish race would have to be killed before a statue of the emperor would be allowed to stand in Jerusalem. Petronius was faced with a dilemma: either to put the obstructing Jews to death, or to put his own life on the line by disobeying Caligula's orders. He chose the latter and returned to Antioch, expecting an early demise. Fortunately for Petronius, by the time the imperial order for his execution arrived from Rome Caligula had already been murdered, and the more conciliatory Claudius proclaimed emperor in his place. For the time being, the fire was subdued, but it was far from extinguished.

Similarly, the economic reality of Roman occupation continued to smoulder. Perhaps the greatest source of tension between Romans and Jews was money. In the republic, Roman administration of a province was synonymous with the extortion, fleecing and exploitation of provincials. 'Words cannot describe how bitterly we are hated among foreign nations owing to the wanton and outrageous conduct of the men whom we have sent to govern,' wrote the senator Cicero in 66 BC.[6] Laws passed by Julius Caesar and Augustus to curb the excesses of Roman governors and grasping soldiers had tackled the problem of corruption, although many cases now went unreported. In Judaea, according to the Gospels, a consensus was reached and advocated by Jesus. When he told the Pharisees in Jerusalem to 'Render unto Caesar the things that are Caesar's, and unto God the things that are God's,' Jesus was acknowledging the acceptable coexistence of taxes paid to Rome and taxes paid to the Jewish Temple. Similarly, when Roman soldiers approached John the Baptist for guidance, his reply did not challenge their presence in Judaea, but recognized it on the following terms: 'Do not extort money and do not accuse people falsely – be content with your pay.'[7] Nonetheless, his answer assumes that the occupying forces, more often than not, did find ways to extort.

In fact, for most ordinary Jews throughout the province, the burden of Roman taxes and other financial exactions chafed from the start. As the years of foreign rule passed, the notion promoted by Jesus of an acceptable Roman administration in Judaea only became harder to stomach. For many peasants, good agricultural land was in short supply. Its possession, or lack of it, sharply divided regional groups in Palestine and Judaea then as today. While the coastal plain had rich soil and rivers to water it, the upland massif of Judaea was rocky and dry, its soil thin. As a result, it was hard enough to make a living, find the land rent, feed a family and pay one's dues to the Temple and tithes to the priests without having to dig even deeper for Caesar when the tax collectors came calling.[8]

But the money-gatherers were unwelcome for another reason. The men who toured the villages of Judaea and relieved the poor of their money were not even Romans. Jewish peasants paid up to a Jewish élite thriving under Roman patronage and tax-collecting contracts. Consequently, the issue of taxes cut a sharp divide in Jewish society. *Pax Romana* enriched some and slowly killed others.

The seeds of these political and economic tensions were sown when Rome took control of Judaea in 63 BC. From that time on they only grew and grew. By AD 66 Judaea was a time bomb. To set it off, all that was needed was someone to press the button. In May of that year Gessius Florus, the Roman procurator, duly obliged.

OUTBREAK

In its last years, the rapacious regime of the emperor Nero needed money, and lots of it. The burden of heavier taxes and forced levies hit the provinces hard. Gaul and Britain suffered; in Africa six landlords who owned half the land of the province were put to death; now Judaea too was about to feel the pinch.[9] One way or another Judaea was going to help make up the shortfall between revenue and Nero's profligate expenditure. Florus announced that the emperor required the massive sum of 400,000 sesterces. He was even prepared to take it from the funds of the Temple treasury, and declared that units of Roman soldiers were going to come to Jerusalem to get it. Since those funds were made up of the sacred dues paid by ordinary Jews for sacrifices to God, Florus's threat amounted to stealing of the most outrageous kind. The Jews in the Holy City were furious.

Gessius Florus was the archetypal greedy Roman governor. He delighted in impoverishing the Jews, boasted about his crimes, and lost no opportunity of turning a profit through extortion and robbery. Indeed, he saw it as a sport.[10] At least this was the view of Joseph ben Mattathias who witnessed the events. Josephus (his Roman name) was a twenty-nine-year-old priest and scholar, scion of an aristocratic Jewish family that could trace its origins in part to an influential dynasty of priests, known as the Hasmoneans, who had ruled Judaea when the Romans first arrived. He had studied the teachings of the three most prominent Jewish sects, and when he could not decide which one to join, he later claimed to have spent three years living with an ascetic hermit meditating in the desert. After some years carrying out his priestly duties in Jerusalem, he then travelled on a diplomatic mission to Rome, where he remained for two years. By May AD 66, perhaps laden with Roman sympathies, he had returned to Jerusalem, only to find it in the crisis provoked by Florus. It was a crisis that would engulf him and change his life for ever. From this point on he became the eyewitness historian of the revolt of the Jews against Rome.

True to his word, Florus in Caesarea ordered his soldiers to take seventeen talents (435 kilograms or nearly 1000 pounds) of silver from the Temple treasury. From this one action all the tensions between the Romans and Jews erupted. Stealing from the very place where King David had founded the Holy City, where King Solomon had built the first Temple, and where the Jews returning from captivity in Babylon had built the second Temple was the greatest violation of their race and history. The Temple was the ultimate symbol of Jewish identity. But Florus couldn't have cared less. In a spirit of reasserting Roman power, he gladly gave the order for the Gentile soldiers to force their way into the most holy of places, upturn the sacred objects, push aside the swarms of priests and protesters who stood in the way, and seize the money.

Stirred up by Jewish nationalists and radicals, there was uproar throughout Jerusalem. When news reached Caesarea that the city was up in arms, Florus dashed off to Jerusalem himself with both an infantry and a cavalry unit to restore order and make sure that he received the money. As he entered the city, some jokers went around mimicking beggars and acting as though they were collecting for the impoverished Roman procurator. Now it was Florus's turn to be angry. He set up a dais in a public space and began an open-air tribunal to bring to justice those who had insulted him. Local leaders formed a line between the Roman leadership and the crowds of angry protesters. Among the moderate priests were Josephus and the high priest Hanan. Apologizing to Florus on behalf of the people of Jerusalem, they desperately tried to calm the crowd and restore order. However, their pleas made no impact. The reality was that the pro-Roman priestly élite was hopelessly exposed. On the one hand, to have tried to bring the culprits before Florus would have resulted in further riots; yet on the other hand, to have sided with the nationalists risked bringing Roman disfavour and an end to their privileges. So at the open-air meeting they compromised and simply begged Florus to forgive the few agitators and extremists for the sake of the many innocent and loyal subjects of Rome. His response, however, only fanned the flames: he sent in the cavalry.

The Roman suppression of protesters in the Upper Market quickly escalated into something much worse. Houses were plundered, over 3000 innocent people were killed, and the instigators of the riot were crucified as a lesson to others. When the Jews plucked up the courage to protest – this time at the massacre – a second bloodbath took place. Once again, the moderates in the Jewish élite were caught in the middle, so they made the traditional signs of supplication: they threw themselves on the ground, covered their heads with dust, tore their clothes and begged the insurgents to stop. They were, they said, only giving the Romans the excuse to plunder further. Once again, the procurator resorted to force. Two more cohorts were drafted in from Caesarea and the soldiers clubbed the protesters to death. When the cavalry pursued those trying to escape, they chased them to the gates of the Antonia Fortress. Here, in the desperate congestion, many were crushed to death and others were beaten to an unrecognizable pulp.[11] With each day full of disasters, the authority of the local leaders and priests collapsed, and popular opinion swung dramatically in favour of the nationalists and armed resistance.

Spoiling for a fight, the nationalists organized retaliation. They barricaded the streets, isolated and hemmed in pockets of outnumbered Roman soldiers, and then, using spears, slingshots and loose bricks and tiles, they attacked, driving Florus and most of his Roman cohorts out of the city. While Florus limped back to Caesarea, the solitary Roman cohort left behind was soon slaughtered. Action was needed, but none of the Roman measures taken had any effect. King Agrippa, the client-ruler of territories partly in Galilee and partly to the north and east of the Sea of Galilee, was called upon. Perhaps he would have more influence over the outraged Jews in Jerusalem. Supervision of the management of the Temple, including the appointment of the High Priest, had been delegated to him by the emperor for over a decade. But when Agrippa entered the Holy City and addressed the hostile crowds, he too was stoned and driven out.[12]

News of the successful resistance in Jerusalem spread across the entire province. In fortress after fortress across Judaea, Roman guards were murdered and Jewish rebels took control.

To restore order, the emperor of Rome and his senatorial advisers turned to Gaius Cestius Gallus, the newly appointed legate of Syria. Perhaps the full might of a Roman legion and numerous other troops would succeed where the meagre auxiliary forces of Judaea had failed. In mid-October AD 66, with 30,000 troops at his side, Gallus marched from Antioch to Jerusalem with the aim of quashing these rebels in a quick, decisive confrontation. But he was the wrong man for the job. A politician more accustomed to the pleasures of provincial peace than the realities of war, Gallus not only failed to take the city, but on his retreat was caught in a desperate trap. This was to prove the moment when a rebellion in a small province of the empire was transformed into war with the superpower of Rome.

As the men of the twelfth legion beat their grinding, demoralized retreat to Caesarea, Gallus failed to take account of one thing: control of the hilltops enclosing the rocky passes through which the Romans marched. When the pass narrowed near Beth-Horon, a huge army of Jewish rebels cut off the road, brought the serpentine column of soldiers to a complete standstill and surrounded them on all sides. Then, from the rocky slopes, they attacked the forces of the occupying power with a barrage of arrows, spears and stones. Unable to defend themselves or keep their formations in a tight defile, the panic-stricken Roman soldiers ducked beneath their shields and suffered hours of painful pounding. Only nightfall provided a temporary respite, and when the next day came, Gallus opted for the ignominy of fleeing. The Romans had been utterly routed, and approximately 6000 of their number had been killed. It was the greatest defeat of regular Roman forces by the people of an established province in all Roman history.[13]

Jews the length and breadth of the province were overjoyed. Many believed their extraordinary victory was a miracle. Prophets, perhaps cooperating with the revolutionary leaders, played their part too in pointing to the hand of God. With His aid, perhaps it was possible for the underdog to defeat the almighty power of Rome. What else could possibly explain such an historic, unprecedented victory? According to Josephus, however, there were many too who viewed their success with dismay. For while the Jews debated the significance of their brilliant, landmark triumph, one thing was certain. The door to negotiations was firmly closed. The Jews, whether they liked it or not, were now committed to war.

In Jerusalem the moderates had regained control of the city. Some ringleaders of the insurrection had been killed, and with their deaths, popular opinion among the majority swung back in favour of the priestly élite. The high priest Hanan and other moderates now pressed home their advantage. If Judaea must fight Rome, they told the people of Jerusalem with renewed authority, at least let us take charge of it.[14] The people agreed and accordingly appointed the priests to lead the war strategy. However, in deciding that, it is reasonable to imagine that Hanan and the élite kept their real intentions secret.

For while the hopes of many people in the city were inflated by the defeat of Gallus and his soldiers, Hanan and his fellow moderates took a more realistic view of the future. To them the more likely outcome of a war was not victory for the Jews, but winning key concessions from Rome. After all, the priestly élite could point out to each other, just six years earlier in Britain the Romans had, with difficulty, put down the revolt led by Boudicca, queen of the Iceni. To avoid another conflict – let alone one that would be long and protracted, and in which many Roman lives would be lost – perhaps the Romans might be prepared to come to new terms?[15] Of one thing, however, Hanan and his fellow priests were sure: they too had to throw in their lot with the rebellion. Their only consolation was that it was they and not the hothead nationalists who were in charge of it.

There was much work to be done. Before the Romans mustered the appropriate military response to Gallus's catastrophic defeat, the Jews needed to organize – and quickly. Hanan urgently required people he could trust to command the rebels in the country at large and prepare the towns for resistance. For the post of commander in Galilee he knew just the right man.

Josephus, Commander of Galilee

When the news of Gallus's defeat reached Rome, the emperor Nero and his advisers saw danger. The rebellion in the little province of Judaea spelt the potential for much worse: the revolt could spread and destabilize the whole of the Roman empire's eastern frontier. One possible fear was that Jews living in Alexandria and Antioch (the second and third greatest cities of the empire) could be persuaded to join their compatriots' fight: the Jewish communities of the eastern Mediterranean represented a 'fifth column' at the centre of the empire. However, there was one area of danger that the imperial advisers may have feared even more: Parthia. The greatest population of Jews outside Judaea resided in Rome's rival empire. Might the Parthians take advantage of the insurrection? Might they see in it an invitation to meddle in the Mediterranean? For help in the crisis, the emperor turned to an unlikely source.

The senator Titus Flavius Vespasianus was a disgraced general living in exile in Greece. The son of a tax-gatherer and the first of his family to reach the Senate, Vespasian had been included in the entourage that accompanied Nero on his tour of Greek festivals in the belief that he would compliantly applaud the emperor whenever he graced the stage. Vespasian repaid the compliment by falling asleep in the theatre and failing to muster even the weariest of claps. Vulgar jokes and ball games were more to his taste. He was simply not cut out to be a patron of the arts. He was a soldier. Burly in physique and bearing a strained expression in his face, he had risen to the ranks of the Senate because of an accomplished military record. He had fought in Germany as a military tribune, but it was in the Roman invasion and conquest of Britain that his reputation soared. Serving under the emperor Claudius, he fought no fewer than thirty battles and was rewarded with triumphal honours and a consulship.[16] In addition to an impeccable military record, Vespasian's location in Greece may have weighed in his favour too: from there he could reach the trouble zone in double-quick time.

But there was one key factor that sealed his appointment. Since Nero was paranoid about rivals among the aristocracy gaining glory and outshining his own, the fact that Vespasian's family could boast no distinguished antecedents was a distinct advantage. This was the ultimate reason why Nero forgave him for his inattentive, ungrateful behaviour on the Greek tour and offered the seasoned general the greatest break of his career: the command of forces in Judaea.[17] However, when the news came, Vespasian could never have imagined quite how radically the appointment would transform his life and that of his wife and two sons.

Needing people he could rely on, Vespasian called upon his eldest son, Titus, to join him in Greece, where together they drew up plans for the Roman campaign. The young man was charming, good-natured and popular. Like his father, he was a strong soldier skilled in horsemanship and the use of weapons, but he was also gifted in other ways. He excelled at singing and playing music, and could compose a speech or a poem in Greek or Latin at the drop of a hat.[18] Now that father and son were together, it was agreed that, although only a quaestor, Titus be given the command of the fifteenth legion based in Alexandria, while Vespasian took charge of the tenth legion and the fifth legion based in Syria. The general decided against making use of the disgraced twelfth legion, defeated by the Jews at Beth-Horon. The three legions would rendezvous at the coastal city of Ptolemais in Galilee before launching their attack on the rebels.

Although these legions might have seemed a massive force, every single soldier in them would be needed. The job confronting father and son was huge. There were many towns and villages to bring into line throughout the province of Judaea, and, according to Josephus's exaggerated figures, each had a population of at least 15,000. Furthermore, the Jews' military tactics of guerrilla warfare were not ones that the Roman legions were best equipped and trained for. Finally, should the Jews retreat to hill-top forts, the Roman forces would face long, demoralising sieges. In taking on these challenges, the relationship between Vespasian and Titus was less that of father and son than a partnership. The two men agreed that the command of forces in Judaea was something in which they could not afford to fail. Through plunder and the selling of prisoners into slavery, there was much money to be made. Success in bringing an end to the rebellion would also bring great glory and acclaim to their name.

While Vespasian organized his army in Syria during the winter of AD 66–7, the commander in charge of the Jewish resistance in Galilee was also making preparations. Josephus took charge of building defences in the towns of Galilee, north of Judaea; he also got to grips with the task of equipping and training the Jewish army. He claimed later to have followed the model of the Roman army, aiming to instil discipline and obedience in his troops, drilling them in the practice of arms, and establishing a clearly organized chain of command. However, the task was proving a miserable, uphill struggle. The aristocratic young scholar found himself in charge of the homeless, of angry peasants and of villagers who had never been to the Holy City. And yet here they were, being asked by an aristocrat, an outsider, to unite behind him and fight a war that was Jerusalem's. Staking his authority over his army would prove a challenge in its own right. Despite these significant difficulties, Josephus's job in Galilee was about to get a lot more complicated.

A local radical called John ben Levi, also known as John of Gischala, his Galilean home town, came and found Josephus. He offered his and his followers' services, which Josephus gratefully accepted. When John energetically organized the rebuilding of Gischala's walls, Josephus was impressed by the man's energy. However, that good impression was not to last. In his account of the war preparations in Galilee, written with hindsight, Josephus's praise quickly turns to venom. John was a 'liar', 'the most unprincipled trickster that ever won ill fame by such vicious habits' and a would-be power-monger who had surrounded himself with a four-hundred-strong private army of thuggish bandits who were prepared to murder for money.[19] Reading between the lines of Josephus's subjective view, John was simply an opportunist with popular instincts, who in the war against foreign oppression was prepared to go to far greater extremes than the well-to-do priest. There was nothing John would not do, no money he would not take, to win power and take the fight to Rome. His presence in Galilee was about to make life hellish for the sensible, moderate commander. More than this, the quarrels between extremist and moderate would give the Romans an unexpected advantage even before they had set foot in Judaea.

When, for example, Josephus gave John permission to provide the Jews in Syria with kosher oil so that they would not have to break their religious code and use foreign-produced olive oil, John seized the opportunity to corner the market in Galilee oil and created a racket. Reselling the produce at eight times the price, he made a fortune for the war effort and, according to Josephus, for himself. Using the profits, he paid for his band of followers to carry out raiding parties on the rich in Galilee. As the havoc increased, so too did the hostility between Josephus and John. Relations soon became so poisonous that the commander believed that John secretly intended to kill him. A scenario ran round and round in Josephus's mind: John wanted to draw Josephus into policing his raids so that, in the fracas, Josephus could be ambushed and killed, and John could seize power. Indeed, Josephus was right to be paranoid. It was not long before John began plotting against his life.

On the pretence of being ill, John gained leave from Josephus to go to the baths in the Galilean town of Tiberias to rest and recover. His actual intention, however, was to stir up a revolt against Josephus through deceptions, lies and bribes. Alerted to the danger by his delegate in Tiberias, Josephus showed the courage for which Hanan had perhaps appointed him commander. Without hesitation, he rushed to the town, gathered the people together and spoke to them forcefully, thus reasserting his authority. John, however, did not give up. Some of his private army made their way through the crowds and, drawing their swords, approached Josephus from behind. People in the crowd shouted to Josephus to watch out, and, with a sharp blade just inches from his throat, he made a narrow escape. He jumped down from the platform on which he had been speaking, and, with the aid of his bodyguard, got away in a boat moored near by.[20]

The episode was enough to swing popular opinion back in Josephus's favour and away from John. The conspirators were rounded up, but John was too quick. He had fled the town and set his sights on rallying followers elsewhere in Galilee. However, it would not be the last time the lives of the two men would cross. Their clash was symbolic of a conflict simmering away throughout the province. Up and down Judaea and Galilee the tensions between the priests' moderate leadership in Jerusalem and the bands of revolutionaries in the country grew steadily worse. In the build-up to war with Rome, others more ideological than John were taking advantage of the chaos and confusion. In the town of Acrabata a peasant leader called Simon ben Gioras had raised his own gang of revolutionaries and was operating independently of the war effort organized in Jerusalem by Hanan and the Temple authorities. The worse the tensions between the Jewish factions, and the more divided the war effort, the easier the anticipated task of Rome would become. However, both revolutionary and moderate alike knew that by the spring of AD 67, the time to pursue their struggles for power had elapsed. The Romans were coming.

Vespasian's three legions amassed at Ptolemais. They were reinforced by a mixture of auxiliary and regular cohorts from Caesarea and Syria, and also with allied forces contributed by the pro-Roman kings in the region – Agrippa, Antiochus and Soaemus. With an army at least 60,000 strong thus deployed, Vespasian and Titus decided on the strategy for war. Some of the commander's officers advised that the cleanest and simplest way to end the rebellion was to go for the jugular and crush resistance in Jerusalem. Vespasian disagreed. He knew that there was one pivotal reason why Cestius Gallus had not been able to take the Holy City: Jerusalem was virtually impregnable.

Built on a rocky plateau with steep and deep ravines on the south, east and west sides, the city was a natural fortress. Adding to its strength were three mighty concentric walls. Even if the city had been built on flat land, Jerusalem would still be impenetrable.[21] To attempt to take the city, went Vespasian's line of reasoning, was a huge gamble and would result not just in a collapse of soldier morale, but also in a massive loss of Roman life. The only safe way to crush the rebellion centred on

Jerusalem was first to take control of the territories around it. The rebels in the towns, villages and guerrilla strongholds of Judaea and Galilee must all be brought into line. However, Vespasian also knew that the manner in which Rome won back the outlying territories was critical.

To win a psychological advantage over the Jewish rebels, Vespasian and Titus decided on a war of terror, a standard Roman tactic. The key principle was to show no mercy: to kill everyone fit to bear arms, and enslave those who could not resist; to plunder and ravage all that came into the Roman army's path. In short, the plan was to terrorize Jerusalem into submission.[22] The sight of the column alone was daunting. Light-armed auxiliaries and bowmen were followed by heavy-armed infantry, some with the responsibility of marking out camps. Then came the road-makers, laden with their tools for levelling surfaces and straightening bends obstructing the path. A cavalry force and body of spearmen protected the personal baggage of the high command. After them could be seen the train of mules carrying the mass of artillery, the battering rams and missile engines. Then came the group comprising Vespasian, Titus and the senior officers with their bodyguard. Appropriately, the military standards, surrounding the symbol of the eagle – 'the king of birds and most fearless of all' – divided the generals from the main body of soldiers, while servants and camp followers brought up the rear.

Invading Galilee from the west, Vespasian first took Gabara, where John of Gischala had taken charge of the rebellion. While John again escaped to regroup elsewhere, the town was less fortunate: it was taken at the first assault. Marching into it, Vespasian executed his plan. He showed no clemency, put to the sword everyone except small children, and then burnt down the town itself and all the surrounding villages. However, when he learnt that the commander of Galilee had rallied the largest stronghold of Jewish resistance in Jotapata, he made that town his next port of call. It too was to become a scene of stark conflict. Vespasian had every intention of going on just as he had begun.

Built on a precipice, Jotapata was a natural hilltop strong-hold, protected on all sides but the north by deep ravines. Inside the town, awaiting the Roman approach, was Josephus. Although by his mere presence the commander of Galilee had raised the morale of the rebels, deep down he had two conflicting feelings. Rationally he knew that it was futile to attempt to defy Roman power. He even claimed to have made a prophecy to that effect: the town would fall on the forty-seventh day. The only real hope of safety was to give in immediately. Josephus even consoled himself that if he went over to the Romans, he would be pardoned, so what was the point in fighting? However, the second emotion was the greater. He would rather die than betray his motherland and flout the trust that his makeshift, peasant army had placed in him.[23] This at least is the picture described by Josephus in his account. It shows signs of the fact that his history was written after the event in an attempt (in part) to present himself to a Roman readership in a good light. One fact was certainly true. Josephus, a Roman sympathizer and unlikely commander, was about to come face to face with the same brute force that had created the Roman empire and was now bloodily stamping out all opposition to it.

It took just five days to clear a road wide enough for the Roman forces to approach Jotapata from the north side. Once in position, Vespasian began the assault. For the first five days the Jews showed an utter disrespect for their vastly superior enemy. Covered by firepower from the town walls, Josephus and his men made daring sallies against the Roman attack, while Vespasian tried to push up the slope and reach the town. After five days of courageous defence, the spirit of the Jews soared with confidence, but then Vespasian changed tack. In order to protect his assault force, he ordered siege towers to be erected against the north wall. Time and again, however, the Roman siege operations were beaten by Jewish resourcefulness.

When the Romans tried to protect the building of the siege towers with hurdles, the Jews made the work difficult by launching rocks from the walls and smashing the Roman defensive works. When the Romans built the siege towers higher, Josephus simply ordered the north wall to be built higher too, his workers protecting themselves with screens made from stretched ox hides. Next, under the combined cover of screens and firepower from a semicircle of 160 artillery engines, Vespasian deployed the unit of soldiers in charge of the battering ram (so called because the iron weight at one end was shaped like a ram's head). When it eventually drew up against the city wall and began pounding, the Jews dropped huge sacks filled with cloth to soften the blows.

However, the Romans raised their game too. When, in one encounter, Vespasian received an arrow in the foot, he used the occasion to inspire his men. He rose above the pain and urged his soldiers on to ever more intense fighting. Josephus saw how a man was decapitated by an artillery stone, 'his head flung like a pebble from a sling more than 600 yards [away]'.[24] Similarly, a pregnant woman was carried 100 metres (135 yards) under the force of another missile. All around the extraordinary Jewish resistance was the rushing sound of approaching missiles, the noise of their final crash and the constant thudding of dead Jewish bodies as they fell from the walls.

Eventually, the Roman attack yielded a prize: a break in the wall. But as the Romans attacked the breach and forced their way into the town, the Jews had one last surprise in store for them. To protect themselves from the barrage of missiles, the

Roman infantry approached in the formation known as the testudo (tortoise). This required twenty-seven men to form up in four ranks and to deploy their shields in a set pattern: some shields protected the sides of the unit, while others were held overhead, each row overlapping with the next. With their protective 'shell' in place, the unit moved slowly towards the north wall. Josephus, however, found a way to neutralize even this. Just as the Romans approached, the Jews poured boiling oil over them. The blistering liquid seeped through every little crack in the *testudo* and threw the Roman units into agony and panic. Some soldiers nonetheless managed to escape and laid a plank in the breach of the wall. The Jews had a plan for this too. They covered it with an oily slick made from boiled fenugreek and thus forced the Romans to slip. Despite these feats of Jewish cunning, nothing could keep the Romans out for ever.

Just before dawn on the forty-seventh day of the siege, Titus led a killing squad noiselessly through the breach. So exhausted with fatigue were the Jews that Titus's men were able to get within reach of the dozing sentry guards, cut their throats and infiltrate Jotapata. Soon the alarm was raised, but it was too late for the Jews to obstruct the legions now charging like ants into the town. Panic-stricken, the rebels dispersed through the narrow streets. Some surrendered, some put up a meagre fight, while others made a desperate bid to take refuge in pits and caves. Most of the rebels were quickly and easily wheedled out and overpowered. However, as the Roman soldiers took control of the town, it was difficult for them to distinguish the insurgents from the surrendering civilians. When one Jew asked a Roman centurion to help him out of a cave, the Roman willingly gave his hand. He was immediately repaid with a quick upward thrust of a sword that killed him instantly. The Romans continued to search high and low for the insurgents, and one man in particular had yet to show his face.

The man who had correctly prophesied that the city would fall on the forty-seventh day (so he said) had also found a hideaway in a pit. Here he joined forty other rebels. For two days they successfully held out, but on the third day one of their party who sneaked out at night to gather provisions was caught and gave away Josephus's whereabouts. Vespasian immediately sent two military tribunes to entice the commander out with the promise of safe conduct. Josephus and his men refused. The rank and file of Roman soldiers gathered at the pit entrance were baying for his blood. However, a third Roman officer, by the name of Nicanor, arrived on the scene and was able to keep them back.

Nicanor was a friend of Josephus whom the priest most likely met in Jerusalem. He now swore on that friendship that Vespasian wanted to save the life of the commander who had put up such an extraordinary defence of the town. Down below in the pit, however, the offer sparked a fierce debate. Josephus wanted to surrender. Interpreting his recent dreams, he believed that God was angry with the Jews and that it was His will that the Romans prosper. The others, however, furious that surrender was even being considered, called Josephus a coward and a traitor. They insisted that suicide was the only honourable way out for all of them. If Josephus refused to join them, they said, they would kill him anyway.

Caught in a dilemma, Josephus at first argued that suicide was an offence against God. The argument only provoked his audience of rebels to violence. They rushed at him with their swords raised, shouting and threatening him. Again Josephus, 'turning like an animal at bay to face each assailant', tried all manner of persuasion: '…he called one by name, glared like a general at another, shook hands with a third, pleaded with a fourth until he was ashamed.'[25] It was no use. Eventually Josephus agreed to the mass-suicide pact. However, he suggested a particular method.

To avoid offending God, lots were to be drawn. Then, beginning with the person who drew the short straw, every third man was to be killed by the man next to him. So began the horrific sight of Jew cutting the throat of fellow Jew. As the lifeless bodies of rebels dropped to the ground, one man was consistently passed over and remained standing. Being a scholar and perhaps well versed in mathematics, Josephus, it seems, had devised the count in such a way that he would always be one of the two survivors. Although the story later inspired a maths problem known as the 'Josephan count', we will never know whether Josephus had used luck or judgement. What is clear is that he now seized his opportunity. He turned to his fellow survivor and desperately tried to convince him to abandon the suicide pact. It must have taken all his powers of persuasion not to be killed for going back on his word after so many had just been murdered, but both men surrendered.

Josephus later put his survival down to the will of God. However, this escape was far from the end of his troubles. The commander of Galilee, the young appointee of Hanan and the Temple authorities in Jerusalem, had failed in his task to resist Rome. He was now a prisoner of Vespasian. Galilee was as good as lost, and Josephus himself faced imprisonment, a long, pathetic journey to Rome and possible execution. Yet the fortunes of Vespasian, Titus and even Josephus were now about to be transformed. With that change of circumstance, the stakes of the war in Judaea were about to be raised.

REVERSALS OF FORTUNE

To raucous jeers from the crowds of Jewish prisoners in the streets of Jotapata, and to a barrage of insults, jabbing elbows and calls for his death from the Roman soldiers, Josephus was dragged out of his hiding place and frogmarched to Vespasian's camp. According to Josephus, it was his noble bearing that now made the general's son, Titus, take pity on him. Indeed, he claimed that it inspired the Roman to reflect on the captive's extraordinary reversal of fortune and ask his father to spare Josephus's life. The reality was perhaps more prosaic. Josephus was not to receive special treatment because of his noble demeanour. The fate awaiting him was that of hundreds of leaders of Rome's vanquished foreign enemies before him: Josephus would be taken to the metropolis, paraded in chains at a triumphal procession, then perhaps ritually executed in the Forum. Before all this could happen, though, he took one of the greatest single gambles of his entire life.

Josephus asked if he could have a private audience with Vespasian and Titus. Having been granted his request, he held his nerve and delivered the words that would make or break him. He told them he came as a messenger of God. There was no point in sending him to Nero, he said, because that man would soon no longer be emperor. The future emperors of Rome, he prophesied, were standing before him. Vespasian must have guffawed at such a preposterous suggestion; emperors of Rome had, after all, always come from a single dynasty of the aristocracy. Perhaps he even grew angry in the belief that Josephus was mocking both Rome and him, an ordinary Roman who had risen through the ranks. He certainly suspected that the scholar and priest was saying anything to save his skin.[26]

In truth, Josephus had taken the messianic prophecy in the Book of Numbers that a saviour would arise from Israel and applied it not to a Jew, but to a Roman. When an officer present asked why, if Josephus was so adept at prophecy, he had not predicted that the town would fall and that he would be captured, Josephus replied that he had. Vespasian's interest was sufficiently pricked by this extraordinary conversation to check on Josephus's prophecy. A messenger soon came back confirming it: Jotapata had fallen on the forty-seventh day, just as Josephus had predicted. It is reasonable to imagine that Titus and his father spied an opportunity. Perhaps this man could somehow be useful to them after all. As far as Josephus was concerned, the gamble had paid off. He was not just safe, but his fortunes had once again taken a rapid u-turn. He was given gifts, clothing and shown every kindness. Although he was still a prisoner, he was now a prized, talismanic one.

As for Vespasian and Titus, their minds soon returned to the more practical matters of war. The campaign of terror in Judaea and Galilee had only just begun. At Tarichaeae, in the kingdom of the Roman client-king Agrippa, 6000 Jews were massacred as Titus made a dramatic amphibious assault on the unfortified part of the city from a lake. After it was taken, Vespasian discriminated between civilian and insurgent, in order to avoid outraging the local population with mass executions and thus make peace-keeping operations easier for Agrippa in the future. However, he broke his promise on the advice of his staff, who feared further insurgency. 'Expediency must be preferred to conventional morality,' was their message.[27] The Jews he had set free were later rounded up in a theatre and 1200 of the old and infirm were slaughtered. The 6000 strongest were sent to Greece to work as slaves on Nero's planned canal in the Isthmus of Corinth. Some 8500 of Agrippa's subjects were returned to him, and the remaining 30,400 were sold into slavery. Similarly, at Gamala the Romans repaid Jewish resistance by putting 4000 Jews to the sword; the remaining 5000 insurgents had already jumped to their deaths in a deep ravine.

While Vespasian surged south, 'liberating' the coastal cities on his march to Judaea, Titus focused on mopping up remaining pockets of resistance in Galilee. In the last conflict of the campaign in AD 67 a surprise lay in store for the Roman general. John of Gischala had been busy rallying and training peasant armies in the Golan Heights and in his home town. Most of these Titus easily crushed. However, when Titus prepared to storm Gischala, John pleaded with him not to attack the town on the Sabbath, but to wait a day. After agreeing to the brief respite, Titus took the town, only to discover that John had vanished. Once again, the rebel leader had made a theatrical, last-minute escape. This time, however, his destination was more predictable: Jerusalem.

In fact, the Holy City was the refuge of every resistance fighter who escaped death or enslavement at the hands of the Roman legions. The result of their arrival in Jerusalem threw the direction of the war into crisis. Many brought with them only bad news. Galilee was lost, they said, and now the Romans were making a slow but unstoppable sweep south. Others, however, violently disagreed. When John and his band of followers rode into Jerusalem they spread their belief that the defeat of the Romans was utterly achievable, that the Jews could still beat them.[28] While the clash of opinions intensified and entrenched the Jewish factions, there was one group caught in the eye of the storm.

The leadership of the war under Hanan and the Temple authorities, cried the nationalist leaders in accusation, had brought only failure after failure. Had the Jewish resistance proved so weak, so ineffectual because the moderate priests wanted all along to surrender the city and Judaea to Rome? With time the argument of the extremist factions only gained momentum; by the end of the year their patience had run out. John's followers first imprisoned and then massacred the moderates. Then they turned their firepower on Hanan and the religious élite. John's faction denounced them as traitors, expelled them from the Temple, then took control of both it and its funds. Soon the Temple complex had become a battle-ground, and by December Hanan and three other leaders from the priestly élite were dead. With their deaths, wrote Josephus, the fall of Jerusalem began.[29]

In the power vacuum left by the moderate leadership, the city fell into the hands of rival factions of nationalists all struggling for supremacy. Over the next year their numbers increased. When, in AD 68, Vespasian's army swept through Judaea, Peraea and Idumaea, the peasant leader Simon ben Gioras and his army also eventually fled to Jerusalem. His arrival provoked further conflict. Informed of the Jews' infighting by deserters, Vespasian's war council urged their commander on. They said that now was the time to attack Jerusalem. Once again, Vespasian disagreed, choosing to avoid a direct assault on the Holy City. Let the Jews destroy themselves, was his view; with the rebels killing each other and deserting to Rome, the Jews of Jerusalem were doing the Romans' work for them. However, it was not for this reason that in July of AD 68 the Roman operations in Judaea suddenly came to a complete halt.

The suicide of the emperor Nero launched the government of the Roman empire into the greatest crisis of its history. Vespasian knew that according to the constitution he needed to be reinstated by the new emperor before pursuing the war. Therefore, while a successor was chosen, he temporarily suspended his campaign.[30] However, the change that was afoot was far greater than a simple switch of personnel. A revolution was under way that would take the Roman empire into a savage civil war. At stake were two questions: which emperor was to run the empire, and on what grounds should he be appointed? Under the empire's first dynasty, the Julio-Claudians, succession was in practice hereditary although in principle it could only be confirmed by the Senate and the Roman people in Rome. That system was now challenged by an extraordinary revelation: the power to appoint new emperors lay not only in Rome, but with armies in the provinces, championing their own generals. 'A well-hidden secret of the empire had been revealed: it was possible, it seemed, for an emperor to be chosen outside Rome.'[31]

From the sidelines of the Roman east, Vespasian and Titus witnessed a series of amazing reversals in fortune. When Nero's first successor, Servius Sulpicius Galba, refused to give traditional cash donations to the military on his accession, the armies that had brought him to power withdrew their support, and his brief administration came to an end. Galba's head was cut off and the Praetorian Guard in Rome declared his successor to be Marcus Salvius Otho. The new emperor's power base, however, did not stretch beyond the metropolis, and soon the army of the Rhine in Germany declared support for their commander Aulus Vitellius. When his armies defeated Otho's at the battle of Cremona, Otho committed suicide and Vitellius became emperor. However, the rule of this aristocrat, like that of the two men who preceded him, was to be short-lived. Now a man not of high birth, but of practical military experience, a man who could command widespread support among the armies of the eastern provinces, was about to step into the running for the most powerful job in the ancient world.

On 9 July AD 69 the armies of Judaea declared Vespasian emperor of Rome. They were quickly joined in their chorus by the armies of the Danube. While Vespasian took control of the critically important province of Egypt, two armies made their way to Italy in his support. One was made up of eastern legions and led by the governor of Syria, Gaius Licinius Mucianus; the Danubian legions, led by Marcus Antonius Primus, formed the other. The legions based on the Danube beat the eastern legions to Italy and prepared to take on the forces of Vitellius. Once again, two Roman armies met at Cremona. In a horrendously bloody conflict, the supporters of Vespasian won. The vicious slaughter of Romans, however, was far from over.

In the capital Vespasian's brother Flavius Sabinus spear-headed an insurrection against Vitellius's forces before the armies of Antonius and Mucianus could join him. The coup failed, so Sabinus and his faction took refuge on the Capitol. In the attack that followed, the ancient Temple of Jupiter went up in flames. Smoked out, Sabinus and his faction were hauled in front of Vitellius and promptly executed. Revenge was not long in coming. Outside Rome, the legions supporting Vespasian brutally forced their way into the city and defeated Vitellius's army. Search parties hunted high and low for the emperor himself. They discovered him hiding in a doorkeeper's lodge beside the palace, the door blocked pathetically by a bed and a mattress. He was then dragged half-naked into the Forum, publicly tortured, beheaded and thrown into the Tiber.[32]

Vespasian received the news of his victory while still in Egypt in December AD 69. But the celebrations could not have been entirely jubilant. His accession had been a vicious bloodbath in which thousands of Romans had lost their lives. It was hardly the glorious start to the principate that Vespasian wanted. In order to justify seizing power by force and to unify the citizens of the empire in support of his regime, the new emperor Vespasian needed a grand military victory, and he needed it fast. He looked to Judaea. He appointed Titus to be commander of the war, and advised him that with the appointment came a new war aim: immediate victory over the Jews at all costs. The future of the new Flavian dynasty now depended entirely on success in Judaea.[33]

The news capped an extraordinary change in circumstances for Titus. The young general had suddenly risen from legionary legate to the dizzying heights of son and heir of the emperor of Rome. Now he was given the go-ahead for a mission to match the transformation of his status: an assault on the one city that Vespasian and he had avoided for the best part of three years – Jerusalem. But Titus was not the only man who could now reflect on his dramatic change in position. Since Josephus's prophecy had come true, Vespasian summoned his prisoner, cut his chains and set him free.

And yet, although his rights had been restored, Josephus soon found out that he had not quite left the firing line. To the young scholar's mind, Vespasian's rise may well have been proof that God was on the side of the Romans and that victory over the Jews was a foregone conclusion, but not to the mind of Titus. The new commander of Roman forces in Judaea needed Josephus's help in facing the greatest challenge of his life.

JERUSALEM

In March AD 70 Titus drew up his army in front of the great walls of the Holy City. To his auxiliary forces and the fifth, tenth and fifteenth legions, Titus had now added another – the twelfth. This was the same legion that had been so disgracefully defeated by the Jews under the command of Cestius Gallus. Now the soldiers of that legion were out for revenge. Yet despite the show of massive Roman force assembling outside the city, inside it the rebel groups of John of Gischala, Simon ben Gioras and Eleazar ben Simon (leader of the Zealots) were in fighting spirits, their hopes riding high. This moment, after all, was the first time that the city had seen Roman soldiers in nearly four years. Gallus, they could tell themselves, had failed to take the city in AD 66, and since that time the Jews of Jerusalem had seen only a reluctance on the part of the Romans even to try to take it.

In fact, many inside its walls believed that Jerusalem was impossible to besiege. The Jews had food and water to last them years, while in the hills of the deserts and woods outside it the Romans would be short of supplies. The great rock of the Temple in Jerusalem was also a natural fortress surrounded by a significant additional defensive structure: three giant walls.

While the Romans delayed their attack on Jerusalem, the rebels had even improved these. Despite squandering much of their time before Titus's arrival on factional warfare, the Jews had completed parts of the unfinished north wall, increasing it to 10 metres (35 feet) in height.

Their final hope of victory, however, resided in the Romans' commitment of troops. With nearly a quarter of the entire Roman army dedicated to the war in Judaea, had not Rome overextended itself? Surely enemies around its empire might take advantage of the war in Judaea? Rather than pursue a long-drawn-out conflict and expose other parts of the empire, surely the Romans would prefer to come to terms? Surely they would be forced to grant Judaea her independence? The Jews were well aware of their advantages. Now, when Titus sent Josephus to approach the walls and negotiate proposals for peace, they announced their confidence with a pithy statement of intent.

Some of the sentry guards manning the walls knew Josephus well. When he drew too close, they addressed the hated traitor not with words, but actions. A single arrow shot through the air narrowly missed him and hit instead his old friend Nicanor in the left shoulder. To the flight of that one arrow Titus responded by pitching the Roman camps 400 metres (450 yards) from the first wall. Then, after reconnoitring the perimeter of the city, he located the weakest points in the wall that would give access to the upper city, the Antonia Fortress and the Temple complex. Next he gave orders for timber to be collected and for three siege engines to be built. Drawn up in front of the north wall, the mobile wooden towers, 21 metres (65 feet) high, were going to provide essential cover for the soldiers manning the battering rams below. So began in earnest the great siege of Jerusalem. Josephus's detailed, eyewitness account would describe its anatomy.[34]

Although the army of Simon ben Gioras had at its disposal the Roman artillery captured from Gallus's attack, the men still did not know how to use it efficiently. As a result, the Romans were able to approach the walls in units and pound away with battering rams. Despite surprise guerrilla attacks by the Jews, the greatest of the rams, nicknamed Victor, eventually smashed a hole in the wall. The detachment of Romans poured in, fought their way through to the gates, opened them and forced the Jews to abandon the first wall. Four days later the Roman war machine had taken the second wall too. That time, however, Titus made a fatal error.

The Roman soldiers had advanced so quickly that they had forgotten to raze a wide section of the wall they had just breached. When the Jews fought back, they trapped the charging Romans against the second wall. Seizing the advantage, the Jews began slaughtering the Roman assault force as they tried to retreat and squeeze their way back through the narrow gap in the wall. The leaders of the rebel armies, John and Simon, were elated, buoyed up by their first success and scenting a Roman massacre. But the joy soon fell from their faces. Titus quickly deployed his bowmen at either end of the street where the fighting was at its thickest. In this way he pinned the enemy back while the Romans reached safety. Simon and John cared so little for the dead Jewish civilians that they temporarily blocked up the breach in the second wall with their dead bodies. Despite this gruesome obstruction, the second wall too eventually fell to the Romans, and the armies of Simon and John retreated once more.

Titus now paused. He knew that in order to bring siege engines against the third wall and attack the Antonia Fortress and the Temple, he needed to build huge platforms on which to stabilize them. Perhaps too, he thought, the breathing space would give the insurgents time to reflect on the Roman offer of peace and the attractions of surrender. While the soldiers gathered more timber from further and further afield and set about the vast construction work, a psychological battle between Romans and Jews now replaced the physical campaign of previous weeks. It would prove just as intense.

Titus played his gambit. He wanted to present John and Simon with an unnerving picture of the sheer strength of the Roman war machine. In a parade that lasted four days, Titus's army marched around the city and, in full battle dress, received their pay. Inside the city the Jews grew demoralized. The parade only reminded them of their weakness. The fact was that food rations had been badly squandered over the years. Supplies were now running out, and thousands of men, women and children were starving to death. John and Simon had an answer to Titus's display of power: terror. The houses of the rich were ransacked for meagre supplies of corn or a loaf of bread, and Jews they suspected of wanting to leave were threatened and killed.

In desperate search of food, some Jews secretly fled the city at night. When they were successfully captured by the Romans, Titus made an example of them: they were tortured and crucified in full view of those remaining in the city. The brutalized, battle-hardened soldiers made a cruel joke by crucifying the bodies in crude, unnatural poses.[35] When the resolve of some Jews wavered at such a sight, again John and Simon responded by raising the psychological pressure. They forced the waverers to look at the crucified bodies and pretended that the grossly mutilated victims of the Romans were not prisoners but suppliants who had gone to them seeking peace. Thus did the war to win over the minds of those caught in the city intensify. Next Titus deployed his secret weapon.

Josephus was sent in once again to circle the walls of the city, shout peace proposals to the sentry guards and appeal for their surrender. Spare your lives and those of your people; spare your country and your temple, he cried out. Was it still not clear to them that God now resided not in Judaea but in Italy? The Romans were invincible, he argued. They were masters of the whole world, and the submission of great nations to them was an ordinary experience. Now that Judaea was an established province of Rome, it was far too late to put up a fight: '...to try to shake off the yoke was to show not a love of freedom, but a morbid desire for death.'[36] His appeals, however, elicited only one response: a volley of jeers, insults and stones.

Seventeen days after the suspension of the siege, the platforms were complete. The full force of the Roman war machine was about to descend on the third wall. Surely a brilliant Roman victory was imminent? John of Gischala, however, had other ideas. During the pause in the fighting, he devised a plan and put it into action. Working day and night, he and his followers dug a tunnel beneath the ground on which the massive platforms had been raised. As they dug their way through, they supported the tunnel with wooden props. In the fierce belief that Jewish ingenuity could beat Roman power, John tirelessly drove his workforce on until the area beneath one of the platforms had been fully excavated. He then daubed piles of kindling wood with pitch and bitumen, brought them into the tunnel, set the whole place alight and fled.

As the fire burnt the wood props, the ground suddenly gave way. The enormous Roman platform, as well as the men and the engines stationed on it, came thunderously crashing down, and with it weeks of Roman exertion. Inspired by John's example, Simon now led a fanatical assault on the other platforms. Seizing firebrands, the vanguard of Jews 'dashed out as if towards friends, not massed enemies' and tried to set fire to the other engines and the battering rams. When the Romans rushed to rescue their precious platforms and put out the fire, more and more Jews ignored any thoughts of their own safety, threw themselves into the fight and sacrificed their lives to keep the flames burning.[37]

When the damage had been assessed, the Romans were plunged into despondency. Titus knew that the slower his progress in the war, the less glorious the victory. Reputations were won by speed as well as success. Under pressure, he held a war council. When some called for an all-out assault and deployment of the full might of the Roman troops, he refused. However, rebuilding the platforms was not an option either. The scarcity of timber in the region required a round trip of 16 kilometres (10 miles) and it was impossible to prevent Jewish guerrilla attacks. It was time to adopt a different tactic – one that combined the safety of his men with speed: to starve the Jews into surrendering their city.

With an ambition that epitomizes the Romans' command of the ancient world, Titus instructed his officers to organize the building of a wall around Jerusalem. It was to be an airtight seal that would prevent anyone from leaving the city and foraging for supplies. The statistics of it are staggering: in three days the Roman legions built a wall 7 kilometres (4¼ miles) in circumference and punctuated it with thirteen forts. Little tasks, said Titus, were beneath the dignity of Rome. For excellence and speed in executing this gargantuan task, legion competed with legion, cohort with cohort. As Titus inspected the work on horseback, he observed how 'the private was eager to please his decurion, the decurion his centurion, the centurion his tribune; the tribunes were ambitious for the praise of the generals; and of the rivalry between the generals, Titus himself was judge.'[38] The plan was that when the siege had sufficiently weakened Jewish resistance, only then would the platforms be rebuilt and the assault reignited. According to Josephus's gruesome account, it was not long before the Roman general reaped his grim rewards.

Starvation was said to have driven a woman to eat her baby, the streets of Jerusalem filled with the dead, and the roofs of houses in view of the Romans were covered with the bodies of men and women too weak even to stand. When the Romans taunted the Jews with displays of food, Simon's and John's determination to fight on became so entrenched that they alienated some of their closest subordinates. When a tower commander named Judas gathered ten people and shouted out to the Romans that they wanted to desert en masse, Simon broke into the tower before they could make their move and executed them. Other Jews, pretending to advance for battle, successfully escaped in their hundreds and handed themselves over to the Romans, only to discover that food was more lethal than the hunger they had left behind. Instead of eating little by little and allowing their bodies to grow accustomed to food again, they ate non-stop and thus killed themselves.

Among the people caught up in the horror of the siege were two whom Josephus was most anxious about: his mother and father. He had learnt that they were alive but imprisoned. Perhaps it was out of fear for their lives that Josephus approached the walls and made another plea for the Jews to surrender. This time the rebels hit their target. Josephus was struck on the head by a missile and knocked unconscious. A race to collect the body of the Jews' most wanted man ensued. The Romans reached it first and rescued their negotiator.

It took twenty-one days for timber to be gathered again and the platforms to be rebuilt. The surrounding countryside reflected the bleak, grinding work: all about were dusty tracts, grassy desert and the sad stumps of dead trees. While the Romans were sapped of all energy by their toils, the armies of John and Simon drew on inhuman reserves of determination. They seemed to rise like ghosts, thriving on famine, fatigue and infighting, only to launch yet another assault and disrupt the

Roman preparations. Although these guerrilla sorties often failed, the fact that they persisted gave the Jews a moral victory.

Soon the Romans were once again pounding at the last wall. Protected from the deluge of missiles, stones and arrows by their shields, the workers ground away with rams, hands and crowbars to lever loose the foundation stones of the wall and cut a breach through it. Eventually, it was not Roman grit that provided the breakthrough, but the tunnel dug by John. While it had once allowed the Jews to destroy the platforms, now it yielded an advantage to Romans: the tunnel fell in and the wall suddenly collapsed in a heap of giant stones. Titus ordered his strongest legionaries to take immediate advantage of this. At two o'clock in the morning an advance unit of Romans charged into the disused tunnel and collided with the armies of John and Simon waiting for them. In the close quarters the Romans jabbed mechanically with their short swords, hardly able to tell Roman from Jew and the direction of advance from retreat. Bodies were crushed underfoot and the noise of groaning and screaming filled the confined, fetid space. Eventually, however, the Roman infantry bloodily pummelled their way through, forcing the Jews to retreat to the holiest part of the city, the Temple complex.

Titus had already taken control of the Antonia Fortress that buttressed the colonnade of the Temple complex. He now ordered it to be razed to the ground: a wide, level access would make the driving ascent of four Roman legions much easier. Before he gave the signal, however, Titus had a final offer to make to the rebels. He turned once again to Josephus, who took his stand in full view of the Jews protected by the Temple enclosure and, speaking in Aramaic, addressed John. Surrender, spare the people and the city, he said, and Rome would still pardon him. This was his last chance. If he persisted in fighting and desecrating the Temple, God would punish him. John launched a torrent of abuse at the turncoat Josephus. Stung, the young priest and scholar gave up. Choking with emotion, he shouted, 'It is God then, God Himself who is bringing with the Romans fire to purge the Temple and is blotting out the city brimful of corruption as if it had never been.'[39] With those words, a monster was unleashed.

The Temple complex was the most well-built part of the city. After six days of battering the walls of its outer court, not a dent had been made. Eventually, the silver gates were set on fire, and as the metal melted, the Romans set fire to the colonnade bit by bit and broke in. As the massive assault drew closer to the inner court and the sanctuary, a heated debate took place between Titus and his officers: what should be done about the Temple itself? Some said that it should be destroyed. If it remained standing, there would never be peace in the Roman province of Judaea. The Temple would remain a symbol around which Jews throughout the world would rally. Others disagreed. It should be spared, they said, but only so long as the Jews did not try to defend themselves in it. If that happened, it would cease to be a holy place and become a military fortress. Titus heard all their opinions, but it was perhaps Josephus who influenced his eventual decision. The commander declared the Temple a precious work of art. In saving it, said Titus, he would bequeath a glorious ornament to the emperor and the Roman people.[40]

In mid-July AD 70, over three months since the start of Titus's campaign, the battle for the outer court of the Temple raged on. The heavy infantry lines of both Roman and Jewish armies were drawn up and warred with each other under a barrage of spears, arrows and missiles of every kind. Gradually the Roman lines, eight ranks deep, advanced and drove the Jews into the inner court. When, after some days, the Jewish army formations broke down and dispersed, the Romans broke through to the inner court. At that moment the battle boiled over and the legionaries cut loose. After the best part of four long, gruelling years of campaign, the Roman soldiers vented their wild hatred on the enemy. Piling through all the entrances, they no longer distinguished between Jewish soldier and civilian. All were indiscriminately slaughtered. The steps of the Temple were awash with blood. In front of them and near the Holy Altar corpses were piled high, those on the top sometimes slithering to the bottom. The din of butchery, however, was about to get a lot worse.

In the chaos a Roman soldier seized a firebrand and threw it through a small opening into the Temple. Soon the building was on fire. A messenger reported the news to Titus. The general leapt up and, with his guard panting after him, dashed towards the sanctuary. Once inside, he saw that the fire could be stopped. He screamed at the soldiers to put it out, but no one paid him any attention. They were too consumed with greed, with getting their just deserts. The slaughter of Jews had given way to mass looting. Darting through the blazing fires, soldiers raided the treasures of the Temple and carried off whatever they could get their hands on. Ancient cups and basins of pure gold, curtains and bejewelled garments, and, most precious of all, the holy seven-branched candelabrum, the shewbread table and the ritual trumpets all fell into the polluted hands of the Roman soldiers. The most sanctified part of the Temple, the iconic epicentre of the Jewish faith, was cleaned out and left to burn.

Plundering was not confined to the Temple alone. In part of the outer court colonnade stood the treasury where the Jews had brought all their gold and precious possessions for safe-keeping during the siege. The Romans now stripped that too before setting it on fire. Coincidentally, a huge crowd of 6000 civilian men, women and children had gathered there in the belief that they would find signs of deliverance from God. According to Josephus, the false prophets who had spread the word were the hired hands of John and Simon; the rebel leaders had told them to issue this prophecy because they wanted to prevent further desertions and thus shore up morale during the battle for the Temple. All the civilians were now helplessly caught up in the flames and met their deaths.

The rebellion of the Jews had been crushed. The insurgents who had fought on in the inner court now burst through the ring of assault surrounding them, and fled into the upper city. The killing squads of Roman soldiers clambered awkwardly over the layer of dead bodies covering the floor of the outer court and gave chase in a blind bid to hunt them down. John and Simon, however, managed to escape. As a mark of Roman supremacy, pagan standards were brought into the Temple complex and erected opposite the east gate. Sacrifices were offered to the emperor and a single cry hailed the victor, Titus. As the city blazed, raucous shouts of 'Commander! Commander!' rose up. Each soldier was so laden with loot that when they later sold their gold for cash, they flooded the market and the value of gold in Syria was halved.[41]

Inside the upper city John, Simon and the Jewish survivors were themselves trapped by the Roman circumvallation. Unable to escape from Jerusalem, they had no option but to ask Titus to talks. Many of their followers, their spirits at last broken, hoped for a pardon. The hardline leaders, however, wanted to leave the city to the Romans and live peacefully in the desert with their fellow survivors. The Roman general was furious. The enemy had been defeated, yet here they were brazenly asking for terms as if they were victors. Taking his stand on a wall that linked the Temple with the upper city, Titus kept his composure as he spoke to John and Simon. He berated the Jews for their ingratitude to Rome, to the power that ruled Judaea.

You were incited against the Romans by Roman kindness. First we gave you the land to occupy and set over you kings of your own race; then we upheld the laws of your fathers, and allowed you complete control of your internal and external affairs; above all, we permitted you to raise taxes for God and to collect offerings, and we neither discouraged nor interfered with those who brought them – so that you could grow richer to our detriment and prepare at our expense to make war on us! Then, enjoying such advantages, you flung your abundance at the heads of those who furnished it, and like beasts you bit the hand that fed you! ... [When my father came into the country] he ravaged Galilee and the outlying districts, giving you time to come to your senses. But you took generosity for weakness, and our gentleness only served to increase your audacity... Most unwillingly I brought engines to bear on your walls. My soldiers, ever thirsting for your blood, I held in leash. After every victory, as if it was a defeat, I appealed to you for an armistice... After all that, you disgusting people, do you now invite me to a conference?[42]

The Jews had broken the *pax Romana*. Nonetheless, Titus made a final offer: if the surviving rebels now surrendered, they would at least be spared their lives. When John and Simon defiantly reasserted their wishes, Titus gave the rest of the city over to his soldiers. The command was to sack, burn and raze.

EPILOGUE

Over the next few days, the principal buildings of Jerusalem, including the Council Chamber, were all destroyed, the remaining treasures were handed over, and the survivors of the Roman terror were rounded up in a part of the Temple complex known as the Court of the Women. The old and sick were killed, and thousands of insurgents were executed, taking the total of those killed in the siege to 1,100,000, according to Josephus. The rest, numbering 97,000, were sold into slavery. The young were sent to hard labour in Egypt, or to become fodder for the gladiators and beasts of Roman arenas throughout the empire. The tallest and most handsome of the rebels, however, were saved for the triumph back in Rome. After hiding in the sewers for weeks, John and Simon eventually surrendered and joined them.

Back in the capital city, the emperor Vespasian was reunited with Titus to the rapturous joy of the Roman crowds. They streamed into the streets to get a view of the victorious general. In the imperial entourage entering the city was Josephus. He would soon be rewarded with Roman citizenship, a handsome pension and lodging in the house in which Vespasian had lived before he became emperor. Here he would sit down to write his history of the Jewish Revolt. A few days after Titus's return, father and son enjoyed their reward too: a magnificent triumph.

Wreathed in crowns of bay leaves and dressed in the traditional purple robes flecked with silver stars of the triumphal general, they rode at the centre of a spectacular procession. They stopped first at the portico of Augustus's sister Octavia, where the senators and knights awaited them and a stage had been set up. Vespasian mounted it and brought the booming shouts of the soldiers and crowds all dressed in their best clothes to a complete hush. With his toga covering his head in the manner of priests, he offered up prayers to the gods.

Then the procession continued. In addition to the thousands of captive slaves, there were also grand floats wrought with gold and ivory, some of them three or four storeys high. On them were borne aloft large tableaux dramatizing scenes from the war in Judaea so that all Rome bore witness to them, as if the people had been there themselves and could rightly share in the celebration of the Roman victory. The crowds gasped too at the spoils. It was as if an exquisite river of gold and silver flowed through Rome. Most prominently displayed were the treasures from the Temple and a scroll of Jewish law known as the Torah.

The parade now approached the Temple of Jupiter on the Capitol. It was still presumably in a state of ruin following the violence before Vespasian's forces had entered Rome and concluded the civil war a year earlier. The procession halted and waited for news from the Forum. Here, according to Roman custom, Simon ben Gioras was dragged out of the Mamertine prison in the northwest corner, beaten up and executed. The sentence on John of Gischala had been more lenient. He faced a regime of hard labour and captivity for the rest of his life. The news of Simon's death was now brought to Vespasian on the Capitol, sacrifices were offered and a rich public feast was devoured.

The imperial public relations machine did not stop there, however. The new dynasty of the Flavians was being founded and legitimized in stone too. Profits from the war in Judaea were ploughed into building the Colosseum. Constructed in part from money raised by the sale of Jewish slaves, it was completed after Vespasian's death by Titus in AD 80, and remains one of the most enduring symbols of Roman power. Vespasian also reconstructed the area around the Capitoline Hill with a glorious temple complex and forum. The message to the Jews – indeed, to any rebels throughout the length and breadth of the empire – could not have been clearer: we destroyed your most holy places, it said, now you can pay for the rebuilding of ours. The emperor dedicated his new temple to peace. Finally, when Titus too passed away after a brief and popular reign of two years, his brother, the emperor Domitian, built the Arch of Titus in his honour. The memory of Rome's insult to Jewish independence was thus kept alive to this day.

In Judaea, Roman mopping-up operations continued until perhaps as late as AD 74. None of the remaining strongholds of rebellion posed any real threat to Rome, but still Vespasian ordered them to be stamped out. The most dramatic conflict was at Masada. Here a Jewish group known as the Sicarii, led by Eleazar ben Yair, took refuge in the fortress perched upon a spectacular outcrop of rock. They held out for years until the Romans built a massive siege ramp that gave access up the steep slope to the top of the rock. But by the time the soldiers reached the fortress, they discovered that all 966 rebels had committed mass suicide rather than become slaves to Rome. Only a woman and her five children survived to report what had happened. The determination of Vespasian in bringing about a total annihilation of Jewish resistance is brought vividly to life today by the extraordinary archaeological remains of the Roman operations at Masada.

When the war was finally over, Roman administration of Judaea was upgraded. A permanent garrison was established and the desolate province became the responsibility of a legate of the emperor. Jerusalem itself was not rebuilt as a civilian settlement for sixty years. In due course, rabbis established new ways to worship without the Temple. Indeed, the situation deteriorated under the emperor Hadrian. When he planned to found a Roman colony, Aelia Capitolina, on the site of Jerusalem, a second rebellion had to be suppressed in AD 135 and, according to Christian sources, the Jews were permanently excluded from the Holy City.

By that time, however, the Roman empire was thriving in a glorious golden age of peace.

Hadrian

In AD 76, the seventh year of Vespasian's rule, Publius Aelius Hadrianus was born in Rome. Although he had no connection to the Flavian dynasty under whose rule he entered the world, just over forty years later Hadrian would become the fourteenth emperor of Rome. He would at that time also become the first emperor in its history to sport a beard. It was close-cropped and carefully trimmed, but unmistakably a beard. Although he was said to have grown it in order to hide the blemishes on his face, Hadrian's beard would become a defining symbol of his age. In microcosmic form it described another revolution – another key transformation in the long life of the Roman empire. It epitomized, as we shall see, the age of the 'good emperors', the high point of the Roman commonwealth, the age of peace that lasted, with the exception of one period of crisis, for over 140 years. The seeds of the shift that heralded this 'golden age' were sown in the reign of Hadrian's predecessor – his beardless cousin Trajan.

The Last Conqueror

Pliny the Younger, a senator and provincial governor who corresponded regularly with the emperor, described Trajan as of 'splendid bearing, tall stature' with a 'fine head and noble countenance'. Even that head's receding hairline only enhanced 'his look of majesty'.[1] It was a portrait that fitted the image. Trajan was of the old school. He was an exceptional and heroic military commander, an *imperator*, holder of the supreme military authority with which emperors ruled the known world. Indeed, on his accession in AD 98 Trajan had a lot to live up to. His father had distinguished himself under Vespasian and Titus as commander of the tenth legion in the Jewish Revolt and had gone on to become governor of the strategically important province of Syria. Appropriately, the way in which Trajan chose to live up to his father's achievements was old-fashioned Roman expansion and conquest. The ripe territory that would be plucked and fall within his grasp was the kingdom of Dacia.

Located in eastern Europe, north of the river Danube, Dacia possessed every ingredient that made it magnetically attractive to the steely embrace of the *pax Romana*. It was an independent kingdom ruled by Decebalus, though Rome of course interpreted that independence as a threat. It was sophisticated and wealthy, thanks to its productive gold and silver mines, which were eyed enviously from afar. Finally, it had made an elementary mistake in offering Rome a case for war. During the reign of Domitian, the last of the Flavian emperors, Decebalus had shown barefaced cheek in crossing the Danube and attacking Roman territory. In the brief war that resulted two Roman commanders had been killed, and Domitian eventually concluded a dishonourable, unsatisfactory peace. Trajan now sought to rectify that. Rome wanted revenge, the exaction of 'justice', the requiting of what was its due.

Between 101 and 106 Trajan launched two wars against the Dacians. When he set out he had no military successes of his own to date; by the time he returned that was no longer the case. The war he waged was the greatest act of aggression since Claudius's conquest of Britain. No one, however, would guess how utterly ferocious these campaigns would be. In an already crowded field, their unstinting brutality was rarely equalled in all Roman history. They far exceeded the 'regime change' goal of toppling Decebalus. The Dacian wars were devoted to nothing less than genocide – the eradication of an ancient 'barbarian' culture, the installation of proper, loyal and civilized colonies of Roman citizens, and the plunder of the region's riches for the betterment of the empire. The complete story is pithily told in Dacia's modern name: Romania.

Only the Romans could celebrate the 'victory' with such extravagance, pride and magnificence. The wealth garnered by Trajan from the war was ploughed into a new harbour at Ostia, the port of Rome. Here was space for concrete moorings and ramps, warehouses and wharves, administrative offices for the provinces (each endowed perhaps with a fitting mosaic to describe the nature or origin of the produce it dispatched), and the wholesale fish, wine and oil markets. The seating capacity of the ancient Circus Maximus was once again expanded, this time to hold 150,000 people. In the heart of the city a magnificent Roman shopping centre went into construction. The expansive marbled piazza was designed to house the rows of temporary stalls, and enclosing it were elegant semicircular tiers of shops and offices terraced into the hillside. This was not, however, the most eye-catching monument to the victory over Dacia.

Trajan's Column, still standing in Rome today, is 30 metres (100 feet) high, made from twenty massive blocks of Carrara marble and is carved with a long, upwardly spiralling series of 155 scenes illustrating the Dacian campaign. The attention to detail is exquisite; almost no set piece is overlooked. Here Trajan addresses his troops, there the soldiers sacrifice a boar, a ram and a bull to purify themselves before battle. Elsewhere the army ships its supplies and builds a fort, and in many other scenes the soldiers pelt their enemy with ballistas fired from their artillery engines and bury their swords deep into Dacian bodies. The Romans are methodical; the Dacians – such as the messenger who appears to fall off his horse – ramshackle. It's a macabre celebration of genocide, but also a highly useful historical document. It reveals the sheer scale, organization and ambition lying behind a Roman military conquest. Inside the column there is further skilled craftsmanship to admire: a spiral staircase winds its way to the top and the chamber at its base would later become the conqueror of Dacia's tomb.

Before Trajan died, however, he had one more ambitious military campaign in him, one more figure to measure up to. Having quite spectacularly outstripped the career of his father, he now wanted to emulate none other than Alexander the Great. To do that he turned his gaze east. The territory of the rich Parthian state stretched from Turkey and the border of Roman Syria all the way across Iraq (Mesopotamia) and into Iran and Afghanistan. A war against Rome's great nemesis would thus take Trajan too on a road of conquest in the direction of the limit Alexander reached: India. The excuse justifying war was a familiar one. The Parthian ruler was interfering once again in Armenia, the buffer-state-cum-client-kingdom loyal to Rome. The balance of power on Rome's eastern frontier was again in jeopardy. Action was urgently required.

In 114 Trajan and his army marched east. The king of Armenia quickly capitulated, and his kingdom soon became a Roman province; so too did northern Mesopotamia, the land en route to a Roman foray into Media (the north of modern Iran). By 116 Trajan was again expanding Roman control and breaking new ground. In that year he reached the westernmost nook of the Persian Gulf, stopped at the shore and stared out to sea. He was looking towards the iconic land he had thus far only imagined. Were he a younger man, he said despondently, he would have followed Alexander's footsteps to India.[2]

Now, exhausted by two years of campaigning in the unforgiving heat of the Arabian deserts, he had to concede that the Greek conqueror was the greater man. Nonetheless, there were extraordinary achievements to note. In his dispatches back to the Senate in Rome the long list of incomprehensibly named peoples whom he had conquered en route was translating into the prospect of an unprecedented glut of triumphs in the metropolis. Trajan, however, would not live to celebrate even one of them.

The collapse of Trajan's achievements happened even faster than their accomplishment. The further east he had ventured, the more exposed and difficult to retain became those places he had already subdued. In 117 Trajan fell ill. His entourage and a column of soldiers made a sombre, mournful retreat back to Italy. By August the supine emperor had reached Selinus on the coast of southern Turkey. There he suffered a stroke and died. He was in his early seventies and left behind no children. He did, however, leave an heir.

That, at least, was the story circulated immediately by those at Trajan's bedside – his wife Plotina and his niece Matidia – the ink of their signatures still wet on the official document specifying the succession. Trajan's adopted son and nominated successor, they announced, was the then Roman governor of Syria. That man was by turns Trajan's cousin, a close companion of Plotina, and the husband of Matidia's daughter Sabina.

A NEW DIRECTION

When the army recognized Trajan's nominee and hailed him emperor, Hadrian's claim to the throne was, if not exactly impeccable and unrivalled, certainly solid. Just to make sure, however, a pragmatic safety measure was required. Although Hadrian denied any involvement to the end of his days, four men in Rome – all influential, able senators and ex-consuls – were murdered within days of the announcement of the new emperor's accession. A story went around that they had been plotting to overthrow Hadrian; according to Dio, however, it was the threat which their wealth and influence posed that was their real undoing.[3] Hadrian's inauguration took place in the Syrian capital of Antioch on 11 August 117.

With his position secured as supreme leader of the vast Roman world, Hadrian took his time journeying from the province of Syria to the capital of what was now his empire. The man who travelled in imperial splendour was fifty-one years old, tall and cut a novel figure for an emperor. Like Trajan, Hadrian's family background was highly unusual. He came not from Rome or even Italy, but from an old, moneyed Italian family who lived in southern Spain near Seville. His ancestors were Roman colonists who had settled there during the Roman conquest of Spain at the turn of the third and second centuries BC. They had invested their money in agriculture and the local silver mines, and the fortunes they made set them up as the bedrock of the wealthy local Roman élite. Hadrian's parochial origins were evident in his voice. When he spoke Latin he did so with a heavy provincial accent, a fact of which he was embarrassed. As Trajan's speech-maker earlier in his career, he had been laughed at whenever he uttered a word. There was also the matter of his beard.

Trajan, the first 'Spanish' emperor, was a classic martial hero. As a result, like Julius Caesar, Augustus and all the Roman emperors before him, he was close-shaved, and his hair, combed forward, was a neatly cropped cap. Hadrian's hair, by contrast, was soft and wavy – a more casual style than that of his predecessors. But it was his facial hair that suggested a clean break with the past regime. Some might have thought it suggested a lack of discipline, the mark of a poor soldier, but that was not the case. In Dacia he had excelled as a commander and had twice been decorated with the highest military honours. He was at ease in conversation and mixing with fellow soldiers of all ranks. His relaxed, open manner was a quality he would carry into his rule, though it was said that this disguised 'a harsh, jealous, libidinous temperament'.[4] Even as emperor he continued to enjoy a military diet of cheese and bacon, he disliked soft mattresses and had an impressive ability to drink copious amounts of alcohol, a talent he had honed on campaign in Trajan's inner circle.

Still, the beard would come to say something different about this man's complex character and the new direction in which he would take the Roman empire. It hinted not at Roman war and conquest, but the culture, the learning and the reflective, intellectual life of the ancient Greeks. Hadrian's aristocratic education paved the way for the passions of his life. He wrote poetry, and he was proud of his skill in playing the lyre and the flute, but above all he enjoyed geometry and sculpture. As a young man, Hadrian had studied in Athens and earned the nickname 'Little Greek'. Like Nero, however, he would take his Hellenistic interests way beyond the standard considered acceptable for an educated Roman aristocrat, let alone a future emperor.

His drive to excel and his inquisitive mind made him, for example, an accomplished, experimenting architect. The building of a temple to Venus would be the very first mark he would make on the city, the first imprint of his reign. He drew up the plans himself. When Apollodorus, the most famous architect of the day, criticized the proportions of the columns on the drafts that, in deference, the emperor had sent to him for approval, the quick-tempered, unforgiving Hadrian promptly had him killed. The criticism did not deter him; rather, it drove him on. The most innovative building that he sponsored was the

Pantheon in Rome, an ambitious rebuilding of the structure first erected by Agrippa in the reign of the emperor Augustus. The idea of a temple dedicated not just to one god but to all the gods of the Roman empire was a thoroughly Roman piece of one-upmanship. That same spirit was reflected in the building's spectacular architecture too, made possible by the Roman invention of concrete. This liberated Hadrian, allowing him to break new ground and experiment with new, non-classical forms. In overseeing the creation of the temple's dome – even greater than that of St Peter's in the Vatican – he outstripped the founding father of the Roman empire. Even today the Pantheon is the most complete of the buildings of ancient Rome to survive. As we shall see, the empire at large was also to benefit from Hadrian's inventive love of architecture.

In his personal life Hadrian lived too as if in imitation of the ancient Greeks. Sexual norms in the ancient world were not the same as our own. For example, there was a strong Greek tradition that a relationship between an older man and a boy on the threshold of manhood was acceptable (the peak of attractiveness was considered to be the moment when the down appeared on a young man's cheek). By contrast, a homosexual relationship between men of equal age and status was not deemed acceptable. The philhellenic Hadrian took the Greek role of the older lover to heart. During his years in Trajan's inner circle, Hadrian was known to be passionately fond of the young men who made up the junior staff in the imperial entourage. Later, in the seventh year of his own rule, Hadrian was travelling with his wife Sabina in Turkey when he met the young, good-looking Antinous. The emperor was smitten. Antinous joined his entourage and for the next seven years, much to the embarrassment of many Romans, never left his lover's side. (The sex was not the problem; it was rather the fact that the emperor seemed so completely devoted to the young man.) Although thirty years his junior, Antinous shared Hadrian's Hellenic loves; they debated in the Museum of Alexandria, and while there together, they visited the tombs of Alexander the Great and Pompey the Great.

In fact, the world over which Hadrian was supreme ruler was largely Greek. The culture of the Romans had grown partly out of ancient Greek culture, partly as a reflection of Greek culture and partly in opposition to Greek culture. In ancient literature there could have been no *Aeneid* by Virgil without the epic *Odyssey* and *Iliad* by Homer. Without the Stoic school of philosophy, the philosophical works of Cicero and Seneca would have lacked their inspiration. Without Epicurus (Hadrian's favourite philosopher) there would have been no Lucretius. Indeed, half the Roman world (the eastern half) spoke Greek, not Latin, as their first language. Now a different kind of man was in charge of this Greek-Roman empire. He was a successful commander, a soldier's soldier and highly popular with the army. He had legitimacy, an undisputed claim to the throne, and he took his Hellenistic leanings seriously. Indeed he had an obsessive desire to be the best. Under this man's rule the old idea that war and conquest alone shaped the Roman world was unceremoniously dumped.

The start of the change was apparent at the very beginning of his reign. Hadrian abandoned Trajan's eastern campaigns. Their failure had discredited the policy of Roman expansion, and the change in direction fitted harmoniously with the mood of the Senate. The priority now was not conquest, but staying within the existing frontiers and reinforcing them. In 121 Hadrian set out from Italy and went to the Rhine frontier. Its strategic importance was reflected in the large number of legions manning it – eight in Germany alone. After arriving on this northern border, Hadrian spent the rest of the year ensuring that the Roman forts, ramparts and watchtowers were strengthened, and that the legions on this and the Danube frontier were drilled to a high standard of military discipline. A determination for the same strategy to be deployed in the empire's most northerly frontier next took Hadrian to Britain in 122. While there it is possible that he initiated the construction of the impressive Pons Aelius, the Roman bridge named after him, which straddled the broad estuary at Newcastle. On the northern side of the river he stood at the site of the future World Heritage landmark, the great symbol of Roman containment that bears his name today.

FRONTIERS

The sheer scale and ambition of Hadrian's vision still staggers. Running 118 kilometres (70 miles) across country, from the North Sea to the Irish Sea, the frontier wall he authorized took ten years to build. Its construction was supervised by the new governor of Roman Britain, Aulus Platorius Nepos. Although just under two-thirds of the wall was made of stone, the last (easternmost) third was originally made of turf and timber. The proportions were as bold as its length. The stone section was 3 metres (10 feet) thick and 4.2 metres (14 feet) high; the turf section matched the stone part for height, but was 6 metres (20 feet) thick. About twenty paces to the north of the wall, and running parallel with it, was a V-shaped ditch 8 metres (26 feet) wide and 3 metres (10 feet) deep. On top of the wall itself was a walkway defended by a crenellated parapet. A Roman soldier walking it would have come across a towered, fortified gateway every Roman mile (approximately 1.5 kilometres), and in between, at every third of that mile (0.5 kilometres) an observation turret. Servicing the wall, as well as forming part of it, were sixteen forts.

One historical summary of Hadrian's rule says simply that the wall divided 'the Romans and the Barbarians'.[5] Touring the wall today, it's tempting to see it as a powerful, entirely defensive structure against an amorphous barbaric enemy. That, however, was not Hadrian's intention, as recent historians have emphasized. A comparison with another Roman feat of engineering is revealing. Hadrian's predecessor Trajan had dammed the river Danube and then built a spectacular bridge across its broad expanse. This became his neat little stepping stone into Dacia. (In the east he even intended to build – but never did – a canal between the Tigris and the Euphrates of Mesopotamia in order to ferry his fleet between the rivers.) Like Julius Caesar's bridge across the Rhine, Trajan's structure in Dacia imposed Roman will on the landscape to make it serve the empire. In the methodical, stately language of architecture and engineering, it loudly proclaimed Roman power.

Hadrian's Wall should perhaps be seen more accurately as his attempt to bellow a similar message of his and Rome's power.[6] Other evidence too suggests that it is misleading to regard the wall as a purely defensive structure. It could, for example, be deployed aggressively; as well as being a sophisticated and powerful bulwark, the wall could also be a starting point for northward attacks and forays. The wall was not just a barrier but a road too, an important line of communication connecting it with a wider network of roads and stopping-off points that scored the breadth of the Roman empire. The administration and domination of the Roman world depended on such lines of communication. As further evidence countering the impression of Hadrian's Wall as a final frontier, there existed under Hadrian many examples of working Roman forts further north of the wall. At the time of the wall's construction, the Roman army was on relatively peaceful terms with the native Britons on either side of it. The peoples to the north and south were not easily distinguished as 'barbarian' or 'Roman'; as in many frontier regions today, they were much more culturally mixed than those terms suggest. The idea of defence, then, was only one aspect of a project that was in fact proud, versatile and dynamic.

The wall increased Roman power in one way above all. It gave the garrisons stationed on it the power of observation. From this stemmed the power of controlling who entered or left the commonwealth of the Roman world, the ability to monitor who traded in it, spoke its language and wore its dress, and the means of regulating who paid its taxes and how that tax was spent. In short it emphasized Roman mastery of their world. Only later, in a less prosperous, more unstable time in the future, would the wall shift in significance, as walls have done throughout history. Only then would it become a symbol of containment, a hermetic seal, the vestigial outpost of a once-vibrant entity.

Although the wall is, then, symbolic of the new direction in which Hadrian would take the empire, this was not a simple about-turn. It was erected not in the spirit of vulnerability or retraction, but quite the opposite.

THE MECHANICS OF EMPIRE

What kind of prospering worldwide empire, then, did Hadrian's Wall enclose at its northernmost point? A thumbnail sketch of the empire at peace might begin with the soldiers inhabiting the barracks close to the wall. The Latin accents and second languages that would have been heard paint a picture of extraordinary fluidity. The soldiers came not only from Britain, but from Belgium, Spain, Gaul and Dacia. Stationed at Arbeia (the fort at present-day South Shields) there was even a naval auxiliary unit from Mesopotamia.[7] The beautifully sculpted tombstone of Regina, the British wife of a man called Barates, tells an equally fascinating story. It shows how this man, possibly a soldier or camp follower, came all the way from Palmyra in

Syria, fell in love with his female slave from Hertfordshire, freed her and settled down to married life in Britain. His valedictory inscription to his dead wife is written in Aramaic, his native tongue. The name of one Arterius Nepos is similarly revealing. It crops up in records in both Armenia and Egypt, before finding its way to northern Britain.

The theme of fluidity is important. The Roman armies on the frontiers were not fixed garrisons. Locally, and from province to province, the legions and the auxiliary units were recruited and deployed with great flexibility; they were constantly on the move. The visibility and presence that this mobility gave them was the key factor in the Roman army successfully controlling an area far larger than it was possible to garrison.

At one fort near the wall, Vindolanda, an unprecedented discovery was made in the 1970s and 1980s – a haul of several hundred wooden writing tablets all found at the one site. Many record administrative matters, such as financial accounts and requests for leave. Others make for more entertaining reading. For example, there is an affectionate invitation to a birthday party from one garrison commander's wife to another, and a soldier's receipt of fresh supplies of socks, sandals and underwear to keep out the winter chills. These letters would have reached the forts from the wider empire through the imperial postal service. Coursing along a network of roads some 90,000 kilometres (56,000 miles) long and connecting Carlisle to Aswan, the letters reached Hadrian's Wall courtesy of the *cursus publicus* (the postal service for official Roman business). Replies were dispersed in exactly the same way. The postmen who collected and delivered these letters stayed at inns en route, and the roads they travelled on were designed for easy drainage and marked by milestones.

The correspondence filtering into the channels of the imperial post also reveal how Hadrian's empire was run. It is extraordinary to think that any one of the empire's 70 million Roman citizens could in theory appeal to the emperor for help. He was the final arbiter. It's no less surprising that citizens could expect a response. As we shall see, emperors such as Hadrian liked to cultivate an ideology of accessibility. The reality of course was very different. The sheer numbers of petitions and requests for imperial favour from this or that community, for adjudication in a matter of law for this or that individual is salutary. Exact figures are not known, but in this period of Rome's golden age the governor of Egypt is said by one source to have fielded an extraordinary 1208 petitions in a single day. One can only imagine how many the emperor Hadrian in Rome received.

Clearly, in order to process all the petitions, the emperor and his provincial governors relied on a huge bureaucracy of administrative advisers with wide, albeit circumscribed, areas of responsibility. The preserved correspondence between the Roman governor of Bithynia-Pontus, Pliny the Younger, and Trajan reflect the vitality of that relationship and where those limits of accountability lay. Pliny's letters to Trajan and others are works of world literature. There was, however, no space for creative flourishes in the bulk of functional, administrative correspondence. In one letter Pliny complains that one of the chores of being a public servant was having to write a vast amount of 'highly illiterate letters'.[8]

Although one might imagine the Roman emperor, governor or commander perfunctorily signing off the replies to the mass of mundane requests that either they or their subordinates had dealt with, one thing is certain. The replies and the resolution of the problems presented – be it a dispute over land, a question of divorce or the matter of citizenship – would transform the lives of the petitioners. The successful running of the empire and the happiness of its citizens thus depended on delegation on a massive scale.

How could the Roman emperor, the Roman governor or the Roman commander be sure that decent, deserving people were appointed to posts in the imperial administration and were able to discharge their duties effectively? As the wooden tablets found at Vindolanda reveal, the imperial post also delivered the all-important letters of recommendation. Among them one can read the advocacy by one friend to another of the virtues and qualities of yet another friend. Such references were vital in selecting people to play a part in the pyramids of bureaucratic administration. In short, what your friends said about you established your reputation and trustworthiness. The logic of this system was simple and effective. The more people wanted to protect their reputation, the less likely they were to recommend a bad egg and thus jeopardize their own standing in the future.

In the hands of administrators appointed by this highly personal Roman system of hiring, most issues were dealt with locally. Only when a matter became a crisis did it come to the attention and decision of the emperor. Beyond this basic prescription for government, Hadrian had also found another way of bringing his rule closer to the citizens of his empire. Under his reign, the presence and visibility of the emperor were stronger than under his predecessors for one simple reason: he liked to travel.

Hadrian spent no less than half of his twenty-one-year rule abroad. Between 121 and 125 his travels took him from his wall in northern Britain to southern Spain, North Africa, Syria, the Black Sea and Asia Minor. Later, the period 128–32 saw him in Greece, Judaea and Egypt. Whether in York, Seville, Carthage, Luxor, Palmyra, Trabzon or Ephesus, Hadrian was always within the bounds of one political state, where Greek and Latin were the commonly spoken languages and over which he was the supreme ruler. He travelled always with his wife Sabina, and their imperial cavalcade of friends, baggage-carriers, guards,

ABOVE: An elegant fresco from *c.* AD 65 decorating a stuccoed ceiling in Nero's Golden House. The private palace, built in the centre of Rome, inspired the acidic graffiti: 'The whole of Rome will become a single house. Romans, emigrate to Veii before that house swallows up Veii too!' The rediscovery of these paintings inspired artists of the Renaissance, such as Raphael.

BELOW: A plan of the rooms of the lower floor of the Golden House. The remains lie under ground, beneath the baths of Trajan, and have recently been restored. Although impressive, this was actually just one part of the whole palace.

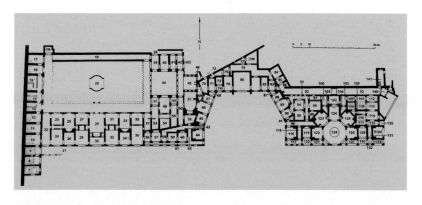

LEFT: Bust of Seneca – senator, philosopher, tragedian, satirist and tutor to Nero. His key philosophical work advised Nero to exercise absolute power with 'clemency'. He was also criticized, however, for being Nero's 'teacher in tyranny'.

ABOVE: A mosaic panel from Pompeii showing a scene from a comedy by the Greek playwright Menander. For most of Roman history Greek culture played a very important, if ambivalent, role. It was acclaimed, but could also be seen as decadent, effete and one reason for that civilization's downfall.

RIGHT: A contemporary bust of Emperor
Vespasian. After the profligacy of Nero, he
stood for a return to financial probity. One
of his new taxes was levied on urine (used, for
example, in Roman laundry). When his son
suggested that this income was undignified,
he picked up some gold coins and replied,
'See, my son, if they have any smell.'

BELOW: A sculpted relief panel from the Arch of
Titus, AD 80s. The monument depicts soldiers
carrying the sacred treasures stolen from the
Temple of Jerusalem after the brutal suppression
of the Jewish Revolt of AD 66–70. It was a
celebration of Roman power designed to
legitimize the rule of the 'victorious'
commanders: the emperors Vespasian and Titus.

ABOVE: The rocky outcrop of Masada, which became the site of the rebel Jews' last defiant stand against their Roman rulers. In AD 74 the commander Flavius Silva first built a wall encircling the plateau, before erecting the massive siege ramp (visible on the right). By the time the Romans reached the fortress at the top, the defenders had chosen suicide over capture or surrender.

BELOW: The aqueduct at Segovia in central Spain was built at the high point of the empire, probably during the reign of Trajan (AD 98–117). An example of Roman engineering bending nature to its will, the aqueduct carried water from hills 15 kilometres (10 miles) away to the city it served below.

ABOVE: A fourth-century Roman floor mosaic from Tunisia vividly depicting the life of a farm centred on a villa in Roman Africa. Labourers harvest crops, seasonal offerings are brought to the lord and lady, animals are gathered in and a peasant sets off to hunt. Such a thriving economic life created the prosperous province known as the 'granary' of the Roman empire.

LEFT: The huge geographical extent of the Roman empire meant that an ever more exotic array of wild animals could be brought to Rome for shows in the arena. In this fourth-century mosaic from Sicily an Arabian oryx (a species of large antelope from the deserts of the Middle East) is hauled on board a Roman trader's ship. Tigers, ostriches and hippopotamuses followed in the animal's wake.

ABOVE: Hadrian's Wall in northern England follows the natural line of the landscape's escarpment. Although we often think of it as a fortified defence against major enemy assaults, the wall was more a line of communication, an observation post and a means of policing trade and migration.

LEFT: A bearded Marcus Aurelius, with his toga drawn over his head, performs a public sacrifice in this second-century relief. Since the time of Augustus, the emperor was also High Priest. The scrupulous state cultivation of the gods through such rituals was considered essential to Rome's success.

ABOVE: Discovered at a Roman villa in Dorset, England, this mid-fourth-century mosaic is perhaps the earliest surviving image of Jesus (identifiable by the XP [chi-rho], the first two letters of the Greek word for Christ). The pomegranate, a symbol of eternal life from Greek myth, has been adapted to stand for the Christian resurrection.

ABOVE: The head of the emperor Constantine the Great in Rome, which once formed part of a colossal statue. Its vast size and the simplicity of its form celebrates the majesty and authority of autocratic power.

RIGHT: Stilicho, pictured in this late fourth-century ivory diptych with his wife Serena and his son Eucherius, was a second-generation Roman of 'barbarian' origins who rose to the top. Upon the death of the emperor Theodosius I (whose niece he married), Stilicho was the western empire's best general and most effective ruler. He paid for his shrewd policy of accommodating the Goths with his own life. Only after Rome was sacked was his strategy finally implemented.

ABOVE: The Mausoleum of Galla Placidia in Ravenna, Italy. Galla Placidia was at once the sister of the Roman emperor Honorius, a hostage of his enemies the Goths, and the wife of the Gothic leader Athaulf, whose brother-in-law, Alaric, sacked Rome in AD 410. She was later forced to marry the man who brought about her husband's defeat: the Roman general Flavius Constantius.

BELOW: 'Destruction' from *The Course of Empire* (1835–6) by Thomas Cole. This imaginative and allegorical painting, part of a five-part work, is thought to allude not only to ancient Rome but to nineteenth-century London and even America.

slaves and secretaries stayed in the palace of the local governor or of a prominent figure from the local élite. Sometimes, in a carefully planned and executed itinerary, the imperial community set up a camp of royal tents en route.

Accordingly, and in contrast to Nero who left Italy only once (for Greece), Hadrian was seen by and interacted with more of his subjects than most Roman emperors. This contributed to his popularity and the image of an accessible, approachable emperor. One anecdote reveals how that visibility mattered. An old woman was said to have spotted the emperor's entourage passing along a road. Sidling up, she tried to detain Hadrian and put a question to him. The wheels of the imperial train, however, did not brake and the woman was left mouthing her words into thin air. Not one to be cowed, she caught up with Hadrian and told him that if he did not have time to stop and hear her request, he did not have time to be emperor at all. Hadrian duly stopped and listened. His standing and popularity, like that of all the emperors at the high point of empire, depended on public opinion. But being highly 'visible' did not in everyone's eyes make a 'good emperor'. To be away from Rome for so long was also the neglectful characteristic of 'bad emperors'.

On Hadrian's travels, the heritage city of Athens, that ancient centre of learning, was of course his favourite destination, and here he made three visits. 'In almost every city he constructed some building and gave public games,' says one account of his rule.[9] The building programme in Athens alone testifies to his favour and philhellenism. He endowed the city with a grand library, a brand new forum and a glorious marble gate. The ancient heart of the city was thus redesigned and made Roman, but Hadrian's fingerprints made an indelible mark in other ways too. The most famous sanctuary, for example, was to Zeus, the greatest of the Greek gods, and the equivalent of the Roman god Jupiter. This temple had been started at the very beginning of the classical period in the sixth century BC; in AD 132 it was completed and dedicated in person by the man whose rule bookends that age. The achievements of the two cultures, one ancient, the other of the imperial present, were fused and celebrated as one.

The classical temples, buildings and monuments he inaugurated (not just in Athens, but in places as far apart as Smyrna in modern Turkey and his family's town of Italica in Spain) were branded with the emperor's name and an inscription. In response, the leading town councillors of the imperial cities that Hadrian had endowed repaid the compliment with the erection of statues, shrines and busts of the emperor. They were to be found in houses, temples and marketplaces. In his beloved Athens there was a statue of Hadrian erected in the Theatre of Dionysus. Even in those places that fell outside Hadrian's favour, the leading citizens honoured the cult of the emperor god. It was a way of demonstrating their loyalty, improving the standing of their community in the emperor's eyes, and putting the emperor under an obligation to help them. Through these symbols of the imperial cult the high profile of the emperor was sustained, even in places where his fondness for travelling did not take him. The same can also be said of the coins, stamped with the emperor's image, that changed hands across the breadth of his empire.

CIVILIZATION AND SLAVERY

Hadrian's Wall, then, encompassed at a northerly point an empire not just of common currency, but of common languages and a classical Greek-Roman civilization. Inside its boundaries the Romans spoke Latin and Greek; outside was the 'bar-bar-bar' of the barbarians. (The Greeks had long ago given this name to those outside their civilization because of the incomprehensible sounds they made, and the Romans had followed suit.) The 270,773 adult citizen males of Rome in 234 BC, the era of the first great revolution in Roman history with which this book started, had boomed in Hadrian's time to a staggering figure 320 times greater. With short life expectancy and low population growth, the life of the empire depended on new blood and the critical willingness of the Roman state to absorb new peoples.

In Britain, for example, Tacitus painted a jaundiced picture of how his father-in-law Agricola had 'Romanized' the sons of the British élite. Under his energetic governorship, Britons had, he said, learnt to speak the language of the Romans, to adopt the toga 'frequently' and had become seduced by the Roman 'vices' of bathing, relaxing under colonnades and attending dinner parties. The Roman culture was in fact nothing more than slavery by another name, said Tacitus. The new 'civilization' had a price tag.[10] By contrast in the east 'Romanization' was really 'Hellenization': men from the eastern élites used their education and the legacy of Greek philosophy, oratory, letters and art to win political power in Rome. That Greek-Roman civilization belied, however, a world of barbaric cruelty and harsh contrasts.

The civilized, cultured Hadrian, for example, was also an avid hunter. His taste for the ancient aristocratic sport was translated into popular form in the spectacular, bloody games he held during his reign. On the occasion of his birthday in January 119, the Romans celebrated by witnessing the killing of a hundred lions and a hundred lionesses. At the high point of the empire the bar for thrilling audiences at Roman games was always being raised in an unending cycle of one-upmanship. The peg holes marking where the bar rested were set to a sliding scale of exotic wild animals provided for metropolitan amusement from the extremely varied geography of Rome's provinces.

Lions and tigers, for example, came from Syria and the Roman east, wild boars from Germany and Gaul, bulls from Greece, horses from Spain, camels and rhinos, leopards, wild asses, giraffes and gazelles from North Africa. Trajan had a fondness for crocodiles from Egypt, and once flooded the Colosseum so that gladiators could do battle with them. There was no end of opportunities for such extravaganzas: under Hadrian, the Roman empire enjoyed more holidays than at any other time in its history. At the end of his birthday games there was a final flourish to the bloodthirsty spectacle: in the theatre and the Circus Maximus he organized a lottery. Hopeful men and women went home clutching their tickets in the shape of small wooden balls.[11]

Other stark contrasts of the time were of a much more sobering nature. Hadrian's prosperous, peaceful empire was, above all, one of extremes of inequality. For example, slaves significantly outnumbered citizens, and this simple fact made the latter nervous. If slaves could organize, they could become a powerful collective force. Another fault line was property. The massive polity primarily served and protected the interests of landowners rather than the peasants who worked the land. While the rich few exploited the well-worn trade routes of the Mediterranean and wowed their friends at dinner parties with a menu of peacock from Arabia, the majority of the poor lived meagrely on what could be produced locally. The rights of citizens too set apart the haves from the have-nots; those without Roman citizenship could earn it, but for most that meant a lifetime of military service in the Roman army.

The empire might have enjoyed a long period of peace, but it remained a dangerous, precarious world too. Away from the big cities and local town councils many areas of life were unpoliced and unpoliceable. The mechanics of Roman justice did not help. The system favoured those with money; redress was produced mainly for advantaged people who had the ability, time and resources to pursue their case. This reality found its way into the Roman code of law. Under Hadrian a disturbing two-tier justice system now began to develop, which distinguished between two kinds of people. The legal punishments of, for example, flogging, torture, beheading, crucifixion and deportation were reserved only for the propertyless 'humble' citizens; more 'respectable' army veterans, town councillors, knights and senators were, by contrast, protected from the sharp edge of Roman law.[12] This divide would become only more acute with time.

In other ways too the golden age of Hadrian's empire had by no means shaken off the rigorous social hierarchy characteristic of the old Roman republic of two hundred years earlier. Despite the homogeneity of language spoken across it, the majority of the Roman world was illiterate. While many had the necessary knowledge for handling army records or an artisan's business accounts, and city dwellers evidently had sufficient understanding to write graffiti and find it amusing, the ability of the minority to write and communicate fluently in the empire's currency of letters gave them a significant advantage over others. However, a closer inspection of the social hierarchy offers surprises. The wealthy élite prided themselves on their private libraries. To cultivate them, slaves were often required to copy texts and act as secretaries. As a result, the unfree were sometimes far more educated and skilled than the millions of poor but free Roman citizens. Cicero's secretary Tiro was one such person; he became a close friend of the Roman senator, held an influential position in his house and was eventually freed. Under Hadrian, some 150 years later, there were many more wealthy 'Ciceros' – not new men from the Italian provinces of Rome, but from her empire-wide territories. Each would have had a small coterie of well-educated 'Tiros'.

The end of Hadrian's reign was marked by sadness. While travelling with Antinous in Egypt in 130, his young lover drowned in the Nile in a mysterious boating accident. To assuage his grief, Hadrian marked the death of the love of his life by founding a city there called Antinoöpolis and by announcing the young man's deification. Henceforth Antinous was worshipped as a god across the empire. Hadrian's travels came to an end in 132. Thereafter he retired to his sumptuous new villa complex at Tivoli, 25 kilometres (15 miles) outside Rome. It was a fitting place to see out his reign. Exquisitely, playfully, artistically its layout forms a grandiose map of the places he had visited in his life. Here there were some buildings called the Academy, after Plato's philosophy school in Athens; there one might while away the hours at a place called Canopus, a sanctuary in Alexandria. The religious afterlife, which fascinated Hadrian, was represented too in places that he named after the domains of the underworld: the 'Elysian Fields' and 'Hades'. In addition, the complex boasted a Greek theatre, a colonnade, some baths, a lavishly endowed private library and a fish pond that housed colourful and novel specimens from across the empire. No expense had been spared in its construction, and this at least 100-hectare (250-acre) retreat had taken as long to complete as his wall in Britain.

The rich and complex golden age enjoyed by the empire girded by that wall continued long after Hadrian's death in 138. Under the emperor Antoninus Pius there was further peace and stability, but in the rule of Marcus Aurelius, another bearded philosopher-emperor, the *pax Romana* was thrown into jeopardy by waves of German invaders. Aurelius's story is full of bitter irony: the man of peace found that in order to save his empire, he had to be almost continuously at war with barbarian armies attacking from the north. The succession of his son Commodus, an indigent, flighty emperor more interested in games and gladiators than Roman security, only saw his father's success in the German wars collapse. In 193 the dynasty founded by Rome's first African emperor, Septimius Severus, ensured that Hadrian's golden age was revived once again. But it was not enough to halt an inevitable slide into decline. By the middle of the third century AD Rome was catapulted into a new period of total crisis and near collapse.

To pull the empire back from the brink, the man responsible for Rome's next great revolution needed, above all, martial prowess and the assured ability to command armies. With his rise to power, one fashion among emperors died abruptly. Beards were out. The clean-cut, close-shaven soldier-emperor was back in style.

| V |

CONSTANTINE

In the distant province of Bithynia-Pontus a trial was causing the Roman governor a headache. Pliny the Younger was a wealthy senator, a refined man of letters, and an enthusiastic gardener. Back in Italy he owned three beautiful villas set amid ideal countryside (two near Lake Como and one in Umbria), and he was considered an enlightened master of no fewer than five hundred slaves. However, now, in AD 111, in the backwaters of Asia Minor close to the Black Sea, those delights of home must have seemed a lifetime away. The tricky case brought before him was proving quite a nuisance.

While Pliny was touring the province to hear legal cases, a group of people had been brought before him and denounced by some locals. Their alleged crime? Being Christians. Pliny gave them every opportunity to prove their innocence. When he interrogated them, however, some confessed that they were followers of Christ. So he gave them another chance after reminding them that the punishment for their crime was death. Again, after the second and third interrogations, they showed not repentance but 'stubbornness' and an 'inflexible obstinacy'. Their faith, he concluded, was 'madness'.[1] The governor was left with no choice: of the guilty, those who were Roman citizens were sent to Rome for an official court hearing, while the non-citizens were executed there and then. If Pliny the Younger thought that would be the end of the matter, however, he was to be sorely disappointed.

News of the case spread around the province. Pliny soon received an anonymous letter listing the names of hundreds of others apparently guilty of the same crime. To make matters worse, when they were brought before him they denied it. The governor, however, was not to be defeated in administering Roman justice. To weed out the guilty from the innocent, he came up with an ingenious solution. He dictated a prayer invoking the pagan Roman gods, asked the accused to repeat it, and requested that they offer up wine and incense to the emperor. The final part of the test was to curse Christ. Some of those who denied being Christian duly followed Pliny's orders. Others revealed that they had been Christians in the past but were no longer and therefore they too agreed to do what Pliny asked of them. Even so, the test had not produced a conclusive verdict. Although some said that they were no longer Christian, did once having been a Christian constitute guilt? To get to the bottom of the crimes they had committed in the past, Pliny's next move was to torture two female attendants of the early Christian Church, known as deaconesses. He found not stories of lechery and cannibalism, as his prejudices might have led him to expect, but only 'depraved, excessive superstition'.[2] What to do with these people? Were they guilty or not? Drawing a blank, Pliny wrote to the emperor Trajan for advice.

The emperor replied that even if there had been suspicions about their past, they should be pardoned. In addition, Pliny was urged not to conduct witch-hunts, not to deliberately seek out Christians. This decision would set the legal standard for 'good' emperors who followed after Trajan. However, the extraordinary exchange of letters between emperor and governor reveals much more. It shows that in AD 111 trials and executions of Christians were an accepted, if legally knotty, procedure.

Persecution of Christians had begun approximately fifty years earlier with the trial in Rome of St Paul, the great first missionary who had taken the message of Christianity to the Roman east. Not long afterwards, the emperor Nero had made scapegoats of the growing community of Christians living in the imperial capital. Looking to take the sting out of the accusation that he himself had started the great fire of Rome in order to build a new palace, Nero famously had them crucified or burnt in the gardens of his residence. The emperor Domitian was accused of similar treatment of the Christians. Although Trajan was lenient in his judgment of Pliny's case, the fact remained that the Christians posed a problem for the Romans. Banding together, worshipping the Christian God to the exclusion of traditional Roman gods was simply intolerable. Trials were brought against them and, if found guilty, the unfortunate believers in this alien religion were treated no better than criminals and prisoners of war. Indeed they often met a similar end – a gruesome death in the Roman arena.

In spite of the hostility and penalties it provoked, Christianity grew and grew. By the beginning of the fourth century, it was an empire-wide phenomenon. It is estimated that at that time perhaps ten per cent of the Roman world was Christian; there were a growing number of churches to be found in all parts of the Roman world; a hierarchy of Christian bishops, presbyters and deacons was developing; and a significant variety of people – from slaves and the poor to the upper classes – were converts to the Christian faith.[3] As a result of this increasingly strong organization, in 303 the Christians faced their greatest persecution yet. The emperor Diocletian issued an edict ordering churches to be destroyed, scriptures to be burnt, some Christians to be stripped of their offices and others to be made slaves.

And yet, within twenty years of Diocletian's persecution, all this changed. Christianity went through a revolutionary transformation in status, rising from being the most despised religion to the most favoured. By 324 it had become the official religion of the Roman world. Devotion to the traditional Roman gods had not disappeared, but, incredible as it would have seemed to people at the time, that religion was no longer a requisite part of what it meant to be a Roman.[4]

The man who initiated this change was the emperor Constantine, the first Christian emperor and the first emperor to publicly sponsor the Christian Church. His decision to support Christianity was perhaps the single most influential turning point in Roman history, if not the history of the world. It was because of Constantine that Christianity thrived throughout the Roman empire and transformed itself into the world religion it is today. The key to this revolution was the exclusiveness of Christianity, the idea that only one god could be worshipped. The one characteristic that had provoked centuries of persecution would, ironically, become for Constantine its most useful, cherished quality. By tapping into Christian faith, Constantine would allow the Roman empire to flourish one last time, and his regime would be hailed as Rome's final golden age.

But the man who was responsible for this religious revolution was not himself an exemplary Christian. Flavius Valerius Constantinus was a man of great contradictions, by turns a soldier, a brilliant general and an astute, dissimulating politician. But was he also a man of genuine faith? A sincere convert to the Christian God? Or was he really a self-interested opportunist and evil genius? Central to the problem of understanding his character are the ancient sources: the pagan authors are highly critical of him, while the Christian writers, particularly Eusebius, the bishop of Caesarea, and Lactantius, produced almost lyrical, heavily partisan hagiographies. Despite the conflicting nature of the sources, one clear picture of the emperor's actions emerges.

To seal his own power and at the same time establish the eminence of the Christian religion required less the Christian virtues of submissiveness, peace and trust than the old Roman virtues of cruelty, vaulting ambition and singular ruthlessness. The people who would fall foul of these characteristics would be not just Constantine's political enemies, but the closest members of his own family.

FOUR EMPERORS

In the third century AD the Roman world was in crisis. In the space of fifty years (235–85) there were no fewer than twenty emperors, each falling in quick succession to political assassination or death on the battlefield. But it was not just the government that was unstable. The security of the empire too was at an all-time low. In 251 the Goths broke through the forts, watchtowers and ramparts along the border of the Danube from a region north of the Black Sea; they defeated the emperor Decius in battle and eventually sacked Athens. In 259 two Germanic tribes, the Alamanni and Juthungi, also smashed their way across the same border and invaded Italy. The worst year was perhaps 260: the Franks breached the border of the Rhine, marauded their way through Gaul and sacked Tarraco. But there was even worse happening on the eastern frontier. The emperor Valerian was captured by the Persians, enslaved and forced to live out his days bending over so that King Shapur could step on his back to mount his horse. Although Valerian died in captivity, in one sense he lived on: in a macabre inversion of deification, his dead body was stuffed and placed in a Persian temple as a warning to future Roman ambassadors. As shocking as these events were, Romans would find that there was worse in store.

For the best part of fifteen years the Roman provinces of Britain, Gaul and Spain seceded from the empire, and in 272 the Romans permanently abandoned the province of Dacia (modern-day Romania). Perhaps the most extraordinary offensive against Rome came from Palmyra, a rich, semi-independent city on the border of Roman Syria. When its king, Septimius Odenathus, died, his widow, Queen Zenobia, took control. Renowned for her extraordinary beauty, intellect and chastity, she orchestrated and led the conquest of the Roman east: Egypt, Palestine, Syria, Mesopotamia and many of the Roman provinces of Asia Minor all fell under her control before she then proclaimed her son emperor and herself took the title Augusta (empress).

The Romans fought back on all fronts. The most successful emperor was Aurelian (ruled 270–5). In the space of just five, brilliant years he won back the eastern Mediterranean, defeated Zenobia and brought her to Rome as the prize prisoner at his triumph. However, the restoration of the Roman east was just one of the many extraordinary achievements of Aurelian's short reign. He also drove the invading German tribes out of Italy, forced them back over the northern borders and made peace with them. When that was done, he went on to restore the seceded provinces of Britain, Gaul and Spain to the empire.

But for all their glory, these exploits could not hide what had become so apparent in the third century: the vulnerability of Rome. The ambivalence of the situation is best summed up by Aurelian's great building legacy. For the first time in the history of the Roman empire the emperor felt it necessary to surround and protect Rome from invaders with a massive wall. It was completed after his death by the emperor Probus (another successful emperor of this period) and still survives in part today. In 285, however, there would come to power a man who would extend that sense of security right across the empire.

Like many emperors of the third century, Gaius Aurelius Valerius Diocletianus (Diocletian) was not from the senatorial and political élite of Rome. He was a low-born soldier from a provincial family who rose to power through the ranks of the military. He had spent most of his time not in the city of Rome, but on the frontiers; in fact, he would travel to the imperial capital only once in his entire life. It was perhaps his experiences on the Danube that spelt out to him the importance of reform if the Roman empire were to survive the preceding decades of crisis. What is certain is that he went about the task of reorganization with extraordinary energy. His reforms focused on money and the army.

The official record of the standing army, the *notitia dignitatum*, shows how he bolstered the strength of the frontiers by creating new legions. He brought the army under central control and improved soldiers' pay and supplies. In order to secure the funding of the army, the empire's economy also needed a radical overhaul. In the course of the third century the coinage of the Roman world had become so debased that the empire reverted to exchanges in kind. Diocletian therefore improved the weight and mint of gold and silver coins, and made them uniform. He also tackled the problem of inflation, and enacted tough social legislation to ensure that tax revenues were successfully and consistently raised. In the process, he established a regular budget for the running of the entire empire.[5]

Finally, the emperor reorganized the provinces. In order to improve imperial administration, Diocletian broke them down into smaller regions; these in turn were grouped under twelve larger administrative units known as dioceses. The new system allowed closer supervision, as well as the resuscitation of law and finance by local governors and their staffs throughout the empire. However, these impressive, innovative measures were not his most celebrated achievement. The grand idea for which Diocletian would go down in history was his decision on 1 March

293 to create a college of four emperors to rule the Roman world. Diocletian was thus the first emperor to accept that the task of running the Roman empire was too big for one man.

The system, known as the tetrarchy (rule by four emperors), worked as follows. The two senior emperors were both given the title Augustus; Diocletian ruled the eastern half of the empire, while his partner Marcus Aurelius Valerius Maximianus (Maximian) ruled the western half. Each Augustus appointed a junior colleague, and these two deputies were both known by the title Caesar. Gaius Galerius Valerius Maximianus (Galerius) joined Diocletian in the east, while Flavius Valerius Constantius, the father of the future emperor Constantine, aided Maximian in the west. The four men resided in imperial centres pointedly closer to Rome's frontiers (see map, page 247). In the east Diocletian's main home was in Nicomedia (modern-day Izmit in Turkey), and Galerius's in Thessalonica (Greece), while in the west Maximian's home was Sirmio (Mitrovitz in modern-day Croatia), and Constantius's was in Trier (Germany). In this way Diocletian ensured that the presence of the emperor of Rome was established in many different areas at the same time.

To shore up the prestige and dignity of the four emperors, uniformity was the key. Each city had an imperial palace, an audience chamber and a hippodrome; each man had his own staff, court and military guard. Diocletian's court in Nicomedia reflected the style of eastern rulers' courts. Subjects paid homage by calling the emperor 'lord' and prostrating themselves before him. Under the four emperors, the signs of despotism were much more overt.[6] However, there was one further, key illustration of the severe nature of the tetrarchy system. A clue lies in the new names that each of the emperors adopted to emphasize the quasi-divine basis of their authority: Diocletian was called Jovius (after the god Jupiter), and Maximian Herculius (after he of the Seven Labours). The underpinning of the new regime was emphatically ancient, traditional and pagan. But in the ointment of Diocletian's drive for uniformity there was a fly.

The single policy of reorganization across the empire for which Diocletian is infamous is his repression of the Christians. Why were they such a threat? Throughout the history of the Roman empire, the favour of the Roman gods was central to its successful creation and survival. With the sweep of conquest, new cults and religions had come within its embrace. Cosmopolitan Rome not only tolerated new religions, but welcomed them too: just as new peoples became Roman citizens, so their religions too were incorporated into the pantheon of Roman gods. Cybele from Asia Minor, Mithras from what is today Iran, Isis and Serapis from Egypt, the goddess Tanit from Carthage – all these gods and their cults came to Rome. They were both worshipped there and took on Roman divine forms. Indeed, their acceptance in Rome meant that the cults grew in stature. The message that their incorporation sent out was clear: even the gods of Rome's former enemies now favoured Rome. The process served to weld the loyalty of Rome's subjects to the empire.

Yet there was a limit to this spirit of Roman toleration for new cults – a line that must never be crossed. A number of small, individual cults posed no threat to state control of religion; indeed, they seemed only to enrich it. But the formation of an organized, alternative community did.[7] The Romans hated Christianity because they considered the worship of its one god dangerously exclusive. It was a rejection of everything it meant to be Roman. By refusing to pray to Roman gods, Christians rejected the Roman race and the Roman order of things. But Christianity posed an even greater threat than this. After decades of crisis, the 'peace of the gods', the unwritten contract by which the Roman gods presided benevolently over the empire in return for worship, was more than a highly guarded prize. On it depended the stability of the entire empire. It was essential to rebuilding security. Loyalty to a Christian God only put that security in jeopardy. Times of greatest crisis entailed the greatest clampdowns.

The first empire-wide persecution of Christians took place in 250. With the northern borders of the empire threatened by Goths, the emperor Decius called for a universal sacrifice in his honour. He wanted to assure himself of divine protection by the gods. Certificates of sacrifice were issued to every citizen, proving that they had participated in them. The Christians who refused were punished with torture and execution. The persecutions ended, but the problem did not. Forty years later, under Diocletian's uniform regime of the four emperors, Roman control of belief was even more paramount. Tradition, discipline and respect for the old gods were the very cornerstones of Diocletian's reforms and the empire's renewal. There was no room for dissent. Unsurprisingly, it was only a matter of time before the tinder was lit and the problem of the Christians flared up violently once again.

In 299 Diocletian learnt of some pagan priests who had tried to divine signs of favour from the gods. When they were unable to find auspicious omens, they blamed their failure on some Christian soldiers who had made a sign of the cross. The reaction that resulted was uncompromising. Diocletian first ordered a purge of the army. After trying to root out Christianity he changed tack and attempted to stop it functioning altogether. He instructed a detachment of the Praetorian Guard in his own imperial city of Nicomedia not simply to burn the local church. Once the flames had subsided, he ordered his soldiers to set to work with axes and crowbars and level it to the ground.

An empire-wide edict followed: Christian meeting-places should be destroyed, scriptures burnt and Christians who held any office should be stripped of it. Depriving Christians of their status deprived them of their legal standing. They were thus liable to summary execution and torture. Christian freedmen were to be made slaves once more. Finally, the bishop of Nicomedia was beheaded and many others were imprisoned and tortured. By ruining Christianity, the persecutors were seeking to foster their traditional religion. In reality, however, the policy had no popular support. It served only to confirm how widespread Christianity had become, and how organized. The campaign had been a bloody, violent failure in an otherwise extraordinarily successful rule.[8] Two years after their initiation, Diocletian called an end to the persecutions in 305.

In that same year Diocletian retired to his magnificent seaside palace at Spalatum (modern-day Split in Croatia), the skeleton of which is preserved today in the form of a medieval town. He was the first and only Roman emperor ever to abdicate voluntarily. His severe, authoritarian work of reform was done, and now he could enjoy the delights of the Dalmatian coast without worry. That at least was his hope. However, with his retirement, the success of the tetrarchy that he had devised began to decline.

Diocletian's ambition was for the system not only to address the problem of security, but also to bring the destabilizing rapid turnover of emperors to an end. The appointment of two Caesars subordinate to two Augusti had made explicit and orderly the means of succession, and thus, it was hoped, would deter usurpers. For all the innovation and success of his other reforms, however, in this ambition his system was a complete failure. All it created was more intense jockeying for power, a new welter of rivalry and competition. It soon became apparent that the only thing that glued the four emperors together was the consent of the others. As soon as that was lost, the government of four would collapse like a sheaf of wheat.[9]

On 1 May 305, at the ceremonies of succession, the cracks were quick to appear. When the former Caesars, Constantius and Galerius, became the new Augusti and took the place of Maximian and Diocletian, one young man at the ceremony in the east had high hopes that he would be appointed as one of the new Caesars. However, it was not the name of Constantine, the son of Constantius, that Diocletian read out, but that of the newly appointed junior emperor Maximinus Daia, a tough, vehemently anti-Christian soldier from Illyria. The overlooked young Constantine had every right to seethe. Not only the son of a Caesar, he was also a man of considerable achievement in his own right. He had proved himself on the battlefield against the Persians on the eastern frontier, and in the north against the Sarmatians. After his father had been sent to Gaul and Britain, he had remained at Diocletian's court. Here he was a high-ranking officer, but his achievement went further than that. In the snake-pit of politics and court life he had perhaps also learnt to be a clever dissimulator. That skill certainly would have been useful at the succession ceremony. However, he was not the only candidate to be unfairly overlooked.

At the western court in Milan, the same ceremony to appoint the new Caesar of the west was being held on the same day. Here Marcus Aurelius Valerius Maxentius, the son of Maximian, Augustus of the west, was passed over in favour of another able army officer called Flavius Valerius Severus. Maxentius had reason to be more than bitter at failing to make the grade. The appointment of Daia in the east had been understandable: he had connections there and was a trusted general and friend of Galerius. But as the son of Maximian, a former Augustus, surely Maxentius had a better claim than Severus to be Caesar in the west? Disappointment turned to suspicion. Severus, like Daia, was an army friend of Galerius. Did his appointment reflect something more sinister? Did the eastern Augustus have designs for control of the west too? The new appointment posed only unanswerable questions. Although the ambitious Constantine and Maxentius did not yet know it, opportunities would come their way to redress the slight they had suffered, and they would not be long in coming. The system of the tetrarchy would soon find itself in meltdown.

According to some sources, the first rift was between the two new Augusti. Constantius perhaps feared that his son would become a political hostage in the court of the eastern Augustus. What is certain is that he sent a dispatch to Galerius requesting that Constantine be allowed to join his campaigns to re-establish Roman order in Gaul and Britain. Galerius was reluctant to do so. Perhaps he also knew that he had a hold over his fellow Augustus as long as Constantius's son was at his court in the east. Following persistent requests, Galerius relented, keeping up the appearance of harmony between the two senior rulers. However, beneath the show of cooperation, so the story goes, he had begun planning Constantine's downfall. Galerius had instructed Severus to intercept and kill the young Constantine. A trap had been set.

Constantine quickly got wind of the plot. One night, he waited until Galerius had retired to his rooms. Then, in the small hours, he took flight. During the long journey west, he skilfully outwitted his pursuers by maiming horses, used for imperial service, which he encountered along the way. Constantine thus threw the potential assassins off the scent of his trail. He was a tall, strong, athletic man and, riding long and hard, he reached his father at Boulogne in Gaul in time to aid him in his last campaign – an expedition across the English Channel to Britain.[10]

The war against the Picts was a great success, and Constantine's role in it was critical. For his valour he earned the title *Britannicus Maximus* (Greatest Briton). The popularity he gained with the army in Britain would prove incredibly influential to his future career. But perhaps equally influential was what he was able to witness. His father was a very different emperor from the eastern rulers, Diocletian and Galerius. Certainly, Constantius had paid lip-service to Diocletian's edict to persecute the Christians; he had, for example, ordered the destruction of some churches. It was not in this action, however that his reputation was anchored. Rather, he was celebrated for protecting the Christians from the brutality that he had witnessed in the east. This was not out of the kindness of his heart; Constantius was a seasoned, unsentimental general from Illyria. The decision came down to a simple political judgement – he saw that persecuting Christians would not help him govern western Europe.

Unfortunately for his son, the reunion they enjoyed was brief. On 25 July 306 Constantius died prematurely at Eburacum (modern-day York). The cause of death was perhaps leukaemia, a possible clue lying in the nickname that was given to him posthumously: 'the Pale'. There was one last, critical action that Constantius took before he died. According to Constantine, his father appointed him Augustus of the west. It was a controversial decision because Constantius had made no attempt to consult with his fellow emperors, least of all Galerius. Nonetheless, the army immediately and joyfully joined in proclaiming the popular Constantine the new Augustus of the west. With that, Diocletian's tetrarchy was, in effect, wrecked. Constantine had broken cover.

Although Galerius, the Augustus in the east, was forced to accept Constantine's elevation in the world, he sent him a purple robe recognizing him not as the new Augustus but as the more junior Caesar. To the position of Augustus in the west he promoted Severus. However, not even Constantine's demotion could hide the new reality of the Roman empire. The government of the tetrarchy was nothing more than a temporary gloss. The four emperors were actually involved in a covert war, each in a bid for more power. Over the next six years that hidden war intermittently broke out into full civil war. The overlooked Maxentius was the first to make his move. He brought his father, Maximian, out of retirement, won over the Praetorian Guard in Rome and in 307 declared himself Augustus with control of Rome, Italy, Corsica, Sardinia, Sicily and North Africa. Galerius sent Severus to deal with the revolt, but Severus was unable to match the combined military forces of Maxentius and Maximian. What troops he could muster deserted him at the gates of Rome. Severus was captured, forced to abdicate power, and then executed at Tres Tabernae, outside Rome, in 307.

From his imperial palace at Trier Constantine had kept a close eye on these events. To maintain his position in a rapidly shifting balance of power, he had even made an alliance with Maxentius and his father. It was sealed by Constantine's marriage to Fausta, Maxentius's sister. All too soon, though, the alliance between the three men broke down in the most spectacular way. First, Maxentius was declared a tyrant and a usurper (with Constantine, Daia, Galerius and a new appointee, Licinius, agreed as the legitimate holders of power). Maximian broke away from his son, but soon, in one last throw of the dice, turned against his son-in-law too and sought to win imperial power in the west for himself. This rebellion now forced Constantine to enter the civil war for the first time. At Arles in Gaul he defeated Maximian, who promptly hanged himself. The response of Maxentius to the news of his father's death was unequivocal. First he ordered the deification of Maximian, then he smashed down the statues and images of Constantine, the icons by which he was recognized as a legitimate emperor, and thus declared war on his former ally. He wanted, he said, revenge for the death of his father.[11]

In 311 Galerius died, and with him the last vestiges of the tetrarchy. The end met by this famous persecutor of the Christians was gruesomely celebrated by the historian Eusebius. Suppurating inflammations and ulcers infested the genitals of the obese emperor. His sick, lumpen body stank. The doctors who were unable to cure him were summarily executed.[12] Was he being punished for his sins against the Christians? This was perhaps the conclusion drawn by Galerius himself: in his last edict, made in his final few days, he renounced the policy of Christian persecution. The tide was turning. But little did he know quite how spectacularly that reversal would soon be transformed into one of the most important revolutions in all history.

Galerius's death left Daia and Licinius disputing control of the east. In the west, two key protagonists also walked the stage: the usurper Maxentius and his brother-in-law Constantine. Constantine was determined that the job of ruling the western half of the Roman empire fell to him alone. However, he wanted to fight on the side of legitimacy and right. His publicly stated aim was to 'avenge the state against the tyrant and all his faction'. Indeed, his biographer and Christian panegyrist, Eusebius, described Constantine's war as a 'task of liberation'.[13]

In reality, Constantine simply wanted to eliminate his rivals. Out of the shambles of the tetrarchy, he would make his bid for sole power. From the seed of that self-interest and ambition, however, would grow one of the most significant moments in European history. The outcome of the war for the west would not only decide the fate of the Roman empire – it would alter the fate of the world.

MILVIAN BRIDGE

Rumours were leaking out of the city of Rome, and they were playing right into the hands of Constantine. The tyrant and usurper Maxentius was the epitome of pure evil, they said, a practiser of witchcraft, a sacrificer of humans. He liked to abduct and rape married women. On one occasion, the city prefect was bullied into allowing Praetorian officers to seize his own wife so that she might become another of Maxentius's victims. But by the time the guardsmen broke down her door, they found she had stabbed herself to death rather than give up her chastity to the self-proclaimed emperor. Maxentius was just as brutal with the citizens of Rome as a whole: when they rioted, he did not flinch in response, but sent in the Praetorians to massacre them. This at least is the portrait of Maxentius given by Eusebius.[14] His Christian-biased work, written more than twenty-five years after the events described, and designed to exalt Constantine by comparison with his enemies, should be taken with a large pinch of salt. The fact remains that in the prelude to war in 312 Maxentius had successfully held on to power in Rome for six years. He must have been doing something right.

Maxentius knew how to make Romans feel good about themselves again. In 306 Rome was in decline, a shadow of its former glorious self. The four emperors barely set foot in the city. As they travelled between the new imperial cities closer to the frontiers of the empire, Rome was ignored because it was off the beaten track. In fact, the people of Rome and Italy could complain that they were being treated like just another province. The year before Maxentius came to power, Italians had lost the privileged tax-free status they had enjoyed for nearly five hundred years. The senators of Rome too had had to make a considerable mental adjustment to the times they lived in: the Senate and the emperor had drifted apart; the senators were eclipsed by the army. Indeed, it was from the military hierarchy on the battlefields of provincial frontiers rather than in the Senate House of Rome that emperors were now made. Romans felt increasingly as though they were living not in the

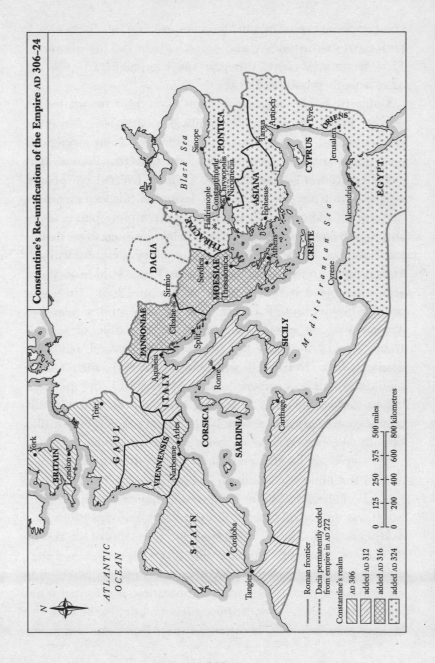

Constantine's Re-unification of the Empire AD 306–24

ATLANTIC
OCEAN

N

York
BRITAIN
London

Trier

GAUL

VIENNENSIS
Narbonne
Arles

SPAIN

Cordoba

Tangier

CORSICA

SARDINIA

ITALY
Aquileia
Rome

PANNONIAE
Sirmio
Cibalae
Split

Carthage

SICILY

Mediterranean Sea

DACIA

Serdica
MOESIAE
Thessalonica

THRACIANE

Athens

Cyrene

CRETE

Black Sea
Sinope

Hadrianople
Constantinople
Chrysopolis
Nicomedia

ASIANA
Ephesus

PONTICA

Tarsus
Antioch

CYPRUS
Jerusalem

ORIENS
Tyre

Alexandria

EGYPT

0   125   250   375   500 miles
0   200   400   600   800 kilometres

Constantine's realm
AD 306
added AD 312
added AD 316
added AD 324

——— Roman frontier
– – – Dacia permanently ceded
from empire in AD 272

329

great imperial capital of a brilliant empire, but in a backwater, a heritage town for tourists, and one decidedly lacking vibrancy.[15] That is until Maxentius began his campaign. His was an unashamedly pro-Roman ticket.

Coins from his illegitimate reign show how he wanted to restore Rome to glory. His political slogan was *Romanitas* (Roman-ness). As a pagan, he appealed to Rome's religious past. It was, after all, the home of all the gods that Romans had collected from all corners of the empire. Everywhere people walked within the city were rich layers of this extraordinary heritage: in addition to the centuries-old temples, statues, altars and imperial mausolea, there were shrines devoted to particular local deities on street corners in every neighbourhood. Maxentius not only rejuvenated pride in Rome's old history, but also encouraged it by giving the city a new look. He was a prolific builder, authorizing a new palace complex near the Appian Way, an enormous hippodrome capable of seating 15,000 spectators, and, his greatest architectural feat, the Basilica Nova. Decorated with marble and detailed stucco mouldings, this government hall could boast of being the city's largest vaulted building. By leaving his stamp on Rome in this way, Maxentius tried to secure his legitimacy as emperor in the west. By 312, however, his appeal was wearing thin.

The buildings he erected cost a fortune. In addition, he had to find the money to maintain the armies with which he had fended off attempts by the legitimate emperors to unseat him. But it was money that Rome did not have. The city, ruled by a usurper, was effectively cut off from the resources of the rest of the empire. As a result, Romans were forced to live on their own means; revenues from the provinces dried up. To make ends meet Maxentius taxed the whole population and forced senators and landowners to contribute gifts of money to the treasury. Making matters worse, another usurper, Domitius Alexander, had taken control of North Africa, thus eliminating Rome's primary source of grain. Food shortages provoked riots, and the full force of the protesters' anger was directed at Maxentius. To maintain control of the city, Maxentius was repressive, and the city of Rome came to resemble more a police state than a glorious reincarnation of the Eternal City. To one man, however, the growing chaos in Rome was wonderful news. This was the man whom Maxentius called the 'son of a whore'; the man whose effigies he jealously destroyed; the man he hated for causing his father's death. This was the man who was now crossing the Alps with an army to 'liberate' and 'rescue' suffering Rome.

Constantine's advisers had not set the best of moods for their general's campaign. Under the influence of pagan priests, they were fearful and hesitant, warning Constantine that the invasion of Italy did not bode well. They had their reasons: they could point to the fact that Constantine had left three-quarters of his army to protect the Rhine frontier from invasion by the Franks, and that he was intending to face the 100,000-strong army of Maxentius (inflated with auxiliaries from Sicily and Africa) with, according to our earliest source, just 40,000 men.[16]

Constantine, in response, disagreed. His soldiers might be outnumbered but, after the wars in Gaul and Britain, they had the advantage of being battle-hardened and fit for war. It was an advantage that would prove to be highly effective. After negotiating the Mount Cenis pass, Constantine and his army entered Italy and promptly defeated the three armies that Maxentius had sent to resist him. By October, Constantine had followed the route of the Flaminian Way and drawn up his troops 15 kilometres (9 miles) north of Rome at Saxa Rubra (Red Rocks). However, the composition of the army that pitched camp there was a little unusual.

In addition to officers and military advisers, Constantine's close entourage also included Christians. Although Maxentius, despite his depiction by Eusebius in the *Life of Constantine*, was not a vehement persecutor of them, Christians had their reasons for hating him. He had banished three bishops from Rome and had failed to restore property that had been confiscated during Diocletian's persecution of the Christians in 303–5. By contrast, Constantine was superficially a much more sympathetic ruler. He was not a Christian, but in Britain and Gaul in 306 he had rescinded Diocletian's edict for the destruction of churches, and had restored Christians' right to worship.[17] This attitude of tolerance made Constantine a candidate for the attention of high-ranking Christians. They had come to his imperial seat at Trier to read aloud their works, and now they formed a small group travelling with him on campaign. One of them was thought to be Ossius, the bishop of Córdoba. It is possible that another was an influential man in his seventies called Lactantius.

A North African by birth, Lucius Caelius Firmianus Lactantius had personally felt the brunt of the Christian persecutions. He had travelled earlier in life to Nicomedia, where he converted to Christianity, and was summoned to Diocletian's court by the emperor as a teacher of Latin rhetoric. During the violence of 303–5, however, he lost his position, and in order to save his life he eventually fled to Constantine's western court at Trier. He met the emperor, composed the Christian work called the *Divine Institutes* between 308 and 309 (dedicating it to Constantine) and would later become tutor to Constantine's son Flavius Julius Crispus, whom the emperor fathered with a mistress before his marriage to Fausta. If he was indeed now in Constantine's camp, Lactantius was probably biding his time. The Christians in the emperor's entourage would certainly have been happy to be on his side, but they would also have been looking to improve on the footholds of influence they had established over the years. All they needed was an opportunity. Whenever and however it came, they were at last in a position to pounce.

South of Constantine's camp, Maxentius was also surrounded by priests. But unlike those in his enemy's camp, they were pagan priests, and, unlike the Christians, they certainly had the emperor's full attention. On 27 October 312, the day before the two sides would join battle, Maxentius was in a panic. He was so anxious about whether he had sufficient support from the Roman people to be assured of victory that he turned to his priests and asked them to read the omens. He desperately needed his confidence to be shored up; only a sign from Rome's traditional gods could do that. The priests cut open the belly of a young animal, delved their hands into its carcass and fingered the intestines. The news was not good.

The augury, so the story goes, indicated that the enemy of Rome would be defeated.[18] The atmosphere in the temple was strained. It is reasonable to imagine that a senator or courtier in the assembled group, desperate to avert a complete collapse in the emperor's morale, tactfully broke the ice. Surely Constantine was the enemy of Rome. Surely *he* would be the one to fall. That, at least, was the way Maxentius chose to interpret the priests' announcement. The imperial court breathed a sigh of relief. Indeed, they had reason to feel confident about their prospects. In addition to their superior number of soldiers, they had devised a cunning plan to scupper Constantine's attack on the city.

To take Rome from the north, Constantine and his army would have to cross the Tiber at Milvian Bridge. (A reconstructed version of this bridge, called the Ponto Milvia, today marks the spot where the original once stood.) Maxentius and his military advisers now made this the central plank of their defence of the city. Maxentius ordered part of the bridge to be destroyed so that the enemy could not cross easily. Alongside it, however, he ordered a temporary floating bridge to be constructed. Crucially, it was made of two parts fastened in the middle by removable iron pins. Maxentius's forces would come out along this bridge and face Constantine. However, should Constantine's army force Maxentius back into the city, the defenders of Rome would be able to cross back over the river and then rely on a devastating counter-attack: they would quickly unfasten the pins, watch the makeshift bridge slide apart and thus prevent Constantine from pursuing them. From the Rome-side banks of the Tiber, Maxentius and his advisers believed, they would watch the enemies of Rome fall like lemmings into the river.[19]

As potentially brilliant as this secret weapon was, Constantine and his army were about to gain their very own psychological advantage. That advantage would spectacularly transform the chances of the outnumbered, anxious Constantine. It would go down in history as one of the most pivotal moments in history, but also one of the most controversial.

Some time before battle was joined, Constantine had a vision. According to Eusebius, at midday, under a bright blue sky, the general saw a shining cross, and inscribed upon it, an instruction: 'By this sign, you will conquer!' Another account elaborates: Christ himself appeared with the cross and the order to be victorious was sung by angels.[20]

Modern historians, suspicious of the fact that Eusebius described the extraordinary moment in great detail in his *Life of Constantine*, but failed even to mention it in his *Church History*, have suggested more rational explanations. Perhaps the vision was a natural astronomical event that produced a 'halo phenomenon'; perhaps Constantine saw a meteor (there is evidence that one landed in this region of Italy at this time). Exactly what he saw, however, is perhaps less important than how he interpreted it. Desperately seeking an explanation, Constantine turned to the Christian priests in his entourage.

Whoever was present, be it Bishop Ossius or Lactantius, they now saw an opportunity and seized it with both hands. This, they said, was a sign from God. It was a sign that He was divinely choosing Constantine to defeat the tyrant Maxentius.[21]

According to Eusebius, Constantine now became convinced that they were speaking the truth. Perhaps he was simply ready and willing to convert. For all his military achievements of the past, he knew he was now facing the most daunting battle of his life. He was leading his soldiers against a vastly superior force and bidding to take the one city that no foreign invader, not even Hannibal, had yet conquered. He needed to put his trust in somebody or something. He needed to know that in return for his devotion there was a god protecting him and his army. Apollo and the monotheistic cult of the Unconquerable Sun had once performed that role: two years earlier Constantine had had another vision in a sanctuary of Apollo in Gaul or Britain.[22] Accordingly, after 310 Constantine had his coins stamped with *Sol Invictus*. But now that pagan deity was being replaced in his thinking by God. For after his spiritual experience before the battle, when he turned to his advisers, he found that this experience was most plausibly explained by the Christians. Constantine was won over.

The Christian priests must not have been able to believe their extraordinary luck. By being in the company of someone who was leaning towards a religious conversion, they had been in the right place at the right time. At last they were not only being listened to by an emperor of Rome, but also obeyed by him.

Constantine wasted no time. Just before battle he made a radical, last-minute change of plan. He ordered all the soldiers to mark their shields in white paint with a sign made up of two Greek letters, chi-rho (XP), the cipher of Jesus Christ. (According to Lactantius, writing four years after the event, Constantine had been given this instruction in a dream before the battle.) Although some of the men would have been Christians, it is likely that the majority were not, so there must have been shock that their commander was asking them to follow him in abandoning the traditional gods. Indeed, at the critical moment before war, when their fears were at their greatest and their superstitions most pronounced, their leader's command must have induced even more terror. It is possible that Constantine went as far as ordering the metalsmiths in his army to adjust the old Roman standards. Even the defining, talismanic symbol of the pagan Roman army was perhaps adapted to signify the cross.[23] The general was determined to take the greatest gamble of his life: to fight the battle under the sign and protection of God.

On 28 October 312 the forces of Constantine and Maxentius collided on a broad plain in front of Milvian Bridge. Maxentius had originally decided to remain in the city, but, buoyed up by his priests' good augury, he too crossed the Tiber over the provisional wooden bridge along with his men. His fragile morale was immediately challenged, however, when he noticed numerous owls landing on the walls of the city.[24] That omen was a fitting symbol of the events that followed. The broad, spacious plain favoured Constantine's cavalry. Sweeping up along the flanks of the enemy, they threw Maxentius's army into utter confusion. The fact was that its commitment to fighting for Maxentius had never been resolute. Those soldiers who did put up a fight were trampled underfoot by horses or routed by the following infantry. Slowly but surely, the army of Constantine forced the defenders of Rome back against the Tiber.

With a sudden, collective failure of heart, Maxentius's troops turned and fled, their general running away faster than any of them. At least, the men perhaps consoled themselves, they could reach their makeshift bridge and make the city their bolt-hole. But Maxentius and his generals had wildly misjudged the effectiveness of their plan B. The temporary bridge could not take the weight of the stampeding survivors from his massive army, and the engineers in charge of unfastening the bolts panicked. Whether spurred by fear or sheer incompetence, they released the metal fastenings too early.

The whole structure collapsed spectacularly. Soldier heaped upon soldier fell into the rushing river and drowned. Others, desperate to save their lives, tried to cross the original bridge. The route was too narrow and they were crushed to death. After the mayhem of the rout had subsided, the banks of the Tiber were littered with thousands of anonymous corpses. One of them, however, was distinguishable by his high-ranking clothes. These clung to the dead body of Maxentius.

The general Constantine had won his greatest military victory. He was now sole ruler of the western empire, and he had achieved the knockout blow under the favour, protection and patronage of the Christian God. His success, it seemed, was thanks to Him. However, Constantine's personal conversion, if indeed he had already converted, had been the easy part. Translating his new religion into the world of Roman politics, to the emperors of the east, and to the pagan majority of Romans throughout the empire was another matter altogether. As it happens, Constantine had only scratched the surface in invoking the protection of God. Although he did not yet know it, the full potential of his new allegiance was yet to be tapped.

LICINIUS, BROTHER IN ARMS

When Constantine the liberator entered Rome, he passed through a pleasant blizzard of incense, flowers and the bright faces of men, women and children shouting his name. They thronged in their thousands to greet him, and joined the celebration 'as if released from a cage'.[25] Constantine rode in a

chariot, and in the procession following him the head of
Maxentius was prominently displayed on a spear. The people
greeted the dead tyrant with vitriolic abuse. By contrast, gifts of
money distributed by soldiers into the eager hands of hungry
Romans were met with cheers. However, despite the jubilation
of Constantine's victory march, the successful general knew that
this was no ordinary triumphal procession.

In reality, he was not simply riding into Rome – he was walking a political tightrope. He owed his victory to the Christian
God; the followers of that God would now expect him to find a
suitable way of recognizing that fact. Yet at the same time the
emperor was entering the ancient city of the traditional pagan
gods, the seat of the Roman senators who upheld those traditional beliefs. To them and the majority of Romans, the
Christians were nothing more than a strange alien group whose
behaviour was highly suspect. They renounced slavery; they led
a humble, ascetic and pleasureless existence; they believed in a
heaven after death; and, for some strange reason, they prized
sexual chastity as a virtue. Pleasing both these audiences was not
going to be easy for the new emperor of the west. By both pagan
senators and the Christians, Constantine's every action was
going to be very closely observed.

For the traditionalists, matters did not start well. Many senators, to their disgust and horror, would have noticed that the
military standards borne into the Forum as part of the procession were certainly not those they were expecting to see. These
ones bore the symbol of Christ. But this was not to be the most
unwelcome surprise in store for them. After Constantine had
exchanged the cuirass and sword belt of a general for the
purple toga, rods of office and laurel crown of an emperor, the
crowds waited expectantly for him to perform the customary
sacrifices to Jupiter. The priests prepared the sacrificial
animal, but Constantine hesitated. He was fearful of his

soldiers' reponse if he refused to participate, but knew that it was not to this deity that he owed thanks. Eventually, he refused to ascend the Capitol to oversee the sacrifice. He did not place a laurel wreath in the Temple of Jupiter, and neither did he take any part in paying tribute to the pagan deity.[26] After these affronts to Rome's traditional past, he would need every bit of political nous when facing his next hurdle: a meeting in the Senate House.

Constantine broke the ice by painting his predecessor as a monster. The regime of Maxentius, he began tactfully, was the responsibility of the tyrant and a few of his henchmen. It was not the responsibility of Rome at large. In this way the senators who had collaborated with Maxentius were excused their guilt. The emperor was equally deft in dealing with Maxentius's army: the compromised Praetorian Guard was to be redeployed on Rome's frontiers. Facing barbarian enemies would be a sure-fire way for them to rediscover their loyalty to the emperor. However, Constantine went much further than excusing the senators and the army: he declared that he wanted to restore their prestige. Under his new regime he would restore authority and responsibility to the Senate. Senators would no longer rest on the laurels of rank and privilege. They, and not just men promoted from the army, would be given an active hand in government once again – as provincial governors, as prefects of Rome, as judges and holders of office.[27] Although this process would actually take place gradually over the years to come, for the moment Constantine had struck just the right note.

In one fell swoop he had extinguished the memory of Maxentius and successfully boosted unity by proposing to make the landed aristocracy of the west his partners. In return, the senators reciprocated his trust. Constantine was declared sole emperor of the west. He received a golden shield and wreath as liberator of Italy, and a statue of Victory was dedicated in his honour in the Senate House. As a final tribute, the grand Basilica Nova adjoining the Forum, which had begun construction under Maxentius, was now completed and dedicated to Constantine. With this last honour, his new recognition of the Christians would be clearly expressed. A colossal statue representing him was to be set up in the west apse, and the statue's hand was to hold the military standard bearing the symbol of Christ.

Over the next few months Constantine remained in Rome. They were critical, highly influential months. It was perhaps during this time that he began to think through what had happened during the battle of Milvian Bridge, what the implication of God's favour on him might be. Perhaps he took an active interest in finding out more about the Christians. Perhaps he visited their communities and discovered how they lived. We know that he invited Christian ministers and bishops to be his guests at dinner during this time. Perhaps Lactantius and Ossius were present too. Certainly the Christians who had travelled unofficially in his entourage on campaign were now promoted to hold the more official posts of court advisers on Church politics and practice during the winter of 312–13. Whatever Constantine discussed with those men in private, it would not be long before the fruits of their deliberations were revealed very publicly.

As Constantine prepared to leave Rome for Milan in mid-January 313, he could look back with pride on a successful few months in the old imperial capital. The clever balancing act between pagans and Christians had so far been expertly and delicately handled. With Rome now rebranded and reconciled, the emperor had successfully consolidated his power in the western half of the empire. Now he set about bringing peace and unity to the east. To that effect, he sent a letter to the eastern emperor. It was a shot across Maximinus Daia's bows. It informed him of

Constantine's new status in the west as conferred by the Senate. It also revealed the western emperor's new religious loyalty by warning Daia to stop persecuting Christians in his domain. However, to bring him to heel, Constantine needed help. He had in mind a new alliance, one to be cemented in the traditional way. The emperor and his entourage set off for Milan: Constantine had a wedding to attend.

The marriage ceremony took place in February in the city's imperial palace, carefully orchestrated and supervised by Constantine himself. The eighteen-year-old bride was the western emperor's sister Constantia. Like many women of the élite in the early fourth century, she was a Christian – faith was important to her, a key part of her personality. It was a personality, however, less suited to what she was being asked to do by her brother: to marry a man many years her senior, whom she did not know, whom she did not love and to whom she was to be wed for political expediency. Undertaking such a task required a much thicker skin than perhaps Constantia possessed. Yet she was given no choice. Constantine insisted that she marry a man who would be crucial to his plans in the east. The name of her groom was Valerius Licinianus Licinius. He too held the title of emperor.

Born of peasants from Dacia (modern-day Romania), Licinius was nearly in his fifties when he married Constantia. Like many of the other tetrarchs, he had risen to prominence as an able and effective soldier. On campaign on the frontiers of the Danube he had become a close friend of Galerius. It was through him that, just as Diocletian's system of four emperors was falling apart, Licinius received his greatest break: in 308, at a conference in Carnuntum, he was appointed to be co-emperor of the west with Constantine in place of the dead Severus. When the eastern emperor Galerius died, however, Licinius negotiated a peace with Daia and took partial control of the dead emperor's territories in the east. But now the fragility of the peace between Daia and Licinius was being exposed. The alliance between Constantine and Licinius, sealed with the dry, diplomatic marriage taking place in Milan, reflected the new lie of the Roman political landscape. The empire was to be shared by the two men alone. There was no room for Daia.

After the marriage ceremony, the alliance was concluded behind closed doors. One can only guess what was said, but the outline is clear. Licinius was to control the east, Constantine the west. Each side would come to the military aid of the other. All was as expected between two emperors redrawing the Roman map. However, Constantine introduced a new, controversial term to their alliance: a policy of toleration of all religions in the Roman world. Although Licinius was not known as a persecutor of Christians, he was certainly pagan in his beliefs. Yet now he was being asked to put his name to a radical new policy in which every Roman was free to worship whichever god he wished. It must have taken him completely by surprise. But if Licinius was reluctant to agree to the policy, Constantine knew how to convince him.

Daia was a renowned persecutor of Christians in the east. The policy of toleration, Constantine might well have suggested, could be the key to winning their support against the eastern emperor. It is easy to imagine that, encouraged by his new Christian advisers, Constantine pressed the importance of this new policy on his pagan brother-in-law. Constantine's belief in the Christian God was apparently sincere, but it could also be highly useful and expedient. Licinius clearly agreed.

The Edict of Milan, as it came to be known later, was soon proclaimed by both men. It was the first government document in the Western world to recognize freedom of belief. Henceforth persecution of Christians was disowned as morally wrong. But the edict's principal benefit was more immediate and tangible than that. It decreed that all Church property previously confiscated from the Christians was to be restored to them. Crucially, it not did favour Christians above pagans, but stressed only their equal rights of worship, granting both full legal recognition to 'follow whatever form of worship they please'. As Licinius did not share his brother-in-law's religious belief, perhaps he had insisted on that detail. Perhaps he had also made sure that the edict did not commit him personally to the Christian faith; the wording 'whatsoever divinity dwelt in heaven' neatly resolved that question.[28] Above all, the edict provided a unifying theme for the new empire; it also gave the government of Constantine and Licinius a unified voice of greater strength.

The agreement bonded two very different men. Constantine was well born, younger than Licinius and, so we're told by Eusebius, charismatic, graceful and good-looking. In winning the west he had proved himself a gifted commander and an astute politician. Licinius, for all his military achievements, was somewhat overshadowed by the western emperor's brilliance. Indeed, he had good reason to be jealous of the young pretender: Licinius had originally been appointed senior emperor in the west, but it was Constantine who, by defeating Maxentius, had successfully secured it for himself. However, there was no time for indulging in past resentments. There was an aggressor to defeat. Before the conference in Milan was finished, news arrived from the east. Daia had made the first move against the allies: he had crossed the Bosporus, invaded Licinius's territories in Asia Minor and laid siege to Byzantium. War had been declared.

It took Licinius only a matter of months to gather an army, give chase to Daia's forces and drive them on to a plain near Hadrianople (modern-day Edirne in Turkey). On 30 April 313, before the battle, Licinius showed he had taken Constantine's message in Milan to heart: he ordered the rank and file of his army to recite, if not a Christian prayer, then a more perfunctory monotheistic one.[29] It seemed to reap immediate dividends. Although Licinius and his 30,000 troops were outnumbered by a 70,000-strong enemy, he and his men enjoyed a comprehensive victory. Daia fled into the Tarsus mountains (in modern-day Turkey) where, to avoid the humiliation of surrender, he committed suicide by taking poison. Buoyed up by his extraordinary victory, Licinius then honoured his agreement with Constantine and, through a letter sent to provincial governors, communicated to the Romans of the east the regime's new policies.

However, any impression that he was behaving out of a new-found sympathy with the Christian faith was quickly dispelled by his next move. To ensure that no one could stake a rival claim to the eastern empire, Licinius ordered a bloodbath. All Daia's sympathizers, court advisers and family were executed. In addition, all the living wives and children of the old tetrarchs Diocletian, Severus and Galerius were hunted down throughout the Roman east and murdered. Although some Christian writers of the time heartily approved of the murder of persecutors, perhaps even they would have been shocked by the clinical nature of the purge. With that accomplished, Licinius, the man who had drifted into a toleration of Christianity for political expediency, took sole control of the east and settled down to administering it from his imperial capital of Nicomedia, with his new young bride alongside. The Roman empire enjoyed a new government and a new cohesiveness. But whereas Licinius's dispassionate toleration of Christianity began and ended with the proclamation and enactment of the Edict of Milan, Constantine's work, undertaken from his base in Trier, was only just beginning.

Publicly, Constantine continued to steer a shrewd non-committal path: although he declined to participate in pagan sacrifices, he still held the highest office of the pagan religious establishment, held by every emperor since Augustus, that of *pontifex maximus* (High Priest). The coins issued in his name were slow to depict any Christian symbolism; instead they carried the name of the monotheistic pagan god Unconquerable Sun, and would do so for many years to come. A speech delivered in 313 at Trier survives: it is a masterpiece of ambiguity, emphasizing Constantine's closeness with the divine, but cleverly not excluding devotion to one faith or another. For all the poise of this balancing act, however, the reality was very different. Constantine had found his unifying theme for the empire. Now he began industriously applying it to the administration and running of the empire.

A letter from 313 shows his first action: Christians, it said, were exempt from civic public duties such as serving as jurors, overseeing the collection of taxes, or organizing building projects, festivals and games. Previously such exemptions had been given to those whose profession benefited the state in other ways, such as doctors and teachers. Now Constantine declared that Christians were just as deserving. Being able to devote more time to worship of the Christian God, said Constantine, would make 'an immense contribution to the welfare of the community'.[30] Christianity, the imperial message made plain, was essential to the good of the empire. In addition, he granted payments to the clergy, and also made Christians of privileged and propertied rank exempt from paying taxes. Indeed, bishops were not only taking on administrative roles at court, but also across the empire: Christians engaged in civil lawsuits were granted the legal right to refer their dispute from a secular magistrate to a bishop. But these utterly unprecedented changes did not just take the form of benefits in rank and privileges. They had a physical manifestation too.

Constantine gave generously from the imperial treasury so that churches across the western empire could be built or improved, or sumptuously decorated. The legacy of his munificence can be seen today in Rome, where he paid for no fewer than five or six churches. The greatest of these was the enormous Basilica of St John Lateran. Although the cathedral that stands there today is a later construction, the proportions of the original building are known. It was no less than 100 metres (330 feet) in length and 54 metres (180 feet) wide. The design of this and other churches was innovative. Although the word 'basilica' is used today to mean a religious building, at the time of Constantine a basilica was simply a secular, public building, normally thought of by Romans as a law court or a marketplace or a venue for public assembly. Under Constantine, this hall-like design now became the structure for the principal church of Rome – and the template for Christian churches in the future.[31]

Normally churches in Rome were built outside the city walls on sites associated with the veneration of apostles and martyrs. The Basilica of St John Lateran, in the heart of Rome, was an exception because it was founded on a plot of land adjacent to an old imperial palace, a residence which Constantine duly donated to the bishop of Rome (namely, the Pope). The Basilica of St Peter's, another church endowed by Constantine, venerated an early Christian cult. On the side of the Vatican Hill, the site of the cult centre of St Peter, a huge terrace was created. The clearing of the ground revealed an ancient pagan and Christian burial ground and it was on top of this that the massive basilica of the first St Peter's was built. In the modern sixteenth-century St Peter's, constructed on the site of Constantine's original church, it is still possible to access the cemetery below.

The new churches not only looked different from pagan temples – they served a different function. The temples had simply housed the deity; the Christian churches, by contrast, were not only houses of God, but places in which His followers could congregate. Here on Sundays, the day that Constantine would later make holy (in 321), Roman soldiers would be seen, for the emperor gave them leave to attend church. When in the house of God, slaves too were given a radical new privilege: they were temporarily free. The sheer physical presence and majesty of these buildings spelt a revolution: Christianity was important and Christians were special.[32]

However, there was one action at this time that above all else revealed the importance of Christianity to Constantine as the glue unifying his and Licinius's new empire. In 313 news reached the emperor that an argument had broken out in the Christian Church of North Africa. It centred on who was the rightful bishop of the province: Caecilian or Donatus. The dispute had arisen because one group believed that Caecilian should not be recognized. He had been ordained, they said, by a bishop who had colluded in the persecutions of Diocletian by handing over holy scriptures to the Roman authorities. As a result, the rival bishop, Donatus, was consecrated. To previous emperors, such a dispute would have been a parochial matter of absolutely no importance. But not to Constantine.

I consider it absolutely contrary to the divine law that we should overlook such quarrels and contentions, whereby the Highest Divinity may perhaps be roused not only against the human race but also against myself, to whose care He had by His celestial will committed the government of all earthly things.[33]

The message was clear: whereas in the past emperors were accustomed to arbitrate petitions or cases of a civil or legal nature brought to them by provincials, Constantine's authority as ruler of the Roman empire was defined as much by his ability to adjudicate disputes within the Church.[34] Dissension among Christians was dissension against the unity of the empire, and in the new regime that was not allowed. Since the persecutions under Diocletian, Constantine had always known that the practice of worshipping one Christian God to the exclusion of all others made imperial unity impossible to achieve. If he were now to break cover and throw in his lot with the Christians, there could be no political advantage if he and his fellow Christians were not themselves united. When the North African dispute rumbled on into the winter of 315–16 the emperor wrote to those involved. He threatened to visit them in person and bash their heads together. By that time, however, there were other, far more pressing matters on Constantine's mind.

The summer of 315 saw the city of Rome in the throes of hosting a grand party. The emperor of the west had left his imperial seat at Trier and, accompanied by an entourage of his family, bishops and court officials, had returned in person to the city he had liberated three years earlier. By way of entertainment, circus races and public games were in full swing. The festival was being held to mark Constantine's *decennalia* – his tenth anniversary of becoming emperor – and now, looking back, there was much to celebrate. He had campaigned against the Germans and secured the Rhine frontier. He had restored peace and stability to an empire that had been falling apart at the seams but was now prospering. The Senate in Rome was once again industrious, a partner in government. Indeed, Constantine had addressed the fear of senators that they, and hence Rome, were no longer important: he increased their number, bestowing the rank of senator on people who were not required to live in Rome or to attend meetings of the Senate. Membership thus became empire-wide rather than local.[35]

The new Christian élite also had cause for celebration. They could now boast a privileged position of influence in

Constantine's court, and the emperor himself, in conversation or in study with Lactantius and Bishop Ossius, was perhaps gaining greater knowledge of his divine protector. His faith was, at least ostensibly, being confirmed. The extent of Christian influence on Constantine can perhaps be gauged in specially minted, commemorative medallions produced in the same year. On them Constantine is depicted wearing the cipher of Christ, the chi-rho, and they were ceremoniously handed out to prominent court officials. Priests, believers and upholders of the traditional Roman religions, however, were not excluded from this prosperity. In the new spirit of toleration their cults too were flourishing. Indeed now, at the festival, a fitting tribute to the emperor's discretion was unveiled and dedicated.

The Arch of Constantine still stands today in the Forum. This major monument marks the transition from classical to a new style known as 'late antique'. In this style reliefs are sculpted depicting Constantine's liberation of Italy: here is a scene describing the defeat of Maxentius, there the drowning of the tyrant's soldiers and in another Constantine's entry into Rome. There is, however, not one Christian symbol to be seen anywhere on it. Quite the opposite was true. Some of the sculptures dated to the reign of Hadrian. They were recycled and remodelled to show Constantine and Licinius, and not the classical emperor, hunting and sacrificing to the Roman gods. This was to be the last time that an emperor would be portrayed performing such pagan activities. For all the strides taken towards favouring Christianity, the reality was that the western emperor could still not yet declare his hand.

Constantine was ambitious to unite the empire. He had now found the means with which to realize that ambition. But for the time being he held himself back. He knew that if he openly supported Christianity he would expose a political flank. The upholders of the traditional gods among the senators, governors and administrators of the empire could still attack him, strategically claiming that he was persecuting pagans. Overt favouring of the Christians, Constantine understood, would not only offend those who supported the traditional gods, but would also expose their weakness, suggesting their disadvantage in the new empire. And with the majority of Roman citizens pagan, there was potentially a plentiful source of support for such rivals to draw on. However, it was not pagan senators that Constantine feared most, but a pagan emperor.

In the same month as the celebrations in Rome took place (July 315), Constantia, the wife of Licinius, gave birth to a son. Just over a year later, on 7 August 316, Constantine's wife, Fausta, also gave birth to a baby boy. But the arrival of these children was not entirely a cause for jubilation because two new chains of legitimacy were being formed. In the minds of Constantine and Licinius it sparked a question that they had not yet confronted: to whom did the empire really belong? Since their alliance had been struck, the answer seemed increasingly to suggest Constantine.

Motivated perhaps by genuine belief, perhaps by calculated self-interest, Constantine's industrious reforms in favour of the Christians were not just unifying the empire with a new theme. They were winning him vital support in Licinius's territory, where the majority of the Roman empire's Christians resided. As Constantine looked at his commemorative arch, he could see how the portraits of both him and Licinius showed the emperors in harmony. Their joint holding of the consulship, and the depiction of both their heads on the coins of the period supported that impression. But Constantine's new brand of government did not fit with the façade. The logical conclusion of one God, one empire was one emperor.

It would not be long before both Licinius and Constantine showed their hands. When that happened, the two men would become rivals and precipitate a new war. It was to be a war between the supporters of Constantine and the radical new religion he had embraced and those who wanted to uphold Rome's traditions. So at least the banners of the two sides would claim. In reality, although dressed up in the robes of a holy war, this conflict was aimed at achieving a time-honoured goal: control of the Roman empire.

WAR OF RELIGIONS

The steps that turned an alliance of emperors into a fierce rivalry are difficult to piece together. Certainly Licinius had reason to be resentful, even jealous.[36] Constantine had taken control of the part of the empire that Licinius believed was rightfully his. To make matters worse, the eastern emperor had only to look around his own territory to see that Constantine enjoyed far greater popularity than he did. Christians of the east offered prayers for Constantine; they hoped that the same largesse he showed their brothers in the west might one day rain down on them too; indeed, because they were prepared to die for their faith, they were prepared to die for him too. They knew that Licinius was neither their saviour nor their voice. In fact, it is possible that it had been Constantine's intention all along to place Licinius in a vice: to use him to settle the eastern empire at the beginning, but then, when that had been achieved, to destabilize him through the instrument of Christianity. Despite envying Constantine's popularity, Licinius harboured a much greater source of bitterness – something that would ultimately push him over the edge.

What most riled the emperor of the east were the steps that Constantine took to cut out Licinius's newborn son from succession to imperial power. In 315 Constantine gave his half-sister Anastasia in marriage to the prominent senator Bassianus. He then sent a delegate to Licinius proposing that Bassianus become deputy emperor in the west. Licinius took offence. It must have occurred to him that it would only require Constantine to appoint his teenage son Crispus as deputy in the east for Constantine to bring the whole empire within the control of his own dynasty. Perhaps it was for this reason that Licinius decided to terminate his friendship with Constantine in the most decisive way: by plotting his assassination.

To carry off such an action, Licinius quickly needed to acquire a pretext and allies. Fortunately, both were easily attainable. He could justify toppling his fellow emperor on the grounds that Constantine had broken the Edict of Milan; he had begun favouring Christians above pagans. If that was not sufficient grounds for action, then, according to a pagan historian, Constantine's infringement of Licinius's territory in the autumn of 315 certainly did the trick.[37] As for help in carrying out the murder of the western emperor, Licinius needed only to look as far as the Senate in Rome.

By 316 some pagan senators, for all the favour that Constantine had promised them, were quietly seething with disaffection. They disapproved of his lavish spending from the imperial treasury to build Christian churches. To them it seemed that only bishops had the emperor's ear and were his favoured dinner guests in the palace. There was no point in expressing ambition, they moaned, for now it was only possible to get ahead in the new regime if you were Christian.

Licinius knew the time was ripe for action. In Nicomedia he asked his court official Senecio to find a willing conspirator in Rome. The ideal assassin needed to have elevated status, be able to gain close access to the emperor and be above suspicion. Senecio had one particularly suitable candidate in mind: his own brother and Constantine's brother-in-law, Senator Bassianus. In setting the plot in motion, however, Licinius had overlooked his own weakness. It is easy to imagine that just as he had been able to find an ally in Constantine's inner court, he had forgotten that the western emperor also had a devout ally in the east. One might speculate that it was she who now passed on a surreptitious alert.

Perhaps Constantia had chanced upon a rumour drifting through the corridors of the Nicomedian palace, or perhaps she herself had accidentally overheard the conversation between Licinius and Senecio. It is even possible that she, on discovering the plot against her brother's life, immediately wrote a letter warning him and dispatched it through a trusted Christian channel of communication. What is certain is that when Bassianus attempted the assassination, he was taken completely by surprise. Constantine had been expecting him. The man who was murdered that night was not the God-beloved emperor, but the putative assassin. When Licinius heard the news he ordered the statues and busts of Constantine in Nicomedia to be smashed. With that, war was declared.

The first encounters between the two armies took place in 316 at Cibalae and Serdica in the Balkans. Although Constantine had the upper hand in both battles, he failed to deliver the decisive blow. As a result, a new alliance was drawn up between the two men. The territories of the Balkans and Greece were ceded to Constantine, while Licinius retained Thrace, Asia Minor, Egypt and the Roman east. The two grudging allies also agreed on the thorny issue of succession: on 1 March 317 Constantine announced from his new seat at Serdica (now Sofia in Bulgaria) that both his sons (his baby by Fausta and Flavius Julius Crispus) and Licinius's child by Constantia were to be declared Caesars – future emperors in waiting. They also agreed to hold the joint consulship for 317, and thereafter to alternate the consulship of each half of the empire between father and son each year. But beneath this paper-thin show of harmony there were deep cracks. In reality, the peace was at best unstable, at worst a piece of diplomatic cynicism on the part of Constantine. The war had simply been shelved.

Between 317 and 321 Licinius endured religious toleration of the Christians. Perhaps he was being kept in line by his wife or by the bishop of Nicomedia, who was based at his court. However, it was a role that the old 'liberator' of the east, the one-time saviour of the Christians, increasingly hated. He had drifted without belief into toleration of the Christians for short-term gain, and now it showed. In the west, by contrast, Constantine the Christian became increasingly strident. He liked to stay up late at night and compose his own rousing speeches. These he delivered to his courtiers, lay sermons expressing his divinely inspired vision for the empire. He put on quite a show. Whenever he mentioned the judgement of God, his face would tighten with intensity, he would lower his voice and point to heaven. His words caused some courtiers in his audience to bow their heads as if he were 'actually flogging them with his argument'. Others clapped loudly, but could not really match the emperor's fervour. Ultimately they ignored his Christian lecturing.[38]

Alongside communicating the awe of God, however, the emperor could still be repressive, even violent. In 317 the Donatist dispute in Africa had not yet been resolved. Constantine lost patience and tried to end it by authorizing exiles and executions. Within a few years, some pagan temples were closed down – the first sign in the west of the slow eradication of the pluralist melting pot of pagan cults. In their place was evidence of a growing new common identity.

Through endowments of property, the high profile of bishops, and charitable gifts of clothes and grain to the poor, orphans, destitute widows and divorcees, churches were fast becoming the centres of local power and organization throughout the provinces of the western empire.[39] Around 321 the judicial authority of bishops was extended, and bequests to churches legalized. It was easy for the provincial élites to buy into the new religion. Upper classes across the empire were becoming increasingly wealthy and self-confident; archaeological finds reveal how the mark of Christ, the chi-rho, began appearing on objects belonging to the wealthy at this time and how new, exquisite villas were rising up across the western empire.[40] Religious conversion had its advantages: it brought with it the new majesty of empire, a new patriotism, and the belief that these would continue to flourish so long as Constantine received not the old Roman 'peace of the gods', but divine protection from God.

In a rare preserved speech known as the 'Oration to the Saints', delivered to a Christian audience on a Good Friday between 321 and 324, Constantine made his position clear. God was responsible for his success. That success put him under a great obligation: to persuade his subjects to worship God, to reform the wicked and unbelieving, and to liberate the persecuted. It was a religious position that had huge political consequences. The stance forced Licinius into a corner, slowly but surely turning the screw on him. It was not long before he handed Constantine a gift, the very thing that the western emperor had perhaps been looking for all along, the very thing that neatly coincided with his faith – a justification for resuming the war.

In Nicomedia the emperor of the east was becoming increasingly suspicious, paranoid even. Were those officials within his own court, he wondered, agents of Constantine? Were they Christian spies? He took them aside and had them interrogated, but could find no evidence of guilt. For one man, so the story goes, he devised a test of loyalty. He asked Auxentius, a legal clerk in his administration, to accompany him to a courtyard in his palace where there was a fountain, a statue of Dionysus and a flourishing vine. Licinius ordered Auxentius to cut the fullest cluster of grapes he could find. When he had done so, the emperor asked him to dedicate the fruit to Dionysus. Auxentius refused. Licinius gave him an ultimatum: lay the grapes at the foot of the statue or leave his court for ever. Auxentius chose the latter; he would later become bishop of Mopsuestia, in modern-day Turkey.[41] This episode was the first of many tests imposed by Licinius. Fear would drive him to far more extreme measures.

In 323 Licinius compelled everyone in his administration to sacrifice or else lose their job. He put the same test of conformity to his army. On the advice of zealous pagan officials, the requirement was forced on civilians, and on 24 December of that year Constantine learnt that bishops were compelled to sacrifice at the festival marking Licinius's fifteen years as emperor. Anyone who refused was to be punished. Councils and assemblies of bishops were forbidden; Licinius did not want them to organize, unite and encircle him, so he forced them to remain in their own cities. Christian meetings of worship could take place only in the open air, and all tax exemptions for the Christian clergy were scrapped. The influence of his devout wife, and his love for her, perhaps prevented him from going further. Other people in his administration had no such compunction. In short, Licinius encouraged a new permissiveness to reign in the east, a sharp whiplash of pagan reaction. Roman governors were free to punish dissident Christians, shut down some churches, demolish others and, in the case of the bishops in the province of Bithynia-Pontus south of the Black Sea, murder key figureheads in the Christian clergy. According to Eusebius, their bodies were chopped up and thrown into the sea as food for fish.[42]

At the imperial palace in Serdica Constantine was urged by Lactantius, his adviser and tutor to his son, to rescue 'the just in other parts of the world'. When Constantine, perhaps deliberately, invaded Licinius's territories in Thrace on the pretext of repelling a Gothic invasion, both parties seized the opportunity to wage war. Constantine's case for hostilities against his brother-in-law and former ally was more wide-ranging than the diplomatic incident suggested. This was a war for the defence of the oppressed, a war of liberation, a war against a persecutor.[43]

The stage was set for one of the last epic confrontations in Roman history. Both sides were quick to mobilize their forces, an extraordinary military feat in its own right. Each side was said to number more than 100,000 infantry and 10,000 cavalry. Even given the propensity of ancient sources to exaggerate, significant numbers of troops had clearly been amassed. Egyptians, Phoenicians, Carians, Greeks from Asia Minor, Bithynians and Africans filled out the ranks of Licinius's forces, while Constantine, in control of a larger part of the Roman empire, relied less on auxiliaries than on standing units of regular Roman legionaries. Eusebius, in contrasting the two armies, had a literary field day. Constantine's troops were, of course, Christian soldiers of God. Licinius's, on the other hand, were motley followers of the traditional gods and eastern mystery cults: wizards, diviners, druggists, seers and meddlers in the malignant arts of sorcery.[44]

Some time before the forces came face to face, Licinius asked his priests to read the omens. The augurers observed the flights of birds and inspected the arrangement of entrails for signs. Their verdict? The omens promised that Licinius would be victorious. The ceremonies continued when Licinius led his closest commanders to a thickly wooded, sacred grove. Pagan statues peeped through the boughs of trees and from behind mossy, rocky springs. The usual sacrifices were made, then Licinius addressed his men. His rhetorical flourish is typical of the way the pro-Christian sources liked to present the conflict.

Friends and comrades, these are our ancestral gods, whom we honour because we have received them for worship from our earliest forefathers. The commander of those arrayed against us has broken faith with the ancestral code and adopted godless belief, mistakenly acknowledging some foreign god from somewhere or other; he even shames his own army with this god's disgraceful emblem. Trusting in him, he advances, taking up arms not against us, but first and foremost against the very gods he has offended. Now is the moment that will prove which one is mistaken in his belief: it will decide between the gods honoured by us and the gods honoured by the other party.[45]

On 3 July 324, at the first engagement at Hadrianopolis in Thrace (modern-day Edirne in Greece), Licinius's hopes for that moment to weigh in his favour were royally dashed.

The two armies had taken up positions on opposite sides of the river Hebrus. For days they eyed each other sullenly. Whenever Licinius's men caught sight of Constantine's standard brightly bearing the sign of Christ, they broke the stillness with jeers and insults. During this strange hiatus, however, Constantine seized the initiative. He fooled his enemy into thinking that he was trying to build a bridge across the river that separated them. He even went through the charade of asking his soldiers to climb a mountain and bring down timber. Secretly, however, Constantine had worked out an alternative, shorter crossing. When his cavalry charged across it, they caught Licinius's army completely unawares. Thrown into confusion, huge numbers of the surprised troops were brutally pursued and cut down. Some gave themselves up in surrender, while others were soundly routed. Licinius was among the latter.[46]

He and his surviving forces quick-marched to the coast, rushed to their ships and tried to flee to safety across the Bosporus. Constantine, however, had prepared for this moment.

He ordered his eldest son Crispus to give chase; at just seventeen years old and now in charge of a two-hundred-strong naval fleet, Crispus seized on his father's instruction. Meanwhile, Licinius's admiral was instructed to stop the pursuit. The two fleets met in the narrow straits of the Hellespont. With a roll of the dice, Crispus chose to leave behind the bulk of his fleet and attack with his eight fastest ships. It proved to be a stroke of genius. His attack was orderly and clinical. Licinius's larger fleet, by contrast, simply crowded out the confined waters and had no room to manoeuvre. The forest of sails and the chaos of chopping, clattering oars brought only confusion. With several of Licinius's ships scuppered, nightfall drew the sea battle to a close. The next day a strong south wind finished off Crispus's work: Licinius's fleet was smashed against the rocks and thus subjected to another crushing defeat. Nonetheless, within a matter of weeks, the eastern emperor regrouped his forces. He had recruited another army from Asia. He faced his enemy once more at Chrysopolis. He was not beaten yet.

The final showdown between Licinius and Constantine took place on 18 September 324. The two emperors drew up their massive armies on a plain midway between Chrysopolis (now a suburb of Istanbul) and the town of Chalcedon. Constantine's army was distinguished once again by its magnificent Christian standard. On the rich tapestry hanging from the crossbar, the sign of Christ (the chi-rho) gleamed with precious stones and glittering streaks of gold. The emperor knew it was vital not to underestimate the importance of this emblem. He ensured that a specially dedicated guard was responsible for it, a group of men who had been selected for their courage and physical strength. Now it was raised proudly above the massed ranks as they waited to launch their attack. Constantine took his time. He was perhaps in his tent, as was his custom, praying quietly to God, waiting and searching for a revelation. When he believed God's will was expressed to him, so it was said, he would rush out of his tent, rouse his troops and order them to draw their swords.[47]

Licinius's army charged first. Perhaps this time, when they spied their enemy's Christian standard held aloft, they viewed it ominously and were silenced. According to Eusebius, Licinius ordered his men not to get close to it, nor even to lay eyes upon it. Indeed, when Constantine's ranks advanced on the enemy and came under a streaming volley of javelins many of them were cut down. Miraculously, so Eusebius claimed, the standard-bearers were saved.[48] Perhaps the heart and power this moment gave the men was contagious, for the confidence to win now spread like an epidemic through Constantine's ranks. As the armies clashed on an incredible scale, the wind, the momentum and the impetus for battle were all with the legionaries of Constantine.

In the face of forceful assault, the fighting spirit had simply left Licinius's men. The battle of Chrysopolis had turned into a massacre on an enormous scale. Over 100,000 of Licinius's army were said to have been killed. The victory of Constantine, of Christianity, was decisive. However, there was one man who had escaped the bloodbath. Licinius slipped away from the battlefield on horseback in the company of some cavalry; as Constantine surveyed the site of the catastrophic defeat his exhausted, destroyed enemy was heading east to the imperial palace at Nicomedia, to his loyal wife and his nine-year-old child. Constantine now followed in pursuit and laid siege to the town.

If Licinius's thoughts had drifted to saving his honour in the traditional way, by turning his sword on himself, perhaps it was the sight of his family as he collapsed at his palace that convinced him otherwise. One ancient source reveals how, during the night of his return home, Constantia persuaded her husband that instead of death it would be better to surrender to Constantine. Once she had gained Licinius's willingness to live on, Constantia slipped out of the palace and entered her brother's military headquarters.

For the first time in nearly ten years Constantine laid eyes on his sister again. This was the woman whom he had wed to his enemy at eighteen years old; this was the wife of the man whom, over the intervening years, Constantine had tried time and again to eliminate so that he could become sole emperor and reunite the Roman empire. Now here she stood amid dirty, exhausted soldiers and bloodied prisoners of war who were being punished 'according to the law of war'. Licinius's commander-in-chief was being held before execution; the captive soldiers were being forced to repent and then acknowledge Constantine's God as the 'true and only God'.[49] In such grim circumstances it must have been hard for brother and sister to look each other in the eye. Nonetheless, Constantia steeled herself and fell on her brother's mercy. Appealing to his Christian values of forgiveness, she begged him to spare Licinius's life. Constantine agreed.

The imperial pageantry of the arraignments contrasted sharply with the miserable ceremony that took place the next day. Constantine, dressed in magnificent robes and now sole ruler of the entire Roman world, sat on a dais in his camp outside the city. He was surrounded by bishops and court officials. Perhaps Lactantius and Ossius were present too, exalting in the victory of their God. Slowly Licinius walked towards Constantine, his former enemies lining the long, humiliating path from the palace to the victor's camp. It is possible that Constantia and her son had to face the ignominy of accompanying the defeated leader. When he reached Constantine, Licinius knelt before the emperor in abject supplication. He had brought with him the purple robes befitting his former office, and with bowed head he offered them up to Constantine. Perhaps Constantine added salt to the wound and asked the former emperor to convert to the Christian faith. What is more certain is Licinius's final indignity: he hailed Constantine 'Lord and Master, begging forgiveness for the events of the past'.[50] Licinius and his family were then officially sent to live out their days in Thessaloniki and in peace.

However, it is easy to imagine that, for all the pomp and ceremony and for all the polite applause, both men knew that nothing had really changed. Within a year of Licinius's surrender and abdication, a detachment of imperial soldiers found him with his family in Greece. When Licinius saw the guards approach perhaps he knew instantly that Constantine had gone back on his word, that the emperor could never allow potential rivals and their heirs to live, could never forgive. The soldiers took him and his son aside and garrotted them.[51]

EPILOGUE

Constantia survived the death of her husband and child. The emperor gave her the title 'Most Noble Lady' and she remained an important figure at her brother's court. Her presence there must have been strained and full of stony recrimination. She died in 330, perhaps no more than thirty-five years old. Constantia, however, was not the only relative to fall foul of her brother's imperial authority.

In 326 Constantine ordered the deaths of both his first son Crispus (whom he had appointed to the rank of Caesar) and his wife Fausta, the woman who had borne him three sons. The cause is shrouded in mystery. There were suspicions at court that Crispus was having an affair with his stepmother; another rumour suggested that it was Fausta who had fallen in love with Crispus, but had been rejected by him. Either way, such immoral behaviour could never be seen to taint the core of the Christian imperial family – the emperor's absolutist legislation on sexual matters forbade it. The short, brilliant career of Crispus ended in execution. The cause of Fausta's death is recorded as suffocation in an overheated steam bath.

Constantine's unsentimental singularity of purpose also showed itself in the religious policy of his later years. In the aftermath of his victory over Licinius, the emperor published several edicts in the east. The persecuted Christians were to be released from prison, they were to have their property restored and they would receive the same privileges as Christians in the west. Bishops were encouraged to repair churches and build new ones. But the preaching tone of these edicts went much further than the Edict of Milan. In the letters accompanying them, Constantine did not force his subjects to abandon paganism and take up Christianity, but he urged them to do so. The Christian God, he wrote, was morally supreme. It was God who had brought an end to persecutors, God who had established the correct observance of religion. Constantine had simply been his instrument.[52] The message rang out: Christianity was now the officially favoured religion of the Roman world. But what about paganism?

Ostensibly the edicts suggest that Constantine was actively campaigning against paganism: some traditional temples were closed, and sacrifices and the consulting of oracles were forbidden, especially by Roman provincial governors and prefects.[53] However, the picture Eusebius describes is misleading. Certainly Constantine wanted to stamp out magic and superstition: he outlawed the private use of diviners, and magic designed to sexually arouse or make an attempt on someone's life. Devotion to the traditional gods, however, was another matter. That form of paganism would be very slow to die out; there was as yet no mass conversion to Christianity.

The imperial ban on pagan sacrifices could never be enforced. They continued in Italy, and in Greece the emperor even lifted the ban so that a cult known as the Eleusinian Mysteries might not be affected. Constantine also allowed a new pagan temple to be built in Italy and dedicated to the imperial family late in his reign. Temples in Rome were granted protection from the emperor, and it remained the job of the prefect of the city to restore and maintain the buildings, statues and centres of the ancient Roman cults in the fourth and fifth centuries. Nonetheless, later emperors would be much harsher in their clampdown on pagan practices. The process of fossilizing Rome's pagan past had begun.

The Church may have become the unifying institution of Constantine's Christian empire. An issue of doctrine, however, was spoiling the picture. When Constantine 'liberated' the east from Licinius, he discovered that the Church there was even more divided than that in Africa. The greatest dispute, however, was not a mere debate over the legitimacy of a bishop, but a philosophical dispute over the relationship between God and Jesus Christ: was God the Father the same as God the Son, or was he inferior? A priest called Arius argued that while God the Father was eternal and indivisible, God the Son had to be created after the Father as His instrument for the salvation of man. Although he was perfect, God the Son was therefore not eternal and could not be called God. Arius's argument sparked an absolute furore and threatened an upheaval in Church unity once again. Constantine stepped in.

In 325 he called together and personally attended the first universal meeting of the Church, known as the Council of Nicaea. The occasion must have been an extraordinary sight. For the first time, over three hundred bishops from all corners of the Roman world came together in an attempt to thrash out the doctrine being disputed by Arius. On the morning of the first day, dressed in the splendour of his bright purple robe embroidered with gold and inlaid with stones, Constantine entered the large, silent hall of the palace at Nicaea. He walked with an elegant, modest gait. A small golden chair was set front and centre before the rows of bishops. Their excitement at the occasion reached a new pitch when the emperor showed deference by waiting for them to sit down before he did. Only when they gave him the signal did he sit first, and then the whole gathering followed suit.[54] From his seat, however, Constantine did much more than invigilate proceedings. He took an active, forceful part.

He was credited, for example, with finding the form of words that resolved the dispute. This stated that God the Son was 'of one substance' in relation to God the Father. The formulation implied that Arius was wrong. Despite this intervention, however, Constantine, the great soldier, the commander who had won the civil war, was less concerned with the intricacies of doctrinal debate. The emperor wanted simply to put out the fire of the controversy and end the dispute. Cajoling, bullying, and slipping between Latin and Greek in his efforts to persuade recalcitrant bishops, Constantine strong-armed the majority into putting their names to the proposed form of words designed to heal the rift. Most complied, but Arius and two of his followers refused and all three men were exiled. Unity, admittedly with the exception of a few dissenters, had prevailed. The grand occasion had been a triumph. Or so it seemed.

Certainly there were striking successes. For the first time the emperor of Rome, the most powerful man in the world, had used his power to establish Christian orthodoxy. On many issues he had won agreement from the vast majority of attendants coming together for the first time. Although Constantine made a show of deferring to the bishops, they had assembled under his authority and the decisions they had reached were universally binding. Indeed, in exiling Arius and his followers the treatment of 'heretics' had been taken out of the hands of bishops and become subject to the criminal law pronounced by the emperor.[55] Religious and imperial power had become one.

In reality dissension had not gone away. Eusebius's account of the Council of Nicaea papered over the very real differences of opinion expressed there. Later on, Arius returned from exile and continued to deliver sermons in his influential city of Nicomedia. Before Constantine died, even the emperor himself would backtrack on the doctrine he had forced the bishops into agreeing. Only with time would the unity that Constantine desired at Nicaea be realized. Indeed, the council produced the 'Nicene Creed'. This is the official summary of the Christian faith, which begins, 'I believe in one God, the Father, the Almighty, maker of heaven and earth...' To this day it is recited by Christians every Sunday. To this day, Constantine's formulation is still the unifying creed of the Church.

Constantine's Christian theme inspired him to breathe new life into his empire in other ways. He helped found Jerusalem as a holy city for Christians as well as Jews, but was ambitious to achieve much more. When, on 8 November 324, with spear in hand, he plotted the site of a new city around the old town of Byzantium (now Istanbul), he founded what he called a 'New Rome'. If Constantine's intention was to rebrand a new Christian empire, what better way to do that than by founding a new imperial capital on the site of his victory against Licinius? And what better place to locate that city than at the strategic point where Europe and Asia meet? With his usual sharp eye for self-promotion, he named the new city after himself. Constantinople was officially dedicated on 11 May 330.

Whereas Rome was defined by its ancient past, former emperors and traditional gods, Constantinople marked the start of a new era. A massive building programme took place: new walls, new forums, a new hippodrome and a new imperial palace all sprang up in the space of just six years. There was also a new

Senate House for the newly appointed Christian senators. As for Christian buildings, the city could boast Constantine's mausoleum, and it is possible that the famous church of St Sophia began its incarnation under the emperor. However, contrary to Eusebius's description, the city that bore Constantine's name was not exclusively Christian. The emperor filled his new city with art treasures from the classical world, making it the showroom of his new empire. Crucially, he did not move the capital city of the empire to Constantinople and thus downgrade Rome. The Eternal City continued to supply senators to help administer the empire. Constantinople was, rather, just another imperial centre, alongside the likes of Trier and Milan, albeit one to which the emperor was highly attached. The better part of his last seven years was spent there.[56]

Constantine died on 22 May 337. His reign had been the longest of any emperor since the very first – Augustus. Some time before his death he was baptized, an indication of the sincerity of his belief. After that time he wore only white, forsaking the robes of imperial purple for the dress traditionally adopted by a Christian initiate. The man who attended his deathbed was a man he had liberated when he defeated Licinius some thirteen years earlier, a man whose company he had often shared since that time, the bishop of Nicomedia.

Christianity continued to thrive on the imperial templates Constantine had set. Only one of the Roman emperors who came after him was pagan. The attempts of Julian the Apostate to turn back the clock between 360 and 363, although vigorous, ultimately failed. At the end of the fourth century, in Rome alone there were seventy priests and twenty-five churches. The sumptuous development of St Peter's reflected the extraordinary patronage of the Roman élite, the Church hierarchy and the emperor himself, and Rome would become a principal destination for pilgrims. However, this success of

Christianity did not hold true for the new, unified and restored Roman empire.

Constantine's successors were his three sons. On his death they had agreed to share power, but almost immediately began arguing and killing each other. The fractures in the Roman empire that Constantine's work had temporarily healed would quickly reappear. Within fifty years they would be gulfs. In 364 a new dynasty was founded under Valentinian I. He chose to divide the empire in half once again, splitting it between an eastern and western emperor. However, the force that would put a fatal stress on the empire came not from weak leadership within, but from the frontiers. The barbarians were coming.

VI

FALL

AD 476 is the official date for the end of the western half of the Roman empire. It fell not with any grand, dramatic fanfare, nor with the crashing boom of fire and iconoclasm, war and revolution. Instead it fell with the gentle rhythmic pounding of a horse's hoofs and perhaps the whirring rumble of wheels on a single imperial wagon. Those sounds belonged to a messenger heading east to Constantinople, rushing across the Roman roads of the empire and carrying with him the imperial vestments, diadem and purple cloak of the western Roman emperor. He had been sent by Odovacar, a Germanic king based in Italy, and instructed to deliver the possessions to the eastern Roman emperor. Odovacar had come to a decision: they wouldn't be needed any more.

Odovacar was, by origin, from the Germanic tribe of the Sciri. He had been a highly successful general in the Roman army in the middle of the fifth century. By 476 so successfully had he built up a loyal power base of Roman soldiers and landowners in Italy that he was able to launch a *coup d'état* and become the effective ruler of the whole peninsula. There was, however, one problem with his complete grasp of power in Italy: there still existed a western Roman emperor. Admittedly, he was a very nominal emperor – a boy of sixteen and the son of a usurper, and since he controlled nothing outside Italy, he posed absolutely no threat to Odovacar's position.

Nonetheless, this was the time to make a clean break – a chance to tie up loose ends.

Odovacar wrote to Zeno, the Roman emperor of the east, informing him that he was going to depose the western emperor. This decision, though, was perhaps less significant than the one that followed. Odovacar also made it clear that he had no intention of appointing another emperor. The ancient post, forged by Augustus over five hundred years earlier, was now so utterly devoid of meaning and power that it really was not worth his while. Zeno's reply implicitly agreed. Although the eastern emperor paid lip-service to constitutional rectitude by telling the king that his status would need to be recognised by the western emperor's predecessor, there was no hiding the reality: Zeno effectively acknowledged Odovacar's seizure of power. When he received that news, King Odovacar ceremoniously dispatched to the eastern emperor the vestments, diadem and cloak of the now defunct western office.

The ancient sources do not tell us very much about the character of King Odovacar. They leave only questions, one of which is whether he had a sense of irony. The name of the boy emperor whom he had just deposed was Romulus Augustulus. The names – one of the mythical founder of Rome and the other meaning 'Little Augustus' – reflect how Roman history had neatly come full circle from Rome's earliest ruler to its most recent; from the first emperor, who had created the age of the Caesars, to its last, a powerless, deposed child. The Roman empire in the west had risen, ruled the Mediterranean world for over seven hundred years and had now fallen, fragmenting into kingdoms ruled by 'barbarians'. While the eastern Roman empire, administered from Constantinople, survived for another thousand years in the form of the Byzantine empire, the western half – Rome, Italy and western Europe – fell into the Dark Ages. How had the greatest, most influential empire of the ancient world come to this? How had it fallen?

The answers given to this, the most enduring question of ancient history, have run well into the hundreds. They range from malaria, lead poisoning and tumours created by too many hot steam baths to soil erosion and climate change; from child-lessness and depopulation to ineffective government and bankruptcy; from the disillusion of provincial élites and the collapse of moral standards to the crumbling of traditional reli-gions and the disintegration of army discipline. In the eighteenth century Edward Gibbon devoted three volumes of his *Decline and Fall of the Roman Empire* to answering the same question. Reflecting the age in which he wrote, Gibbon chron-icled the best part of three hundred years of Roman history in the West (from 180 to 476) and pinpointed Christianity as a chief culprit. Belief in the afterlife, he suggested, utterly sapped Romans of the steely resolve and discipline required to suffer hardships for the sake of maintaining the empire. Gibbon's view of an inevitable, slowly evolving and complex process was highly influential over the centuries that followed him. Recent scholarship, however, has taken a different view. The Roman empire collapsed staccato style; it did so not inevitably, but under the impact of key, spectacular shock waves in its last hundred years; and the people who created those crises were barbarian invaders.[1]

This chapter will focus on one of those critically decisive moments: the sack of Rome in August 410. It will tell the story of how the greatest city of the ancient world, the city-state that ruled a massive empire for over seven hundred years, fell to barbarians and was ritually sacked. The destruction of the ancient city is an enlightening, pivotal moment because the forces that brought about the sack epitomize the shock waves that shattered the western Roman empire between 376 and 476.

Perhaps the greatest of these forces was the motivation of the barbarians. Their invasions came down to a single belief – that the Roman empire was an El Dorado that offered a chance for a better life. They came not to destroy Rome, but to become part of it. However, in trying to win acceptance within the empire, to win peace terms and a slice of that prosperity, destroying the empire is exactly what would happen.

The man who led the sack of Rome was a Goth by the name of Alaric. Almost everything about him and his vast number of followers subverted the Roman concept of a 'barbarian'. He was no mindless, irrational thug, but a Christian and a man of his word. His troops were no hot-headed, marauding horde, but an organized and efficient army. They besieged Rome not for immediate, smash-and-grab looting of gold and treasure, but with foresight, with a view to executing a long-term plan. In short, Alaric the Goth, the barbarian, the sacker of Rome, was much more of a Roman. Extraordinarily, he had fought and trained in the Roman army and showed a strategic thinking and determined, calculating mind that resembled not barbaric invaders but the greatest Roman generals – a Caesar or an Augustus, a Vespasian or a Constantine. In one respect, though, he was very un-Roman. The sack of a foreign city would not, for him, rate as a success or victory, but as a complete and utter failure.

This is the story of how ambition, betrayal and internecine conflict felled the greatest city of the ancient world. The same themes on which Romulus had founded Rome some 1200 years earlier would come back to haunt the city once again at the very moment of its destruction.

BREACHING THE EMPIRE

AD 376. The Roman empire had for over a decade been unofficially divided into two halves. The emperor Valens ruled in the

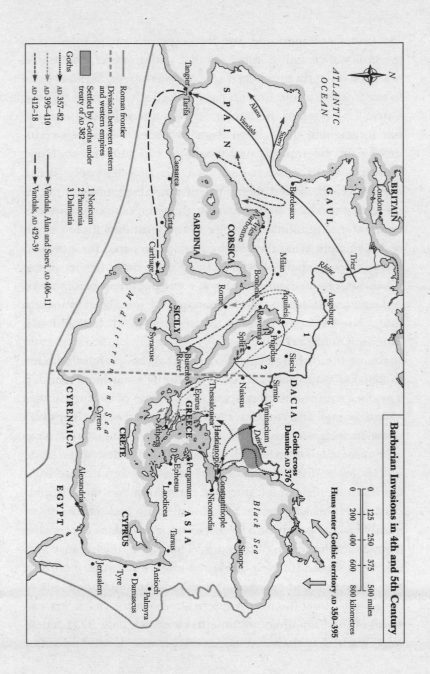

Barbarian Invasions in 4th and 5th Century

Legend:
- Roman frontier
- Division between eastern and western empires
- Settled by Goths under treaty of AD 382
- Goths
- AD 357–82
- AD 395–410
- AD 412–18
- Vandals, AD 429–39
- Vandals, Alan and Suevi, AD 406–11

1 Noricum
2 Pannonia
3 Dalmatia

Goths cross Danube AD 376

Huns enter Gothic territory AD 350–395

Scale: 0 — 125 — 250 — 375 — 500 miles
0 — 200 — 400 — 600 — 800 kilometres

BRITAIN, London, ATLANTIC OCEAN, GAUL, Rhine, Trier, Augsburg, Bordeaux, SPAIN, Tangier, Tarifa, Caesarea, Cirta, Carthage, SARDINIA, CORSICA, Narbonne, Arles, Milan, Bononia, Aquileia, Ravenna, Frigidus, Split, Rome, SICILY, Syracuse, Mediterranean Sea, Siscia, DACIA, Danube, Sirmio, Viminacium, Naissus, Thessalonica, EPIRUS, GREECE, Athens, Hadrianople, Constantinople, Nicomedia, Pergamum, Ephesus, ASIA, Laodicea, Tarsus, Sinope, Black Sea, CRETE, CYPRUS, Antioch, Tyre, Damascus, Palmyra, Jerusalem, Alexandria, EGYPT, CYRENAICA, Cyrene, Busento River, Alans, Vandals, Suevi

373

east from Constantinople, and the emperor Gratian ruled from the imperial capital of Milan. In that year, however, Valens was not to be found in his eastern seat of government. He was closer to the frontier of the Roman east, in Antioch, trying to put out a fire: King Shapur, the leader of a resurgent Persian empire, was threatening the eastern Roman border. Valens was channelling all the resources he could to face the threat. Huge numbers of the eastern army at his disposal were being deployed, and to feed them, Valens was taking a bigger cut of the agricultural tax. In the mid-fourth century the economy and manpower of the Roman empire were robust enough to sustain such demands. What the empire was not prepared for, however, was a dramatic chain of events taking place on its border in the northeast. On the river Danube, at some point between modern Bulgaria and Romania, the Roman empire was about to witness the greatest refugee crisis of the ancient world. It would also find itself fatally exposed.

Facing the rushing expanse of the Danube, perhaps as many as 200,000 Goths had gathered on Rome's northern frontier. They were not an invading army, but a nation of Gothic families – men, women and children seeking asylum en masse. They had come in their wagons, with their livestock, ploughs and whatever possessions they could carry – chairs, hides, wheelmade pottery, silver drinking vessels and utensils of bronze and iron. On reaching the border, they had camped out on the northern bank of the broad river, and their leadership had sent an envoy humbly asking permission from the emperor Valens to cross the frontier and live in his dominions.[2] They had come because they had been forced to: life outside the empire's northern borders had become too dangerous. They had been hounded out of their lands along the northwestern shores of the Black Sea and south of the Carpathian mountains (see map, page 373). These were lands that they had occupied because it was here they could settle, establish their farms and benefit from the economies of the client-states of Rome – the communities in the regions bordering the Roman empire who traded with the Romans. However, in the year 376 the wealth of the lands the Goths had adopted had come under the envious eyes of others who wanted a slice of the action.

The people who had set the crisis on the Danube in motion, the people who were 'the seed-bed and origin' of the crisis, were the Huns. The best Roman historian of this period, Ammianus Marcellinus, describes them as abnormally 'savage', possessors of 'squat bodies, strong limbs and thick necks', a people 'so prodigiously ugly and bent that they might be two-legged animals'.[3] A less partisan, more modern view, however, reveals that they were a nomadic people, expert in the use of the bow, who came from the Eurasian steppes. This was terri-tory that stretched from Mongolia to the eastern margins of Europe. The poor quality of the land and the unfriendly weather conditions there dictated the people's roaming way of life. Perhaps spying the wealth of the Black Sea region, the Huns had moved west, causing havoc by raiding and destabiliz-ing Gothic territories en route. This was the 'big bang' moment – the moment that forced the Goths off their lands and on to the Roman empire's frontiers.

In approaching Rome, however, the Goths, a nation of farm-ers, were taking a huge gamble. Seeking asylum was a decision they had pondered for a long time. It was true that the Roman empire represented a stable, developed economy, that life within its frontiers offered the chance for a better, more protected future than life outside. That old life was now over-shadowed by the constant threat of assault from the Huns. Yet at the same time, in crossing the frontier they were putting their entire nation at the mercy of Rome; they were exposing them-selves to a new potential threat – that of slavery or death. The

Gothic leaders had eventually made up their minds: life under Rome would be the lesser of two evils. Cautiously they sent their request to Emperor Valens. Little did they know that they were not the only ones to handle the crisis tentatively.

In the east Valens should have been delighted by the news of the Goths' arrival: they represented the prospect of raw recruits for the Roman army. Indeed, by filling the ranks with them, said the flatterers in Valens's court, the empire would stand to make more money from the provinces. In place of the usual levy of troops, the eastern Roman court could ask the provinces to contribute gold instead. The truth, though, was very different. Valens and his advisers were more probably thrown into a complete panic over the situation on the Danube. With the bulk of the Roman army on the eastern frontier, the troops in the west were spread very thinly along its northern borders. The shortage of soldiers meant that far from being in control of the situation, the Romans were in no position whatsoever to police the refugee crisis. Nonetheless, Valens gave permission for one of the Gothic tribes to cross the Danube. Transported in Roman ships day and night, the Tervingi tribe was ferried across the dangerous rapids of the river, and poured over the frontier like 'lava from mount Etna'. Meanwhile, the Roman forces available patrolled the river, keeping out the Greuthungi tribe. To those who made it over the border, however, it would quickly become apparent just how unprepared the Romans were for their arrival.[4]

During the winter of 376–7, while the Roman generals on the border waited for Valens to spare troops from the eastern frontier to help deal with the refugees, the Goths endured a long, agonizing delay. The sea of tents and makeshift homes on the Roman side of the Danube belied the horrendous conditions they experienced that bleak, freezing winter. Poor sanitation and a crippling shortage of food made their life hell. The Roman generals had no inclination to do anything about it. In fact, they were quite prepared to make it worse. Turning black marketeers, they seized an opportunity to make a quick profit out of the suffering 'barbarians'. In exchange for slaves and even children of some of the poorer Gothic citizens, the Roman generals gave the starving refugees fresh food. The Goths who had traded must have been doubly revolted to discover that they had bartered away children for dog meat.[5]

Tensions between Roman and barbarian quickly reached boiling point. In order to prevent the crisis spiralling out of control, the chief Roman general ordered the Goths to move on to the Roman regional base at Marcianople. However, he did not have enough soldiers both to police the frontier and to accompany the Tervingi Goths. The Greuthungi Goths, realizing that the border was no longer being patrolled, secretly crossed the river in makeshift rafts and canoes made from hollowed tree trunks, and thus slipped quietly into Roman territory. With the Greuthungi following at a significant distance behind, the Tervingi and the Greuthungi reached Marcianople. They were, however, in for another nasty surprise.

The majority of the Goths were kept outside the walls of the town by Roman soldiers. Inside, the Roman generals invited the 'barbarian' leaders to a sumptuous dinner. Perhaps in a bid to throw the Goths into confusion and thus seize control of the situation, the Romans made a botched attempt to assassinate the Gothic leaders. For the Goths, after their months of misery, this was the last straw. When their people outside Marcianople heard about the assassination attempt they were incandescent with rage. Hearing the riotous fury outside, the Gothic leaders thought quickly on their feet: they told the Romans that if they pressed ahead and killed them, there would certainly be a war. Only by setting them free could that be avoided.

Given the shortage of troops, the Romans were forced to release the Gothic leaders. But this was the most disastrous of all outcomes. The masses of refugees were not only starving, but utterly alienated and seething with anger. Once reunited with their angry, disenchanted leaders, the refugee Goths quickly overcame the Roman soldiers guarding them and pillaged Marcianople. War had been declared.

The war took place between 377 and 382, and the battlefield was the Balkans. Valens made a hasty peace with the Persian king, released whatever forces he could from the eastern frontier and raced to tackle the Goths. Although the conflict was unfolding in his half of the Roman empire, Valens nonetheless called upon the western emperor to help. Gratian agreed, but was unable to release his army immediately; he was preoccupied with securing the middle Danube from a further breach in the frontier made by a Germanic tribe called the Alamanni. During this delay, the Goths raided freely just to survive, and the people of Thrace bore the violent brunt of Roman inaction. Soon, however, the Goths would be brought into line again. It would not be long before they faced the full force of the Roman army.

The great conflict between the Goths and Valens's troops turned on the events of 9 August 378. The battle was fought at Hadrianople (modern-day Edirne in Turkey) and it was riven with mistakes from the start. As the weeks of the summer passed and Gratian's army failed to appear, Valens's troops grew demoralized. Then, when the Romans believed they had the Goths in a position to engage them in battle, a fateful Roman council of war was called. Valens's generals informed him that the enemy army was much smaller than it really was. Furthermore, while some officers advised caution, others did not. The latter were in belligerent mood, and in order to get their way, they knew how to press the emperor's buttons. Valens was jealous of Gratian's military success in the west. This was his chance, they now told him, to show what the eastern empire was made of. Valens had long ago run out of patience waiting for Gratian to arrive. Now, piqued and prodded by his hawkish generals, he decided to go it alone, to deal with the Goths once and for all. His advisers were right, he believed: he really did not need Gratian.[6]

After a forced march of eight hours over rough country and under a scorching August sun, Valens's army was given neither food nor rest. All the soldiers received was the order to advance. When the two sides clashed, Valens and his men discovered to their horror that the Goths were no bedraggled barbarian horde. They were an organized, well-equipped and disciplined army 20,000 strong. The wings of the Gothic cavalry immediately wiped out the Roman left wing. Then the Goths brought all their power to bear on the Roman centre. Close-packed and with their shields raised, the Romans were too huddled together to draw their swords and use them to any effect. In addition, a cloud of dust blew up above the place where the fighting was at its fiercest and camouflaged the javelins and spears that rained down upon the Romans. The enemy fire was picking them off one by one.

Exhausted and confused, the soldiers of the Roman army thrust with their swords as best they could without any purpose or plan. Some killed their own men. Eventually, the Roman line gave way and the massacre reached its climax. By nightfall even the emperor's bodyguard had been murdered, and Valens himself had been mortally wounded. What was unthinkable to the Romans had actually come to pass: a barbarian force had cut the heart out of the eastern Roman army, which had vastly outnumbered it. The principal general, no fewer than thirty-five military tribunes and perhaps as many as 13,000 soldiers had all died. The battle of Hadrianople was the worst Roman defeat at the hands of a foreign enemy since Hannibal's annihilation of the Romans at the battle of Cannae nearly six hundred years earlier. By the time Gratian arrived on the scene, there was nothing to see but a field dark with blood and covered with Roman corpses.

The defeat sent a shock wave throughout the Roman world. Hadrianople had smashed the idea of an invincible Roman empire. Its integrity had been breached, and Rome would never get it back again. Goths were now the conquerors of the Balkans, free to roam as they pleased, free to stay. A region of the empire had been lost, but the reality of a Gothic nation camped out on Roman territory presented an even more threatening situation. The Goths continued to war with the Romans for six years and the result was the ravaging of the countryside, the wiping out of agricultural produce and the erosion of the empire's tax base. A diminished tax base spelt a reduction in imperial expenditure on the army – bad news when two-thirds of the money paid into the imperial treasury was usually spent on the military. The bottom line revealed a truly bleak state of affairs: the circumstances in which the emperors of Rome most needed the army occurred at exactly the moment when their ability to pay for it was most under threat. Something had to be done.

Valens's successor as emperor of the east was Theodosius I. He raised a new army, but that too was defeated. Having utterly failed to overcome the Goths in war, on 3 October 382 he was forced to talk peace. The terms of the treaty agreed with the Gothic leaders allowed the tribes of the Tervingi and the Greuthungi to settle in the Balkans, not as Roman citizens but as virtually autonomous allies of Rome. In Constantinople a spokesperson for Theodosius's regime put a positive spin on the peace, casting it as a victory. The Goths, he said, had exchanged war for farming. The reality was very different. Throughout Roman history it had always been the Romans who controlled whether to accept immigrants or not. If they did, it was because the barbarian had sufficiently prostrated himself and abjectly begged to be a part of the empire and the Romans had benevolently, powerfully bestowed the gift of admittance.[7] In 382, however, it was the immigrant Goths who, to a large part, had dictated terms to the Romans. The balance of power had shifted, but it would soon shift again.

Despite Roman attempts to treat the Goths fairly and equally, the Goths suspected that their improved status in Roman eyes was only a temporary measure. Indeed, they believed that the Romans were secretly looking for any excuse to undo the peace agreement. Their suspicions centred on the one clause in the treaty that made the peace so uneasy: should the emperor call upon them, significant parts of the Gothic army were required for service in the Roman army. Might the Romans use this to weaken the barbarian allies? In the minds of many Goths those suspicions were about to be resoundingly confirmed.

In early September 394, by the river Frigidus in modern-day Slovenia, Theodosius I had amassed a huge Roman army. The ranks of soldiers were lined up to face the rebellious forces of Eugenius, a usurper of the western empire. Before attacking, Theodosius placed the Gothic contingent, several thousand men strong, in the vanguard of the assault. When battle was joined, the Goths inevitably suffered the worst of the casualties on a calamitous first day of fighting. Although Theodosius eventually won the battle, for the Goths it was an overwhelmingly pyrrhic victory: approximately 3000 of their men are understood to have died. What further proof was needed, the Goths asked themselves, of the plain truth that the Romans considered them nothing but expendable, second-rate citizens?

One of the Gothic leaders who voiced the widespread discontent had been a mere boy when the Goths first crossed the Danube in 376. In 394, at the battle of Frigidus, he was the young general in charge of the Gothic allies fighting alongside the Romans. In the following year, when Theodosius I died, he was appointed leader of the united Tervingi and Greuthungi tribes. His name was Alaric and his message was clear. The Goths would avenge their catastrophic losses at Frigidus; they would fight until the treaty of 382 was rewritten; they would fight for a better, more secure future.

The very same force that was once at the service of Rome and that had secured the key Roman victories at the end of the fourth century, was now about to be turned against it. But there was one man who would stand in Alaric's way. He was a Roman general who had also fought at the battle of Frigidus – as Alaric's colleague. Intriguingly, however, Flavius Stilicho would become not only Alaric's great nemesis, but also his lifeline and ultimately his ally.

ALLIANCE OF ENEMIES

Before he died at the start of the year 395, the emperor Theodosius I wanted to establish a new imperial dynasty. He made his two sons, Arcadius and Honorius, emperors of the east and west. However, Arcadius, the ruler of the east, was only seventeen years old, while Honorius, the emperor of the west, was just ten. The man Theodosius turned to on his deathbed and asked to act as the boys' guardian was his most successful and distinguished general – Flavius Stilicho. Stilicho, however, was not a typical Roman.

While his mother was Roman, his father, a cavalry general, was a Vandal. The Vandals were a Germanic people who possibly came from the Przeworska culture located in modern-day Poland. Through his extraordinary achievements on the battlefield under Theodosius, Stilicho had risen to the highest ranks of Roman politics, had become the emperor's chief adviser and had married his niece. His official title was *magister militum* – commander-in-chief of the Roman army. At the end of the fourth century the people who had risen to the top of the army were also the top politicians of the day and the most influential figures in the imperial court. So when Theodosius died, Flavius Stilicho, a soldier of Vandal origin, became the most powerful man in the entire Roman world. In both east and west, he was the empire's effective ruler.

Although we don't know much about his character, one incident suggests that he was a man of considerable tenacity and ambition. While his regency over Honorius, the emperor in the west, was accepted, Stilicho claimed that he was also regent to Arcadius in the east. We have only Stilicho's word that this was Theodosius's dying wish because he alone was present at the old emperor's deathbed.[8] It is possible that Stilicho made it up in order to maintain the unity of the empire that Theodosius had brilliantly but briefly resurrected. If that was Stilicho's ambition, it was short-lived. As soon as Arcadius was settled in Constantinople, the imperial court officials in the east refused to be ousted by a mere Vandal in the west, and intrigued for control of the young man. Stilicho was forced to shelve his ambitions in the east and to focus, for the time being, on guiding Honorius and governing the west. Within a few years of his charge's accession, he married Honorius to his own daughter. Over the next thirteen years Stilicho would become like a father to the young emperor. Indeed, the young man on the throne was going to need Stilicho's firm grip to retain it. The rumble of war was building once again to a crescendo. Alaric had begun his rebellion.

Under Alaric's leadership, the Goths first set their sights on forcing the eastern empire into a new deal. To help encourage Arcadius's court to come to the negotiating table, Alaric decided to apply some pressure. Departing from their base in Bulgaria, the Goths ransacked their way through the Balkans, into Greece and along the Adriatic coast. The display of violence paid off and a deal was soon forthcoming, but it did not last. When the conciliatory court official responsible for brokering the deal with Alaric was toppled by more hawkish colleagues, the agreement was torn up. Reaching a dead end, Alaric decided to exploit the division in the Roman empire, to play one side off against the other. He turned the full firepower of his army on the west, and in 402 invaded Italy. Perhaps, thought Alaric, force would prove more fruitful there.

Alaric's demand was simple: long-term legal recognition for his people. This he wanted to achieve in two ways. The first step was his appointment to *magister militum* because he hoped that this high-ranking military position would help him make the Gothic allies legitimate and equal partners in the Roman army. The second step was a food subsidy. He wanted Stilicho, his former comrade in arms, to grant the Goths part of the agricultural produce from the region they had settled. It was to be levied as a tax dedicated to the Goths. Stilicho, however, had other ideas. He was not about to give in to these demands; he was not prepared to stake his entire political career on a peace with the Goths just because they were prepared to put a knife to the western empire's throat. It was not a political gamble he wanted to take.

As a result, the armies of Stilicho and Alaric clashed on two occasions, but in both battles there was no decisive outcome. Negotiations by war seemed to have reached stalemate. Cut off from his food supplies and with no victories to his name, Alaric was forced to make a weary, miserable retreat from northern Italy back to the Goths' base south of the Danube in modern-day Bulgaria. His policy to get a better deal from Rome seemed to be going nowhere fast. He could not then have imagined how, within a few years' time, all that would change. In 406 Stilicho was prepared to make a pact with the devil.

Stilicho sent his negotiator, Jovius, to Alaric: the regent ruler of the west had a message for him. It revealed that, far from thinking the Goths were a thorn in his side, Stilicho now saw them as the key to fulfilling his plans. He wanted to kill three birds with one stone. First, he wanted to grant the Goths the legal rights to the land they occupied. If he did this, he would achieve his second aim, which was to use the Gothic army to secure the northeastern Roman frontier from further invasion. However, there was a problem. The lands where Alaric and the Goths were settled – Dacia and Macedonia (east Illyricum) – belonged not to the western empire, but to the eastern half. If Stilicho were able to remove that province from the eastern imperial court through a display of military muscle, he would gain a third advantage – an excellent and much-needed recruiting ground for soldiers for the western army. And so, on behalf of Stilicho, Jovius proposed the following: in exchange for granting Alaric's demands, the Goths would join forces with Stilicho and together they would march on the eastern empire. Alaric agreed.[9] But just when peace between Romans and Goths was at last in sight, all prospect of it was hopelessly shattered.

Alaric waited for Stilicho's army, but it never arrived. A year passed and there was still no sign of it. Stilicho had been detained by events way beyond his control. A second massive shock wave had been sent rippling through the Roman empire, leaving only chaos in its wake. The year 406–7 had just become a second critical moment in the collapse of the western empire.

In the space of approximately twelve months Stilicho had to confront not one but three crises in the west. All three events were provoked by a second wave of Hunnic raiders overrunning the lands to the northeast of the Roman empire. First, another Gothic king, Radagaisus, accompanied by a huge following, crossed the Danube and invaded Italy. He reached as far as Florence, where Stilicho met him and, with the best Roman army he could muster, overcame his forces. Radagaisus was executed and thousands of his troops were drafted into

Stilicho's ranks. Much more crippling, however, was the second crisis to swamp Stilicho: the breaching of the empire's northern frontier by a new wave of barbarian invaders.

This group was made up of Vandals, Alans (a nomadic people from the Black Sea) and Suevi (a Germanic-speaking people who had long been based on the Hungarian plain). Together they crossed the river Rhine near the town of Worms in Germany, sacked the old imperial capital of Trier, wreaked havoc across Gaul, and eventually crossed the Pyrenees to reach Spain. Thus a second vast group of barbarians had breached the Roman frontier, ravaged Roman territory and had no intention of going back.

The third crisis originated with the army in Britain. At this time, the western Roman army consisted of garrison forces stationed along the frontiers, large field armies in Gaul and Italy, and smaller field units in North Africa and Britain. In 407, that army in Britain proclaimed the self-styled Constantine III as the rightful emperor of the western empire. When Constantine crossed over to Gaul and tried to stem the flood of the Vandals, Alans and Suevi into the west, his popularity soared and he won over the Gallic field army too. The provinces of Britain, Gaul and Spain thus fell into his control. It was a potent power base from which to launch an attack on Italy.

Under the impact of these three blows, the western Roman empire was on the brink of collapse. Stilicho was still in control of the large field army of Italy, the same force that had neutralized Radagaisus's invasion. But while this army may have been sufficient to defend the country from the likes of Radagaisus, they were not strong enough, however, to attack either Constantine the usurper or the combined invading force of the Vandals, Alans and Suevi. And as for the proposed venture with Alaric's Goths in the Balkans – that was now out of the question. Suddenly the great generalissimo of the west found his hands tied behind his back. The full effects of the crisis, however, were only just beginning to be felt.

Finding new forces to fight back required money. But at the start of the fifth century, money in the western Roman empire was in short supply. Now, in 406–7, with the western empire convulsed by both the arrival of tens of thousands of barbarian invaders and the seizure of Britain, Gaul and Spain by the usurper Constantine, tax revenues in those provinces were, for the time being, as good as lost. Money was scarcer than ever before: only Italy, Sicily and North Africa were paying into the imperial coffers. Now the crisis was about to get worse. The Goths, tantalized by the prospect of Stilicho's hand of peace, were beginning to get itchy feet.

After waiting over a year to pursue Stilicho's planned attack on the east, Alaric knew full well that the alliance with the western Roman empire was slipping away once again. Nonetheless, he expected payment for maintaining his army at Stilicho's request during that time. He therefore sent a message requesting 4000 pounds (1800 kilograms) of gold. It was money the west could ill afford. To put teeth into his request Alaric advanced his army closer to Italy, pitching camp in Noricum (modern-day Austria). When the request reached Stilicho, he travelled to Rome to consult the emperor Honorius and the Senate about what to do. The matter sparked a furious, barnstorming debate.

The majority of the senators offered a succinct and brutal response to Alaric's invoice. It merited nothing less, they said, than a declaration of war – a war to wipe out the threat of the wretched Goths once and for all! Stilicho's, however, was the voice of restraint: we must pay the money, he said, and maintain our peace with the Goths. This controversial position only caused more of a furore. Why on earth, the senators demanded to know, should Rome suffer the dishonour and shame of paying such a vast sum of money to these miserable barbarians? Stilicho's reply was plain: it was as a result of his alliance with the Goths. This had been agreed with a view to winning back for Honorius the critical province of east Illyricum from the eastern court. It was also intended, he reminded the right honourable senators, to settle the Goths, bolster the northeastern frontier and rejuvenate the depleted army with new recruits.[10]

This was the policy on which Stilicho had staked his political clout in 406. Now, in the crisis enveloping the western empire, he had to stick with it. Rome had no choice. Beneath the debate there lurked an impasse. While the majority of senators advocated war, Stilicho knew full well that the western empire had no forces with which to fight the Goths. Stilicho, it was becoming clear, was right to advocate paying Alaric. One hawk, called Lampadius, conceded to Stilicho's policy, but accepted defeat ungraciously. 'This,' he cried out, 'is not a peace but a pact of servitude!'[11] However, there was another man present in the Senate who was quietly prepared to take the long view.

Olympius was an insidious senator, a highly ambitious courtier and the unofficial leader of the hawks in Honorius's administration. As he watched the debate go Stilicho's way, he could console himself that as soon as the threat from Constantine III had been dealt with, the full western Roman army of Britain, Gaul and Italy could regroup and fight the Goths another day. Indeed, it is easy to imagine why Olympius's thoughts might have drifted to the future. The emperor Honorius was still young, suggestible and weak. He had known only the flatteries of court life and nothing of the real world. Stilicho's hold over him was slipping away day by day. Yes, it was true that the great general had won the debate in the Senate, but he had done so at the cost of expending all his reserves of political capital. To Olympius, the high-wire act of Stilicho's

Gothic policy was looking decidedly perilous. It was only a matter of time before he lost his balance. Olympius would soon be proved right.

When Honorius's brother Arcadius, the eastern Roman emperor, died in 408, Stilicho fell out with his adolescent charge. Honorius said that, as western emperor, he wanted to go to Constantinople and arrange affairs for the smooth hand-over of power. Stilicho disagreed. Perhaps he believed that Honorius was too inexperienced to take on such a responsibility. Perhaps he was simply unwilling to surrender the power to which he, as the young emperor's guardian, had become accustomed. No, insisted the general, he was the one who should go to Constantinople. The reason? There was no money to pay for the imperial entourage to travel east. What's more, said Stilicho, the situation in the west was too precarious. With Constantine III so close in Arles, Italy needed Honorius. Bruised, bitter and sulking, Honorius gave way. As soon as Stilicho had gone, Olympius spied his opportunity and moved in for the kill.

With an affected display of modesty and Christian rectitude disguising the fork in his tongue, Olympius sidled up to Honorius as they travelled together to review the army at the military headquarters in Ticinum (modern-day Pavia). Perhaps he reminded the emperor of the crisis the west was in. Constantine in Gaul was virtually on Italy's doorstep; the Vandals, Alans and Suevi were making themselves at home in Spain; and Alaric and his army of Goths were at a loose end, still hovering menacingly in Noricum. This, he would have argued, was the fault of one man and one man alone: Stilicho. To cap it all, that same man was once again pursuing his ambitions to control the east as well as the west – just as he had tried to do from the start of Honorius's reign. He had gone to the east, said Olympius, not to manage the situation there, but to seize the 'opportunity of removing [Arcadius's chosen successor] the young Theodosius, and of placing the empire in the hands of his own son, Eucherius'.[12]

Stilicho had been the closest thing to a father that Honorius had known. The emperor was, of course, married to Stilicho's daughter. Nonetheless, Olympius seemed to be winning over the young man's attention. If there was any residue of feeling for his old guardian, the uncertain, peeved Honorius probably did not show it. Olympius would now have had one final argument up his sleeve, one final dagger to plunge. Let's not forget, he perhaps suggested, that Stilicho himself is one of 'them' – a barbarian.

It would have been quite normal for someone like Olympius to use such a tack in casting a slur on a man's character. The old, deeply ingrained prejudice of the Romans was a reworking of Aristotle's view of human nature and ran as follows. All humans were made up of rational and animal elements. In Romans the rational element was dominant. It gave them the capacity, in war and politics, for foresight, for holding strong under pressure and determinedly persevering towards an agreed goal in spite of short-term failures encountered along the way. In barbarians, by contrast, the animal element was dominant. They were rash, fearful, disorganized. They were prone to panicking and losing their heads in the face of adversity, victims of the slightest vicissitude of fortune.[13] Above all, as Olympius no doubt pointed out, they were not to be trusted.

Honorius remained for four days at Ticinum, rallying and encouraging the soldiers for the fight against the rebel Constantine. During his review of the ranks, Olympius maintained his show of Christian piety by visiting the sick and the wounded from the recent military engagements with the usurper. In reality, he was doing no such thing. Among the officers whom he could trust he was spreading the same insinuations he had made to Honorius: the Romans, he whispered, needed to be rid of the barbarians once and for all – and who better to start with than Stilicho? It was all part of a covert, carefully organized plan to reverse Stilicho's policy of pragmatic toleration towards barbarians and end his influence. But the subtlety of Olympius's infiltration of the Roman army disguised the utter brutality of his desired effect.

On Honorius's last day at Ticinum, Olympius gave the signal. The soldiers who were in on the plan turned on Stilicho's allies in the army and the imperial court and started killing. To the shock and horror of many, a bloody military coup had come from nowhere and was now raging viciously. Unsuspecting commanders of the cavalry and infantry, prefects of the court, magistrates, treasurers, heralds and stewards of the emperor were all murdered for their association with Stilicho. If they tried to escape, they were swiftly hunted down. Honorius could do nothing about it. He rushed out of the palace dressed in no more than his undergarments and a short cloak, ran into the city centre and shouted out unheeded orders to stop. Ticinum was in chaos. But it was only the beginning.[14]

In his proposed journey east Stilicho had got no further than Bononia (Bologna), 160 kilometres (100 miles) south of Ticinum. Perhaps, for reasons that are not clear, he never intended to go to Constantinople.[15] When he heard news of the mutiny at Ticinum, he was distraught. He immediately called a council of some soldiers who had accompanied him. These were the recently drafted Goths from the army of Radagaisus. It is revealing that these 'barbarians' were now the ones who were determined to place their loyalty with Stilicho and the Roman emperor. It was decided that if the emperor had been killed in the mutiny, Stilicho's force of 12,000 Goths would march on Ticinum and punish the Roman soldiers who had carried out the atrocity. When news arrived that the emperor was safe, however, the plan was dropped. The general knew that inflicting heavy losses on the military establishment of northern Italy would only open the door to either Alaric or Constantine III. Indeed Stilicho, the dutiful officer, faithful to the status quo and to the integrity of the western Roman empire, had no intention of upsetting the balance between Romans and barbarians by inciting his largely Gothic Roman soldiers against native Roman soldiers. It was simply not the honourable thing to do. He had devoted his entire career to achieving just the opposite and he was not going to change now.

Eventually he decided to return to Ravenna, Honorius's preferred imperial capital, and to confront the new situation.[16] As he made his way there, he had perhaps already guessed that he could no longer trust Honorius's friendship. However, he was not expecting quite such a cold welcome. Olympius, now 'master of the emperor's inclination', had sent out orders to soldiers at Ravenna to arrest Stilicho at the earliest opportunity. Getting wind of this on the night of his arrival, Stilicho took refuge in a church. He knew that no one could touch him there. What's more, the sanctuary would give him valuable time to talk with the allies and friends who had accompanied him and to work out what to do.

The following morning Olympius's soldiers came knocking on the church door. They presented the bishop with a letter from Honorius permitting them to put Stilicho in custody. They swore to the bishop that Stilicho would not be killed. Against the wishes of his allies Stilicho agreed to leave the church, but as soon as he did so a second letter was produced. It pronounced that for his crimes against the western empire, Stilicho was to suffer the punishment of death. The throng of Stilicho's supporters went mad with fury and promised that they would find a way to rescue him. In an angry, menacing tone of voice, Stilicho told them to stop such talk. It would only make the situation worse. With that, he calmly submitted himself to the soldiers, laid bare his neck and was beheaded on 22 August 408.[17]

The violent fallout from Stilicho's death was as devastating as it was clinical. Olympius damned all memory of his predecessor by extracting false accusations against him under torture. His chosen method was to have his victims bludgeoned. In this way he forged evidence that Stilicho 'coveted the throne'.[18] Stilicho's son, some of his relatives and all his remaining allies in the army and administration were murdered. His daughter, the emperor's wife, was lucky; she was unceremoniously removed from Honorius's presence and sent to live with her mother. The tentacles of the purge reached as far as Rome. Olympius ordered the confiscation of all property from those who had held any office under Stilicho. The soldiers in Rome took this as their cue, indeed, as their licence, to vent some repressed rage. They raided houses both in Rome and in cities up and down Italy, and fell upon every man, woman and child of barbarian origin, slaughtering them in their thousands. The purge had now become a massacre, an ancient Roman pogrom.

One contemporary historian's epitaph for the dead general described him as 'the most moderate and just of all the men who possessed great authority in his time'.[19] Perhaps he had been overly ambitious for power, but this ambition was focused on the preservation of the western state. Stilicho's great virtue had been his loyalty – to emperor and to Rome. Apart from being Rome's greatest general in the late Roman empire, Stilicho was the lynchpin of relations between Roman and barbarian. He had seen that accommodating and Romanizing the Goths was the key to maintaining the future and, above all, the military security of the western Roman empire. Once he had gone, that policy vanished with him. Olympius's hawks shrieked for war.

The massacre, however, had not accounted for everyone. Some 10,000 Gothic soldiers from the army of Radagaisus had escaped the pogrom. They turned to the only person who would offer them sanctuary – Alaric, in the mountains and hills of Noricum. When they reported the horrific news from Italy, Alaric knew that the tables were turning against him once again. With the death of Stilicho, he knew he had lost not just his once great adversary, but also his greatest ally. With a wholesale change of personnel at the western court complete, he knew he had also lost his greatest hope for peace. When his initial offers for terms were rejected by the new regime, the sheer callousness of Honorius's rejection must only have added salt to the wound.

Faced with a new deadlock, Alaric was left with only one option. It was the option he least wanted: to use force, to take the dagger of his Gothic army – now swollen to 30,000 soldiers – and place it at the throat of the western Roman empire. At the end of the calamitous year 408, Alaric invaded Italy. This time he was not going to leave without getting what he wanted.

ALARIC'S PEACE

In quick succession the northern Italian towns of Aquileia, Concordia, Altinum, Cremona, Bononia, Ariminum and Picenum all fell to the Goths under Alaric's furious assault in the autumn of 408. However, there was one city that the Gothic leader omitted: the imperial seat of Ravenna. It was a natural fortress, which was why Honorius had retreated there even though Milan was the imperial capital of the west. For the same reason Alaric decided that, even with his substantial army, he could not take his fight directly to the emperor. Rome, the revered ancient capital of the old Roman empire, would be a much softer target, a much more attractive hostage to take. By November Alaric's army had surrounded the city. Forces were garrisoned outside each of the thirteen gates, and a blockade of the Tiber cut off the city's access to its port at Ostia, and thus its grain supplies from North Africa. A neat, hermetically sealed siege of the ancient treasure chest of the western empire would, thought Alaric, be the best way to hurt Honorius.

Within a matter of weeks, the city-state that had ruled the known world, the home of the ancient gods, the God of the Christians and the Senate, became a tomb, a desolate, morbid ghost town. Gothic boats patrolled the river, and sentry guards kept an eye on every inch of the city's walls. Inside those walls the daily food rations for the city's inhabitants were cut by two-thirds, and people died in their thousands. Corpses could not be taken out of the city, so they littered the streets, their stench a miasmic mantle hovering over everything. As the winter drew closer, there were those who would turn to cannibalism. Only the wealthy could draw on secret reserves of food. While some, no doubt, desperately hoarded their goods, the wife and mother-in-law of Gratian, the former emperor of the west, were known for their philanthropic handouts.[20] Among the well-to-do caught up in Alaric's grip was someone whose presence in Rome would have added to the impact the siege had on Honorius in Ravenna. Galla Placidia was none other than the emperor's sister. Despite this, however, the obstinate Honorius did not lift a finger to help Rome. Indeed, the first delegation the Gothic leadership received came not from Ravenna, but from two of the city's leading senators. Far from being humbled by the siege, they were in a blustering mood.

The two men had a simple message for Alaric: Rome was armed and ready for a fight. 'The thicker the grass,' replied Alaric, 'the more easily it is cut down!' And with that he let out a big belly-laugh. He was not alone in finding the pathetic, pumped-up posturing of the senators amusing. When he had first reached Rome, Alaric had sent for reinforcements, and his brother-in-law Athaulf had duly arrived with additional forces of Goths and Huns. Perhaps Athaulf now shared in his brother's joke.

Realizing that their diplomacy had got off to a disastrous start, the Roman envoys changed tack. They adopted a more modest tone and tried to find a way of ending the crippling siege. The Gothic brothers conferred. Yes, there was something that could be done to alleviate matters somewhat: all the city's gold, silver, movable items and barbarian slaves resident in the city might do the trick. 'But if you take all these things, what would be left for those inside the city?' 'Their lives,' came Alaric's cold, terse reply.[21]

Within days, a spectacular, unprecedented procession of wagons left the city of Rome. They carried 2250 kilograms (2 tons) of gold, 135,000 kilograms (13 tons) of silver, 4000 silk tunics, 3000 scarlet-dyed fleeces and 1350 kilograms (3000 pounds) of pepper. Since the imperial treasury in Rome was entirely empty, the senators had to pull every string, use every form of compulsion to levy the goods. Even precious statues from the ancient temples were melted down.[22] In return, Alaric and Athaulf agreed that the siege be lifted for three days only. The ports and markets opened once again, food entered the city and Rome breathed a sigh of relief.

But while Athaulf perhaps rejoiced at receiving the treasure and enjoyed the sight of Goths dishing out to Rome her just deserts, the gold and other riches were not what Alaric wanted. True, he knew they were needed urgently in the short term: he had fresh recruits, as well as his original force of 20,000 men, to keep happy and loyal. He needed to reward them, to assure them of their prestige. But in the long term Alaric wanted Gothic prestige to take an entirely different form – a form much more durable than the transitory gleam of lucre. To that end he again approached the Roman senators. He had a little task for them.

While the siege was temporarily lifted, Alaric urged the senators to use the time wisely. They should go to Ravenna as his ambassadors and bring the emperor Honorius to the negotiating table. Alaric wanted to discuss terms for the one thing he really wanted, the one reason why he was besieging the city: a permanent peace and alliance with Rome. The senators duly set off.

At the emperor's palace in Ravenna the senators found an imperial court unhappy and under the thumb of Olympius. Honorius had divorced his wife (Stilicho's daughter) and had thus cut the last tie to the old regime of his dead father-in-law. Yet now that Stilicho was gone for ever, the emperor was perhaps realizing just how valuable he had been. Indeed, Stilicho's skills as a general and a leader at the service of the empire were just what was needed now. Without them, none of the problems affecting the west had shown any sign of improving; in fact, they had just stagnated and grown worse. As a result, when the senators arrived at the imperial palace, the emperor was no longer willing to reject out of hand Alaric's request for negotiation.

Honorius agreed in principle to a military alliance with Alaric. The details of land settlement, of a secure source of revenue, were not, for the time being, on the table. Nonetheless, the offer was an important step in the right direction. Or so it seemed. On closer inspection, Honorius's response revealed the fingerprints of Olympius's influence. Perhaps the emperor's chief adviser had reminded him that the granting of a new land settlement spelt only more trouble. The tax revenues from Rome and Italy were already decimated thanks to Alaric's ravaging of the peninsula. Any further handing over of land to the Goths would only make matters worse: no land meant no tax revenues; no money meant no army; and no army, perhaps suggested Olympius, rising to his theme, meant no empire. Ultimately, the greatest advantage of the non-committal agreement was that it bought the emperor more time. He could profitably expend this precious time trying to gather the Roman forces to face Alaric on an even military footing so that he would never have to honour the agreement anyway. So, while promising much, the offer actually gave nothing away. Batting the ball straight back into Alaric's court, Honorius dismissed the senators to Rome.

The Goth was delighted at the news. Peace, he believed, was within sight. Since his plan of besieging Rome seemed to be reaping rich dividends, he and his army agreed to withdraw from Rome and headed north. What Alaric had failed to realize, however, was a lesson he should have learnt long ago. He was trying to forge an alliance with people who believed he was nothing more than an uncouth barbarian leading an uncivilized rabble. The fact was that Honorius had no intention of honouring an alliance. As Alaric waited patiently in northern Italy for a proper agreement to come, the duplicity of the western court soon became painfully apparent.

Honorius had used the hiatus to try to reinforce the defences of Rome. He had dispatched to the city an élite corps of 6000 soldiers, the cream of the Roman army in Italy. Before they even reached Rome, however, Alaric's men had spotted them. Immediately, Alaric amassed the totality of the Gothic army, sent it in pursuit and promptly wiped out all 6000 Roman soldiers. Later on there were further indignities for the imperial forces to endure. When Athaulf and a detachment of Goths stationed near Pisa were peremptorily assaulted by an army led by Olympius himself, they were taken completely by surprise. The Goths lost over a thousand men in the conflict, but as soon as they had reorganized, they revealed to the Romans the full extent of their numbers and fury. Olympius's pathetic army retreated to Ravenna in disgrace.[23]

As the unscathed Roman soldiers beat their hurried, ignoble retreat and scurried through the Golden Gate of Ravenna, perhaps Honorius looked on from a window in his palace. The sorry picture threw the contrast between Olympius and Stilicho into stark relief. Shortly afterwards some eunuchs in the emperor's court spied an opportunity for the kind of wholesale blood-letting common to autocratic regimes throughout history. In front of the emperor they accused Olympius of heaping more disasters upon the state. The emperor saw absolutely no reason to disagree. Indeed, disillusion quickly turned to anger. As if waking from a drug-induced stupor, Honorius was perhaps at last seeing things clearly; or perhaps he was just lurching petulantly from one ill-judged strategy to another. The sources don't say. Either way, the young Honorius finally made a decision. As quickly as he had been adopted as the emperor's unctuous chief counsellor, so Olympius was unceremoniously dumped.[24]

On a black winter's night in Italy, some time in early 409, the signs that the future of the western empire had once again hit rock bottom were to be seen in three places at once. Somewhere north of Ravenna, in a dismal bid to save his life, the deposed, ruthless courtier Olympius was in flight to Dalmatia (modern-day Croatia) and anonymity. Further south, Alaric was wasting not a moment to vent his scorching fury. Perhaps vowing never again to be made a fool of, never again to be so roundly dishonoured and insulted by the Romans, he gave his army clear instructions to return to Rome, to put it again under siege, and to make the city suffer once more. Meanwhile, in the imperial palace of Ravenna, the forlorn Honorius was in despair. His hated enemy Alaric would soon be slowly strangling the life out of Rome and, while the Roman army in Italy was stretched to its limit in its failed efforts to deal with the Goths, day by day the usurper and self-proclaimed emperor Constantine III in Gaul grew in stature and power. Indeed, Honorius was at such a low ebb that around this time he even dispatched the purple imperial robes of office to his rival emperor and formally recognized

Constantine's claim to power. The real ruler of the west had clearly come to the depressing conclusion that he might, after all, need the armies of Britain and Gaul under the usurper's command. And yet, despite the gloom, there was a glimmer of hope for Honorius.

It came in the forms of his Praetorian prefect, Jovius, and his most senior general, Sarus. The latter was a military commander of considerable experience, who had proved his abilities under Stilicho and Olympius. Indeed, the Italian army could still boast a total of 30,000 soldiers, and Honorius could rely on Sarus to lead them. But the general had another key quality: he was by origin a Goth, a nobleman, a man of the same stock as Alaric. The two men came from rival Gothic families, and it is very possible that Alaric had beaten Sarus to the leadership of the Goths in 395. That contest would not have been the clean-cut election of modern politics, but something closer to a blood feud, the vanquished possibly losing not just his chance to lead, but his family too in the victor's cull of potential rivals. Sarus, rejected by his own, had taken his military skills to the emperor and the service of Rome.[25] A Goth with a bitter, ancient grievance against the enemy of the emperor – who better to help Honorius outwit Alaric? Jovius, however, was even more key to the emperor's future.

Jovius had been Stilicho's chief administrative officer in Dalmatia. As such, his responsibility had been to help supply Alaric's Goths and organize them for the planned joint attack on the east back in 406. Jovius was the man who had negotiated that old agreement between Alaric and Stilicho, the man who had spent days in the company of the Goth in Epirus (modern-day Albania), the man who could almost call Alaric his friend. Honorius now turned to Jovius and promoted him to chief adviser. Perhaps, thought the young emperor, there was a way out of this awful mess after all.

THE SACK OF ROME

The historian Zosimus tells us that Jovius was conspicuous for his 'education'.[26] He now used his wisdom, tact and diplomacy to advocate to Honorius the only viable solution to the spiralling crisis: peace with Alaric.

Jovius knew that Alaric had the western empire exactly where he wanted it. The Gothic army had an extraordinary force of 40,000, their numbers recently swollen by runaway slaves. That mighty force was surrounding Rome, and Honorius could do nothing about it. True, the Roman army in Italy could be deployed against them, but since their numbers were evenly matched a fight was far too much of a gamble – there could be no guarantee that the Romans would win. True, Honorius's recognition of Constantine III had taken the sting out of his rival's threats for the time being, but both he and Jovius were not yet prepared to capitulate the entire western empire to the usurper. By the spring of 409 Constantine III had elevated his sons to emperor, thus establishing a new dynasty, and had also established his 'imperial' seat at Arles in southern Gaul. He had his feet firmly planted on the doorstep of Italy. Should Honorius's forces be weakened by Alaric, Constantine was ready to break in: to cross the Alps and add the remainder of the western empire to his swag bag of imperial domains.[27] Honorius had decidedly run out of bargaining chips.

Alaric knew this too. So when Jovius sent a delegation to Rome informing him of the Roman about-face and inviting him and Athaulf to Ariminum (Rimini) near Ravenna to negotiate a settlement, Alaric was, most probably, not in the least surprised.[28] Although the worth of the emperor's word and the meaningfulness of so-called Roman honour and justice had become seriously devalued commodities, he was nonetheless persuaded.

Admittedly, he had Rome under siege and had once again pinched an artery of the western empire, but he had no intention of executing his threat and sacking it. That would be futile and result only in failure: he would be forsaking the chance of a permanent, long-term peace for short-term gains that would only mean more running, more looking over his shoulder, more insecurity for his people. It would be the political equivalent of banging his head against a brick wall. Slowly he picked himself up, begged his disaffected brother-in-law to lend him his support, and together the disgruntled men headed north to meet Jovius. He was at last going to prise all he could out of the Romans.

Alaric put his terms on the table. He wanted an annual payment of gold, an annual supply of grain, and an agreement that the Goths could settle in the Roman provinces of the two Venetias (the region around Venice), Noricum and Dalmatia. His final term – a senior generalship for himself in the Roman army – would secure his influence at court and a voice to protect the interests of his people. The terms were dispatched to Honorius, and Jovius, Alaric and Athaulf awaited the emperor's response. When it came back the letter was read out and at first it sounded promising. Honorius agreed to the corn and the gold, but he made no mention of the land question. And as for the generalship… Allow a barbarian a principal role in his government? No, that was absolutely out of the question![29]

Alaric flew into a rage. Thumping his fist on the table, he threatened the immediate burning, sacking and destruction of Rome, and promptly marched out. Jovius left too, though for Ravenna, and more out of fear that the deal had blown up in his face. It took some days for Alaric to regain his composure. Finally, he asked some bishops to act as his emissaries and sent the emperor a radically revised offer. He did not want the money or the position, or even Venetia or Dalmatia. All he wanted, he said, was the measly province of Noricum for his people, a province that was 'situated at the far end of the Danube, was continuously harried by invasions, and contributed little tax to the treasury'.[30]

This was an extraordinary moment. Here was a man who could have destroyed the western empire at the nod of his head, who had all the power and held all the aces. Yet he was prepared to sacrifice that power in return for a durable peace, a stable home and a permanent end to the suffering of his people. Ultimately, he wanted the Roman empire to survive just so long as his people had a place in it. Even Honorius was astounded. When the bishops read out Alaric's offer, 'everyone alike was amazed at the man's moderation'.[31] Incredibly, however, the callow, capricious emperor refused Alaric's request. The sources don't make clear exactly why. Perhaps in the end he preferred to sacrifice the city of Rome rather than come to terms with his enemy. Ultimately, he was prepared to allow even the city in which his sister was held hostage to be destroyed rather than suffer the humiliation of having to make the Goths Roman partners on Roman soil.

For the third time Alaric marched on Rome. Athaulf and his generals, snorting plumes of scorn and hatred for Honorius and the western empire, must have bayed for their leader to honour his threat. Alaric, however, was not going to attack yet. Admittedly, he had now given up on the western Roman emperor, but he was determined not to give up on the western Roman empire. In the summer of 409, to the problem of how to apply pressure without resorting to violence, Alaric devised a cunning solution. He recruited in Rome the help of an ambitious, patrician senator with a fondness for Rome's ancient past and ideas above his station. The Goth sanctioned this man's appointment by the Senate to the rank of emperor, and set up a new seat of power in the ancient capital to rival that of Honorius in Ravenna. As a result, in the summer of 409 there were, unbelievably, three 'emperors' in the west: Honorius, Constantine III and now Attalus. Alaric at last had a temporary place in the western Roman state: as Attalus's commander-in-chief.

The bold plan certainly hurt Honorius. As Alaric's army won over northern Italy to Attalus's cause, Honorius was sent spinning into a panic. He even considered abandoning the western empire, and had some ships prepared to whisk him off to Constantinople. His resolve to face the enemy was given a much-needed injection of steel only when 4000 reinforcement soldiers from the eastern empire arrived just in time and defended Ravenna. Soon, however, perhaps urged by Jovius, Honorius came up with a way to counter the rebellion.

The province of North Africa, on whose grain supply Rome relied for food, was still loyal to Honorius, so the one legitimate western emperor simply ordered it to be cut off. Attalus's brief, insubstantial regime quickly became discredited. Even Alaric, who had effectively promoted him to emperor, grew disillusioned with, and tired of, this irritating, pathetic mock-emperor. He stripped him of his imperial robes and sent them to Honorius to prove his change of strategy once again. In the end, Alaric took Galla Placidia, Honorius's sister, hostage. Cocooned in Ravenna, the insensitive Honorius still turned a blind eye to the ancient capital on its knees. And still the Goth did not attack Rome.

Alaric's decisiveness, his foresight and determination to achieve his vision are all the more astonishing because the stakes were now higher than ever. He had a new battle on his hands – this time with his own administration. Not to punish Rome violently for Honorius's treatment of the Gothic nation encamped on Italian soil was a highly unpopular policy. Athaulf and others would have made their position clear: a treaty with the Romans was simply pie in the sky. The Romans could not even be trusted to keep their word! Athaulf and the restless administrators had reason on their side. Indeed, it was now so difficult to sell a policy of negotiation rather than force that Alaric's leadership was on the line. Nonetheless, with the odds utterly stacked against him, he was prepared to stake all his quickly evaporating political clout on one final throw of the dice.

When he sent one last delegation to Ravenna little did he know it, but Honorius was, most probably, finally ready to make peace. A deal was on the table. But if Honorius and Alaric were expecting to resolve the great problem of the Goths by negotiation, their hopes were to be shattered in the most unexpected and tragic way. As Alaric, Athaulf and their detachment of Gothic soldiers made their journey north and reached to within 12 kilometres (7 miles) of Ravenna, they were ambushed by the Roman general Sarus. Alaric was completely stunned.

Unbeknownst to the emperor, Sarus had decided to act on his own initiative. He knew that any settlement between Alaric and the Romans would have completely jeopardized his own hard-earned position at the Roman top table. If there were to be an agreement, it had to involve him. If not, he would lose his position and probably his life. His attack also gave him a chance to settle an old score against his rival. Just at the moment when there was a real chance of peace between Roman and Goth, he was utterly determined to torpedo it. Acting out of spite and revenge a Goth, not a Roman, finally scuttled any chance of negotiation.

When Honorius heard the news of the ambush, perhaps he felt that the whole sorry episode proved his old prejudice: no barbarian, not even a Romanized one such as Sarus, could ever be trusted. Heading south, having narrowly escaped with their lives, Alaric and Athaulf too were licking the wounds of a prejudice they believed had been painfully confirmed. Honorius, they thought, had proved to be the same cowardly embodiment of deceit he had always been. They had been betrayed one last fatal time. In the heat of a mid-August day in 410 the Goths' leaders returned for the final time to Rome.

Arranged in neat columns around the city wall was the most extraordinary sight: an army of 40,000 men, the equivalent of eight old Roman legions. The city had last been sacked by the Celts in 390 BC. Now, some eight hundred years later, a new force of soldiers thronged outside. The more senior commanders and noblemen wore helmets, body armour and short capes of wolfskin or sheepskin. Their swords would have been carefully engraved with herringbone patterns, sheathed in scabbards of wood or leather, and lined with fur. The ranks of Gothic soldiers had only the protection of their short tunics and trousers, and their armoury of shields, barbed javelins, bows and throwing axes.

The tall, graceful Athaulf felt vindicated. With his brother's policy of reason utterly destroyed, he was in belligerent mood, urging on the ranks as they beat their weapons against their shields. The clatter that greeted Alaric as he left his tent to take command built to a crashing, unstoppable crescendo. Rome was utterly hamstrung, on its knees. Nearly two years earlier, Alaric had first raised the sword over the city's neck. Now he let it fall. But when he gave the signal to attack, on 24 August 410, the proud, ambitious Alaric knew that he had failed.[32]

The city was easy to overpower. On the night of the assault somebody opened the Salarian Gate for the Goths. According to a later account, a noblewoman had taken the action out of a desperate desire to put the city out of its prolonged misery. More probably, whoever invited the Goths in had been bribed.[33] Inside too there was little resistance: Rome had no army – only a small, ramshackle ceremonial guard. There is no detailed account of what happened over the next three days. What is clear is that in all the chaos there was a surprising level of order and restraint. This was not quite the uncivilized act of savagery by a barbarian horde one might have expected.

Alaric was not only a Christian, but a Christian who had been helped over the previous two years by bishops. Out of respect for them and his faith, the basilicas of St Peter's and St Paul's became places of sanctuary. With the exception of a massive silver Eucharist cup donated by Constantine, Christian treasures and the churches that housed them were respected and preserved.[34] In contrast to the infamous Roman sacks of Carthage and Corinth in 146 BC, in which wholesale destruction, mass slaughter, enslavement and looting were the standard, the sack of Rome was very un-Roman indeed. Nonetheless, although Alaric and his Goths may have been Christians they were not saints. They had come to plunder, to exact revenge.

Perhaps guided by the slaves who had defected to Alaric, Gothic squads searched the streets for the houses of the rich. When they found them they put the sharp blade of an axe at their victims' heads and demanded all their gold, silver and treasures. The pagan temples were looted for movable statues and precious objects, and the treasures from the Temple of Jerusalem, the victims of a Roman sack some 350 years earlier, were stolen once again. Some Romans escaped to the places of asylum, but the many who resisted or could not flee were killed, tortured or beaten up. The stories of defiant heroic women who resisted rape, or who were battered but mustered the courage to protect another (found in the writings of Orosius, Sozomen and Jerome), suggest that for widows, married women and virgins quite the opposite was true.[35]

On the third day the Gothic army, its efficient and horrific work complete, reassembled. Some grand houses and public buildings – notably the mansion of Sallust, the Basilica Aemilia and the old Senate House – were set on fire. With the thick black smoke of this last act rising above the Salarian Gate, the Goths abandoned the battlefield of their 'victory' over the Romans. The army was laden down with loot, but Alaric, with no homeland and no peace, came away empty-handed.

EPILOGUE

The after-shock of the disaster reverberated across the breadth of the Roman world. In Jerusalem St Jerome lamented how, 'In one city the whole world perished'.[36] Pagans and Christians alike used the destruction of the Eternal City to score points. For pagans the sack was proof that once the traditional gods had been rejected and had left the city, so too had its protection. To St Augustine in North Africa, however, the lesson to be learnt was quite different. He met eyewitnesses who had fled to that province to escape the Goths, and what he learnt from them confirmed only one thing: Rome had been on a slippery slope of moral decline ever since the sack of Carthage in 146 BC. Without the fear of that Mediterranean power to keep it in check, Rome had free reign to indulge in the selfish passions of greed and domination. Now, in the sack of Rome, that process had come to its logical, revolutionary conclusion. All human, earthly cities – even the new Christianized Rome of Constantine – were transitory and ephemeral, concluded St Augustine.[37] Only the City of God in heaven was eternal and supreme. The natural order of the world, the ancient scheme of things, anchored in the city that had dominated the Mediterranean world for hundreds of years had gone topsy-turvy.

The Gothic invasion of Italy, its culmination in the sack of Rome, and the western emperor's utter inability to find a solution to the crisis had dealt the western Roman empire a critical death blow. But it was not knocked out yet. Certainly the facts painted a bleak picture. The barbarian grouping of Vandals,

Alans and Suevi still occupied territories in Spain; Constantine III still had his ambitions and controlled Britain, Gaul and the rest of Spain; and Alaric's Gothic nation was still in Italy. Yet the Roman state in the west had by no means fallen.

Indeed, against the odds, the western Roman empire would be pieced back together again. The architect of this extraordinary resurgence was a brilliant general and politician who took on the dual role of *magister militum* forged by Stilicho; he was the commander-in-chief of Roman forces in the west and, overshadowing the weak emperor Honorius, effective ruler of the western empire. Indeed, Flavius Constantius, an utterly ruthless career soldier born in Naissus (modern-day Nis in Serbia), was one of the last great leaders of the Roman world, an individual in the mould of Julius Caesar, a man who, by the mere fact of his existence, could turn the course of history.

First, Constantius's hands were significantly freed when the Goths eventually left Italy. After the failure to negotiate a peace with Honorius, Alaric planned to make a home for the Goths in North Africa. However, before this could occur, the man who had promised so much met an anticlimactic end. Seized by a violent fever, Alaric died in 410 perhaps without having reached even his fortieth birthday. He received a Gothic burial fit for a king: the Busento river in Cosenza (in modern-day Calabria) was diverted, and in the river bed was dug a grave. Once Alaric's corpse had been laid to rest in it, the dam was broken and the waters rushed over his dead body. The Roman captives who had carried out the burial were afterwards executed to keep its precise location a secret for ever. Athaulf now succeeded his brother, abandoned the plan for North Africa and, plundering Italy along the way, moved the Goths to southern Gaul in 412. In the hopes of coming to an alliance with the western court, Athaulf had brought with him a bargaining chip. The Roman princess Galla Placidia was still a hostage of the Goths and would soon become Athaulf's wife and mother of his son. Should Athaulf succeed in winning a place at the imperial court, that child would be a potential emperor in waiting.

With strategic room to manoeuvre, Flavius Constantius finally moved the Roman army in Italy against Constantine III and defeated him. The usurper was captured, executed and his head taken to Honorius at Ravenna. With the Roman armies of Britain, Gaul, Spain and Italy united once more, Constantius now had the military muscle to seek a permanent settlement with the Goths – but on his terms. In particular, Constantius refused to make Athaulf an equal partner in the Roman admin-istration. For Athaulf this was a deal-breaker. His obstinacy proved very unpopular when Constantius applied force and tried to starve the Goths into an agreement by blockading them at Narbonne (southwestern France). The Goths eventually toppled their leader, and a moderate successor agreed terms with Constantius. In 418 Alaric's dream of a homeland for his nation was realized. The Goths were finally settled in Aquitaine in the Garonne valley of southwest Gaul (modern-day Bordeaux). In keeping with the return of advantage to Rome, Galla Placidia was handed back to Honorius and married off, against her will, to Flavius Constantius. Her son by Athaulf having died prematurely, she would, in due course, bear her new husband two children.

The final parts of the jigsaw were the Vandals, Alans and Suevi. Constantius now used his peace with the Goths to his advantage. Reinvigorating his Roman army with Gothic allies, he moved south to Spain, defeated the Vandals, Alans and Suevi, and brought the Iberian provinces back under Roman control. In the space of just ten years Constantius had brilliantly extricated the western Roman empire from the crisis that had nearly killed it. He pulled together once more all the threads of the western domains that a decade earlier had looked to be hopelessly untangling, and held them in the grip of his hand. In achieving this brilliant feat, however, there had been a high price to pay.

The years of looting and the ravages of warfare across the west meant that agricultural produce, and hence revenues, were down. With the Goths settled in Gaul, there was a much smaller area of provincial territory able to deliver tax into the imperial coffers. For example, the island of Britain, ignored by Constantius as his army focused on putting out fires in Gaul and Spain, was now detached from the western empire and lost for ever. Henceforth it could not rely on the protection by the western empire's forces. As a result of such changes, there were few resources to rejuvenate a western army that had been reduced by almost half in the wars against the barbarians during the critical years of Honorius's reign (395–420). Although the emperor remedied the western army's huge losses by providing more units, the majority of these were not new field army units, but lower-grade auxiliary units that had been upgraded and reclassified. The money did not stretch far enough for anything more than a military facelift.[38]

The final hangover from the years of invasion was widespread disaffection among the provincial landowning élites. These were the local self-governing centres of power that organized tax-gathering, and on whom the imperial centre of the west depended for the task's successful administration. They were not happy, and their disaffection centred on one simple fact. The emperor Honorius had not been able to keep his side of the bargain – to provide military protection for their property in exchange for the collection of taxes. After years of upheaval and diminishing security, it was becoming obvious that the ancient contract between emperor and local élite was slowly being torn up.[39]

This disaffection could easily turn to outright defiance. The train of thought perhaps ran as follows: if life under a Gothic or

Vandal king would prove safer, if it offered the benefits of protection from war, and if it proved more conducive to sustaining their lifestyle, why bother to be part of the Roman empire at all? In the early fifth century cases of local élites breaking away from the centre were isolated, but this could and would become a trend. With five per cent of western Roman citizens owning 80 per cent of the land, the loosening of this old cornerstone of the Roman empire was a critical effect of the barbarian invasions – another hammer blow in the fall of the western empire.

Consequently, despite Constantius's success, the same forces that had so rattled Italy under the impact of Alaric's Goths had returned to wreak havoc on the western empire during Constantius's years of regaining control. Like a convalescent from major surgery, the western empire was now well again, but it was a pale shadow of its former self. Soon it would have to find the strength to stomach further pummellings. The most fatal of these centred on the rich Roman province of Africa, the granary of the western empire.

In 421 Constantius, now appointed co-emperor, fell ill and died unexpectedly. When Honorius passed away two years later, a protracted struggle for power was let loose with one brief regime swiftly falling prey to the bloody cull of another. Eventually, Valentinian III, the six-year-old son of Constantius and Galla Placidia, was promoted to emperor. The real ruler, the man who had actually won the power struggle in 431, was a worthy successor to Constantius. Known as the last great Roman commander, Flavius Aetius had his hands full when he became commander-in-chief of the Roman forces. During the fight for succession, the regrouped and revitalized Vandals had crossed from Tarifa in southern Spain, landed in Africa in May 429 and began heading east. Either by assault or by treaty, they gradually took control of what is now Morocco and Algeria. By

439 they had captured the empire's third largest city – Carthage. By taking this province, the Vandals had their hands at the west's jugular.

In the early fifth century, Africa was the chief source of grain and revenue for Rome and Italy. Under Julius Caesar, 50,000 tonnes of grain in a year was shipped from Carthage, and since that time shipments had continued from the massive extended Roman docks there. For this reason Africa was the western empire's lifeline. Now Aetius set about resuscitating it. During the 430s he had been detained from taking action against the Vandals by a new wave of barbarian invasions and rebellions in the western provinces. By 440, however, he had brought those under control, had won – through brilliant diplomacy – assistance from the eastern empire, and had amassed an extraordinary allied fleet in Sicily. The aim of the united forces of the eastern and western Roman empire was the reconquest of the key province of Africa. However, at the moment when Aetius should have given the order for the 1100-ship fleet to sail, the mission was suddenly abandoned. The eastern forces, said the emperor of the east, were urgently required back in his half of the empire because Constantinople was facing an invasion like no other. The decision to ditch the attack on North Africa would prove to be the last critical turning point in the collapse of the west. The man who had provoked it came from the very same people who, in 376, had sparked the first 'big bang' moment in the fall of the west, the first invasion of Rome's northern frontiers. His name was Attila the Hun.

Just as the Huns began the story of the fall of the western Roman empire, so they end it. During his campaigns of the 430s, Aetius had temporarily engaged the services of the Hunnic forces. However, now, in 440, with their leadership united under Attila and their ascendant empire stretching from the Black Sea to the Baltic and from Germany to the central

Asian steppes, the Huns were back for much more than a lucrative military partnership. In two devastating sweeps through the Balkans in 441 and 447, Attila invaded the eastern empire and made a mockery of the Roman army's resistance. The effectiveness of his forces came down not only to the use of the bow. The Huns were the first barbarian force to work out how to storm well-defended fortress towns. The secret of their success lay in the skilful use of siege engines, battering rams and scaling ladders, which they had simply copied from the Romans. By ransacking the eastern empire in this way, Attila was able to extort incredible amounts of gold out of Constantinople. In 451, however, he received an invitation to lay his hands on new riches. Allegedly enticed by a rescue plea-cum-marriage proposal from the rebellious sister of the emperor Valentinian, Attila turned his attentions to the west.

In perhaps the last great military encounter in the history of the western Roman empire, Aetius managed to pull together an army of Romans, Goths, Franks, Burgundians and Celts, and with it decisively defeated his enemy at the battle of the Catalaunian Plains (modern-day Châlons) in Gaul. At the Huns' second attempt, however, in 452, Aetius could offer little resistance. Attila invaded Italy and sacked several cities in the north. His greatest triumph was the successful siege of the imperial capital of Milan, and in a moral victory he also forced Valentinian III to flee from Ravenna to Rome in terror. However, at the river Po disease and inadequate supply lines brought the Huns' campaign to a stuttering halt and they eventually retreated. Attila died that same year. According to one source, he met his end not fighting but, bizarrely, on his wedding night. He had been feasting to celebrate his marriage to a beautiful Gothic princess by the name of Hildico, and after retiring to their nuptial quarters, the great Hunnic leader suffered a nosebleed and choked to death on his own blood.

As quickly as Attila's empire sprang up, so it disintegrated after his death. By that time, however, the death blow to the west had been dealt. Aetius may have successfully seen off Attila, but he lacked the military firepower to take North Africa back from the Vandals. He did not live to see the proof of that stark fact. In return for brilliantly defending the western empire from the blistering assault of Attila's forces, Aetius – the 'last Roman' – was thanked by Valentinian III with assassination in 454. The emperor was fearful and envious of his commander's power. Over a decade after Aetius's death in 468, the eastern empire made one final play for North Africa. In a sea battle off the coast of what is now Libya, however, the Byzantine fleet was roundly defeated by that of the Vandals.

After the loss of Africa, the only revenues the western empire could rely on were those of Italy and Sicily. These were not nearly enough to pay for an army large enough to dictate terms to the multitude of barbarians settled in the west: the Goths, Burgundians and Franks of Gaul, the Goths and Suevi of Spain, and the Vandals of North Africa. The balance of power between the Roman army and the forces of barbarians, between the western emperors and the barbarian kings had fatally, permanently shifted. The reality of where power now lay was most clearly pronounced in the accession in 455 of Emperor Avitus. The one thing that had secured his rise to 'power' was a military alliance with Theodoric II – a barbarian king. In due course, further treaties were struck between the imperial administration at Ravenna and the Goths and Vandals, whom the administration acknowledged, in effect, as legitimate possessors, inheritors and partners in the west. Bit by bit the remaining Roman territories splintered out of central control. The last breath of the western empire, however, was gasped in Italy.

By 476, the financial and military muscle of the central authorities of Italy were so limp, so withered that they were no longer able to maintain themselves let alone keep intruders firmly in check. The lines defining Roman and barbarian were becoming increasingly blurred, the histories of citizen and invader ever more fused. However some distinctions were still visible, some did still matter. Take Odovacar, for example. This man made the gentle transformation from top Roman general to Germanic king when he settled his Roman soldiers in Italy. Indeed, that little rump of the Roman army in Italy wasn't really Roman either. The soldiers were Germanic mercenaries who, like their leader, came from the people of the Sciri. Odovacar had no money to give them, so he paid them with land – possibly as much as one-third of Italy once its current Roman owners had been booted off. There could be no clearer statement of who were now the successors to the old western empire.

Odovacar thus became sole effective ruler of Italy. With the loyalty of his settled Scirian soldiers, he had now secured his personal power base too. There remained one awkward distinction left to resolve – the small anomaly of Romulus Augustulus. The office of the western Roman emperor had long been a quaint tradition in the process of fossilization, the ceremonial appointee of some barbarian commander or king. Little Romulus, however, took this trend to a new extreme. He was a sixteen-year-old boy and the son of a usurping army commander recently toppled by Odovacar. He controlled nothing outside Italy, Odovacar controlled everything within it. Legitimacy, if it existed at all, belonged really to the man whom Romulus and his father had usurped, Julius Nepos, the last emperor to be formally recognized by the eastern emperor. So, why bother keeping Romulus? Indeed, why bother finding a replacement? Surely it would be better to send him back to his family in Campania, to give him a decent pension and to let him live in peaceful obscurity?

Taking the side of caution, however, Odovacar despatched an

embassy to Zeno, the eastern emperor. Why didn't Zeno take over sovereignty of both halves of the empire, proposed Odovacar, while the Germanic king administered everyday affairs in Italy? The suggestion posed an awkward dilemma. For Zeno, deposing Romulus was not a problem – Constantinople had never recognised him anyway. The problem was Nepos whom he had recognised. But while he realised that Nepos no longer held any sovereignty, the eastern emperor did not want to be the one who effectively sanctioned the handover of power to the Germanic king, the one who formally ended the western state. Chance, however, offered him a solution.

Coincidentally Zeno had in his possession a letter from Nepos. The usurped western emperor had written to Zeno to request his help in making a last bid for power, a last bid to win back the Roman state in the west. After some reflection, Zeno made two deft, sidestepping replies. To Odovacar he said that the king needed to offer his allegiance to Nepos because the last formally recognised western emperor was the only person who could legitimately acknowledge Odovacar's status. To Nepos, however, he made an apology: he could not offer him any practical assistance in recovering the west. Such an endeavour, he implied, was utterly futile. And with that Zeno had accepted – without having to spell it out – that the western empire was lost and Odovacar had seized power

In Italy, with Romulus deposed, Odovacar tended to one last tidying up exercise. What to do about the ceremonial robes of office of the western Roman emperor? He was certainly not going to be wearing them. He was not a sovereign Augustus – that was not his role nor the basis of his power. He was happy to call himself king. No, perhaps the best place for them was in the east, with the emperor Zeno. A messenger was summoned and the imperial vestments, diadem and purple cloak were dispatched to Constantinople.

If Odovacar was tempted to see the occasion as momentous or somehow ominous, maybe he reassured himself that there could well be another emperor some time in the future. There might one day be the occasion for just such a leader, but there was certainly no need for one now, not in his Italy. The ancient Roman authority of an Augustus, the power which had created and ruled an empire for centuries and which was embodied in those imperial signs of office, was, at least for the time being, leaving the west.

NOTES

SEVEN HILLS OF ROME

1. Virgil, *Georgics*, Book 4. 8ff.
2. Ibid., 73–4.
3. Peter Jones and Keith Sidwell (eds), *The World of Rome: An Introduction to Roman Culture* (Cambridge, 1997), p. 7.
4. Polybius, *Histories*, Book 6. 52.
5. Livy, Book 1. 32.

I REVOLUTION

1. Polybius, *Histories*, Book 6. 54.
2. Ibid., 53.
3. Polybius, *Histories*, Book 1. 1.
4. Ibid., 20 & 59.
5. Livy, Book 21. 35.
6. Livy, Book 26. 11.
7. Peter Jones and Keith Sidwell (eds), *The World of Rome: An Introduction to Roman Culture* (Cambridge, 1997), pp. 20–1.
8. Appian, *Roman History*, Book 8. 116.
9. Polybius, *Histories*, Book 36. 9.
10. Sallust, *Conspiracy of Catiline*, 10.
11. Appian, *Roman History*, Book 8. 69; W.V. Harris, 'Roman Expansion in the West' in A.E. Astin, F.W. Walbank, M.W. Frederiksen and R.M. Ogilvie (eds), *Cambridge Ancient History* (Cambridge, 1989), vol. 8, p. 154.
12. Livy, *Periochae*, 47; W.V. Harris, 'Roman Expansion in the West' in A.E. Astin, F.W. Walbank, M.W. Frederiksen and R.M. Ogilvie (eds), *Cambridge Ancient History* (Cambridge, 1989), vol. 8, p. 149.
13. Appian, *Roman History*, Book 8. 81–3.
14. Polybius, *Histories*, Book 36. 2.
15. Polybius, *Histories*, Book 31. 23.
16. Plutarch, *Life of Tiberius Gracchus*, 2.
17. Isidore, *Etymologies*, 2. 21. 4; Jones and Sidwell, *World of Rome*, p. 106.
18. Appian, *Roman History*, Book 8. 128.
19. Ibid., 129–30.
20. Ibid., 130–31.
21. Homer, *Iliad*, Book 6. 448–9.
22. Appian, *Roman History*, Book 8. 132.
23. Plutarch, *Life of Tiberius Gracchus*, 4; Appian, *Roman History*, Book 8. 133.
24. Appian, *Roman History*, Book 8. 134.

25. Plutarch, *Life of Tiberius Gracchus*, 8; Mary Beard and Michael Crawford, *Rome in the Late Republic: Problems and Interpretations* (London, 1999), p. 55.
26. Beard and Crawford, *Rome in the Late Republic*, p. 14.
27. Sallust, *Conspiracy of Catiline*, preface passim.
28. Appian, *The Civil Wars*, Book 1. 7.
29. Beard and Crawford, *Rome in the Late Republic*, p. 68.
30. Livy, *Periochae*, 55.
31. Plutarch, *Life of Tiberius Gracchus*, 8.
32. Ibid., 5.
33. Ibid.; Appian, *Roman History*, Book 6. 80.
34. Cassius Dio, Book 24. 83; Cicero, *de haruspicum responsis*, 43.
35. Plutarch, *Life of Tiberius Gracchus*, 8.
36. Ibid., 9.
37. Appian, *Civil Wars*, Book 1. 11.
38. Cicero, *pro Sestio*, 103; Appian, *Civil Wars*, Book 1. 10.
39. Plutarch, *Life of Tiberius Gracchus*, 12.
40. Ibid., 14.
41. Ibid.
42. Ibid., 16.
43. Ibid., 17.
44. Ibid., 18–19.
45. Ibid., 19.

II CAESAR

1. Cassius Dio, Book 43. 44.
2. Mary Beard and Michael Crawford, *Rome in the Late Republic: Problems and Interpretations* (London, 1999), p. 5.
3. Valerius Maximus, Book 6. 2.
4. Plutarch, *Life of Caesar*, 4; Suetonius, *Life of the Deified Julius Caesar*, 45.
5. Plutarch, *Caesar*, 4.
6. Suetonius, *Deified Julius Caesar*, 10.
7. Cicero, *To Atticus*, 2. 1.
8. Plutarch, *Caesar*, 13.
9. Suetonius, *Deified Julius Caesar*, 18.
10. Ibid., 22.
11. Cicero, *To Atticus*, 2. 19.
12. Cicero, *On the Consular Provinces*, 33.
13. Caesar, *Commentaries on the Gallic War*, Book 1. 14.
14. Ibid., 1.
15. Caesar, *Gallic War*, Book 4. 17.
16. Caesar, *Gallic War*, Book 7. 1; Cassius Dio, Book 39. 53.
17. Suetonius, Deified Julius Caesar, 26.
18. Sallust, *War with Jugurtha*, 86.
19. Plutarch, *Life of Pompey*, 52.
20. Ibid., 53.
21. Sallust, *Histories*, Book 4. 69. 18: 'Only a few prefer liberty, the majority seek nothing more than fair masters.'
22. Plutarch, *Pompey*, 54.
23. Letter from Caelius to Cicero in Cicero, *Letters to Friends*, 8. 1.
24. Caesar, *Gallic War*, Book 7. 1.
25. Ibid., 4.
26. Ibid., 8.
27. Plutarch, *Caesar*, 25.
28. Caesar, *Gallic War*, Book 7. 71.
29. Plutarch, *Caesar*, 15.
30. Caesar, *Gallic War*, Book 7. 86.
31. Plutarch, *Caesar*, 27.
32. Caesar, *Gallic War*, Book 7. 88.

33. Suetonius, *Deified Julius Caesar*, 25.

34. Plutarch, *Caesar*, 27.

35. Suetonius, *Deified Julius Caesar*, 26.

36. Caesar, *Gallic War*, Book 3. 10.

37. Letter from Caelius to Cicero in Cicero, *To Friends*, 8. 5.

38. Plutarch, *Pompey*, 55.

39. Letter from Caelius to Cicero in Cicero, *To Friends*, 8. 8.

40. Plutarch, *Pompey*, 57.

41. Ibid.

42. Letter from Caelius to Cicero in Cicero, *To Friends*, 8. 14.

43. Appian, *The Civil Wars*, Book 2. 30.

44. Ibid., 31; Cicero, *To Atticus*, 7. 8.

45. Caesar, *The Civil War*, Book 1. 1.

46. Appian, *Civil Wars*, Book 2. 32.

47. Ibid., 33.

48. Plutarch, *Caesar*, 32.

49. Ibid., 32; Appian, *Civil Wars*, Book 2. 35.

50. Suetonius, *Deified Julius Caesar*, 32.

51. Letter from Caesar to Cicero in Cicero, *To Atticus*, 9. 7.

52. Cicero, *To Atticus*, 8. 13

53. Cassius Dio, Book 41. 5.

54. Plutarch, *Caesar*, 33.

55. Lucan, *Civil War*, Book 2. 22ff.

56. Plutarch, *Pompey*, 61.

57. Cicero, *To Atticus*, 8. 2; 9. 18.

58. Plutarch, *Caesar*, 34; Cicero, *To Friends*, 14. 8; Cassius Dio, Book 41. 9.

59. Caesar, *Civil War*, Book 1. 26.

60. Ibid., 26.

61. Ibid., 26–8.

62. Ibid., 29; Plutarch, *Caesar*, 35.

63. Lucan, *Civil War*, Book 3. 110ff.

64. Caesar, *Civil War*, Book 1. 32–3.

65. Plutarch, *Caesar*, 35.

66. Caesar, *Civil War*, Book 3. 3.

67. Suetonius, *Deified Julius Caesar*, 58.

68. Caesar, *Civil War*, Book 3. 48.

69. Plutarch, *Caesar*, 41.

70. Ibid., 41.

71. Caesar, *Civil War*, Book 3. 85; Plutarch, *Pompey*, 68.

72. Lucan, *Civil War*, Book 7. 257ff; Plutarch, *Caesar*, 42.

73. Lucan, *Civil War*, Book 7. 319ff.

74. Caesar, *Civil War*, Book 3. 91.

75. Plutarch, *Caesar*, 45.

76. Plutarch, *Pompey*, 72.

77. Caesar, *Civil War*, Book 3. 99; Plutarch, *Caesar*, 46; Suetonius, *Deified Julius Caesar*, 75.

78. Plutarch, *Pompey*, 80; Plutarch, *Caesar*, 48.

79. Plutarch, *Caesar*, 67.

AUGUSTUS

1. Suetonius, *Life of the Deified Augustus*, 79.

2. Suetonius, *Life of the Deified Julius Caesar*, 88.

3. Suetonius, *Deified Augustus*, 10.

4. Cassius Dio, Book 47. 3; Appian, *The Civil Wars*, Book 4. 5. For other acts of savagery by Augustus, see also Suetonius, *Deified Augustus*, 15.

5. Cassius Dio, Book 51. 1.

6. Suetonius, *Deified Augustus*, 35; Cassius Dio, Book 54. 18.

7. Suetonius, *Deified Augustus*, 101.

8. Keith Hopkins, 'Taxes and Trade in the Roman Empire (200 BC to AD 400)', *Journal of Roman Studies* 70 (1980), pp. 101–25.

9. Suetonius, *Deified Augustus*, 23.

10. Augustus, *My Achievements*, 26.

11. Suetonius, *Deified Augustus*, 28.

12. Ibid., 29.

13. Ibid., 30.

14. Suetonius, *Life of the Deified Claudius*, 21.

15. Suetonius, *Deified Augustus*, 69.

16. Ibid., 99.

17. Strabo, *Geography*, Book 5. 3. 9.

III NERO

1. Peter Jones and Keith Sidwell (eds), *The World of Rome: An Introduction to Roman Culture* (Cambridge, 1997), p. 60.

2. Miriam Griffin, *Nero: The End of a Dynasty* (London, 1984), pp. 189ff.

3. David Shotter, *Nero* (London, 2005), p. 5.

4. Seneca, *The Pumpkinification of the Divine Claudius*, 10.3 – 14.1.

5. Tacitus, *The Annals of Imperial Rome*, Book 12. 68.

6. Suetonius, *Life of Nero*, 28.

7. Tacitus, *Annals*, Book 13. 14.

8. Ibid., 16.

9. Tacitus, *Annals*, Book 14. 1.

10. Seneca, *On Clemency*, 1. 1. 2.

11. Griffin, *Nero*, p. 66.

12. Suetonius, *Nero*, 26.

13. Ibid., 20; Pliny the Elder, *Natural History*, Book 19. 108; Book 28. 237.

14. Cornelius Nepos, *Lives*, preface; Tacitus, *Annals*, Book 14. 20; Griffin, *Nero*, p. 41.

15. Cassius Dio, Book 61. 17.

16. Cassius Dio, Book 62. 13.

17. Tacitus, *Annals*, Book 14. 56.

18. Cassius Dio, Book 62. 28.

19. Tacitus, *Annals*, Book 14. 60.

20. Cassius Dio, Book 62. 15.

21. Suetonius, *Nero*, 31; Tacitus, *Annals*, Book 15. 42.

22. Suetonius, *Nero*, 31.

23. Martial, *Book on the Spectacles*, 2. 4; Suetonius, *Nero*, 39; Suetonius, *Life of the Deified Vespasian*, 9.

24. Tacitus, *Annals*, Book 15. 44.

25. Ibid., 45.

26. Suetonius, *Nero*, 31.

27. Griffin, *Nero*, pp. 205ff.

28. Tacitus, *Annals*, Book 15. 58.

29. Ibid., 66.

30. Tacitus, *Annals*, Book 16. 5.

31. Cassius Dio, Book 62. 28.

32. Cassius Dio, Book 63. 1.

33. Griffin, *Nero*, p. 205.

34. Cassius Dio, Book 62. 28.

35. Tacitus, *Histories*, Book 2. 8. This shows how Nero remained popular with ordinary Roman citizens across the empire even after his death; the succession of people who falsely claimed to be the dead emperor were greeted with excitement.

36. Cassius Dio, Book 63. 12.

37. Ibid., 18.

38. Ibid., 13; Suetonius, *Nero*, 28.

39. Mary Beard, *The Parthenon* (London, 2002), p. 108.

40. Cassius Dio, Book 63. 21.

41. Suetonius, *Nero*, 41.

42. Ibid., 44.

43. Pliny the Elder, *Natural History*, Book 18. 35.

44. Suetonius, *Nero*, 47.

45. Tacitus, *Histories*, Book 1. 72.

46. Suetonius, *Nero*, 48.

47. Ibid., 49.

48. Tacitus, *Histories*, Book 1. 16.

49. *Law on the Power of Vespasian*, in

Hermann Dessau (ed), *Inscriptiones Latinae Selectae* (Berlin, 1892-1916.) no. 244, AD 69/70.
50. Griffin, *Nero*, p. 207.

IV REBELLION

1. E. Mary Smallwood (ed.), *The Jewish War* (London, 1981), p. 463.
2. Martin Goodman, *The Ruling Class of Judaea: The Origins of the Jewish Revolt Against Rome, AD 66–70* (Cambridge, 1987), p. 115.
3. The Acts of the Apostles 25:22ff; G. Woolf (ed.), *The Cambridge Illustrated History of the Roman World*, (Cambridge, 2003), p. 350.
4. Josephus, *The Jewish War*, Book 2. 266.
5. Barbara Levick, *Vespasian* (London, 1999), p. 25; Josephus, *Jewish War*, Book 2. 197.
6. Cicero, *On the Manilian Law*, 65.
7. Woolf, *Illustrated History of the Roman World*, p. 350.
8. Neil Faulkner, *Apocalypse: The Great Jewish Revolt Against Rome, AD 66–73* (Stroud, 2002), pp. 47–50. Faulkner estimates that the Jewish peasants paid not less than 15 per cent of their annual income to the Romans (p. 61).
9. Cassius Dio, Book 63. 22; Pliny the Elder, *Natural History*, Book 18. 35.
10. Josephus, *Jewish War*, Book 2. 277.
11. Ibid., 326.
12. Ibid., 342ff.
13. Ibid., 546ff; Fergus Millar, *The Roman Near East, 31 BC – AD 337* (Cambridge, Mass.; London, 1993), p. 71.
14. Josephus, *Jewish War*, Book 2. 562.
15. Goodman, *Ruling Class of Judaea*, p. 177.
16. Suetonius, *Life of the Deified Vespasian*, 10 & 4.
17. Ibid., 1 & 4; Tacitus, *Histories*, Book 2. 76.
18. Suetonius, *Life of the Deified Titus*, 3 & 8.
19. Josephus, *Jewish War*, Book 2. 585.
20. Ibid., 614.
21. Tacitus, *Histories*, Book 5. 11.
22. Josephus, *Jewish War*, Book 3. 62.
23. Ibid., 406 & 135.
24. Ibid., 245.
25. Ibid., 383.
26. Ibid., 403.
27. Ibid., 536.
28. Josephus, *Jewish War*, Book 4. 121ff.
29. Ibid., 318.
30. Goodman, *Ruling Class of Judaea*, p. 180.
31. Tacitus, *Histories*, Book 1. 4.
32. Suetonius, *Life of Vitellius*, 16–17.
33. Goodman, *Ruling Class of Judaea*, p. 231ff.
34. Josephus, *Jewish War*, Books 5–7. These give the full account of the siege of Jerusalem which took place between March and September AD 70.
35. Josephus, *Jewish War*, Book 5. 451.
36. Ibid., 365.
37. Ibid., 466ff.
38. Ibid., 503.

39. Josephus, *Jewish War*, Book 6. 110.
40. Ibid., 241.
41. Ibid., 316.
42. Ibid., 333ff.

HADRIAN

1. Pliny the Younger, *Panegyric*, 4.
2. Cassius Dio, Book 68. 29.
3. Cassius Dio, Book 69. 2.
4. Danny Danziger and Nicholas Purcell, *Hadrian's Empire: When Rome Ruled the World* (London, 2005) p. 15. A contemporary description of Hadrian's character.
5. Imperial History, *Life of Hadrian*, 11.
6. Danziger and Purcell, *Hadrian's Empire*, p. 178.
7. Ibid., p. 177.
8. Pliny the Younger, *Letters*, 1. 10. 9.
9. Imperial History, *Life of Hadrian*, 19.
10. Tacitus, *Agricola*, 21.
11. Cassius Dio, Book 69. 8.
12. Robin Lane Fox, *The Classical World: An Epic History from Homer to Hadrian* (London, 2005), p. 595.

V CONSTANTINE

1. Pliny the Younger, *Letters*, 10. 96.
2. Ibid.
3. Peter Brown, *The Rise of Western Christendom* (Oxford, 2002), pp. 18ff; Keith Hopkins, *Journal of Early Christian Studies* 6 (1998), pp. 185–226.
4. Mary Beard, John North and Simon Price, *Religions of Rome* (Cambridge, 1998), vol. 1, p. 365.

5. Averil Cameron, *The Later Roman Empire* (London, 1993), pp.33–7.
6. Ibid., p. 42.
7. Peter Jones and Keith Sidwell (eds), *The World of Rome: An Introduction to Roman Culture* (Cambridge, 1997), pp. 172–4.
8. Eusebius, *Church History*, Book 8. 2; Cameron, *Later Roman Empire*, p. 44.
9. Cameron, *Later Roman Empire*, p. 32.
10. Lactantius, *On the Deaths of the Persecutors*, 24; Zosimus, *New History*, Book 2. 8. For Constantine's physical appearance see Eusebius, *Life of Constantine*, Book 1. 19.
11. Lactantius, *Deaths of the Persecutors*, 44; Zosimus, *New History*, Book 2. 14.
12. Eusebius, *Church History*, Book 8. 16.
13. Inscription from the Arch of Constantine in Rome; Eusebius, *Life of Constantine*, Book 1. 27.
14. Eusebius, *Life of Constantine*, Book 1. 34–6.
15. Cameron, *Later Roman Empire*, p. 7; Beard, North and Price, *Religions of Rome*, vol. 1, p. 364.
16. *Latin Panegyrics*, 9 (12). 3. 3 & 5. 1–2. Zosimus (*New History*, Book 2. 15) gives even more inflated battle figures: 170,000 infantry and 18,000 cavalry for Maxentius versus 90,000 infantry and 8,000 cavalry for Constantine.
17. Lactantius, *Divine Institutes*, 1.
18. Eusebius, *Life of Constantine*, Book 1. 37; Lactantius, *Deaths of the Persecutors*, 44.
19. Zosimus, *New History*, Book 2.

15; Eusebius, *Life of Constantine*, Book 1. 38.

20. Eusebius, *Life of Constantine*, Book 1. 28; Sozomen, *Church History*, Book 1. 3.

21. For modern interpretations of the sign see Averil Cameron and Stuart G. Hall, *Eusebius: Life of Constantine* (Oxford, 1999), pp. 207–10.

22. *Latin Panegyrics*, 7 (6). 21.

23. Eusebius, *Life of Constantine*, Book 1. 30.

24. Zosimus, *New History*, Book 2. 16.

25. Eusebius, *Life of Constantine*, Book 1. 39. The distribution of money by the soldiers to the people of Rome is recorded on reliefs on the Arch of Constantine.

26. *Latin Panegyrics*, 12 (9). 19; Zosimus, *New History*, Book 2. 29; Eusebius (*Life of Constantine*, Book 1. 48) gives 315 (the date of his return to Rome to celebrate his ten-year anniversary of being emperor) and not 312 as the date when Constantine made no pagan sacrifices in Rome.

27. Timothy Barnes, *Constantine and Eusebius* (Cambridge, Mass.; London, 1981), pp. 44ff.

28. Lactantius, *Deaths of the Persecutors*, 48.

29. Ibid., 46.

30. Eusebius, *Church History*, Book 10. 7.

31. Beard, North and Price, *Religions of Rome*, vol. 1, p. 369.

32. Ibid., pp. 368–9.

33. *Corpus Scriptorum Ecclesiasticorum Latinorum (CSEL)*, vol. 26, no. 206.

34. Beard, North and Price, *Religions of Rome*, vol. 1, p. 370.

35. Cameron, *Later Roman Empire*, p. 8.

36. Eusebius, *Life of Constantine*, Book 1. 49–50.

37. Zosimus, *New History*, Book 2. 18-20.

38. Eusebius, *Life of Constantine*, Book 4. 29; Cameron, *Later Roman Empire*, p. 57.

39. Eusebius, *Life of Constantine*, Book 4. 28.

40. Peter Heather, 'Senators and Senates' in Averil Cameron and Peter Garnsey (eds), *Cambridge Ancient History* (Cambridge, 1997), vol. 13, pp. 184–210.

41. Philostorgius, *Ecclesiastical History*, Book 5. 2.

42. Eusebius, *Life of Constantine*, Book 2. 2.

43. Lactantius, *Divine Institutes*, 1; Eusebius, *Life of Constantine*, Book 2. 3.

44. Eusebius, *Life of Constantine*, Book 2. 4.

45. Ibid., 5.

46. Ibid., 4; Zosimus, *New History*, Book 2. 22.

47. Eusebius, *Life of Constantine*, Book 2. 12.

48. Ibid., 16.

49. Ibid., 18.

50. Zosimus, *New History*, Book 2. 28.

51. Ibid.

52. Eusebius, *Life of Constantine*, Book 2. 24–42.

53. Beard, North and Price, *Religions of Rome*, vol. 1, pp. 372–5, 382; Naphtali Lewis and Meyer

Reinhold (eds), *Roman Civilization: Selected Readings* (New York, 1990), vol 2, no. 180; Cameron, *Later Roman Empire*, p. 57.

54. Eusebius, *Life of Constantine*, Book 3. 10.

55. Beard, North and Price, *Religions of Rome*, vol. 1, p. 371.

56. Cameron, *Later Roman Empire*, pp. 63–4.

VI FALL

1. The case for this view has been made most recently and most persuasively by Peter Heather in *The Fall of the Roman Empire* (London, 2005).

2. The principal account of the Goths seeking refuge in Roman empire in AD 376 is in Ammianus Marcellinus, Book 31 – the most detailed and lively narrative of the period AD 354–376.

3. Ammianus Marcellinus, Book 31. 2.

4. Ibid., 4; Heather, *Fall of the Roman Empire*, p. 158.

5. Ammianus Marcellinus, Book 31. 4.

6. Ibid., 12.

7. Heather, *Fall of the Roman Empire*, pp. 72–3.

8. Claudian, *Against Rufinus*, 2. 4–6; Heather, *Fall of the Roman Empire*, p. 217.

9. Zosimus, *New History*, Book 5, 29; Heather, *Fall of the Roman Empire*, pp. 215–16.

10. Zosimus, *New History*, Book 5. 29. Zosimus was a sixth-century east Roman historian and Books 5 and 6 in his *New History* give, relatively speaking, the most comprehensive account of events leading up to the sack of Rome in AD 410; most importantly, he made use of the contemporary histories of Eunapius and Olympiodorus, which today are only fragmentary.

11. Ibid.

12. Ibid., 32.

13. Heather, *Fall of the Roman Empire*, pp. 67–72.

14. Zosimus, *New History*, Book 5. 14.

15. Ibid., 33.

16. Ibid., 34.

17. Ibid.

18. Ibid., 35.

19. Ibid., 34 (following Olympiodorus, *Histories*, fragment 17).

20. Ibid., 39.

21. Ibid., 40.

22. Ibid., 41.

23. Ibid., 45.

24. Ibid., 46.

25. Heather, *Fall of the Roman Empire*, p. 227.

26. Zosimus, *New History*, Book 6. 1.

27. Heather, *Fall of the Roman Empire*, p. 222.

28. Zosimus, *New History*, Book 5. 48.

29. Ibid., 48–9.

30. Ibid., 50.

31. Ibid., 51.

32. Heather, *Fall of the Roman Empire*, pp. 228–9.

33. Sozomen, *Church History*, Book 9. 9; an alternative story is told by Procopius in *History of the Wars*, Book 3. 2. 7–39.

34. Heather, *Fall of the Roman Empire*, p. 227.

35. The sources for Alaric's sack of Rome are collated in Pierre Courcelle, *Histoire littéraire des grandes invasions germaniques* (Paris, 1964), pp. 45–55.

36. Jerome, *Commentary on Ezekiel*, Book 1, preface.

37. Augustine, *City of God*, Book 2. 29; Heather, *Fall of the Roman Empire*, pp. 229–32.

38. Heather, *Fall of the Roman Empire*, pp. 246–8.

39. Ibid., pp. 138–40.

FURTHER READING

FOREWORD

Woolf, G. (ed), *The Cambridge Illustrated History of the Roman World* (Cambridge, 2003)

Cornell, T. J., *Beginnings of Rome: Italy and Rome from the Bronze Age to the Punic Wars* (London, 1995)

Woolf, G., *Et Tu Brute? The Murder of Caesar and Political Assassination* (London, 2006)

Wyke, M., *Projecting the Past: Ancient Rome, Cinema and History* (New York; London, 1997)

Hopkins, Keith and Beard, Mary, *The Colosseum* (London, 2005)

Bowman, A. K., *Life and Letters on the Roman Frontier: Vindolanda and its People* (London, 2003)

ANCIENT SOURCES
Available in translation:

Cicero's Letters to Atticus (London, 1978)

Cicero's Letters to his Friends (London, 1978)

Tacitus, *The Annals of Imperial Rome* (London, 1989)

Petronius and Seneca, *The Satyricon, The Apocolocyntosis* (*The Pumpkinification of the Divine Claudius*) (London, 1977)

Suetonius, *Lives of the Caesars* (Oxford, 2000)

Plutarch, *Fall of the Roman Republic* (London, 1972)

Caesar, *The Civil War* (London, 1967)

Josephus, *The Jewish War* (London, 1981)

SEVEN HILLS OF ROME

Jones, Peter and Sidwell, Keith (eds), *The World of Rome: An Introduction to Roman Culture,* (Cambridge, 1997)

Woolf, G. (ed), *The Cambridge Illustrated History of the Roman World* (Cambridge, 2003)

Hopkins, Keith, *Conquerors and Slaves* (Cambridge, 1978)

Griffin, Jasper, *Virgil* (London, 2001)

Jenkyns, Richard, *Virgil's Experience: Nature and History, Times, Names, and Places* (Oxford, 1998)

ANCIENT SOURCES
For Rome's early history see the following Penguin translations:

Polybius, *Histories: The Rise of the Roman Empire* (London, 1979)

Livy, *The Early History of Rome* (Bks 1–5) (London, 2002)

Livy, *Rome and Italy* (Bks 6–10) (London, 1982)

For Virgil, see:

Georgics (Oxford, 2006) and *The Aeneid* (London, 1990)

I REVOLUTION

The most accessible narrative account of the life of Tiberius Gracchus can be found in:

Richardson, Keith: *Daggers in the Forum: The Revolutionary Lives and Violent Deaths of the Gracchus Brothers* (London, 1976).

Other key works are:

Astin, A. E., *Scipio Aemilianus* (Oxford, 1967)

Stockton, David, *The Gracchi* (Oxford, 1979)

Astin, A.E.; Walbank, F.W.; Frederiksen, M.W.; Ogilvie, R.M. (eds), *Cambridge Ancient History*, Volume 8: 'Rome and the Mediterranean to 133 BC' (Cambridge, 1989)

Beard, Mary and Crawford, Michael, *Rome in the Late Republic: Problems and Interpretations* (London, 1999)

Brunt, P. A., *Italian Manpower* (Oxford 1971)

ANCIENT SOURCES

For the Roman conquest of the Mediterranean see:

Polybius, *Histories: The Rise of the Roman Empire* (London, 1979) (selected excerpts)

Livy, *The War with Hannibal* (Bks 21–30) (London, 1970)

Livy, *Rome and the Mediterranean* (Bks 31–45) (London, 1976)

In Loeb Classical Library edition see:

Polybius, *The Histories* (Cambridge, Mass., 1922–27)

Appian, *Roman History* (Cambridge, Mass., 1912–13) both of which give the full Greek text and translation.

For accounts of the lives of Tiberius Gracchus and Gaius Gracchus see:

Plutarch, *Makers of Rome* (London, 1965)

Appian, *The Civil Wars* (London, 1996)

All the primary sources relating to the Gracchus brothers have been usefully collated in:

Stockton, David, *From The Gracchi To Sulla: Sources for Roman History, 133–80 BC* (London, 1981)

II CAESAR

The most accessible, well-researched and exciting narrative of the fall of the Roman republic can be found in:

Holland, Tom, *Rubicon: The Triumph and Tragedy of the Roman Republic* (London, 2003)

Two authoritative biographies of Caesar are:

Gelzer, Matthias, *Caesar, Politician and Statesman* (Oxford, 1968)

Meier, Christian, *Caesar* (London, 1996)

Other key works for the late Republic are:

Beard, Mary and Crawford, Michael, *Rome in the Late Republic:*

Problems and Interpretations
(London, 1999)

Weinstock, Stefan, *Divus Julius*
(Oxford, 1971)

Crook, J.A.; Lintott, Andrew;
Rawson, Elizabeth (eds) *Cambridge
Ancient History*, Volume 9: 'The
Last Age of the Roman Republic,
146–43 BC' (Cambridge, 1989)

ANCIENT SOURCES

There is a wealth of ancient sources
for this period of Roman history.
For Caesar's writings see:

Caesar, *The Gallic War* (Oxford,
1996)

Caesar, *The Civil War* (London,
1967)

For the contemporary letters of
Cicero and his correspondents
see:

Cicero's Letters to Atticus (London,
1978)

Cicero's Letters to his Friends (London,
1978)

Cicero, *Selected Letters* (London,
1986) (one volume)

For the ancient biographies of
Pompey and Caesar see:

Plutarch, *Fall of the Roman Republic*
(London, 1972)

Suetonius, *Lives of the Caesars*
(Oxford, 2000) (Julius Caesar)

Other ancient narratives of the last
decades of the republic are:

Appian, *The Civil Wars* (London,
1996)

Lucan, *Civil War* (Oxford, 1999)
(poetic account)

AUGUSTUS

Wallace-Hadrill, Andrew, *Augustan
Rome* (Bristol, 1993)

Zanker, Paul, *The Power of Images in
the Age of Augustus* (Ann Arbor,
1988)

Beard, Mary; North, John; Price,
Simon, *Religions of Rome*: Volume
1: 'A History' (Cambridge, 1998)

Galinsky, Karl (ed), *The Cambridge
Companion to the Age of Augustus*
(Cambridge, 2005)

Bowman, A.K.; Champlin, Edward;
Lintott, Andrew (eds), *Cambridge
Ancient History*, Volume 10: 'The
Augustan Empire, 43 BC–AD 69'
(Cambridge, 1996)

Syme, Ronald, *The Roman
Revolution*, (Oxford, 1939)

Price, S. R. F., *Rituals and Power: The
Roman Imperial Cult in Asia Minor*
(Cambridge, 1984)

Jones, Peter and Sidwell, Keith
(eds), *The World of Rome: An
Introduction to Roman Culture*,
(Cambridge, 1997)

Barchiesi, Alessandro, *The Poet and
the Prince: Ovid and Augustan
Discourse* (Berkeley, 1997)

ANCIENT SOURCES

The key ancient texts for the life
and rule of Augustus are:

Suetonius, *Lives of the Caesars*
(Oxford, 2000)

Cassius Dio, *The Roman History: The
Reign of Augustus* (London, 1987)

For Augustus's own account of his
reign (*My Achievements*) see:

*Res Gestae Divi Augusti, The
Achievements of the Divine Augustus*,
(ed) P. A. Brunt and J. M. Moore

(Oxford, 1967) which has original text, translation and commentary
The primary sources on all aspects of Augustan age have been usefully collated in:
K. Chisolm and J. Ferguson (eds), *Rome: The Augustan Age, A Source Book* (Oxford, 1981)

III NERO

An excellent and authoritative account of the crisis of Nero's reign is:
Griffin, Miriam T., *Nero, The End of a Dynasty* (London, 1984)
Two short introductions to Nero's rule can be found in:
Shotter, David, *Nero* (London, 2005)
Malitz, Jürgen, *Nero* (Oxford, 2005)
Other key works are:
Grant, Michael, *Nero* (London, 1970)
Champlin, Edward, *Nero* (Cambridge, Mass.; London, 2003)
Beacham, Richard C., *The Roman Theatre and its Audience* (London, 1991)
Beacham, Richard C., *Spectacle Entertainments of Early Imperial Rome* (New Haven; London, 1999)

ANCIENT SOURCES

For Tacitus's works for this period see the following translations:
Tacitus, *The Annals of Imperial Rome* (London, 1989)
Tacitus, *The Histories* (London, 1972)
For Suetonius's life of Nero see:
Suetonius, *Lives of the Caesars* (Oxford, 2000)

For Cassius Dio's account of Nero's reign see Loeb Classical Library edition:
Cassius Dio, *Roman History*, Volume 8 (Cambridge Mass., 1925)
Seneca's *The Pumpkinification of the Divine Claudius* can be found in:
Petronius and Seneca, *The Satyricon, The Apocolocyntosis (The Pumpkinification of the Divine Claudius)* (London, 1977)

IV REBELLION

The most authoritative accounts of the origins and context to the Roman war against the Jews in AD 66–70 are:
Goodman, Martin, *The Ruling Class of Judaea: The Origins of the Jewish Revolt Against Rome, AD 66–70* (Cambridge, 1987)
Goodman, Martin, *The Roman World 44 BC–AD 180* (London, 1997)
A new history of the Romans and Jews between the first and the fourth centuries aimed at a general readership and by the same author was published in January 2007:
Goodman, Martin, *Rome and Jerusalem: The Clash of Ancient Civilizations* (London, 2007)
Other key works are:
Millar, Fergus, *The Roman Near East, 31 BC–AD 337* (Cambridge, Mass.; London, 1993)
Levick, Barbara, *Vespasian* (London, 1999)
Sanders, E. P., *Judaism: Practice and Belief* (S.C.M.P., 1992)
Faulkner, Neil, *Apocalypse: The Great Jewish Revolt Against Rome AD 66–73* (Stroud, 2002.)

Woolf, G. (ed), *The Cambridge
Illustrated History of the Roman
World* (Cambridge, 2003)
For the military aspect of the Jewish
Revolt (and the Roman army in
general) see:
Peddie, John, *The Roman War
Machine* (Stroud, 1994)
Gilliver, Catherine, *The Roman Art of
War* (Stroud, 1999)
Goldsworthy, Adrian, *The Complete
Roman Army* (London, 2003)
Connolly, Peter, *Greece and Rome At
War* (London, 1998)

ANCIENT SOURCES
For the key primary source see:
Josephus, *The Jewish War* (London,
1981)
For Josephus's own account of his
life see in Loeb Classical Library:
Josephus, *The Life and Against Apion*
(Cambridge Mass., 1926)
For the account of the Roman civil
war AD 68–69 (the 'year of the four
emperors') see:
Tacitus, *The Histories*, (London,
1972)
For Suetonius's lives of Vespasian
and Titus as well as the emperors of
AD 68–69, Galba, Otho and
Vitellius, see:
Suetonius, *Lives of the Caesars*
(Oxford, 2000)

HADRIAN

An auhoritative and accessible new
history of Hadrian's rule is:
Danziger, Danny and Purcell,
Nicholas, *Hadrian's Empire, When
Rome Ruled the World* (London,
2005)

Other useful works for this period,
Birley, Anthony, *Hadrian: The
Restless Emperor* (London, 1997)
Salway, Peter, *A History of Roman
Britain* (Oxford, 2001)
Bowman, A. K., *Life and Letters on the
Roman Frontier: Vindolanda and its
People* (London, 2003)
Lane Fox, Robin, *The Classical
World: An Epic History from Homer to
Hadrian*
(London, 2005)
Scarre, Christopher, *The Penguin
Historical Atlas of Ancient Rome*
(London, 1995)
Jones, Peter and Sidwell, Keith
(eds), *The World of Rome: An
Introduction to Roman Culture*,
(Cambridge, 1997)
The Vindolanda tablets are also
available online at:
http://vindolanda.csad.ox.ac.uk

ANCIENT SOURCES
For Pliny's letters see:
The Letters of the Younger Pliny
(London, 1963)
For Pliny's Panegyric of Trajan, see
Loeb Classical Library edition:
Pliny, *Letters and Panegyricus*
(Cambridge, Mass., 1969)
For Cassius Dio's account of the
reign of Hadrian see Loeb Classical
Library edition:
Cassius Dio, *Roman History*, Volume
8 (Cambridge Mass., 1925)
For the Imperial History, *Life of
Hadrian*, see:
Lives of the Later Caesars (London,
1976)
For Tacitus's account of Roman
Britain, see:

Tacitus, *The Agricola and The Germania* (London, 2003)

V CONSTANTINE

A good, authoritative introduction to this period of Roman history can be found in:

Cameron, Averil, *The Later Roman Empire, AD 284–430* (London, 1993)

Other key works are:

Brown, Peter, *The Rise of Western Christendom: Triumph and Diversity AD 200–1000* (Oxford, 2002.)

Brown, Peter, *Power and Persuasion in Late Antiquity: Towards a Christian Empire* (Madison, Wis.; London, 1992)

Odahl, Charles, *Constantine and the Christian Empire* (London, 2004)

Barnes, Timothy, *Constantine and Eusebius* (Cambridge, Mass.; London, 1981)

Drake, H. A., *Constantine and the Bishops: The Politics of Intolerance* (Baltimore, Md.; London, 2000)

Digeser, Elizabeth DePalma, *The Making of a Christian Empire: Lactantius and Rome* (Ithaca, N.Y.; London, 1999)

Southern, Pat, *The Roman Empire from Severus to Constantine* (London, 2001)

Beard, Mary; North, John; Price, Simon, *Religions of Rome. Volume 1: A History* (Cambridge, 1998)

Lenski, Noel (ed), *The Cambridge Companion to the Age of Constantine* (Cambridge, 2006)

Cambridge Ancient History, Volume Bowman, Alan; Cameron, Averil;

Garnsey, Peter (eds), 12: 'The Crisis of Empire, AD 193–337', (ed) (Cambridge, 2005)

ANCIENT SOURCES

For Eusebius's works see:

Eusebius, *Life of Constantine*, (ed) Averil Cameron and Stuart G. Hall (Oxford, 1999) which has introduction, translation and commentary

Eusebius, *The History of the Church from Christ to Constantine* (London, 1989)

For Lactantius's works see:

Lactantius, *De Mortibus Persecutorum* (*On the Deaths of the Persecutors*), (ed) J. L. Creed (Oxford, 1984) which has parallel Latin and English text.

Lactantius, *Divine Institutes*, (ed) Anthony Bowen and Peter Garnsey (Liverpool, 2003) which has original text, translation and commentary.

For Zosimus's *New History* see:

Zosimus, *Historia Nova, The Decline of Rome* (San Antonio, 1967)

VI FALL

The most up-to-date, accessible and authoritative history of Rome's decline is:

Heather, Peter, *The Fall of the Roman Empire* (London, 2005)

Other key works are:

Heather, Peter: *Goths and Romans 332–489* (Oxford, 1991)

Heather, Peter, *The Goths* (Oxford, 1996)

Matthews, John, *Western Aristocracies and Imperial Court, AD 364–425*

(Oxford, 1975)

Ward-Perkins, Bryan, *The Fall of Rome and the End of Civilization* (Oxford, 2005)

Cambridge Ancient History, Volume 13: 'The Late Empire, AD 337–425' Cameron, Averil; Garnsey, Peter (eds), (Cambridge, 1997)

ANCIENT SOURCES

For Ammianus Marcellinus's history see:

Ammianus Marcellinus, *The Later Roman Empire: AD 354–378* (London, 1986)

For Zosimus's *New History* see:

Zosimus, *Historia Nova, The Decline of Rome* (San Antonio, 1967)

For the fragments of Olympiodorus' *Histories* see:

Blockley, R. C. (ed) *The Fragmentary Classicising Historians of the Later Roman Empire: Eunapius, Olympiodorus, Priscus and Malchus,* Volume 2 (Liverpool, 1983) which has Greek text, translation and notes.

ACKNOWLEDGEMENTS

Creating this book has been a team effort. On the BBC series production team I am grateful to the executive producer, Matthew Barrett, and to the series producer, Mark Hedgecoe, for their advice and for being such a pleasure to work with and learn from; to the series directors Chris Spencer, Nick Green, Nick Murphy, Andrew Grieve, Tim Dunn and Arif Nurmohamed, whose scripts significantly helped to shape the main chapters; to Christabelle Dilks, the series script editor; and to the series researchers Rebecca Snow, Sarah Jobling and Annelise Freisenbruch for their brilliant research which forms an integral part of this book. I would like to thank Annelise too for her kindness in taking the time to read the second half of the manuscript and also for researching the chapter on Augustus. I would also like to express my thanks to Ann Cattini and Anna Mishcon for generously allowing me the time to write this book, and especially Laurence Rees, whose support has been a constant and much appreciated source of encouragement.

At BBC Books my sincere thanks go to Martin Redfern, the commissioning editor, for his trust, patience and guidance during the writing of this book; to Eleanor Maxfield for managing the project so amicably and tirelessly; to Trish Burgess for editing and always improving the text; to Sarah Hopper for her wonderful picture research; and to Martin Hendry for working around the clock on the design.

This book would not have been possible without the generous advice of the academics who acted as consultants on the project. I owe a great deal of thanks to Martin Goodman and Averil Cameron for their responses and corrections to chapters IV and V respectively. I am also grateful to Peter Heather from whose counsel and recent book, *The Fall of the Roman Empire*, chapter VI benefited considerably. My greatest debt and warmest thanks, however, are owed to Mary Beard who has been so kind in sharing ideas, reading the manuscript, replying to emails in record time and making countless life-saving corrections. She has been an inspiration to work with, and her expertise forms a major part of this book.

On a personal note, my warm thanks go to my teachers Simon Price, Laetitia Edwards, Peta Fowler, James Morwood and Bruce McCrae; to Jonathan Stamp; to my brother, Matthew, for his brilliant company while wandering around the Roman ruins of the Mediterranean; to Harriet and Clayton for the Roman coins; and finally, for their affectionate support during the writing of this book, to my mother, Patsy, to Martyn, Sylvie and Kate, and to my friends, especially Kari Lia, Sam Sim, Paula Trybuchowska, Mark Williams, Helen Rumbelow, Tony Pritchard, Carl Siewertz and Helen Weinstein.

INDEX